ORACLE SQL
HIGH-PERFORMANCE TUNING

Guy Harrison

To join a Prentice Hall PTR Internet mailing list, point to:
http//www.prenhall.com/mail_lists

Prentice Hall PTR
Upper Saddle River, NJ 07458
http://www.prenhall.com

D1472935

Library of Congress Cataloging in Publication Data

Harrison, Guy.
   Oracle SQL high-performance tuning / Guy Harrison.
      p. cm..
   Includes bibliographical references and index.
   ISBN 0-13-614231-1
   1. Relational databases. 2. Oracle (Computer file) 3. SQL
   (Computer program language)
   QA76.9.D3H365154 1997   97-1168
   005.75'65--dc21   CIP

Editorial/production supervision: *Nicholas Radhuber*
Manufacturing manager: *Alexis Heydt*
Acquisitions editor: *Mark Taub*
Marketing manager: *Dan Rush*
Editorial assistant: *Tara Ruggiero*
Composition: *Mary Strunk*
Cover design: *Anthony Gemmellaro*
Cover design supervisor: *Jerry Votta*

Prentice Hall books are widely used by corporations and government agencies for training, marketing, and resale.

The Publisher offers discounts on this book when ordered in bulk quantities.
For more information, contact:
        Phone: 800-382-3419 Fax: 201-236-7141
        E-mail: corpsales@prenhall.com
        Or write: Prentice Hall PTR
        Corporate Sales Department
        1 Lake St.
        Upper Saddle River, NJ 07458

Printed in the United States of America
10 9 8 7 6 5 4

ISBN 0-13-614231-1

Prentice-Hall International (UK) Limited, *London*
Prentice-Hall of Australia Pty. Limited, *Sydney*
Prentice-Hall Canada Inc., *Toronto*
Prentice-Hall Hispanoamericana, S.A., *Mexico*
Prentice-Hall of India Private Limited, *New Delhi*
Prentice-Hall of Japan, Inc., *Tokyo*
Simon & Schuster Asia Pte. Ltd., *Singapore*
Editora Prentice-Hall do Brasil, Ltda., *Rio de Janeiro*

CONTENTS

PART TWO: Practical SQL Tuning

PART THREE: Beyond SQL Tuning

PREFACE

Over recent years, the popularity of the Oracle Relational Database Management System (RDBMS) has increased dramatically. Along with this heightened popularity has come an increasing interest in improving the performance of Oracle-based systems. The heightened emphasis on performance can be attributed to a number of factors:

❑ Oracle databases now tend to be substantially larger than they were in the past. Five years ago, average Oracle databases would have been measured in hundreds of megabytes or less. Nowadays, even "small" Oracle databases are measured in gigabytes.

❑ As the average size of the database increased, so has the user population which the database is expected to support. In its infancy, Oracle databases generally supported non-critical, small-scale applications. Today, Oracle databases increasingly support mission-critical, high-performance, high-volume applications.

❑ The expectations of computer users have increased. Response time delays and throughput rates which would have seemed tolerable in the past are no longer acceptable.

It's quite common for the performance of an Oracle application to appear to be acceptable during development only to abruptly degrade when the application encounters production data volumes and transaction rates. While there are a number of reasons why this occurs, inefficient SQL which fails to maintain good performance as data volumes increase is a major factor.

Poorly performing SQL arises in applications for a number of reasons. Although SQL is a relatively easy language to learn, its non-procedural nature tends to obscure performance-related issues. As a result, it's much harder to write efficient SQL than it is to write functionally correct SQL. Additionally, there seems to be insufficient awareness of the need to carefully monitor and tune SQL performance and the tools and techniques needed to tune SQL are not widely known.

Another factor which has increased the importance of well-tuned SQL is the emergence of "data warehouses" and On-Line Analytical Processing (OLAP) systems. These databases are often extremely large and are subject to a great deal of ad hoc query activity. If the SQL which supports these queries is inefficient, then queries may take hours or even days to complete or may fail to complete at all.

When Oracle applications start to misperform, it's typical for performance experts to be called in to perform benchmark tests or tune the Oracle database engine. For the most part, they will tune the operating system, change Oracle configuration parameters, reconfigure I/O and so on. At the end of the process, you can (if you are lucky) expect a 10 to 20 percent improvement in performance.

What is usually apparent during these tuning exercises is that it is the SQL contained within the application that is the most important factor in determining performance. If the SQL can be tuned, then performance increases of 100 percent or more are not uncommon. But a dilemma exists—by the time performance problems are recognized, it is often difficult to make changes to the production SQL. Furthermore, performance experts usually don't have the application knowledge required to understand and tune the SQL, while the developers don't have the necessary understanding of SQL performance tuning.

It follows that the best way to substantially improve the performance of most Oracle applications is to improve the efficiency of the application SQL. To make this happen, developers needed to acquire SQL tuning skills together with a commitment to tuning.

The objective of this book is to provide SQL programmers with the theory and practice of SQL tuning together with hints and guidelines for optimizing specific SQL statement types. We'll see how to diagnose and correct problems with existing SQL and briefly explore performance issues beyond SQL tuning—such as design and server tuning. By following the guidelines in this book, SQL programmers should be able to write SQL which will perform well both in development and in production and will be able to detect and correct inefficiencies in existing SQL. The result will be SQL which performs to its peak potential.

WHY THIS BOOK?

With the Oracle server documentation set consisting of more than a dozen manuals—including a tuning guide—and a couple of independent Oracle tuning texts on the market, is there really a need for this book?

There is a need, and the basis for this need lies in two fundamental imperfections in all alternative tuning guides—they are aimed almost exclusively at Database Administrators (DBAs), and they gloss over the processes of tuning SQL statements. There is a need for a book which is aimed not at the administrators of the Oracle databases, but at those writing the access routines (e.g., the SQL) for the database—such as application developers, users of data warehouses and others whose work involves writing high-performance SQL.

Additionally, while tuning the database engine can help poorly performing applications, nothing can match improving the efficiency of SQL for getting massive performance improvements. The Oracle tuning guide and other performance tuning texts give primary attention to database server tuning.

WHO SHOULD USE THIS BOOK?

This is not a book for Oracle DBAs (Data Base Administrators), although DBAs should find things of interest here. Rather, this is a book for anyone who needs to write SQL which has a performance requirement.

People who need to write high-performance SQL are:

❑ Developers of Oracle-based applications. These developers will typically need to embed SQL statements within the code of the development tool (such as SQL*Windows, Powerbuilder or Visual Basic). Alternately, the SQL may be contained within stored procedures which they will call from their client tool. These SQL statements will need to be efficient, otherwise the applications concerned will fail to meet reasonable performance requirements.

❑ Those querying data warehouses or decision-support type databases. These databases are typically very large and hence these queries must run efficiently, otherwise they may take an unreasonable time to complete (or not complete at all).

❑ Anyone who writes Oracle SQL statements and cares about their response time or throughput.

HOW TO USE THIS BOOK

Very few people read a book of this type from beginning to end. Depending on your background, you may wish to skip sections which review database theory and jump right into the details of SQL tuning. However, apart from the "Review of SQL" and the "Beyond SQL Tuning" section, most readers should attempt to read or at least review most of this book.

The book has the following major sections:

Introduction	This section (the preamble to which you are reading now). This section contains a review of the importance of SQL tuning and an overview of the tuning process.
Review of SQL	This section reviews the history and basic functionality of the SQL language and may be useful for those who are relatively new to SQL. The section defines basic SQL concepts which are used later in the book. Those experienced in SQL will probably skip or only skim this section.
SQL Processing and Indexing	This section explains the mechanisms by which Oracle interprets an SQL statement and retrieves or alters the data specified. This section introduces a number of very important topics, such as the role of the query optimizers, indexing and hashing concepts; SQL parsing; and basic data retrieval strategies. Although this section is heavy on theory, it's difficult to successfully tune SQL without at least a broad understanding of these topics. All readers are encouraged to read this section.
Tracing SQL Execution	This section explains how SQL processing can be traced and interpreted. Understanding the tracing and diagnostic utilities is a basic prerequisite for SQL tuning. Unless you feel very familiar with the *tkprof* tool and the EXPLAIN PLAN statement, you should not skip this chapter.
Tuning SQL	This section contains specific tuning guidelines for specific SQL statement types and circumstances. While it will be useful to read this section from start to finish, this is a part of the book

which may be used as a reference. You may wish to consult the relevant portions of this section as appropriate tuning requirements arise. Specific chapters in this section are:

- ❏ Tuning table access
- ❏ Tuning joins and subqueries
- ❏ Sorting and aggregation
- ❏ Data Manipulation Statements
- ❏ PL/SQL statements
- ❏ Parallel SQL
- ❏ Miscellaneous topics

SQL Tuning Case Studies This section consists of a number of SQL tuning examples, showing SQL statements and traces from the start of the tuning process to the end. In a practical sense, this section is intended to illustrate the theory, techniques and principles covered in previous sections. As such, it tends to reinforce and complement previous sections.

Beyond SQL Tuning This section introduces techniques for improving the performance of SQL which is already fully tuned. These techniques involve some understanding of the Oracle architecture and internals and involve some undocumented Oracle facilities. This section could therefore be characterized as "advanced" and may not interest the mainstream of readers. We will also discuss design issues which can affect the performance of your SQL.

Glossary and appendices The glossary contains definitions for many of the technical terms used in this book. While technical terms are usually defined within the main text when they are first used, the reader who skips sections may find the glossary useful. The appendices contain details of configuring client programs and the Oracle server for specific circumstances, a reference guide and a guide to further reading and other resources.

THE SAMPLE DATABASE

Whenever possible, any SQL tuning principle in this book will be illustrated with an example SQL statement. Usually, these SQL statements will be based on the sample database shown in the diagram below. This database is not intended to illustrate good or bad data modeling principles—but to be a basis for illustrating a wide range of SQL statements.

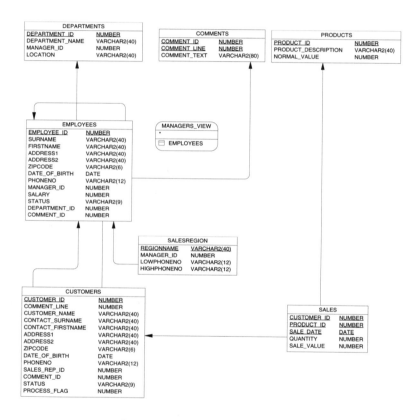

Structure of the sample database

Many of the examples contained in this book are accompanied with a graphical illustration of the performance gains which can be achieved by various optimizations. These performance measurements were collected on a range of computer hardware, ranging from a high-end UNIX SMP host to a 486 laptop running personal Oracle. Performance measurements are shown in either elapsed times or logical database I/Os ("block reads"), whichever was most appropriate to the optimization being performed.

ACKNOWLEDGMENTS

This book would not have been possible without the support and encouragement of my family. Undertaking a major writing project while simultaneously working long hours as a consultant resulted in many family sacrifices. This book is therefore dedicated to my wife, Jenni, and my children, Christopher, Katherine and Michael.

Invaluable technical and general advice and corrections were contributed by my colleagues and friends Steve Adams, Nick Goldsmith and Michael Farrar. Tony Jambu also provided some significant contributions. Their contributions are very much appreciated.

Over the past few years, a world-wide community of Oracle professionals has developed both through the International Oracle User Group (IOUG) and in internet mailing lists, newsgroups and web sites. Many of the participants of this community unselfishly share their time, knowledge and expertise assisting less experienced users and increasing the enlightenment of Oracle users everywhere. I've benefited enormously from this community and would like to thank all those who have contributed to it.

In Australia, Peter Sharman (psharman@au.oracle.com) runs an Oracle DBA mailing list which contains a wealth of technical information and advance notice of new features in the Oracle RDBMS. The mailing list was of great help to me while developing this book. Thanks for providing such a fantastic service, Peter.

Sections of Chapters 5 and 8 first appeared in the *Oracle Technical Journal* (now named "OReview: The Independent Voice of the Oracle Community"). Thanks to Kathleen O'Connor for allowing these sections to be re-used and for publishing the works in the first place.

Mark Taub from Prentice Hall first suggested this book and encouraged me throughout the project. I would also like to thank the production editor at Prentice Hall, Nick Radhuber.

I'd finally like to say hello to my nieces, Angela, Evelyn, Maree and Catherine. Catherine, although I couldn't dedicate the book to you, I do dedicate this sentence!

INTRODUCTION TO SQL TUNING

INTRODUCTION

The objective of this book is to help the reader write efficient, high performance SQL in the Oracle environment and to improve the performance of existing SQL. As argued in the preface, improving SQL performance is usually the most effective way of improving the performance of Oracle applications. Additionally, it is an approach which is available to a wide range of developers and users of Oracle databases and which can improve performance at all stages of the application development life-cycle.

In this chapter, we examine in some detail the incentive to tune SQL, the effects of poorly tuned SQL and the performance benefits which can be obtained from SQL tuning. We'll also examine some of the common objections to SQL tuning.

We will then move to a discussion of the SQL tuning process. This will include:

❏ The place of SQL tuning in overall performance management.

❏ The establishment of an effective tuning environment.

❏ Skills and tools required for a successful SQL tuning effort.

❏ An overview of the steps involved in SQL tuning.

WHY TUNE SQL?

To some, the objectives and importance of SQL tuning is so self-evident that there seems little need to articulate it. However, before we undertake any exercise as time-consuming and potentially difficult as SQL tuning, we need to understand what we are trying to achieve and the costs and benefits we can expect.

THE INCENTIVE FOR TUNING

Tuning SQL is not always easy. As often as not, the effort of tuning a piece of SQL takes more time than writing and testing the SQL in the first place. So why bother?

There are a number of reasons why we undertake the sometimes difficult process of SQL tuning. Some of these reasons are:

❏ To improve interactive response time of an Oracle-based application. A major component of the response time of these applications is the amount of time taken to retrieve or update data in the database. By tuning the SQL underlying these applications, response times can be reduced from excessive to acceptable—or even sensational!

❏ To improve batch throughput. Batch systems may be required to process thousands or millions of rows of data within some rigidly defined "batch window" (the period of time allocated for batch jobs). Improving the SQL which drives these batch jobs will allow more rows to be processed within a given time period and allow these jobs to complete within their allotted time. Often problems within batch reports are not noticed until a steadily degrading batch job suddenly exceeds its time limit—for instance, when the daily report takes longer than 24 hours to run.

❏ To ensure scalability in our application. As we increase the load on our system (as measured by the number of users connected to our system or the data volumes in our database), we hope that our performance (as measured by response time or throughput) degrades gradually. The sad truth is that many applications degrade anything but gracefully as load increases. Figure 1.1 graphically illustrates some of the ways application performance degrades under increasing load.

❏ To reduce system load. Even if performance is strictly speaking within acceptable bounds, tuning the application can free up system resources for other purposes.

❏ To avoid hardware upgrades. This reason is a powerful incentive for those who actually have to pay for computer hardware. It's not uncommon for hardware upgrades to be recommended as a solution for poorly performing applications. This solution, while having the advantage of avoiding tuning, is often ultimately futile—since a non-scalable application may require an escalating series of hardware upgrades which rapidly reach the limits of what is available or affordable.

Scalability

Figure 1.1 illustrates some common patterns of application scalability.

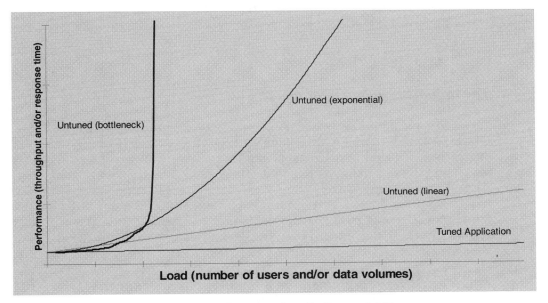

FIGURE 1.1   Patterns of application scalability.

A well-tuned application will continue to deliver required performance as the user population or data volumes increase. An inadequately tuned application will exhibit degradation of performance as increasing demands are encountered. This degradation might be:

❏ Increasing steadily (linear degradation). This is the least serious case because the degradation tends to be predictable and responsive to hardware upgrades.

❏ Increasing at an increasing rate (exponential). This is more serious because the exponential increase is not always recognized and tends to "creep up." Hardware upgrades are likely to be ultimately ineffective.

❏ Abruptly encountered (bottleneck). In this case, an abrupt degradation ("we hit a brick wall") is encountered. Frequently, there is no
advance warning and no hardware upgrade solution.

COMMON OBJECTIONS TO SQL TUNING

Because producing high performance SQL is so much more difficult than producing functional SQL, it's possible to encounter resistance to the tuning process.
Some of the common objections which you might encounter are:

❏ The Oracle optimizer automatically tunes SQL statements.
❏ Tuning SQL statements is not within my area of specialty.
❏ I'll write the SQL—someone else can tune it.
❏ I'll tune the SQL later.
❏ We can't afford to tune our SQL.

The optimizer will do it for me

We discuss the optimizer in detail in Chapter 3. The optimizer is that part of the
Oracle server which tries to determine the most efficient way to execute your SQL
statements. While the optimizer gets smarter with every release of the Oracle software and can often make very good decisions, it lacks critical information which
the SQL programmer is likely to possess regarding the distribution and nature of
data in your application. Also, you might be able to spend hours or days determining the best approach, while the optimizer must make a decision in a "split-
second." In short, the optimizer can help, but usually cannot do as good a job as
the experienced SQL programmer/tuner.

I'm not a SQL programmer, I'm a [insert your specialty here]

In the dominant client-server development environment, SQL coding is often the
responsibility of those whose primary expertise is in a front-end development
tool—for instance Powerbuilder, SQL*Windows, C, Microsoft Visual Basic or
other similar tool. These programmers might regard SQL programming as a
"side-line" and feel that SQL tuning is not their responsibility. This is a dangerous
attitude, since poorly tuned SQL is likely to have an impact on overall application
performance far more severe than anything contained in the front-end code. In
general, if you write the SQL, you need to take responsibility for it—and that
includes performance.

I'll write the SQL—someone else can tune it

It's often believed that it's the responsibility of some other team member—possibly the DBA—to tune the application SQL. Regardless of whether or not this other person has the time, mandate or skills necessary to tune the SQL, it's usually the person who writes the SQL who has the critical knowledge required for tuning.

For instance, when trying to tune someone else's SQL, a DBA will have to expend a fair amount of effort in determining what the SQL is trying to do. They will need to understand the underlying data at least as well as the author of the SQL and may be concerned that in tuning the SQL, they might inadvertently change the *semantics* (the meaning) of the SQL.

Generally, only the author of the SQL has all of the knowledge required to tune the SQL. All that might be missing is the necessary SQL tuning principles—and that's the purpose of this book.

I'll tune it later

The problem with this attitude is the same as the problem with procrastination in general, and specifically with delaying quality control in software development. It has become fairly well understood that the cost of fixing a software defect increases throughout the software development life-cycle. For instance, it may take one hour to fix a software defect if it is picked up in development, 10 hours to fix if picked up in system testing and 20 hours if picked up in production.

The same principle holds true for SQL tuning. Usually, the longer you wait, the more difficult it is to tune. For instance, the data model may be finalized—preventing *denormalization*—or the code may now be in production and can't be fixed without an extensive quality assurance and change control process.

Don't put it off—tune your SQL as you write it.

We can't afford to tune it

In reality, you probably can't afford not to tune. Failure to implement efficient SQL leads to unnecessary hardware upgrades, to lost productivity by system users, to end-user dissatisfaction and often to the cancellation of software projects.

Failure to tune early in the development life-cycle usually leads to a more substantial tuning effort later. Almost always, untuned systems are running on hardware much more expensive than would be required for a tuned system. It's possible for literally millions of dollars to be spent on hardware upgrades which could have been avoided by a couple of weeks of application tuning.

SQL tuning is always cost-effective.

The place of SQL tuning in the overall tuning process

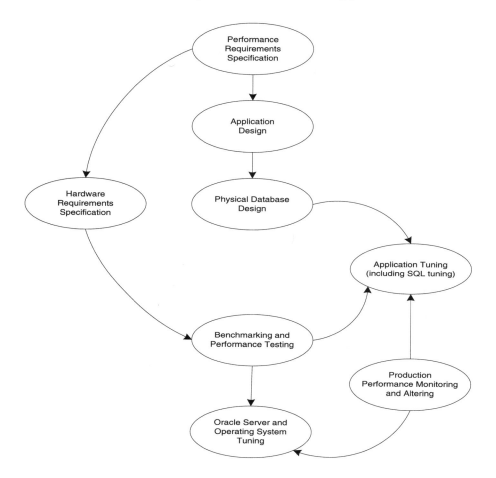

FIGURE 1.2   A view of the overall performance management process.

SQL tuning is only one of a number of aspects of the total tuning process. One view of this total process is given in Figure 1.2. Some of the other tuning components are:

❏ **Performance requirements specification.** During the initial requirements specification phase, the performance requirements of the application should have been identified. These requirements can be specified in terms of transactions per second, response times or some other measure. These requirements set the performance objectives which will be used to determine the success of subsequent tuning efforts.

❏ **Application design.** During this stage, the functionality and architecture of the application are determined. The functionality determines the deliverables of the application, and the architecture determines how the application will provide these deliverables. Decisions made at this stage can determine both the performance requirements and possibilities of the system. This stage also incorporates the development of a *logical database design*.

❏ **Physical database design.** While the *logical model* defines the data which will be held within the database, the *physical model* describes how this data is stored in the real-world database of tables, indexes, etc. The physical design usually determines the ultimate limits on the performance of your application. Usually, it is difficult to change the data model substantially once the model is beyond the design stage because of the impact on existing programs. For instance, you may be able to add an index to the physical database, but you probably won't be able to merge two tables without re-coding substantial portions of the application.

Application and database design changes often offer the most significant performance improvements. Unfortunately, changing the application or database design after implementation is often impractical at worst, or costly at best. It's therefore important to attempt to optimize the design before implementation. Chapter 14 discusses some aspects of application/database design.

❏ The **hardware requirements specification** will usually be developed before the application is ready for benchmark and performance testing. The capacity of the hardware platform will have a significant effect on the system performance. Chapter 15 discusses some issues involved in sizing a hardware platform.

❏ **Application tuning (excluding SQL).** This usually involves changing the application's algorithms to improve performance. For instance, you might change the application so that it reads some file into memory and caches it there, rather than re-reading the file every time it is required.

❏ **Application tuning (SQL).** For database-centric applications, the most significant improvements in performance are often realized by the tuning of application SQL. Improving SQL performance is the major focus of this book.

❏ **Benchmark and performance testing** often occur prior to implementation of a system to ensure that the performance requirements specifications can be met. In some cases, benchmark testing might occur prior to the finalization of the hardware requirements specification.

❏ **Oracle server tuning** is the process of improving database performance without changing the application SQL or data model. This might require changing configuration parameters or spreading database files across multiple disks.

❏ **Operating system tuning**. This is similar to tuning the Oracle server. We might change configuration settings or reorganize the machine's resources. Additionally, we may acquire more resources if deemed necessary.

Tuning Oracle and/or your operating system can lead to significant improvements in performance, although not usually as substantial as those realized by tuning your SQL. Tuning the Oracle server or the operating system is particularly effective when contention for a resource or a bottleneck in processing exists. In Chapter 16, we introduce ways of identifying and addressing such bottlenecks.

❏ **Hardware upgrades** can result in substantial improvements to performance, but are often a very costly solution. Additionally, upgrading hardware can be ultimately futile if your application scalability is very poor. For instance, you may have to quadruple your hardware resources in order to get a two-fold improvement in performance.

Figure 1.3 shows the potential improvement you might expect out of each of these measures. We can see from the figure that SQL tuning can offer very substantial improvements in performance, without the cost of hardware upgrades and without the difficulty of changing the design of a production application.

WHEN SHOULD SQL BE TUNED?

Ideally, SQL should be tuned as it is written. As we progress through the normal system development life-cycle (design-development-test-implementation), it becomes increasingly costly to tune SQL, and the performance improvements we can expect to achieve diminish. There are a number of factors to this:

❏ Certain aspects of the application become impossible to change without re-implementing large portions of the design. For instance, the design of the database can form the basis for all application programs. We can change it quite easily in the design stage, but changing it at a later stage might require that we re-code every program to adjust to the new data model.

❏ If we tune the SQL when it is first written, then we only have to test the SQL once. However, if we have to tune the SQL following its first round of testing, then those tests will have to be repeated once the SQL is tuned. Furthermore, when the SQL is first being constructed, the functional requirements, underlying table designs and other critical information will already be at hand. Returning to tune an SQL statement at some later date will require a review of the purpose and logic of the SQL.

❏ Once SQL enters a production system, there are often restrictions on the tuning measures which can be put in place. For instance, building or altering an index on a large table may require substantial time, during which the application will be unavailable. For applications which are required to be available around the clock, creating such a new index might be a major problem.

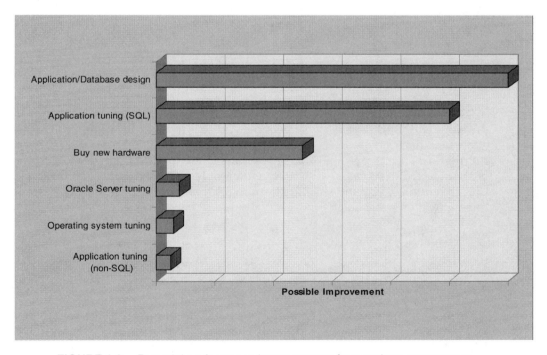

FIGURE 1.3   Potential performance improvements from various components of the total tuning process.

Figure 1.4 illustrates the cost and benefit of tuning during various stages of the application life-cycle.

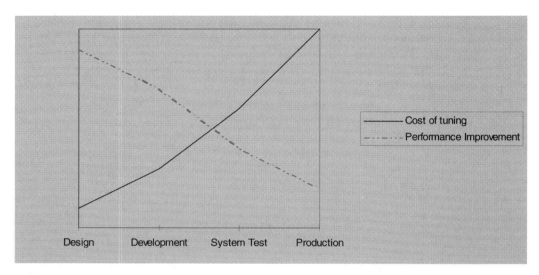

FIGURE 1.4 Costs and benefits of tuning during the system life-cycle.

It follows from this discussion that tuning should be introduced into the development process as early as possible and that to do so is both more effective and economical.

Performance issues are often ignored until an application is deployed, or at best, subjected to a stress test shortly before implementation. Although this makes the job of tuning SQL more difficult, tuning SQL is still the best hope for improving application performance.

THE SQL TUNING PROCESS

Although this book contains an abundance of SQL tuning techniques, guidelines and examples, it cannot provide a rule or an example for every circumstance. What it can do presents an effective approach to tuning which will result in well-tuned SQL statements and offers some suggestions for common situations.

There is a very substantial element of trial and error in SQL tuning. However, this trial and error is characteristic of a scientific process rather than a random process—the expert SQL tuner is formulating and evaluating theories and *iteratively* establishing the best SQL. Like the scientist, the SQL tuner collects data, formulates theories, tests those theories and repeats the process until the best SQL statement is found.

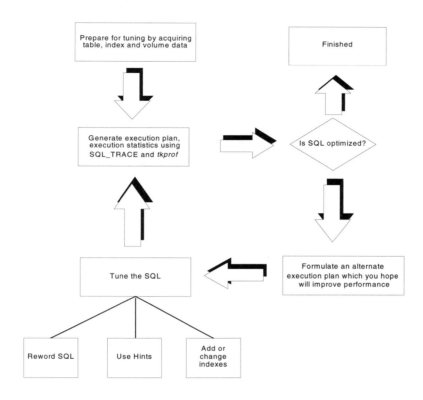

FIGURE 1.5 A view of the SQL tuning process.

There are three aspects to Figure 1.5 which should emphasized:

❏ First, it's an iterative process. That is, we repeat the process until we reach a satisfactory outcome.

❏ Second, the concept of measuring SQL performance is critical. Without measurement, we have no way of knowing the effect of our tuning efforts. We therefore have to be very familiar with the tools which are available for measuring performance.

❏ Third, tuning the SQL can involve a range of methods, such as altering the text of the SQL statement, creating or altering indexes, etc. To do this effectively, you need to understand how Oracle processes SQL and you need to have some familiarity with the options for improving performance. Therefore, this book contains details of Oracle SQL processing together with examples of improving specific types of SQL statements.

SETTING UP THE TUNING ENVIRONMENT

Before you can start to tune, you need to establish an environment which promotes an efficient and accurate measurement of SQL. You also need to have on hand details of your database structure and volumes.

There are many projects in which tables that have millions of rows in production contain only a few tens of rows in development, where developers have no idea what indexes exist, and where developers don't know about the tools which exist to tune SQL. In such an environment, tuning SQL is impossible.

The ideal tuning environment is one in which:

❑ Data volumes are realistic.

❑ Data model documentation is available and is easy to understand.

❑ System performance requirements are spelled out.

❑ Validation of performance requirements is built in to the quality assurance process.

Realistic data volumes

Plenty of systems seem to be performing quite well in development, but suffer drastic and dramatic performance problems in production. Generally, these systems were developed in an environment where the amount of data in the database was totally unrealistic. In fact, it's not at all uncommon to find that developers are writing SQL statements against empty tables—tables which will contain millions of rows in production.

Using realistic data volumes has at least two desirable effects:

❑ Any problems with the performance of SQL are noticed before they hit production.

❑ Tuning efforts which work in development will also work in production.

What are "realistic" data volumes?   In an ideal tuning environment, the data volumes and distribution would be exactly the same as that in the target or production environment. Unfortunately, processing and resource restrictions often make it difficult to realize this ambition.

If you can't populate your tuning environment with the same volumes as your target environment, you may be able to use your target environment for some of your tuning. If your SQL is query only (e.g., does not change any of the data in the target environment) and you have an off-peak or non-critical window in your target system, then testing your SQL against the target environment can be an option.

However, in many cases, there is no window of opportunity for running ad-hoc SQL against the production environment, or production control procedures prohibit such activities.

The following principles may help when establishing data volumes in the development or tuning environment:

❏ Small tables, such as code and reference tables, should be the same size in the tuning environment as in the target environment.

❏ Larger tables should be larger than the small tables mentioned above. They should also be large enough so that reading every row of the table takes at least 10 to 100 times longer than reading a single row from an index.

❏ These larger tables should be scaled down by approximately the same degree. That is, if one of the tables is five percent of its size in the target environment, then all of these larger tables should be five percent of their target size. This preserves the relative sizes of the tables.

For example, in the sample database outlined earlier, you might set up a tuning environment as shown in Table 1.1.

TABLE 1.1 Possible tuning environment data volumes for the sample database.

Table Name	Size in target environment (production database)	Size in tuning database (development database)	Comment
DEPARTMENTS	100	100	Reference table—Maintain same volumes
PRODUCTS	100	100	Reference table—Maintain same volumes
EMPLOYEES	5,000	1,000	20% sample
PRODUCTS	30	30	Reference table—Maintain same volumes
SALES	1,000,000	200,000	20% sample

TABLE 1.1   Possible tuning environment data volumes for the sample database. *(Continued)*

Table Name	Size in target environment (production database)	Size in tuning database (development database)	Comment
CUSTOMERS	20,000	4,000	20% sample
SALES REGION	500	500	Reference table—Maintain same volumes
COMMENTS	250,000	50,000	20% sample

Documentation

When tuning an SQL statement, you need ready access to your database structure —table definitions, index definitions, table sizes, relationships between tables, etc. If you don't have this information at hand, you will find yourself working in the dark. If your database was generated by a CASE tool, then the same tool can generate this information. Otherwise, you can obtain the necessary information from the data dictionary. The script *dbschema.sql* in the companion CD-ROM will generate concise table, index and view definitions.

Know your system requirements

It's always a good idea to define what the performance requirements for the database system actually are. In other words, how fast is "fast enough"? For instance, for an on-line system, how quickly should an query return the data? five seconds, one second, less than one second? This information will allow you to determine when your tuning efforts have succeeded.

MEASURING SQL PERFORMANCE

Oracle provides tools which reveal the way in which Oracle is processing your SQL and the resources (CPU, I/O, etc.) expended. These tools are:

❏ The EXPLAIN PLAN statement—which can be used to show Oracle's strategy for retrieving the data requested by your SQL statement.

❏ The SQL_TRACE facility—which generates a trace of your SQL statements' execution.

❏ The *tkprof* utility—which transforms this trace file into useful output.

These tools are powerful, but unfortunately not always easy to use. Guidelines for using these tools are contained in Chapter 5.

TUNING SQL

Improving the performance of your SQL can be achieved using a number of techniques:

❏ Re-wording your SQL.

❏ Giving Oracle explicit instructions (called *hints*) which direct Oracle to use particular approaches to retrieving and processing data.

❏ Creating or changing indexes or clusters.

❏ Changing the table structure.

Determining which combination of approaches is likely to result in performance improvements requires the following:

❏ An understanding of how Oracle processes SQL.

❏ An understanding of how you can influence Oracle's processing.

❏ An understanding of how to make the most of indexes and clustering.

❏ An awareness of the possible alternative approaches to various types of SQL statements.

Some additional skills will help you ensure that your SQL is getting every opportunity to work effectively:

❏ Effective application and database design are an essential ingredient for a high performance application. Tuning SQL may be futile if the underlying design is flawed.

❏ A knowledge of Oracle server performance monitoring and tuning can be invaluable. It may be that although your SQL is optimally tuned, bottlenecks in the Oracle server are preventing it from reaching its full potential.

> Try to establish a productive environment in which to tune your SQL. Obtain realistic or representative data volumes for your key tables. Ensure that application and database design information is at hand and that tuning tools are available.

CHAPTER SUMMARY

As the database size, user populations and performance expectations of Oracle databases have increased, so has the interest in improving the performance of Oracle applications. Much of this interest has focused on tuning the configuration of the database server while the tuning of application SQL has been somewhat neglected.

Tuning SQL can improve the response time, throughput and scalability of an application and can help to avoid costly hardware upgrades. Tuning SQL is a very cost-effective way of improving system performance because it can yield substantial improvements at any stage of a system's life-cycle—although addressing SQL tuning during earlier stages will result in the greatest performance gain.

Tuning SQL involves measuring the performance and characteristics of the SQL to be tuned. The performance of SQL can be improved in a number of ways, including:

- ❏ Adding or changing Oracle indexes.
- ❏ Re-wording the SQL statement.
- ❏ Using Oracle hints.
- ❏ Changing the database structure.

Best tuning results will be obtained if you establish an effective tuning environment with representative data volumes, clearly defined performance objectives and comprehensive database documentation.

To effectively tune SQL, you will need the following:

- ❏ An understanding of how Oracle processes SQL.
- ❏ An understanding of Oracle indexing facilities.
- ❏ An ability to use Oracle SQL tuning tools, such as *tkprof*, EXPLAIN PLAN and hints.
- ❏ Methods for improving the performance of specific categories of SQL.
- ❏ An elementary understanding of database and application design principles.
- ❏ Some familiarity with Oracle server architecture and how bottlenecks in that architecture might affect the performance of your SQL.

Chapter 2

REVIEW OF SQL

INTRODUCTION

In this chapter, we briefly review the SQL language. This chapter is intended for readers who are relatively new to the SQL language or for those who need to refresh their knowledge of SQL functionality. This chapter is not a comprehensive guide to the facilities of either ANSI standard or Oracle SQL.

The topics we shall cover include:

- ❏ The history of SQL and the relational data model.
- ❏ ANSI standard SQL and Oracle SQL.
- ❏ Categories of SQL statements such as queries, Data Manipulation and Data Definition language statements.
- ❏ The use of NULL values.
- ❏ Grouping of SQL statements into indivisible transactions.
- ❏ Types of SQL query operations including joins, subqueries, set and aggregate operations.
- ❏ The performance impact of the non-procedural nature of SQL.

HISTORY OF SQL

PRE-SQL DATABASES

Prior to the development of SQL and the relational model, the predominant models for database systems were the *network* model and the *hierarchical* model. The hierarchical model is best represented by a number of successful mainframe-based database packages—IMS being a good example—and the network model is often associated with the CODASYL database standard and such databases as Cullinet.

The hierarchical model represented data as a tree of parent and child records. A special language, DL/I, was used to navigate this tree and retrieve records. Since not all data structures can easily be represented by a hierarchy, the special work-arounds had to be developed for some applications.

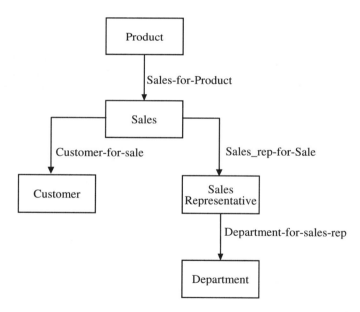

FIGURE 2.1   A hierarchical data model. In this implementation, information about customers, sales representatives and departments would need to be redundantly repeated for each sale.

The network model was capable of more flexibly representing data structures. In the network model, records are linked via pointers. For instance, there could be a pointer in a child record to the parent record. This pointer facility made the network model fairly efficient, but meant that data could not easily be accessed in ways which had not been anticipated.

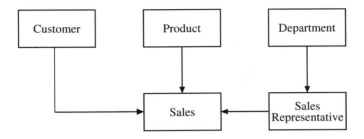

FIGURE 2.2   Network data model.

Both models presented substantial obstacles to the storage and retrieval of data. In general, only professional programmers could write the programs needed to extract the data. Consequently, long backlogs of report requests built up in MIS departments. Furthermore, the implementation of these databases was very complicated. The data model design essentially determined the queries which could be executed. If a need arose to combine data in an unexpected way, this typically could not be done easily or efficiently.

THE RELATIONAL MODEL

In June 1970, Dr. E.F. Codd presented a paper called "A Relational Model of Data for Large Shared Data Banks." In this paper, Dr. Codd described a model for storing data in computer systems which was based on mathematical set theory.

Although the mathematical underpinning of the relational model is moderately complex, the implementation typically appears fairly simple to the end user—data is represented as a set of two-dimensional tables (or relations). Rows in the table correspond to records in a traditional dataset and columns in the table correspond to fields. One or more of the columns is defined as a *primary key* and this column or combination of columns will uniquely define the row.

In a relational database implementation, tables are related by the shared column values and not by pointers or other artificial structures.

Operations in a relational database are not processed record-at-a-time as in other implementations, but instead groups of data are processed in single operations. The output of relational operations is itself a table (or a *relation* or *result set*) which can be processed by further relational operations.

In the relational model, the logical representation of data is unaffected by its physical representation. That is, users of a relational model can manipulate the data without needing to know the details of its actual location or storage method.

The first relational database system was a prototype called System R, developed by IBM between 1974 and 1978. This system used a language called **S**tructured **E**nglish **QUE**ry **L**anguage or SEQUEL. In subsequent implementations, the name was shortened to SQL.

The first commercial relational database was Oracle version 2 (version 1 was a prototype) in 1979. IBM released SQL/DS in 1981, followed by the successful mainframe relational database DB/2 in 1983.

Despite misgivings about poor performance, the relational model quickly gained ground over hierarchical, network and other database models. By 1985, it seemed that a database system could not survive unless it at least claimed to be relational. Many commercial databases of this time which claimed to be relational were, in fact, variations on the network model.

However, as the relational database concepts became more widely understood, most "pretend"-relational databases gave way to "nearly"-relational databases (few databases can claim to implement all the features of the relational model). Most popular non-relational databases withered and died fairly rapidly, and the relational model became the dominant paradigm for database systems in the late 1980s and 1990s.

SQL AND THE RELATIONAL MODEL

A relational database is required to support a "data sub-language" which implements relational operations. In general, this will require that the language:

❏ Supports operations on sets or groups of data (i.e., the opposite of record-at-a-time processing).

❏ Is able to refer to data independently of its physical storage. For instance, there should be no requirement to specify the name of the file in which a table is stored—the table name alone is sufficient.

❏ It should be non-procedural. That is, it does not instruct the DBMS how the data is to be retrieved. It only needs to unambiguously describe the data to be retrieved.

SQL is the implementation of such a sub-language in almost all relational databases, including Oracle.

Prior to the relational model, the language used to access database languages was procedural. That is, the request would include the instructions required to access the data as well as the data to be retrieved. For instance, the following instructions might be required to total all the sales for a customer:

```
MOVE '9999' TO CUSTOMER-NO IN CUSTOMER
OBTAIN CALC CUSTOMER
LOOP:
```

```
      OBTAIN NEXT SALES WITHIN CUSTOMER-SALES
      ADD SALE-AMOUNT IN SALES TO SALES-TOTAL
      ... Do something with the data ...
GOTO LOOP
```

The above example illustrates two common features of non-relational databases:

❑ The DBMS is told exactly how to obtain the required data.

❑ Data is processed one row at a time.

By contrast, a relational model must support a non-procedural language for retrieving information. This means that the language will specify the data to be retrieved, but will not specify how the data is to be obtained:

```
SELECT SUM(SALE_VALUE)
   FROM SALES
  WHERE CUSTOMER_ID=9999
```

In the first example, the order and exact method of retrieving the rows is specified. In the second example, the order in which the tables is to be accessed is undefined, and the use of indexes or other access methods is left to the discretion of the database management system.

SQL (Structured Query Language) was developed by IBM for the SQL/DS system and is an example of such a non-procedural data access language. Although "SQL" and "relational database" seem somewhat synonymous today, SQL itself is not part of the relational model, and hence a database may implement a non-SQL access language and still be truly relational.

Although a number of non-SQL access languages were developed (the most notable being QUEL in early versions of INGRES), SQL rapidly gained acceptance as the de-facto "standard" for database access languages.

THE ANSI STANDARD

The ANSI SQL standards committee was formed in 1982 and the first standard was released in 1986. This standard is commonly known as SQL-86 and is the basis for most SQL implementations known today. It was amended in 1989— hence SQL-89. A major revision to the standard, SQL-92, was released in 1992.

The SQL-89 standard provided the basis for most SQL dialects in common use today—including Oracle's. SQL-89 provided definitions of the common SQL operations—queries and data manipulation—but omitted facilities to alter database schema, control security and implement data integrity. SQL-92 implements many of these features, together with some substantial changes to SQL grammar and capabilities.

FUTURE OF SQL

The current evolving ANSI standard, known as SQL3, is still under development. This standard will encompass:

❑ Procedural extensions to SQL, such as stored procedures and triggers.

❑ Hierarchical queries, sometimes refered to as the "explosion of parts."

❑ Support for object-oriented methods. This will likely include user defined datatypes of arbitrary complexity and the ability to encapsulate data (tables) and methods (stored procedures).

TYPES OF SQL STATEMENTS

QUERIES

The most common SQL operation is the query or select statement. This statement implements the standard relational operations such as SELECTION, PROJECTION and JOIN.

This is the simplified syntax for an Oracle select statement:

```
SELECT (column_list)
  FROM table_list
[WHERE join conditions and query conditions]
[GROUP BY (column_list)]
[HAVING (condition)]
```

The SELECT statement forms the basis for many other SQL operations. SELECT statements are used when creating views, in sub-queries or when creating a table defined as the result of a query.

DATA MANIPULATION LANGUAGE (DML)

DML statements allow data in the database to be added, amended or deleted. This functionality is provided by the INSERT, UPDATE and DELETE statements.

INSERT

The INSERT statement adds new rows to a single table. Its simplest syntax is:

```
INSERT INTO (table_name)
        (column_list)
VALUES (value_list)
```

Often a query is used to populate rows:

```
INSERT INTO (table_name)
    query_statement
```

For instance:

```
insert into customers
        (customer_id,Customer_name , Contact_Surname,
        Contact_Firstname , Address1 ,Address2 , ZipCode,
        Date_of_birth, PhoneNo, Sales_rep_id)
    select customer_id,Customer_name , Contact_Surname,
        Contact_Firstname , Address1 ,Address2 , ZipCode,
        Date_of_birth, PhoneNo, Sales_rep_id
    from customer_upload;
```

UPDATE

The UPDATE statement allows rows in a single table to be updated. Its simplified syntax is:

```
UPDATE (table_name)
    SET (column_list)=(value list)
    WHERE query_condition
```

The value list can be a subquery (see subqueries, below). For example:

```
UPDATE GIRLS
        SET height=(select height
                            from PEOPLE
update customers c
    set sales_rep_id=(select manager_id
                        from employees
                      where surname=c.contact_surname
                        and firstname=c.contact_firstname
                        and date_of_birth=c.date_of_birth)
    where (contact_surname,contact_firstname,date_of_birth) in
        (select surname,firstname,date_of_birth
            from employees)
```

DELETE

The DELETE statement allows one or more rows in a table to be deleted. The syntax is:

```
DELETE FROM (table_name)
    WHERE query_condition
```

DDL

The Data Definition Language allows database objects to be created or altered. You should refer to the Oracle Server SQL reference manual for detailed definitions. Some of the Oracle DDL statements are:

❏ CREATE TABLE
❏ DROP TABLE
❏ ALTER TABLE
❏ CREATE INDEX
❏ DROP INDEX
❏ ALTER INDEX
❏ CREATE SEQUENCE
❏ DROP SEQUENCE
❏ CREATE SCHEMA
❏ DROP SCHEMA
❏ ALTER SCHEMA

Of particular note (from the terms of SQL tuning) are the DDL statements which are based on queries. In particular, the CREATE TABLE statement and CREATE VIEW statement can be defined in terms of a query. For example:

```
create table customer_sales_totals
   as
select  customer_name,sum(sale_value) sale_total
  from sales s,customers c
 where s.customer_id=c.customer_id
 group by c.customer_name
```

Another DDL statement which is of particular importance to SQL tuning is the create index statement which is used to index selected rows to improve retrieval performance or to enforce uniqueness.

QUERY OPERATIONS

SUBQUERIES

A subquery is an SQL statement which occurs within another SQL statement. Such a "nested" SQL statement can be used in many SQL statements, such as SELECT, DELETE, UPDATE and INSERT statements.

The following statement uses a subquery to count the number of employees who share the minimum salary:

```
select count(*)
  from employees
 where salary=(select min(salary)
                 from employees)
```

CORRELATED SUBQUERY

A correlated subquery is one in which the subquery refers to values in the parent query. A correlated subquery can return the same results as a join, but can be used where a join cannot, such as in an UPDATE, INSERT and DELETE statement. For instance, the following statement assigns the sale representative for a customer who is also an employee to the employee's manager.

Note the reference in the subquery to the CUSTOMERS table—this is the *correlated* part of the subquery.

```
update customers
   set sales_rep_id=(select manager_id
                       from employees
                      where surname=customers.contact_surname
                        and firstname=customers.contact_firstname
                        and date_of_birth=customers.date_of_birth)
 where (contact_surname,contact_firstname,date_of_birth) in
       (select surname,firstname,date_of_birth
          from employees)
```

JOINS

The join operation allows the results from two or more tables to be merged based on some common column values.

Inner join

The inner join is the most common type of join operation. In this case, rows from one table are joined to rows from another table based on some common ("key") values. Rows which have no match in the other table are not included in the results. For instance, the following query links employee and department details:

```
select department_name,surname,salary
  from employees e,departments d
 where e.department_id=d.department_id
   and e.surname='SMITH'
```

Equi-joins and theta join

An equi-join is one in which the equals operator is used to directly relate two values. This is very commonly used to look up a unique key or to join master and detail tables—such as in our previous inner-join example. A join which uses an operator other than the equals operator (such as >, BETWEEN or !=) is called a *theta* join.

```
select customer_id,regionname
  from customers, salesregion
 where phoneno between lowphoneno and highphoneno
```

outer join

The outer join allows rows to be included even if they have no match in the other table. In Oracle, the outer join operator is "(+)"—but note that this is one of Oracle's major deviations from the ANSI standard. The following query illustrates the outer join:

```
select department_name,surname
  from departments d,
       employees   e
 where d.department_id=e.department_id(+);
```

The effect of this outer join is to include departments without employees in the results.

anti-join

A common requirement is to select all rows from a table which do not have a matching row in some other result set. This is typically implemented using a subquery and the IN or EXISTS clause. Oracle Corporation has recently taken to calling such an operation an "anti-join." The following examples illustrate the anti-join using the EXISTS and IN operators. Each example selects employees who are not also customers.

```
select surname,firstname,date_of_birth
  from employees
 where (surname,firstname,date_of_birth) not in
          (select contact_surname,contact_firstname,date_of_birth
                  from customers)

select surname,firstname,date_of_birth
  from employees
 where not exists
             (select *
                from customers
               where contact_surname=employees.surname
```

```
                           and contact_firstname=employees.firstname
                           and date_of_birth=employees.date_of_birth)
```

self join

In a self join, a table is joined to itself. This is performed in exactly the same manner as any other join. The following example shows the employees table in a self join to link employees with their manager:

```
select m.surname manager ,e.surname employee
  from employees m,
       employees e
 where e.manager_id=m.employee_id
```

SET OPERATIONS

SQL implements a number of operations which deal directly with result sets. These operations, collectively referred to as "set operations," allow result sets to be concatenated, subtracted or overlaid.

The most common of these operations is the UNION operator, which returns the sum of two result sets. By default, duplicates in each result set are eliminated. The UNION ALL operation, by contrast, will return the sum of the two result sets, including any duplicates. The following example returns a list of customers and employees. Employees who are also customers will only be listed once:

```
select contact_surname,contact_firstname,date_of_birth
  from customers
union
select surname,firstname,date_of_birth
  from employees
```

MINUS returns all rows in the first result set which do not appear in the second result set. The following example returns all customers who are not also employees:

```
select contact_surname,contact_firstname,date_of_birth
  from customers
minus
select surname,firstname,date_of_birth
  from employees
```

INTERSECT returns only the rows which appear in both result sets. The following example returns customers who are also employees:

```
select contact_surname,contact_firstname,date_of_birth
  from customers
 intersect
select surname,firstname,date_of_birth
  from employees
```

All set operations require that the component queries return the same number of columns, and those columns need to be of a compatible datatype.

AGGREGATION

Aggregate operations allow for summary information to be generated, typically based upon groups of data. Data can be grouped using the GROUP BY operator. If this is done, the select list must consist only of columns contained within the GROUP BY clause and *aggregate functions*.

Some of the aggregate functions are:

❑ AVG   - Calculate the average value for the group.

❑ COUNT   - Return the number of rows in the group.

❑ MAX   - Return the maximum value in the group.

❑ MIN   - Return the minimum value in the group.

❑ STDDEV   - Return the standard deviation for the group.

❑ SUM   - Return the total of all values for the group.

The following example generates summary salary information for each department:

```
select department_id, sum(salary)
   from employees
 group by department_id
```

VIEWS

Views can be thought of as "stored queries" or "virtual tables." A view appears logically to the user as a table, but is defined in terms of a query. A view can be based on more than one table, and a view can be updated if logically possible. An alternative to creating the CUSTOMER_SALES_TOTALS table in the previous example would be to create a view:

```
create view customer_sales_totals_v
   as
select  customer_name,sum(sale_value) sale_total
  from sales s,customers c
 where s.customer_id=c.customer_id
 group by c.customer_name
```

NULLS AND THREE-VALUED LOGIC

NULL values are used to indicate that a data item is missing or undefined. The use of NULL values in relational databases is a hotly debated topic because of the misleading or unexpected results which sometimes occur. For instance, the following query does not include all rows in the table, because it will not include rows where JOB is NULL:

```
SELECT count(*)
    FROM PEOPLE
WHERE JOB='ACCOUNTANT'
    OR JOB!='ACCOUNTANT'
```

The concept of NULL or missing values extends the traditional and intuitive two-valued logic (TRUE/FALSE) to a new, three-valued logic (TRUE/FALSE/UNKNOWN). Using this three-valued logic, if a job is UNKNOWN, it is also unknown whether JOB!='ACCOUNTANT.' While this fairly trivial example seems somewhat reasonable (after all, if job is unknown, then it *might* be 'ACCOUNTANT'), many people argue that three-valued logic leads to "wrong answers" and should be abandoned.

We can't pursue this debate here, but will later see that note that NULL values are important in SQL tuning because they are not included in indexes. Operations which search for NULL values therefore pose particular tuning challenges as well as running the risk of unexpected results.

TRANSACTIONS

A transaction is an indivisible logical unit of work. In practice, a transaction is a collection of SQL commands which will either succeed or fail as a unit. The following properties of a transaction are important:

❑ A transaction is commenced when a DML statement is issued—that is, the first time data is modified. In Oracle, a transaction can also be commenced using the ALTER SESSION SET TRANSACTION statement or by the DBMS_TRANSACTION.BEGIN_DISCRETE_TRANSACTION call.

❑ Changes to rows made during the transaction are not visible to other sessions.

❑ Rows which have been changed within the transaction are locked and may not be altered by other sessions until the transaction has completed.

❏ A transaction is terminated with the COMMIT or the ROLLBACK statement, by a DDL statement (which implicitly commits) or by program termination (which issues a COMMIT for a normal termination and a ROLLBACK for an abnormal termination).

❏ If a COMMIT is issued, changes made during the transaction become permanent and are made visible to other sessions. All locks are released.

❏ If a ROLLBACK is issued, changes made during the transaction are discarded. All locks are released.

ORACLE EXTENSIONS TO THE ANSI STANDARD

The ANSI standard allows for three levels of ANSI compliance: "entry," "intermediate" and "full."

As of Oracle 7.3, Oracle conforms to the entry level of the SQL-92 standard. This is the lowest level of compliance with the ANSI standard, but does require Oracle to comply with the "core" ANSI model. Entry level SQL-92 is very similar to SQL-89 and in fact, Oracle SQL has changed only slightly over the past five years.

Oracle provides a number of enhancements to the ANSI standard. Some of these cover features are not included at all in the ANSI standard, while in other cases, Oracle may have implemented a feature which was later defined in the ANSI standard, but in a different manner. If ANSI compatibility is a concern, you can identify statements which contain any extensions with the following SQL command:

```
ALTER SESSION SET FLAGGER ENTRY|INTERMEDIATE|FULL|OFF
```

"ENTRY," "INTERMEDIATE" and "FULL" correspond to the levels of ANSI compliance mentioned above.

HIERARCHICAL QUERIES

A "hierarchical" query is one in which parent and child rows exist in the same table. This is also often referred to as the "explosion of parts" query. In a simple self join, a child row is joined to a parent row. In a hierarchical query, the child is joined to the parent row, the parent row is joined to its parent row, and so on, until the entire hierarchy is exposed.

For instance, in the EMPLOYEES table, the column manager_id points to the employee_id of the employees manager. We can easily display the manager for each employee by issuing a self join:

```
select e.surname employee ,m.surname manager
  from employees e,
       employees m
 where e.manager_id=m.employee_id;
```

```
EMPLOYEE          MANAGER
---------------   ---------------
RAMPTON           EVANS
STOKES            MILLS
NUTTALL           LEE
LEE               MCDOWELL
PARKES            LEE
EVANS             PATCH
GOSLEY            REID
FRYER             KNOTT
LITTLE            LEE
ALEXANDER         EVANS
BATTERHAM         EVANS
POUND             LEE
BOSWOOD           WORLAND
```

If we want to display the employees in the command hierarchy, we can use the hierarchical operators CONNECT BY and START WITH.

```
select rpad(' ',level*3)||surname employee
  from employees
 start with manager_id=0
connect by prior employee_id=manager_id;
```

```
EMPLOYEE
------------------------------
    REID
        GOSLEY
        POOLE
        JENSEN
        KEYWORTH
            WALKER
            JAMES
            FRYER
            MILLS
                STOKES
                BURNS
                JOHNSON
```

This query shows that REID is the senior employee in the hierarchy. WALKER reports to KEYWORTH who reports to REID and so on.

ANSI standard SQL does not provide a simple method for performing such queries (although a definition is expected in SQL3).

OUTER JOIN

SQL-92 does provide a means of performing an outer join. The OUTER JOIN operation can appear in the from clause to indicate that the join is to be an outer join. In the following example, at least one row will be returned for each department, even if the department has no employees.

```
select department_name,surname
   from departments d left outer join employees   e
      on d.department_id=e.department_id;
```

Oracle's implementation of the outer join, which predates the SQL-92 standard by several years, is to use the (+) operator in the WHERE clause. The following example shows Oracle's implementation of the outer join:

```
select department_name,surname
   from departments d,
        employees   e
  where d.department_id=e.department_id(+);
```

Oracle's implementation can be rather confusing and it is fairly common for users to place the (+) operator on the wrong side of the expression. You may find it useful to think of the (+) as going on the side of the comparison which will return nulls if there is no match—in other words: "add nulls here."

SOME COMMENTS ON THE SQL NON-PROCEDURAL APPROACH

The movement from procedural, record-at-a-time processing used in pre-relational databases to the non-procedural, set-oriented processing using in SQL has had a major effect on the ease and efficiency of data access.

Early critics of relational databases frequently claimed that the relational model could not deliver acceptable performance. This criticism was largely based on the relational model's reliance on indexes rather than pointers for data navigation. The perceived performance problems impeded take-up of relational databases for some time, but eventually were overcome by the theoretical and practical benefits being delivered by the relational model—together with improvements in the performance of relational databases and computer hardware.

Today, the average database size of relational databases is probably 10 to 100 times greater than that of the early 1980s. User requirements for throughput and response time are higher than ever. Relational database vendors constantly release competing benchmark results to support the proposition that their implementation is the fastest. Clearly the user community is still concerned with the performance of relational databases.

While relational databases can provide adequate performance for almost any application type, many relational databases are performing several levels below their potential. It may be that a major reason for this failure to perform is the "non-procedural" nature of SQL. SQL encourages the user to specify the data to be retrieved without giving any thought to the way it will be retrieved. Since the retrieval path is absolutely central to the performance of the query, SQL actively discourages users from thinking about, or optimizing, performance.

It may be that eventually, relational database engines will be so advanced that no SQL tuning effort will be needed. However, this is definitely not the case at present. Whatever happens in the future, the simple fact now is that to implement high performance relational systems, substantial investment in SQL tuning must be made. The philosophy of "state what you want, not how to get it" is a philosophy which should be rejected if optimal performance is the target.

CHAPTER SUMMARY

A relational database presents data to the user as a series of tables. Tables are linked by common data values. Users can issue commands against a relational database without needing to know the physical implementation details for the database. Relational databases have become the dominant model for database management because they offer flexible access to data. SQL (Structured Query Language) is a language designed for the retrieval and manipulation of data in relational databases.

SQL is defined by ANSI standards. Oracle SQL conforms to the "entry level" ANSI 92 standard for SQL. Extensions to Oracle SQL include a facility for hierarchical queries and a facility to perform outer joins.

The major categories of SQL are:

❏ Queries, which are represented by the SELECT statement.

❏ Data Manipulation Language (DML) to UPDATE, DELETE AND INSERT data.

❏ Data Definition Language (DDL) to create tables, indexes and other database objects.

Issuing queries is one of the primary operations of the relational database. Some typical query operations are:

❏ Joins, which allow rows from two or more tables to be combined based on common key values.

❏ Subqueries, which are select statements which may appear within other SQL statements.

❏ The ORDER BY clause, which allows results to be returned in sorted order.

❏ The GROUP BY operator, which allows aggregate information for groups of rows to be calculated.

A NULL value is one which is missing or unknown. The use of NULLs results in three-valued logic—TRUE, FALSE or UNKNOWN—rather than the two-valued logic typical of many computing environments.

Groups of SQL statements can be combined into a transaction. Statements in a transaction will succeed or fail as a unit. The COMMIT statement causes statements in a transaction to be made permanent and the rollback statement causes the changes to be aborted.

Chapter 3

SQL PROCESSING

INTRODUCTION

In this section, we look at how Oracle turns your SQL statements into results—either returning or changing data within the database. Processing SQL statements is, from one point of view, all that relational databases do, so understanding SQL processing requires an understanding of how Oracle works.

It's possible to tune an SQL statement without having a full understanding of how Oracle processes SQL—but having such an understanding usually saves a lot of wasted effort. As we discussed in Chapter 1, tuning SQL is a repetitive process which can involve a fair deal of trial and error. With an understanding of Oracle's processing techniques, you should be able to reduce the number of errors and move more directly to the best result.

The major aspects of SQL processing which we will discuss in this chapter are:

❑ The overall procedure which Oracle undertakes from the receipt of your SQL statement to its successful execution.

❑ The process of SQL *parsing*—in which Oracle checks your SQL for errors, checks for existing identical SQL statements and prepares the SQL for execution.

❑ A brief overview of Oracle's data retrieval mechanisms, such as table scans, index fetches and sorts.

❏ An overview of multi-table operations, such as joins and set operations.

❏ An overview of Oracle transaction processing.

❏ A detailed examination of the Oracle query optimizers.

OVERVIEW OF SQL PROCESSING

Figure 3.1 displays an overview of the steps involved in executing an SQL statement.

CURSORS

A *cursor*, or *context area*, is an area in memory in which Oracle stores your SQL statement and associated information. This includes the parsed and unparsed representation of your SQL statement, the execution plan and a pointer to the current row.

When SQL statement execution is complete, the memory associated with the cursor can be freed for other purposes or can be saved for re-execution.

In most tools, the allocation of cursors is performed by the client tools and is transparent to the programmer. In the *programmatic interfaces* (for instance, *PRO*C* or *Oracle Call Interface* [OCI]) and in some other tools, the programmer may create and destroy cursors explicitly.

PARSING

Parsing is the process of preparing your SQL statement for execution. This process is analogous to the process a language compiler or interpreter must undertake in order to translate high level statements into machine code. The parse process will include the following phases:

❏ Check that the SQL statement is *syntactically* valid: that the SQL conforms to the rules of the SQL language, that all keywords and operators are valid and correctly used.

❏ Check that the SQL is *semantically* valid. This means that all references to database objects (i.e., tables, columns) are valid.

❑ Check security: that the user has permission to perform the specified SQL operations on the objects involved.

❑ Determine an execution plan for the SQL statement. The execution plan describes the series of steps which Oracle will perform in order to access and/or update the data involved.

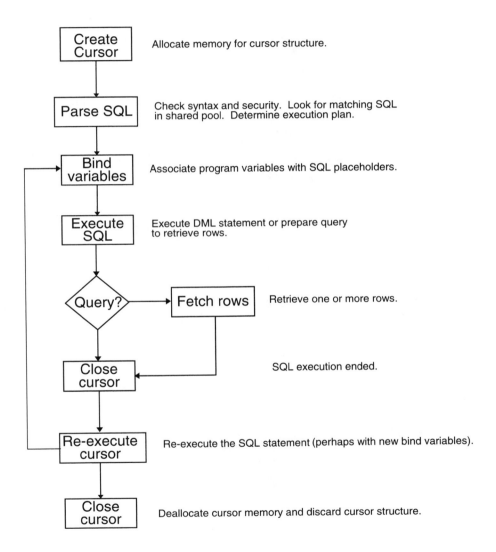

FIGURE 3.1 Simplified overview of Oracle SQL processing.

Parsing can be an expensive operation, although often its overhead is masked by the greater overhead of high IO requirements. However, eliminating unnecessary parsing is always desirable.

SHARED SQL

In order to avoid unnecessary parsing, Oracle maintains a *cache* of recently executed SQL statements together with their execution plans. Technically speaking, this cache is maintained in the *SQL Area* of the *Shared pool* (see Chapter 15 for more details on the shared pool). Whenever a request to execute an SQL statement is issued, Oracle looks for a matching statement in this cache. If a matching statement is found, Oracle uses the execution plan stored in the cache and so avoids most of the overhead involved in parsing.

Oracle uses a *hashing* algorithm in order to locate a matching statement in the shared pool. This means that it uses a mathematical process to translate the SQL text into a number and uses that number to find that SQL in the shared pool. It therefore stands to reason that for a match to be found, the SQL must be *exactly* identical—including spaces, upper/lower casing, use of aliases, etc.[1]

You may see a recommendation—based on the implications of this hashing algorithm—to code SQL identically throughout your application. This allows SQL with the same functionality—but contained within separate programs—to share the same slot in the shared pool. However, you'll rarely see much advantage from such an approach—the SQL cache is big, and there is room enough for a few "nearly" identical SQL statements coming from different modules.

A much more common reason why SQL cannot be found in the shared pool is because it contains hard-coded literals instead of bind variables.

BIND VARIABLES

An SQL statement may contain variables which change from execution to execution. These variables are typically parameters to the SQL statement which define the rows to be processed or new values to be inserted or updated. We can specify these variables either as *literals* or as *bind variables*.

For instance, using literals, we could retrieve details for employee 1234 with the following SQL statement:

```
SQL> select firstname,surname
2    from employees
3    where employee_id=1234
```

---

[1]In fact, to speed the comparison process, most versions of Oracle only compare part of the SQL statement—perhaps the first and last 64 bytes.

The next time we wished to select an employee, we would change the "1234" literal to the new value and re-execute. This will work, but remember that the SQL statement must be absolutely identical if a match is to be found in the shared pool. Since the employee_id is likely to be different for every execution, we will almost never find a matching statement in the shared pool and consequently the statement will have to be reparsed every time.

An alternative approach is to specify these variable portions with *bind variables*. Bind variables (sometimes called host variables) are fixed references to variables contained elsewhere in the programming language or development tool. Within most languages or tools, bind variables are recognizable because they are prefixed by a colon. For instance, in the following statement, the value of employee_id is stored in a bind variable (the SQLPLUS VAR command allows us to define a bind variable):

```
SQL> variable employee_number_ws number

SQL> select firstname,surname
2     from employees
3     where employee_id=:employee_number_ws
```

Two very strong advantages of bind variables are:

❏ If the value of the bind variable changes, you don't need to create a new cursor or re-parse the SQL statement when re-executing the SQL.

❏ If another session executes the same SQL statement, it will find a match in the shared pool, since the name of the bind variable does not change from execution to execution.

Conversely, if you use literals instead of bind variables, you'll suffer from the following problems:

❏ Every time you change the value of a literal, you (or your software tool) will have to request that the SQL be re-parsed.

❏ When you do request the parse, the chance of finding a match in the shared pool will be negligible.

❏ The SQL cache will fill up with "on-off" SQL, and may need to be bigger than it otherwise would be.

❏ When an Oracle session wants to place a new SQL statement in the shared pool, it has to acquire an Oracle internal lock (a *latch*). Under extreme circumstances in some versions of Oracle, contention for these latches can result in a performance bottleneck at best or dramatic performance problems at worst.

Figure 3.2 illustrates the flow of activities which occur when Oracle is required to parse an SQL statement. Note the amount of processing which is avoided if we can avoid re-parsing the SQL statement or if a matching SQL statement is found in the shared pool.

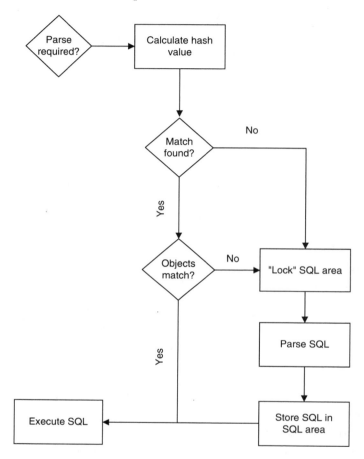

FIGURE 3.2 Flow of processing during parsing of an SQL statement.

RECURSIVE SQL

Recursive SQL is SQL which Oracle generates on your behalf in order to parse or execute your SQL. For instance, in order to determine that all table and column names in your SQL are valid, Oracle must check a number of tables collectively known as the *data dictionary.* Usually this information can be found in memory (in the *dictionary cache* or *row cache*). However, if the information cannot be found in memory, then Oracle will issue a *recursive SQL* statement to retrieve it.

Since recursive SQL is frequently generated during parsing operations, reducing parsing will reduce recursive SQL.

REDUCING PARSING

❏ Parsing is an expensive operation. In extreme cases, excessive parsing can completely bottleneck your application system.

❏ If you are going to re-execute your SQL but use different parameters, use bind variables to define these parameters. This will minimize parsing.

Depending on your development tool, reducing parse overhead may be automatic or may require careful coding. Guidelines on reusing cursors and using bind variables within some popular development tools can be found in Appendix C.

EXECUTING SQL

EXECUTING AND FETCHING

Once the SQL statement is parsed and all variables are bound, Oracle is ready to execute the statement. In the case of DML (INSERT, UPDATE, DELETE), executing the statement results in the SQL being actioned immediately (although the changes do not become permanent until a COMMIT is issued).

In the case of a SELECT statement, the execute call readies the cursor for fetch operations. In the case of certain queries (for instance, where the rows must be sorted or locked), opening the cursor makes Oracle retrieve all the rows to be returned. In other cases, opening the cursor simply locates the record pointer at the first row.

Regardless of whether the open call must access all rows to be returned, it is the *fetch* call which returns data to the client environment. The fetch call retrieves one or more rows from the database and stores the results in host variables which can be manipulated by the program.

Array fetch

Each fetch request can return more than one row. When a fetch returns a batch of rows in this manner, it is known as an *array fetch*. Array fetches are much more efficient than fetching a row at a time.

Often your client tool (for instance, SQL*PLUS) will automatically perform array fetches. Other tools might require that you explicitly perform an array fetch (for instance, PRO*C or PRO*COBOL). See Appendix C for guidelines on configuring array fetch in various development tools.

RESULT SETS

The output from an SQL query is referred to as a *result set*. A result set consists of rows and columns and may be thought of as a temporary table containing the queries results. Result sets are also created during intermediate operations. For instance, in a join of tables A, B and C, table A is joined to B creating an intermediate result set. This result set is then joined to table C to create the final result set which is returned to your program.

RETRIEVING DATA

Oracle can retrieve your data in a number of ways. The most common techniques for retrieving table data are to:

❑ Read the entire table using a *full table scan*.
❑ Access a specific row using its *ROWID*.
❑ Use an index to locate the rows.
❑ Use a hash key lookup.

Here we will briefly examine each access mechanism. Detailed guidelines for optimizing table accesses are contained in Chapter 6.

Full table scan

The full table scan is the simplest way for Oracle to get your data. In a full table scan, every row of data in the table is read into memory. This access mechanism is always available to Oracle.

To perform a full table scan, Oracle reads all *blocks* (the basic unit of data storage) allocated to the table, starting with the first block and continuing until it reaches the *high water mark*. The high water mark is the "highest" block in the table which has ever held data. For instance, immediately after creating a table, the high water mark will be set at five blocks. As rows are inserted into the table, the high water mark will move up. However, even if all rows in a table are deleted, the high water mark never moves down. The only way to reset it is to truncate or recreate the table.

ROWID access

The *ROWID* is a pseudo-column—which means that although you can SELECT it, it isn't really part of the table data. The ROWID represents the physical location of a row. Accessing a row by its ROWID is usually the quickest way to get the row, since the ROWID tells Oracle exactly where the row is in the database.

ROWID accesses typically happen for one of the following reasons:

❑ The ROWID was obtained from an index which was used to locate the rows.

❑ The ROWID was obtained via a hash key lookup (see below).

❑ The ROWID was obtained from a currently open cursor (using the WHERE CURRENT OF CURSOR clause).

Index lookups

An index allows rows matching values stored in the index to be quickly retrieved. Oracle will search the index for matching key values. The index links these key values to the ROWIDs of matching rows. The ROWIDs can be used to quickly retrieve the matching rows from the table.

Oracle supports two types of indexes—B*-tree and bitmap indexes. Details of the construction of these indexes is contained in Chapter 4.

Hash key lookup

A *hash function* is a mathematical function which can be applied to a column value to obtain a *hash value*.

A *hash cluster* is a table in which data is physically stored according to the hash value of a key column. To find rows corresponding to some key value, Oracle can apply the hash function to some key value and then access the rows corresponding to the resulting hash value. Hash clusters are discussed in detail in Chapter 4.

JOINING TABLES

Joins allow rows from two or more tables to be merged, usually based on common key values. Most non-trivial SQL statements involve joins. The different types of join operations supported by the relational model are described in Chapter 2. Here, we discuss the variety of techniques which Oracle can employ to efficiently perform your join. Optimization of joins is discussed in detail in Chapter 7.

Oracle supports three join techniques:

❑ The sort merge join.
❑ The nested loops join.
❑ The hash join.

The sort merge join

The *sort merge join* is a join method which does not require indexes. When applying the sort merge algorithm, Oracle sorts each table (or the *result set* from a previous operation) on the column values used to join the two tables. Oracle then merges the two sorted result sets into one.

You can conceptualize this process by imagining that you have two piles of numbered pages (perhaps odd numbers in one pile and even in the other) in some random order. To get these two piles into a single pile in correct order, you would arrange each pile in sorted order and then interleave the odd and even pages.

The nested loops join

The *nested loops* join is a join algorithm which usually involves an index (or hash cluster) on at least one of the tables.

In a nested loops join, a full table scan is done on one of the tables or result sets (probably either the smaller table or the table which does not have an index on the join column). For every row found in this result set, a lookup—usually involving an index—is performed on the second table and the matching row is retrieved.

You can imagine doing such a join yourself if you had two piles of paper, one sorted—one not, and you wanted to find matching numbers in each pile and you didn't care about the order of the final pile. You could do this by going through the unsorted pile sheet by sheet. For each sheet, you could quickly find the matching sheet in the other pile (since that pile is sorted). When you had finished going through the unsorted pile, you will have matched sheets in both piles. However, the resulting pile would not be in any particular order.

The hash join

In a hash join, a *hash table* (a sort of on-the-fly index) is constructed for the larger of the two tables. The smaller table is then scanned, and the hash table is used to find matching rows in the larger table.

This can work very well, especially if the hash table can fit in memory (otherwise, temporary tables have to be allocated). It performs particularly well if the two tables are of different sizes. Hash joins also work well for "anti-joins" and with parallel SQL.

SORTING AND GROUPING

Following the accessing and joining of raw table data, the SQL statement may require that the data be:

- ❏ Returned in sorted order (due to ORDER BY).
- ❏ Aggregated (due to GROUP BY, DISTINCT, MAX or other statistical operators).
- ❏ Compared with some other result set (UNION, INTERSECTION, MINUS).

These operations all need to sort the final or intermediary result set. To do this, Oracle allocates an area of memory (defined by the configuration parameter *SORT_AREA_SIZE*) which it will use to perform the sort. If the memory allocation is insufficient to perform the sort, a *temporary segment* is allocated and the sort becomes a *disk sort*. Optimizing operations which involve sorting and aggregation is the topic of Chapter 8.

MODIFYING DATA

Data Manipulation Statements (DML) allow data to be inserted, deleted or updated. Optimization of DML statements, and of DML statements grouped in transactions is discussed in Chapter 9.

Typically, most of the overhead involved when you UPDATE or DELETE data is in locating the data to be processed. Once the rows to be altered are retrieved and loaded into Oracle shared memory, they may be altered or deleted with only a small overhead. However, if a column to be updated is heavily indexed, or a row is deleted from a heavily indexed table, finding and modifying index entries may be expensive.

INSERTS and free lists

When an INSERT statement is executed, Oracle must find a block which has sufficient free space to accommodate the new row. To do this, Oracle maintains one or more lists of free blocks for each table, called a *free list*. If there are multiple concurrent inserts into a table, there can be contention for these free lists and it may be necessary to create multiple lists. Chapter 16 contains a discussion of multiple free lists.

Array INSERTS

The array INSERT is similar to the concept of the *array fetch* and allows Oracle to insert rows in batches. Array INSERTs are much more efficient than inserting a row at a time. See Appendix C for guidelines on implementing array processing in various client tools.

Locking

Like all RDBMSs, Oracle implements a locking scheme to prevent concurrent updates to table rows. Oracle's locking scheme has the following features:

❏ Only the rows which are updated or deleted are locked. In the case of a table with a unique index, an insert locks the index row with that unique value.

❏ Locks do not prevent the row from being selected. However, the row values seen by other processes will be the row values *before* the update occurred (providing that it is not yet committed).

❏ All locks are released when a COMMIT or ROLLBACK is issued.

❏ Entire tables can be locked explicitly using the LOCK TABLE command.

❏ Rows may be locked without being altered with the FOR UPDATE clause of the select statement.

❏ Implementing bitmapped indexes may cause locks to be applied to entire blocks of data.

❏ Implementing referential integrity can cause table locks to be applied.

Committing

Changes made during your transaction are not being made directly to the database files on disk. Instead, they are being made to copies of the disk blocks contained in Oracle's *buffer cache* within the *SGA*—this means that changes are initially made in memory only.

A COMMIT causes all changes made in the transaction to become permanent. In order for Oracle to guarantee that no committed data will be lost, the transaction details must be written to disk. When you issue a COMMIT, Oracle writes the transaction details to a transaction log known as the *redo log*. You have to wait for this disk write to occur before continuing. Therefore, when inserting or updating large quantities of data, it can be advantageous not to commit too often, since every commit requires some disk I/O.

QUERY OPTIMIZATION

For almost all SQL statements, there will be more than one way for Oracle to retrieve the rows required. When Oracle parses an SQL statement, it must decide which approach will be fastest. The process of determining this "optimal" path to the data is referred to as *query optimization*.

Query optimization is applied to all queries and to any other statement (for instance, UPDATE, INSERT, DELETE, CREATE TABLE AS *queries*) which contains a query or which contains a WHERE clause.

The part of the Oracle software which performs query optimization is referred to as the *optimizer*.

Oracle supports two approaches to query optimization:

❑ The *rule based optimizer* is the older of the two optimizers and has its roots in the origins of the Oracle RDBMS. This optimizer makes its decisions based on a set of rules and on the rankings of various access paths. The rule based optimizer is not aware of—and cannot take into account—data volumes. For instance, the rule based optimizer will always prefer an index lookup to a full table scan. However, the rule based optimizer cannot distinguish between a full table scan of a table with two rows, and that of a table with two million rows.

❑ The *cost based optimizer* was introduced in Oracle 7. It incorporates may features of the rule based optimizer, but has the advantage of being able to take into account statistical information relating to the volume and distribution of data within tables and indexes. This optimizer can therefore distinguish between a two row table and a two million row table and may generate different execution plans for each.

THE OPTIMIZATION PROCESS

The aim of both optimizers is to establish an effective *execution plan*. Because SQL is a non-procedural language, the SQL itself does not include instructions for retrieving the data. It is up to Oracle to devise a means of retrieving the data and the resulting scheme is referred to as the *execution plan*.

For instance, consider the following SQL:

```
select distinct customer_name
  from customers c,
       sales     s,
       employees e
 where s.sale_date>sysdate-7
   and e.surname='Flintstone'
   and e.firstname='Fred'
   and c.sales_rep_id=e.employee_id
   and s.customer_id=c.customer_id
```

In English, this query might be stated as "give me the names of all Sales Representative Flintstone's customers who have bought something in the past week."

The optimizer has to decide which is the best way to get the data. Some possible approaches are:

1. Get all sales for the past week. Then, get the names of all the customers matching those sales. Then, filter out any customers who aren't handled by Mr. Flintstone.

2. Get Flintstone's employee_id. Using that id, get all customers handled by Flintstone. Then filter out any customers who haven't bought anything in the last week.

3. Get all customers. Then filter out those who aren't represented by Flintstone. Then filter out those who haven't made any sales.

It is apparent that the decision on which approach to take will make a very significant difference to the amount of time taken to retrieve the results. It may also be obvious that the last approach is likely to be the worst, since all customer records would have to be read—so we hope the optimizer won't pick that path.

CHOOSING THE OPTIMIZATION APPROACH

Despite the fact that the cost based optimizer has been around for some years, many systems are still using a rule based approach. There are a number of reasons for this:

❏ Early versions of the cost based optimizer contained significant deficiencies, and better performance could often be achieved by using the rule based optimizer.

❏ Converting existing systems to the cost based optimizer can be a substantial task, since existing SQL will be tuned for the rule based optimizer and may need to be re-tuned to take advantage of cost based optimization.

❏ Developers and DBAs were used to the rule based optimizer. Using the cost based optimizer required training and familiarization.

❏ Execution plans from the cost based optimizer could change when the data changed. This made the cost based optimizer less predictable. It also meant that queries developed in small to medium development environments could behave differently in the larger production environments.

Despite these drawbacks, the cost based optimizer is the correct decision for almost all new projects and a valid migration option for many existing systems. Cost based optimization represents the future of Oracle query optimization; while the rule based optimizer is likely to be discarded at some time during the life of Oracle version 8. Improvements to the cost based optimizer have been made in each release of Oracle and now the cost based optimizer will almost always choose an execution plan which is as good or better than that which the rule based optimizer would choose. When it doesn't, you can use *hints* to adjust the execution plan.

While the cost based optimizer has been improved with every release, the rule based optimizer is virtually unchanged since the first release of Oracle 7.

Cost based optimization can be particularly good for "untunable" SQL. "Untunable SQL" is SQL you have no control over, such as the SQL generated by a third party tool (such as Microsoft Access) or ad hoc SQL entered by casual users. These sorts of SQL are very common in decision support or data warehousing environments and here the cost based optimizer can be particularly helpful.

Despite the advantages of cost based optimization, you should not conclude that the cost based optimizer will relieve you of the need to tune SQL. The cost based optimizer can make the tuning process easier, since it will usually pick the best (most *selective*) of all available indexes and choose a good *driving table*. However, the cost based optimizer can't rewrite badly formulated SQL and it certainly can't create an index if a useful one is missing. Whichever optimization approach you choose, it is still up to you (or the author of the SQL) to ensure that it is properly tuned.

DETAILS COMMON TO BOTH OPTIMIZERS

While the two flavors of optimization use totally different techniques to determine the "optimal" execution plan, there are a number of initial steps and restrictions which they share.

Statement transformation

Certain SQL statements are transformed into logically equivalent statements.

A statement which incorporates a subquery involving the IN clause can often be represented as a join. For instance, the statement below selects all employees who work for departments in the Melbourne location.

```
select employee_id, surname,firstname
  from employees
 where department_id in
       (select department_id
          from departments
         where location = 'Melbourne')
```

The same query can be expressed as a join:

```
select e.employee_id, e.surname, e.firstname
  from employees e,
       departments d
 where d.location='Melbourne'
   and d.department_id=e.department_id
```

Using join logic to resolve statements of this type is usually more efficient than using IN logic, so Oracle automatically transforms statements with correlated subqueries using an IN into a join where possible.

Another example of automatic transformation is the transformation of statements containing OR conditions. A statement involving an OR condition may be expressed as a UNION ALL. For instance, the following query retrieves the names of all departments in Melbourne and London:

```
select department_name
  from departments
 where location = 'Melbourne'
    or location = 'London'
```

Rather than use an OR clause, the same query can be expressed using a UNION, as follows:

```
select department_name
  from departments
 where location = 'Melbourne'
UNION ALL
select department_name
  from departments
 where location = 'London'
```

The UNION approach promotes the use of indexes, and so Oracle may translate statements using OR into UNIONS.

If a statement references a view, the definition of the view can be "pushed into" the SQL statement. For instance, if we had a view defined as follows:

```
create or replace view MANAGERS_VIEW as
select *
from EMPLOYEES
where MANAGER_ID is null;
```

and a query on that view like this:

```
select firstname,surname
   from managers_view
 where salary >100000
```

The optimizer might insert the view definition in the SQL so that it looks like this:

```
select firstname,surname
  from EMPLOYEES
 where MANAGER_ID is null
   and salary >100000
```

Other similarities in the approach

Both optimizers must compare a number of possible access paths and join orders. The questions the optimizers will consider are:

- ❏ For each table, what options do I have for retrieving the data?
- ❏ With which table should I start? In what order should the tables be joined?

Depending on the complexity of the SQL, there may be hundreds of possible combinations of access paths and join orders.

Regardless of the optimizer selected, the following rules apply:

- ❏ If a join would result in a single row only (perhaps both tables had a primary or unique key lookup specified in the where clause) then that join will be given preference.
- ❏ If there is an outer join, the outer join table (the table which may not have matching rows) will only be joined after the other (*inner*) table.

DETAILS OF THE RULE BASED OPTIMIZER

The basic approach of the rule based optimizer is:

1. For each table in the where clause, every possible access path is considered and ranked.
2. The access path with the lowest rank is selected.
3. For each remaining table, every possible access path is considered and ranked.
4. The access path with the lowest rank is selected.
5. And so on until every table is joined.

Table 3.1 shows the access path rankings for the rule based optimizer.

TABLE 3.1   Access path rankings for the rule based optimizer.

Rank	Operation
1	Single row by ROWID
2	Single row by cluster join
3	Single row by hash cluster key with unique or primary key

TABLE 3.1   Access path rankings for the rule based optimizer. *(Continued)*

Rank	Operation
4	Single row by unique or primary key
5	Cluster join
6	Hash cluster key
7	Indexed cluster key
8	Composite key (but only if all keys are used)
9	Single column indexes
10	Bounded range search on indexed columns
11	Unbounded range search on indexed columns
12	Sort merge join
13	MAX or MIN of indexed column
14	ORDER BY on indexed columns
15	Full table scan

These access path rankings can be hard to remember, so you may wish to remember just a few basic principles:

❑ Single row lookups are preferred to multiple row lookups.
❑ Indexes are preferred to table scans or sort merges.
❑ Equality lookups are preferred to range lookups.
❑ Bounded ranges (for instance, BETWEEN) are preferred to unbounded ranges (e.g., GREATER THAN).
❑ Using every column of an index is preferred to using only some columns of a concatenated index.

The rules for determining join order can be complex, but it boils down to the following principles:

❑ The rule based optimizer will tend to choose the join order with the least number of unoptimized joins. "Unoptimized" joins are generally those which don't use indexes.
❑ The rule based optimizer will choose as the "driving" table (first table in the join order) the table with the lowest ranking access path.

DETAILS OF THE COST BASED OPTIMIZER

The cost based optimizer also compares between many possible access paths. The cost based optimizer then constructs a list of possible execution plans and tries to estimate the "cost" which would be required to satisfy each execution plan. The execution plan with the lowest "cost" is selected.

The calculation of "cost" is based on a number of factors, including:

❑ Estimated number of database reads required.

❑ Requirements for sorting.

❑ Availability of the parallel query option.

The cost based optimizer may not consider all possible plans, as this may result in an excessive overhead. The higher the cost of the SQL statement, the more plans the cost based optimizer will consider.

This cost based approach is somewhat less predictable than the rule based optimizer, since the execution plan selected will depend on the statistics collected for a table, which are subject to change, and on its costing algorithms, which are unpublished and also subject to change.

Collecting optimizer statistics

The statistics which the cost based optimizer uses to calculate execution plan costs are collected using the ANALYZE table command. The analyze table command has the following (simplified) syntax:

```
ANALYZE TABLE table_name [CALCULATE STATISTICS|ESTIMATE
STATISTICS [SAMPLE n ROWS|PERCENT]]
```

The analyze command collects information from the nominated tables and its indexes and stores them in data dictionary tables which can be accessed by the cost based optimizer to calculate SQL statement costs. The following statistics are always collected:

❑ For a table, number of rows, number of blocks used and empty, average row length and average amount of used space within each block.

❑ For indexes, number of distinct keys, number of *leaf blocks*, and depth of the *b-tree* (see Chapter 4 for a detailed explanation of these terms).

The ANALYZE command allows you to read all table and index blocks to generate exact statistics (the COMPUTE STATISTICS option) or to sample a certain percentage or certain number of rows (ESTIMATE STATISTICS). For instance, the following command estimates statistics for the EMPLOYEES table using a 10% sample:

```
ANALYZE TABLE employees estimate statistics sample 10 percent
```

Examining every row using the CALCULATE STATISTICS option is usually impractical for very large tables—it will either take too long, or fail completely due to insufficient temporary segment space. In these cases, ESTIMATE STATISTICS, using a sample size of between 10 to 25% (perhaps even smaller for huge tables) will generate statistics which are sufficiently accurate.

Histograms

Prior to Oracle 7.3, the optimizer would know the number of unique keys in an index, but would not know the distribution of the key values. This would often cause the optimizer to disregard an index which had a small number of key values, even if some of those values were very infrequent and therefore good candidates for index lookup.

For instance, consider a database which contains details of handedness (e.g., right-handed, left-handed, ambidextrous). An index on this column will only contain three values and as a result, will not be selected by the cost based optimizer. This decision would be sensible if the query involved searching for right-handers, since over 90% of the database would be selected and an index would not be appropriate. However, if searching for ambidextrous individuals, the index would be very useful since less than one percent of rows would be selected.

The introduction of histograms allows Oracle to recognize selective values within otherwise unselective columns. The histogram stores information about the frequency of various column values which Oracle can use to decide whether or not to use the index.

To create a histogram, you use the following syntax in the analyze command:

```
ANALYZE TABLE table_name [ESTIMATE...|CALCULATE...]
FOR COLUMNS column_list|
FOR ALL COLUMNS|
FOR ALL INDEXED COLUMNS
SIZE n
```

You can choose to generate histograms for all columns in the table, for all indexed columns or for selected columns only. Normally, you would choose to create histograms only for columns where the data was not evenly distributed (e.g., is "skewed").

Histograms and bind variables   Oracle cannot use a histogram if the values to be selected are contained in bind variables. As we saw earlier, bind variables are an alternative to hardcoding the query parameters, and are beneficial because they reduce the overhead of parsing the SQL statement.

However, if Oracle is to make use of histograms which may have been created on a column, then it will be necessary to explicitly include the value in the SQL statements. This is because Oracle determines the access path for a statement without examining the values in bind variables. For instance, the following statement cannot make use of a histogram:

```
max_salary:=100000;
select count(*)
    into :output_bind
    from employees
 where salary > :max_salary
```

However, the following statement would be able to make use of a histogram on salary:

```
select count(*)
    into :output_bind
    from employees
 where salary > 100000
```

Therefore, you may decide not to use bind variables if you believe that the SQL statement will benefit significantly from the use of histograms. The trade-off between histograms and bind variables is discussed in more detail in Chapter 6.

Guidelines for using cost based optimization

Using the cost based optimizer can yield better results than the rule based optimizer, and can make SQL tuning easier. However, there are a few things you need to do to ensure that the cost based optimizer reaches its full potential:

1. Analyze your tables regularly.

2. Analyze *all* your tables. The cost based optimizer can make poor decisions if only some of your tables are analyzed.

3. All other things being equal, the CBO will use the leftmost table in the FROM clause as the driving table and will use the left-right order of tables in the FROM clause as the join order. Bear in mind that this is the *opposite* of what the rule based optimizer would do. If you have a preferred join order, list your tables in that order in the FROM clause.

4. Create histograms for columns which have an uneven distribution and/or a small number of distinct values. When wanting to take advantage of the histograms, make sure that you explicitly include the search values within the SQL statement itself rather than as bind variables.

5. Ensure that your development/tuning environment has similar or representative volumes and data characteristics as the production environment. It's not much good to optimize your SQL in development only to have changes in the data volumes cause the plan to change in production.

6. Watch out for tables which are loaded during batch runs. When analyzed (perhaps by a nightly or weekly analyze job) these tables may

have been empty. If you load thousands or millions of rows to these tables during batch processing, Oracle will continue to treat these tables as if they are empty unless you specifically analyze them after they have been loaded.

SETTING OPTIMIZER GOAL

The optimizer goal determines the overall approach that the optimizer takes in determining an execution plan. There are four possible settings for the optimizer goal:

1. RULE—which specifies that the optimizer is to take the rule based approach to optimization.

2. CHOOSE—which specifies that the optimizer is to use the cost based approach if *any* of the tables in the SQL statement have been analyzed. If no tables have been analyzed, then use the rule based approach.

3. ALL_ROWS—use the cost based optimizer (regardless of the presence of statistics) and choose an execution plan which will minimize the cost of processing all rows specified. This is the default behavior for the cost based optimizer. It is suitable for batch processing and reporting queries.

4. FIRST_ROWS—use the cost based optimizer and choose an execution plan which will minimize the cost of retrieving the first row. This setting can be useful for interactive applications because the critical performance measure may be the time taken to display the first row or page of information.

There are three ways to set the optimizer goal:

1. You can specify a default for the entire database in the database configuration file (the *init.ora* file). For instance, the following line sets the default goal to be a cost based optimization of response time:

```
OPTIMIZER_MODE=FIRST_ROWS
```

If no setting is specified in the init.ora file, then the default setting is CHOOSE.

2. You can change the default setting for your session by using the ALTER SESSION statement. For instance, after issuing the following statement, the optimization mode will be set to RULE for all subsequent statements (unless another ALTER SESSION command changes this):

```
ALTER SESSION SET OPTIMIZER_GOAL=RULE
```

3. You can change the optimization goal for an individual statement by using a *hint*. (We'll discuss hints in detail in a moment.) For instance, the following statement will be optimized for throughput using cost based optimization:

```
SELECT /*+ ALL_ROWS*/
   FROM EMPLOYEES
 WHERE MANAGER_ID=(SELECT EMPLOYEE_ID
   FROM EMPLOYEES
 WHERE SURNAME='Flintstone'
   AND FIRSTNAME='Fred')
```

INFLUENCING THE OPTIMIZER USING HINTS

Hints are instructions which you can include in your SQL statement to instruct or "guide" the optimizer. Using hints you can specify join orders, type of access paths, indexes to be used, the optimization goal and other instructions.

An optimizer hint appears as a comment following the first word of the SQL statement (e.g., SELECT, INSERT, DELETE or UPDATE). A hint is differentiated from other comments by the presence of the plus sign ("+") following the opening comment delimiter ("/*"). For instance, the following statement will be processed using the rule based optimizer:

```
SELECT /*+ RULE */ *
FROM EMPLOYEE
WHERE SALARY > 1000000
```

Table 3.2 lists some of the more commonly used hints. A more complete list can be found in Appendix A.

TABLE 3.2 Some commonly used hints.

HINT	USE
CHOOSE	Use the CHOOSE optimizer goal (see above).
RULE	Use the RULE optimizer goal (see above).
FIRST_ROWS	Use the FIRST_ROWS optimizer goal (full).
ALL_ROWS	Use the ALL_ROWS optimizer goal (see above).
FULL(*table_name*)	Use a full table scan to access the nominated table, even if there is an appropriate index path to the data.

TABLE 3.2 Some commonly used hints. *(Continued)*

HINT	USE
INDEX(*table_name index_name*)	Use the specified index on the specified table.
HASH(*table_name*)	Use hash cluster based retrieval on the specified table (this will obviously only work if the table is in a hash cluster).
INDEX_DESC(*table_name index_name*)	Use the specified index on the specified table, but scan the index from high values to low values. Normally, if an index is used to scan a range, the scan occurs from low value to high value.
AND_EQUALS(*table_name index_name index_name index_name ....*)	This hint instructs the optimizer to merge the specified indexes when retrieving rows for the specified table.
USE_NL(*table_name*)	This hint specifies that when this table is first joined, the nested loops approach should be used.
USE_MERGE(*table_name)*	This hint specifies that when the table is first joined, the merge join approach should be used.
USE_HASH(*table_name)*	Use the *hash join* technique when joining this table.
MERGE_AJ(*table_name)*	This hint is placed in a subquery which is referred to by NOT IN in the main query. The hint specifies that an *anti-join* is to be performed using the sort merge method.
HASH_AJ(*table_name)*	This is used in the same context as HASH_AJ and specifies that the *anti-join* should be performed using the hash join method.
PARALLEL(*table_name parallelism*)	This hint directs that the table should be accessed via parallel table scan. The parallelism parameter determines how many query processes shall be used. See the section on parallel query tuning for more information.
NOPARALLEL(*table_name*)	Don't use parallel query, even if table or database default would normally result in parallel processing.

TABLE 3.2 Some commonly used hints. *(Continued)*

HINT	USE
CACHE(*table_name*)	When performing a full table scan, encourage the caching of the table within Oracle shared memory. NOCACHE has the opposite effect.
ORDERED	Use the order of tables in the FROM clause as the join order. This overrides normal preference for an alternative join order based on cost calculations.

Multiple hints can appear in the same comment, separated by a space. For instance, the following hint requests a full table scan on both DEPARTMENT and EMPLOYEES:

```
select /*+ FULL(E) FULL(D) */
       e.employee_id, e.surname, e.firstname
  from employees e,
       departments d
 where d.location='Melbourne'
   and d.department_id=e.department_id
```

Using hints to change the access path

One of the most frequent uses of hints is to force a particular access path to be selected, and typically, this means forcing the use of a particular index.

The simplest hint for forcing an index is the rather appropriately named INDEX hint. Typically, the INDEX hint is used to force the use of a particular index in this manner:

```
select /*+ index(e,employee_mgr_idx) */ surname
  from employees e
 where department_id=:1
   and manager_id=:2
```

However, you can also instruct the optimizer to choose between a subset of indexes by specifying multiple index names:

```
select /*+ index(e,employee_sal_idx,employee_mgr_idx) */ surname
  from employees e
 where department_id=:1
   and manager_id=:2
```

And you can simply specify that you want an index to be used, but leave it up to the optimizer to choose the appropriate index:

```
select /*+ index(e) */ surname
  from employees e
```

```
   where department_id=:1
     and manager_id=:2
```

You can also specify that you would like multiple indexes to be merged using the AND EQUALS hint (although most of the time, merging indexes suggests you are missing an appropriate concatenated index):

```
select /*+ and_equal(e,employee_dept_idx,employee_mgr_idx) */ surname
  from employees e
 where department_id=:1
   and manager_id=:2
```

By default, Oracle scans indexes in ascending order. You can, however, specify that you wish the index to be scanned in descending order, for instance:

```
select /*+ index_desc(e,employee_sal_idx) */ surname
  from employees e
 where salary < :1
```

If you don't want to use an index, you can use the FULL hint. You might want to do this if:

❑ You're using rule based optimization and the optimizer is selecting a very unselective index.

❑ You're using cost based optimization and the optimizer is using an index which appears to be selective (e.g., has a large number of distinct values) but you happen to know that the particular value being searched is not selective (for instance, you have a query which is using an index to get all people under 100 years of age).

Example of using the full hint:

```
select /*+ full(e) */ surname
  from employees e
 where department_id=:1
   and manager_id=:2
```

Using hints to change the join order

The other common reason for using hints is to change the join order, or to change the type of joins performed.

The ORDERED hint instructs the optimizer to join tables in the order in which they appear in the from clause. If all other factors are equal (perhaps both tables are the same size and both have equivalent indexes), then the optimizer will join tables in this order anyway—so it's a good idea to always specify tables in the order you want them joined. However, the cost based optimizer will usually be able to pick a specific join order based on the statistics collected for the table. By using ORDERED, you can force the join order to be the same order as in the FROM clause.

```
select /*+ordered*/ d.department_name,e.surname
  from employees e,
       departments d
 where d.department_id=e.department_id
   and d.department_name=:1
```

As we've seen, the two common types of joins in Oracle are the *nested loops* join and the *sort merge* join. You can force the use of these methods by using the USE_NL or USE_MERGE hints.

```
select /*+ordered use_nl(d)*/ d.department_name,e.surname
  from employees e,
       departments d
 where d.department_id=e.department_id
   and d.department_name=:1
```

Errors in hint specifications

If you make an error in a hint specification—for instance, forgetting the plus sign or specifying an invalid hint—Oracle will ignore the hint without generating an error or warning. Therefore, it is very important that you validate that your hint worked (using the *explain plan* or *tkprof* utilities documented in Chapter 5).

It's particularly easy to make mistakes when specifying table names. If the table name is given an alias in the FROM clause, you *must* specify this alias in the hint. However, you must not specify an owner (or "schema") name, even if it appears in the FROM clause.

For instance, assume this is the query:

```
select surname,firstname
    from employees e
   where salary=0
```

The following are some valid and invalid hints:

/*+ INDEX(e salary_idx) */	Correct usage. Then index salary_idx will be used.
/* INDEX(e salary_idx) */	Invalid, because the "+" is missing after the opening comment marker.
/*+ INDEX(employees salary_idx) */	Invalid, because employees is given a table alias in the from clause, but not in the hint.

/*+ INDEX(e, salary_idx */	Invalid, because the ending bracket is missing.
/*+ INDEX(e, salary_idx) */	Valid, although the comma following the table alias is not necessary.
*+ INDEEX(e salary_idx) */	Invalid, because the hint is misspelled.

INFLUENCING THE RULE BASED OPTIMIZER

Before the introduction of the cost based optimizer and the advent of hints, SQL programmers were still able to influence the query optimizer. They did this by disabling certain access paths and by using the order of tables in the FROM clause. These methods still work, although hints are more powerful and self-documenting.

Disabling access paths

If a column in the WHERE clause is modified by a function or other operation, an index using that column cannot be used. By disabling certain indexes, you can prevent the optimizer using certain access paths. By disabling the access paths you do not want the optimizer to use, you hope that the optimizer will eventually use the access path of your choice.

For example, in the following query, Oracle could choose to use the index on either the surname columns or on the salary column:

```
select *
  from employees e
 where e.salary > 100000
   and e.surname like 'S%'
```

By modifying the surname column (concatenating a blank), we prevent any index on surname being used, hence forcing the salary index access path:

```
select *
  from employees e
 where e.salary > 100000
   and e.surname||'' like 'S%'
```

In the case of numeric or date columns, you can get the same effect by adding 0 to the column, for instance:

```
select *
  from employees e
 where e.salary+0 > 100000
   and e.surname like 'S%'
```

Changing the join order

Sometimes, you can change the join order by suppressing various access paths using the "trick" above. If this doesn't work, the order of tables in the from clause does influence the cost based optimizer. If access path rankings are equal, then the table specified last in the from clause will be the first table in the join order.

For instance, Oracle resolves the following SQL statement by performing a full tablescan of SALESREGION and then using an index to find matching records in DEPARTMENTS:

```
select /*+RULE*/ department_name,regionname
  from departments d,
       salesregion s
 where d.manager_id=s.manager_id
```

However, if we change the order of the tables in the from clause, the opposite join order results: a full table scan of departments is used.

```
select /*+RULE*/ department_name,regionname
  from salesregion s,
       departments d

 where d.manager_id=s.manager_id
```

CHAPTER SUMMARY

In this chapter, we looked at how Oracle processes SQL statements. Understanding Oracle's approach to SQL processing can be of great assistance when tuning SQL.

- ❑ A cursor is an area in memory which contains the essential information about your SQL statement which Oracle needs in order to process the SQL statement efficiently.

- ❑ Parsing—preparing an SQL statement for execution—can consume precious CPU resources. You can reduce the number of parses required by reusing *cursors*, and by using *bind variables*.

- ❑ Oracle can retrieve (*fetch*) or insert data in arrays or batches. Making use of this array interface often leads to a 100% improvement in throughput.

- ❑ The process of determining the most efficient way to get or change the data requested by the SQL statement is called query optimization. There are two query optimizers: the rule based optimizer—which uses the characteristics of tables and indexes to determine the best path—and the cost based optimizer—which also takes into account the size of tables and the number of keys in an index. The cost based optimizer is the best choice in most circumstances.

❏ Whichever optimizer is chosen, it's up to the SQL programmer to ensure that the best execution plan has been chosen. The SQL programmer knows more about the application and data characteristics than the optimizer and has the benefit of possessing both more time to decide on the optimum path and a superior query optimizer (i.e., the human brain). Simply put, both the *rule based optimizer* and the *cost based optimizer* can make poor decisions.

❏ The optimizers must determine the way in which table data is to be accessed (the *access path*) and the order in which tables will be joined (*join order*).

❏ The major factors influencing both join order and access paths are the presence or absence of indexes (both optimizers) and the size and distribution of table and index data (cost based optimizer only).

❏ When using the cost based optimizer, make sure you analyze your tables regularly or when they have realistic data volumes.

❏ You can influence either optimizer by using hints, which are comments embedded in the SQL statement which contain instructions to the optimizer.

PRINCIPLES OF INDEXING AND CLUSTERING

INTRODUCTION

In this chapter, we will examine the indexing and clustering facilities provided by Oracle.

Indexes and clusters are features offered by Oracle which exist primarily to enhance performance. Understanding and using indexes or hash clusters effectively is of paramount importance when optimizing SQL. Effective indexing can result in huge improvements to SQL performance.

The advantages of indexes do not come without a cost. Creating the index can be a very time-consuming process and often can't be done on-line. In addition, indexes must be updated during inserts, deletes and updates and this can slow down these operations. Finally, indexes take up storage space; it's not uncommon for indexes to take as much disk space as the tables to which they refer.

Indexing and clustering decisions are important and can be complex. Simply indexing everything is not usually a good idea since updates will be degraded. On the other hand, almost any database of a significant size is going to require indexes in order to perform effectively. The solution, of course, is to index or hash selectively, creating indexes or hash clusters only when you get a benefit from it.

In this chapter, we'll examine the implementation of Oracle indexes and clusters. Specifically:

❏ The structure of the B*-tree index—Oracle's default index structure.

❏ Multi-column (concatenated) indexes.

❏ Implicit indexes created by referential integrity constraints.

❏ Clustering one or more tables on common key values (an index cluster).

❏ Clustering a table using hash key values (a hash cluster).

❏ Bitmapped indexes.

THE B*-TREE INDEX

The B*-tree ("Balanced Tree") index, is Oracle's default index structure. Figure 4.1 shows the structure of a B*-tree.

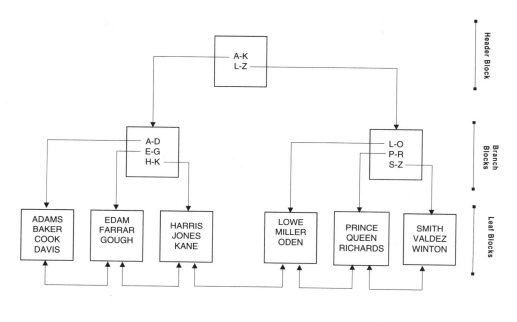

Index Blocks are linked in both directions.

FIGURE 4.1 Structure of a B*-tree index.

The B*-tree index has a hierarchical tree structure. At the top of the tree is the *header block*. This block contains pointers to the appropriate *branch block* for any given range of key values. The branch block will usually point to the appropriate *leaf block* for a more specific range or, for a particularly big index, point to another branch block. The leaf block contains a list of key values and pointers (ROWIDS) to the appropriate rows in the table.

Examining the diagram in Figure 4.1, let's imagine how Oracle would traverse this index. Should we need to access the record for "BAKER," we would first consult the header block. The header block would tell us that key values starting with A through K are stored in the leftmost branch block. Accessing this branch block, we find that key values starting with A through D are stored in the leftmost leaf block. Consulting this leaf block, we find the value "BAKER" and its associated ROWID, which we would then use to get to the table row concerned.

Leaf blocks contain links to both the previous and the next leaf block. This allows us to scan the index in either ascending or descending order and allows range queries using the ">," "<" or "BETWEEN" operators to be processed using the index.

Each leaf block is at the same depth; that is, every leaf block can be accessed by accessing the header block and one (usually) or two branch blocks.

B*-tree indexes have the following advantages over traditional indexing strategies (for instance, indexed sequential [ISAM]):

❏ Because each leaf node is at the same depth, performance is very predictable. In theory, no row in the table will be more than three or four I/Os away.

❏ B*-trees offer good performance for large tables, again because the depth is at most four (one header block, two levels of branch blocks and one level of leaf block). Again, no row in even the biggest table would take more than four I/Os to locate. (In fact, because the header block will almost always be already loaded in memory, and branch blocks usually loaded in memory, the actual number of physical disk reads is usually only one or two.)

❏ The B*-tree index supports range queries as well as exact lookups. This is possible because of the links to the previous and next leaf blocks.

The B*-tree index provides flexible and efficient query performance. However, maintaining the B*-tree when changing data can be expensive. For instance, consider inserting a row with the key value "NIVEN" into the table index diagrammed in Figure 4.1. To insert the row, we must add a new entry into the "L-O" block. If there is free space within this block then the cost is substantial, but perhaps not excessive. But what happens if there is no free space in the block?

If there is no free space within a leaf block for a new entry, then an *index split* is required. A new block must be allocated and half of the entries in the existing block moved into the new block. As well as this, there is a requirement to add a new entry to the branch block (in order to point to the newly created leaf block). If there is no free space in the branch block, then the branch block must also be split.

These index splits are an expensive operation: new blocks must be allocated and index entries moved from one block to another.

Index splits can be avoided if key values are inserted in ascending sequence. This is one of the advantages of using an *artificial key* (artificial keys are discussed in Chapter 14). You can also reduce index splits by increasing the amount of free space kept within the index for new entries. This is defined by the PCTFREE clause of the CREATE INDEX statement.

INDEX SELECTIVITY

The selectivity of a column or group of columns is a common measure of the usefulness of an index on those columns. Columns or indexes are selective if they have a large number of unique values or few duplicate values. For instance, the DATE_OF_BIRTH column will be very selective while the GENDER column will not be selective.

Selective indexes are more efficient than non-selective indexes because they point more directly to specific values. The cost based optimizer will determine the selectivity of the various indexes available to it, and will try and use the most selective index.

UNIQUE INDEXES

A unique index is one which prevents any duplicate values for the columns which make up the index. If you try to create a unique index on a table which contains such duplicate values you will receive an error. Similarly, you will also receive an error if you try and insert a row which contains duplicate unique index key values.

A unique index is typically created in order to prevent duplicate values rather than to improve performance. However, unique index columns are very often effective query keys—they point to exactly one row and are therefore very *selective*. Both the rule based and cost based optimizers will tend to prefer unique indexes to non-unique indexes.

IMPLICIT INDEXES

Implicit indexes are indexes which are created automatically by Oracle in order to implement either a primary key or unique constraint.

You may recall from our earlier discussion of relational database principles that every row in a table must have a unique identifier and that this unique identifier is known as the *primary key*. As well as the primary key, there may be a number of *candidate keys* which are also unique. Oracle allows you to define these keys (and also foreign keys) when you create a table. In order to implement either a primary or unique constraint, Oracle creates a unique index. As well as enforcing uniqueness, these indexes are also available to enhance the performance of queries.

CONCATENATED INDEXES

A concatenated index is simply an index comprising more than one column. The advantage of a concatenated key is that it is often more *selective* than a single key index. The combination of columns will point to a smaller number of rows than indexes composed of the individual columns. A concatenated index which contains all of the columns referred to in an SQL statement's WHERE clause will usually be very effective.

If you frequently query on more that one column within a table, then creating a concatenated index for these columns is an excellent idea. For instance, we may often query the employees table by surname and firstname. In that case, we would probably want to create an index on surname *and* firstname. For instance:

```
Create index employee_name_idx on employee(surname,firstname)
```

Using such an index, we could rapidly find all employees matching a given surname/firstname combination. Such an index will be far more effective than an index on surname alone, or separate indexes on surname and firstname.

Figure 4.2 compares I/O requirements for various access paths. Clearly, the concatenated index offers the most efficient retrieval.

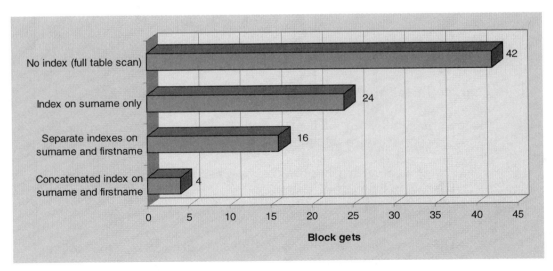

FIGURE 4.2 Comparisons of access paths for employee name retrieval.

ORDER OF COLUMNS IN A CONCATENATED INDEX

If a concatenated index could only be used when *all* of its keys appeared in the WHERE clause, then concatenated indexes would probably be of pretty limited use. Luckily, a concatenated index can be used providing any of the initial or *leading* columns are used. Leading columns are those which are specified earliest in the index definition. For instance, with the concatenated index we created on the employee table (on surname, firstname), we could use the index to retrieve employees matching a surname, but not employees matching on firstnames (a full table scan would be required).

To extend this example, imagine a concatenated index on surname, firstname, date_of_birth. Table 4.1 shows how this index can be used. Only the leading, or leftmost, parts of the index can be used.

TABLE 4.1   Using an index on surname, firstname, date_of_birth.

Columns specified in the WHERE clause	Columns in the index which can be used
surname,firstname,date_of_birth	Surname,firstname,date_of_birth: all columns in the concatenated index are specified.
surname,firstname	Surname,firstname: The two columns are leading columns, so both can be used.
surname,date_of_birth	Surname only. Date_of_birth cannot be used, because it comes after firstname, which is not specified.
firstname	None! The index cannot be used unless the first column is specified.

Guidelines for concatenated indexes

The following guidelines will help in deciding when to use concatenated indexes, and how to decide which columns should be included and in which order.

- ❑ Create a concatenated index for columns from a table which appear together in the WHERE clause.
- ❑ If columns sometimes appear on their own in a WHERE clause, place them at the start of the index.
- ❑ The more *selective* a column is, the more useful it will be at the leading end of the index.

We'll discuss the optimization of concatenated indexes in greater detail in Chapter 6.

INDEX MERGES

If more than one column from a table appears in the where clause and there is no concatenated index on the columns concerned but there are indexes on the individual columns, then Oracle may decide to perform an *index merge*.

In order to perform an index merge, Oracle retrieves all rows from each index with matching values and then merges these two "lists" or result sets and returns only those which appear in each list. For instance, consider the case in which there is an index on employee(surname) and another index on employee(firstname). If we issued a query for "Ian Smith," we would first retrieve all employees with the surname of "Smith," then retrieve all employees with the firstname of "Ian." The two lists would be merged, and only employees in both lists would be returned.

Performing index merges is almost always less efficient than the equivalent concatenated index. If you see an index merge (shown in execution plans with the AND EQUALS operator), consider creating an appropriate concatenated index.

NULL VALUES

When an indexed column is NULL, or when all columns in a concatenated index are NULL, then the row concerned will not have entry in the index. In other words, *nulls are not indexed*. This is a fundamental and important concept, since it is not possible to use an index to find NULL values, although it is possible to find a value NOT NULL. If you find yourself coding an IS NULL condition in the WHERE clause, be sure to consider the potential performance impact of the resulting full table scan.

FOREIGN KEY INDEXES AND LOCKING

You can declare referential integrity constraints to prevent rows being inserted into detail (or "child") tables which do not have a matching row in a master (or "parent") table. This facility preserves the integrity of your data and is implemented automatically by most CASE tools. For instance, the following statement creates a foreign key constraint between EMPLOYEES and DEPARTMENTS:

```
alter table EMPLOYEES
add constraint fk1_employees foreign key (DEPARTMENT_ID)
references DEPARTMENTS (DEPARTMENT_ID);
```

Once the constraint is enabled, attempting to create an EMPLOYEE row with an invalid DEPARTMENT_ID, or to delete a DEPARTMENT row which has matching employees will generate an error. However, in order to prevent inconsistencies during the operation, Oracle applies table level locks (rather than the usual row level locks) to one of the two tables during an update.

In version 7.0 and 7.1, an insert into the child table (in our example, EMPLOYEES) would cause the parent table (e.g., DEPARTMENTS) to be locked against update. In 7.2 and 7.3, an update to the PARENT table (e.g., DEPARTMENTS) would cause the child table (e.g., EMPLOYEES) to be locked against update.

These table locks are not required if there is an index on the foreign key in the child table (for instance, an index on EMPLOYEES.DEPARTMENT_ID). Often, you will create such an index anyway in order to optimize joins and queries. However, if you omit such a foreign key index and if the parent table is subject to update, you may see heavy lock contention. If in doubt, it's safer to create indexes on all foreign keys, despite the possible overhead of maintaining unneeded indexes.

INDEX CLUSTERS

Index clusters are a mechanism for storing related rows from one or more tables in the same segment. Rows which have common *cluster key* values are stored together. In theory, this will speed up joins because the rows to be joined are stored in the same block. In practice, index clusters are of severely limited value and should only be used when the tables are *always* referenced together. Here are some of the disadvantages of index clusters:

❑ Full table scans against only one of the tables in the cluster will be slower, since blocks for other tables in the cluster will also have to be scanned.

❑ Inserts can be slower because of the additional effort required to maintain the cluster.

❑ The performance benefit for joins may be minimal.

Figure 4.3 shows how an index cluster would be implemented for the PRODUCTS and SALES tables. We'll examine the effect of index clusters on join and scan performance in greater detail in Chapter 7.

Product Table

Product ID	Product_description	Normal Value
10	Excelsior Mk 10	30000
20	Defiant 101	20000
30	Entabe 1701	80000

Sales Table

Product ID	Customer	Sale_date	Other Columns....
10	13	12-May-96	
10	18	2-May-96	
20	12	7-May-96	
30	1	1-Jan-96	
30	2	12-Dec-96	

Index Cluster of Sales and Product

Product ID	Product_description	Normal Value
10	Excelsior Mk 10	30000
Customer ID	Sale_date	Other columns....
13	12-May-96	
18	12-May-96	
Product ID	Product_description	Normal Value
20	Defiant 101	20000
Customer ID	Sale_date	Other columns....
12	7-May-96	
Product ID	Product_description	Normal Value
30	Entabe 1701	80000
Customer ID	Sale_date	Other columns....
1	1-Jan-96	
2	12-Dec-96	

FIGURE 4.3 Structure of an index cluster.

HASH CLUSTERS

The term *hashing* refers to the process of using a mathematical transformation which translates a key value into a storage address. In Oracle hash clusters, key values are translated into hash keys, and rows with the same hash key are stored together. The hash key tells Oracle where these blocks are located. In this way, Oracle can go directly to the blocks required without expending any I/O on an index lookup.

Hash clusters minimize the number of block reads required to locate a row using the hash key. With a hash cluster, retrieving the row in question may require only one block access—the access of the block containing the row. In comparison, a B*-tree index will require at least four block reads (index header block, index branch block, index leaf block and table block).

REQUIREMENTS FOR HASH CLUSTERS

The cluster key should have a high cardinality (large number of unique values). In fact, unique or primary keys are usually good candidates for the hash key.

The hash key should normally be selected by an exact match, rather than by a range or "like" condition. For example, if we created a hash cluster based on the employee table, we could not use the hash cluster to enhance the search to scan for all employee_ids between one and ten.

STRUCTURE OF HASH CLUSTERS

When a hash cluster is created, it is necessary to specify the number of hash key values which are expected; this is done using the HASHKEYS clause of the CREATE CLUSTER statement. The SIZE clause of the CREATE CLUSTER statement determines the number of hash key values stored in each block. The overall initial size of the hash cluster will therefore be dependent on the setting of these two values.

The setting for SIZE and HASHKEYS is critical to the performance of the hash cluster. If HASHKEYS is set too high, then the hash cluster will become sparsely populated and full table scan performance will degrade. On the other hand, if HASHKEYS is set too low, then multiple cluster keys will be allocated the same hash key. These *collisions* can result in the block allocated for the hash cluster overflowing and additional blocks being chained. Once chaining occurs, cluster key lookups can require more than one I/O to resolve and the benefit of the hash cluster is reduced or eliminated.

By default, Oracle uses an internal algorithm to convert the cluster key into a hash value. This algorithm works well for most circumstances. However, you can also use the cluster key (if it is uniformly distributed) or you can specify your own function (written in PL/SQL).

Figure 4.4 shows an example of a hash cluster. The diagram illustrates some important principles:

❑ The hash key serves as a relative offset into the hash cluster. That is, once Oracle calculates the hash key, it can move directly to the relevant block in the hash cluster.

❑ The same amount of space is allocated for each hash value. If the space allocated is too high, then space will be wasted and the cluster will be sparsely populated—and this will degrade full table scan performance (for instance, the space allocated for hash key 2 is completely unused).

❑ If the amount of space allocated for a hash value is too high, then additional blocks will have to be chained. This degrades lookup performance, since Oracle must perform additional I/Os to get to the rows stored in these chained blocks. For instance, in Figure 4.4 the data for employee 69 is stored in a chained block. Retrieving his details will require an additional I/O.

WHEN TO USE HASH CLUSTERS

You could consider using hash clusters in the following circumstances:

❑ Data in the table is accessed primarily by an EQUALS TO condition on the cluster key.

❑ Range scans on the cluster key are rarely, if ever, performed.

❑ Full table scans are rarely, if ever, performed.

❑ The table is either static in size, or you are prepared to rebuild the cluster periodically when the size changes.

We'll discuss the optimization of hash clusters in detail in Chapter 6.

Employee Table (unclustered)

Employee_id	Surname	Firstname	Date of Birth
10	Potter	Jean Luc	21/04/23
11	Smith	Ben	23/05/78
12	Thomas	Dianna	5/08/47
15	Jones	Katherine	11/11/34
89	Smith	Montgomery	19/02/20
34	Cane	Beverly	0/09/38
54	Main	Leonard	7/05/30
69	Ryder	William	3/06/40

Cluster key	Hash key
10	0
11	1
12	2
15	0
89	4
34	4
54	4
69	4

Table of conversion from cluster key to hash key

Hash key	Employee_id	Surname	Firstname	Date of Birth
0	10	Potter	Jean Luc	21/04/23
	15	Jones	Katherine	11/11/34
1	11	Smith	Ben	23/05/78
2	12	Thomas	Dianna	5/08/47
3				
4	89	Smith	Montgomery	19/02/20
	34	Cane	Beverly	9/09/38
	54	Main	Leonard	7/05/30

Hash Cluster of the Employee Table

4	69	Ryder	William	3/06/40

FIGURE 4.4   Structure of a hash cluster.

BITMAPPED INDEXES

Bitmapped indexes are the newest addition to Oracle's indexing/hashing strategy and were introduced in Oracle 7.3. In a bitmap index, Oracle creates a bitmap for each unique value of the column in question. Each bitmap contains a single bit (0 or 1) for every row in the table. A "1" indicates that the row has the value specified by the bitmap and a "0" indicates that it does not. Oracle can rapidly scan these bitmaps to find rows matching a specified criteria. Oracle can also rapidly compare multiple bitmaps to find all rows matching multiple bitmapped criteria.

Bitmaps suit columns with few distinct values are often queried in combination. If there is only a single column condition, then a full tablescan will probably outperform the bitmap lookup (for the low cardinality columns involved).

Figure 4.5 shows an example of bitmapped indexes on an imaginary table called SURVEY (perhaps a survey of prospective customers). Bitmapped indexes exist on gender, marital status and own_home (e.g., owns their own home). To find all single males who own their own home, Oracle extracts each bitmap and finds rows who have a "1" in each bitmap.

FEATURES OF BITMAP INDEXES

❏ Bitmap indexes offer fast retrieval for columns which have only a few distinct values and which are often queried together. However, full table scans will usually be more efficient if the columns are queried individually.

❏ Bitmapped indexes are especially suitable for large tables and for aggregate (e.g., "how many") queries.

❏ Bitmapped indexes can be used in any order and in any combination, so they are more flexible than a corresponding concatenated index, which requires that you use at least the first column in the index.

❏ If used appropriately, bitmapped indexes are very compact—much more compact than the equivalent concatenated index.

❏ Columns in a bitmapped index should be of low cardinality—that is, the columns should have only a few distinct values. Otherwise, too many bitmaps must be constructed and maintained.

❏ Merging multiple bitmaps is an operation which can be performed very efficiently by the computer (bit operations are very fast).

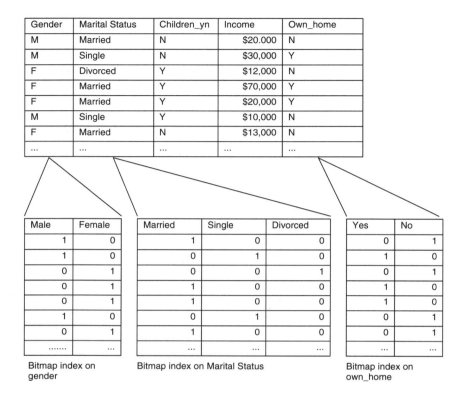

Gender	Marital Status	Children_yn	Income	Own_home
M	Married	N	$20.000	N
M	Single	N	$30,000	Y
F	Divorced	Y	$12,000	N
F	Married	Y	$70,000	Y
F	Married	Y	$20,000	Y
M	Single	Y	$10,000	N
F	Married	N	$13,000	N
...	...	...	...	...

Male	Female
1	0
1	0
0	1
0	1
0	1
1	0
0	1
....	...

Bitmap index on gender

Married	Single	Divorced
1	0	0
0	1	0
0	0	1
1	0	0
1	0	0
0	1	0
1	0	0
...	...	...

Bitmap index on Marital Status

Yes	No
0	1
1	0
0	1
1	0
1	0
0	1
0	1
...	...

Bitmap index on own_home

Select * from survey where sex='Male' and marital_status='Single' and own_home='Yes'

Male		Single		Yes		
1		0		0		0
1		1		1		1
0	AND	0	AND	0	EQUALS	0
0		0		1		0
0		0		1		0
1		1		0		0
0		0		0		0
...		...		...		...

◄—— **This row satisfies the query.**

FIGURE 4.5   Example of a bitmap index. Bitmaps for "male," "single" and "own_home" are used to rapidly find single men who own a home in the SURVEY table.

DRAWBACKS OF BITMAP INDEXES

❑ Oracle is unable to lock a single bit, and consequently, locking for bit-mapped indexes is at the block (or page) level. Since a very large number of rows (or bits) can fit in a single block, many rows will be locked. This makes bitmap indexes inappropriate for applications with even moderately high transaction rates.

❑ Bitmap indexes are not suitable for range queries, or for columns with large numbers of distinct values. Use B*-tree indexes, if necessary, for these columns.

INDEX ONLY TABLES

Earlier in this chapter we considered the importance of including all required columns in a concatenated index in order to optimize query performance. It is also a significant optimization to include all columns which appear in the select list in the concatenated index so that we can satisfy the query using the index alone without a table access.

Imagine a table for which every column was included in such a concatenated index and for which all queries were satisfied using that index. In this circumstance the table itself has become superfluous—it is the index alone which stores the data required and which is used to satisfy queries. However, the table still exists and consumes valuable disk storage and incurs an overhead when rows are added, removed or modified. We might wish we could dispense with the table altogether and keep just the index.

Oracle version 8 allows us to create *index only tables*. These may be used in the same way as other tables but are stored internally in a B*-tree index format. By storing a table in a B*-tree index format, we avoid the duplicating data in both the table and the index, and ensure that queries which access the table by its primary key are very fast, since only an index lookup—without the normal corresponding table access—will be required. We create an index-only table using the ORGANI-ZATION keyword of the CREATE TABLE statement, e.g.:

```
create table iot_table
(pk_col1    number not null,
 pk_col2    number not null,
 data_col1  varchar2(30) not null,
 data_col2  long ,
 constraint iot_table_pk primary key (pk_col1,pk_col2))
organization index
pctthreshold 50
overflow tablespace long_tbs;
```

Index-only tables are organized as a B*-tree index constructed against their primary key. The primary key plus additional columns are stored in the leaf blocks of the B*-tree—however, only the columns which contribute to less than PCTTHRESHOLD percent of the total row length stored in the B*-tree leaf blocks. The remainder of the row is stored within chained blocks in the OVERFLOW TABLESPACE. In the above example, any portions of the row accounting for more than 50% of the total row length would be stored in the tablespace "long_tbs." In practice, this would result in columns PK_COL1, PK_COL2 and DATA_COL1 being stored in the leaf block, while the long column DATA_COL2 would be stored in the overflow block.

The ability to relocate longer columns away from the B*-tree structure allows Oracle to keep the B*-tree relatively small and efficient, while keeping small, frequently accessed columns in the B*-tree. When creating an index-only table, define frequently accessed, small columns early in the column list and large, infrequently accessed columns later in the list. Define PCTTHRESHOLD so that only the frequently accessed columns are retained in the B*-tree. The primary key should include all columns which might appear in the WHERE clause.

It is not possible to create a secondary (e.g., non-primary key) index on an index-only table. This is because the index-only table rows are not associated with a ROWID and hence there is nothing for the secondary index to point to.

Index-only tables are suitable in the following circumstances:

❏ All queries on the table can be satisfied using the primary key. No secondary indexes are required.

❏ A table contains a few frequently accessed short columns and infrequently accessed long columns.

❏ Either the total row length—or the length of frequently accessed columns—is relatively small.

CHAPTER SUMMARY

Effective indexing or hashing is essential if your SQL is to perform at peak efficiency. Oracle supports four indexing/hashing schemes:

❏ B*-tree indexes, which offer flexible and fast retrieval for range or equality lookups for tables of all sizes.

❏ Index clusters, which may be useful to physically co-locate two or more tables which are often joined together.

❏ Hash clusters, which can optimize lookups of single values for static tables.

❑ Bitmapped indexes, which may be useful if you need fast resolution of aggregate queries incorporating multiple columns with few unique values for large tables.

B*-tree indexes are suitable for the vast majority of applications. Use the following guidelines when creating B*-tree indexes:

❑ Create indexes for columns which have a large number of distinct values.

❑ Consider indexes for columns which are used in the where clause to select rows or to join tables.

❑ There is an extra overhead in maintaining an index on columns which are frequently updated—so avoid indexing these columns.

❑ Consider creating multi-column (concatenated) indexes when columns are queried together in the where clause. Put the most selective and frequently queried columns at the leading edge of the index (first in the list of columns).

❑ Consider indexing foreign key columns if you implement referential integrity.

Use the following guidelines when contemplating clustering or bitmapped indexing:

❑ Be wary of implementing index clusters. The small potential benefit in join performance is often not worth the cost in table scan performance.

❑ Consider using hash clusters for tables where you need to optimize the lookup of a key value using an EQUALS TO condition and where full table scans are not required. If you implement a hash cluster, make sure you carefully configure its storage—see Chapter 6 for details on doing this.

❑ Consider bitmap indexes for large tables with low update rates, for which you wish to query on multiple, low *cardinality* columns. Decision support systems and "data warehouses" may find bitmapped indexes useful.

❑ Oracle 8 provides "index only" tables. These are tables which are stored internally in a B-tree format. Index-only tables are suitable for tables with a narrow search criteria—since no secondary indexes can be defined. They also suit tables with long, infrequently accessed columns.

TRACING ORACLE SQL

INTRODUCTION

In this chapter, we'll explore the tools provided by Oracle which allow you to examine how your SQL statement is or will be executed. Without these tools, you will have only a vague understanding of how your SQL is being processed. You will only know if it's "running fast" or "running slow." Using the tools covered in this chapter, you'll be able to determine exactly how Oracle processes your SQL and you'll also be able to measure exactly the resources required to execute it. Effective measurement of SQL statement execution, and a determination of the execution plan used by Oracle to execute the SQL, are essential prerequisites for efficient SQL statement tuning.

The tools we discuss here are:

❏ EXPLAIN PLAN, which can reveals how Oracle will obtain your data (the execution plan).

❏ SQL_TRACE, which generates a trace file containing SQL statements executed by your session and their resource requirements.

❏ *tkprof*, which formats the output of SQL_TRACE.

❏ The SQL*PLUS AUTOTRACE command, which allows execution plans and statistics to be displayed from within an SQL*PLUS session.

There are many third party tools available which can assist in tuning SQL. You'll find demonstration versions of some of these on the companion CD-ROM. These tools can be useful but are not always available. The tools discussed in this chapter are part of the default Oracle distribution and hence are always available. Although they may not be as easy to use as some of the graphical third party tools, they are capable of providing all the information you need to effectively tune SQL.

EXPLAIN PLAN

The EXPLAIN PLAN command allows you to determine the execution plan Oracle will apply to a particular SQL statement. The execution plan is inserted into a "plan table" which you can query to extract the execution plan.

EXECUTING EXPLAIN PLAN

The EXPLAIN PLAN command has the following syntax:

```
EXPLAIN PLAN [SET STATEMENT_ID = `statement_id`}
             [INTO table_name ]
    FOR sql_statement
```

The options for EXPLAIN PLAN are:

statement_id   Some unique identifier for your SQL statement. By using a statement identifier, you can store multiple SQL statements in one table.

table_name   The name of the plan table you want to use to store the execution plan. This table must already exist and must conform to the standard structure of a plan table (see below). If you don't specify a plan table, EXPLAIN PLAN will attempt to use the name "PLAN_TABLE."

sql_statement   The SQL for which you wish to determine the execution plan. The SQL must be valid and you must have sufficient privileges to run the SQL. The SQL may contain bind variables.

THE PLAN TABLE

Oracle distributes an SQL script to create the plan table with the Oracle server software. The script is called *utlxplan.sql* and is usually found in the *rdbms/admin* subdirectory of the software distribution. You can copy and edit this script to change the name of the plan table (if you use the "INTO table_name" option of the EXPLAIN PLAN command) or you can use the script "as is" to create a plan table called PLAN_TABLE.

The EXPLAIN PLAN command will insert a row into the plan table for every step of the execution plan.

The structure of the plan_table is shown in Table 5.1.

TABLE 5.1 The structure of the plan_table.

Column Name	Description
STATEMENT_ID	The statement identifier provided by the SET STATEMENT_ID clause.
TIMESTAMP	The date and time the explain plan statement was executed.
REMARKS	Not populated by the EXPLAIN PLAN command, but you can insert your own comments here.
ID	A unique identifier for the step.
PARENT_ID	The parent of this step. The parent step is the step which is processed *after* the current step. In other words, the output of a step is fed into its parent step.
POSITION	If two steps have the same parent, the step with the lowest position will be executed first.
OPERATION	The type of operation being performed. For instance, TABLE ACCESS or SORT.
OPTIONS	Additional information about the operation. For instance, in the case of TABLE SCAN, the option might be FULL or BY ROWID.
OBJECT_NODE	If this is a distributed query, this column indicates the database link used to reference the object. For a parallel query, it may nominate a temporary result set.
OBJECT_OWNER	Owner of the object.
OBJECT_NAME	Name of the object.
OBJECT_INSTANCE	Location of the object in the SQL statement.
OBJECT_TYPE	Type of object (TABLE, INDEX, etc.).
OPTIMIZER	Optimizer goal in effect when the statement was explained.
SEARCH_COLUMNS	Unused.

TABLE 5.1   The structure of the plan_table. *(Continued)*

Column Name	Description
OTHER	For a distibuted query, this might contain the text of the SQL sent to the remote database. For a parallel query, the SQL statement executed by the parallel slave processes.
OTHER_TAG	Indicates the type of value in the OTHER column. This can denote whether the step is being executed remotely in a distributed SQL statement or the nature of parallel execution.
COST	The relative cost of the operation as estimated by the cost based optimizer.
CARDINALITY	The number of rows that the cost based optimizer expects will be returned by the step.
BYTES	The number of bytes expected to be returned by the step.

FORMATTING PLAN TABLE OUTPUT

The most common way of making sense of the plan_table data is to execute a hierarchical query against the table. The PARENT_ID and ID columns allow for a self-join, which can be implemented using the CONNECT BY clause of the SELECT statement.

A common representation of such a query is :

```
select rtrim(lpad(' ',2*level)||
       rtrim(operation)||' '||
       rtrim(options)||' '||
       object_name)   query_plan
  from plan_table
connect by prior id=parent_id
   start with id=0;
```

This produces the typical nested representation of an explain plan. For instance, if we EXPLAIN the following statement:

```
explain plan for
select /*+RULE */
       e.surname,e.firstname,e.date_of_birth
  from employees e,
       customers c
 where e.surname=c.contact_surname
   and e.firstname=c.contact_firstname
   and e.date_of_birth=c.date_of_birth
 order by e.surname,e.firstname
```

The execution plan query will produce the following output:

```
query_plan
------------------------------------------------------
SELECT STATEMENT
    SORT ORDER BY
        NESTED LOOPS
            TABLE ACCESS FULL CUSTOMERS
            TABLE ACCESS BY ROWID EMPLOYEES
                INDEX RANGE SCAN EMPLOYEE_BOTHNAMES_IDX
```

INTERPRETING THE EXECUTION PLAN

Interpreting a formatted execution plan such as that shown in the previous section requires practice and often some degree of judgment. However, the following fundamental principles guide the interpretation:

1. The more heavily indented an access path is, the earlier it is executed.

2. If two steps are indented at the same level, the uppermost statement is executed first.

3. An access path may be comprised of a number of steps in the execution plan. For instance, an index access is shown as an INDEX SCAN together with a TABLE SCAN BY ROWID. In this case, the indentation level of the outermost access determines the precedence of the execution. For instance, in the explain plan above the most heavily indented operation is the index range scan of an EMPLOYEES index. However, this operation is combined with the ROWID access of the EMPLOYEES table. It's therefore the CUSTOMERS access which is the first step executed.

With these principles in mind, let's interpret the execution plan shown in the previous section.

1. The most heavily indented statement is the index scan of index, EMPLOYEE_BOTHNAMES_IDX. However, this is an index scan associated with a table lookup. As we said earlier, an index lookup coupled with a table lookup is effectively a single step, and so the index lookup is *not* the first step in the execution plan.

2. The uppermost and most heavily indented step is therefore the full table scan of the CUSTOMERS table. This step is therefore the *driving access path* and CUSTOMERS is the *driving table*.

3. The index lookup of EMPLOYEES is at the same level of indentation as the scan of EMPLOYEES. This indicates that the steps have a common parent. We therefore need to examine the parent step to establish the relationship. The parent step is "nested loops," which means that the two tables are joined using the nested loops method described in Chapter 3.

4. The next step is the SORT ORDER BY step. This step simply supports the ORDER BY clause in the SELECT statement.

COMMON EXECUTION STEPS

Table 5.2 describes some of the common execution steps which you may encounter. These steps are defined by the combination of the OPERATION and OPTION columns of the PLAN_TABLE.

TABLE 5.2 *Descriptions* of the operations and options reported by EXPLAIN PLAN.

Category	Operation	Option	Description
Table Access Paths	TABLE ACCESS	FULL	The well-known full table scan. This involves reading every row in the table (strictly speaking, every block up to the high water mark).
	TABLE ACCESS	CLUSTER	Access of data via an index cluster key.
	TABLE ACCESS	HASH	A *hash key* is issued to access one or more rows in a table with a matching *hash value*.
	TABLE ACCESS	BY ROWID	Access a single row in a table by specifying its ROW-ID. ROWID access is the fastest way to access a single row. Very often, the ROWID will have been obtained by an associated index lookup.

TABLE 5.2 *Descriptions* of the operations and options reported by EXPLAIN PLAN. *(Continued)*

Category	Operation	Option	Description
Index Operations	AND-EQUAL		The results from one or more index scans are combined.
	INDEX	UNIQUE SCAN	An index lookup which will return the address (ROW-ID) of only one row.
	INDEX	RANGE SCAN	An index lookup which will return the ROWID of more than one row. This can be because the index is non-unique or because a range operator (e.g., ">") was used.
Join Operations	CONNECT BY		A hierarchical self-join is performed on the output of the preceding steps.
	MERGE JOIN		A merge join performed on the output of the preceding steps.
	MERGE JOIN	OUTER	An outer join implemented by a merge join.
	NESTED LOOPS		A Nested loops join is performed on the preceding steps. For each row in the upper result set, the lower result set is scanned to find a matching row.
	NESTED LOOPS	OUTER	An outer join implemented by a nested loops join.
Set operations	CONCATENATION		Multiple result sets are merged in the same way as in an explicit UNION statement. This typically occurs when an OR statement is used with indexed columns.

TABLE 5.2 *Descriptions* of the operations and options reported by
EXPLAIN PLAN. *(Continued)*

Category	Operation	Option	Description
	INTERSECTION		Two result sets are compared and only rows common to both are returned. This operation usually only takes place as a result of an explicit use of the INTERSECTION clause.
	MINUS		All result sets in the first result set are returned, except those appearing in the second result set. This occurs as a result of the MINUS set operator.
	UNION-ALL		Two result sets are combined and rows from both are returned.
	UNION		Two result sets are combined and rows from both are returned. Duplicate rows are not returned.
	VIEW		Either a view definition has been accessed or a temporary table has been created to store a result set.
Miscellaneous	FOR UPDATE		The rows returned are locked as a result of the FOR UPDATE clause.
	FILTER		Rows from a result set not matching a selection criteria are eliminated.
	REMOTE		An external database is accessed through a database link.
	SEQUENCE		An Oracle sequence generator is accessed to obtain a unique sequence number.

TABLE 5.2 *Descriptions* of the operations and options reported by
EXPLAIN PLAN. *(Continued)*

Category	Operation	Option	Description
	SORT	ORDER BY	A result set is sorted in order to satisfy an ORDER BY clause.
Aggregation	COUNT		Count the rows in the result set in order to satisfy the COUNT() function.
	COUNT	STOPKEY	Count the number of rows returned by a result set and stop processing when a certain number of rows are reached. This is usually the result of a WHERE clause which specifies a maximum ROWNUM (for instance, WHERE ROWNUM <= 10).
	SORT	AGGREGATE	This occurs when a group function is used on data which is already grouped. For instance, SELECT MAX(AVG(SALARY)) FROM EMPLOYEES GROUP BY MANAGER_ID.
	SORT	JOIN	Sort the rows in preparation for a merge join.
	SORT	UNIQUE	A sort to eliminate duplicate rows. This typically occurs as a result of using the distinct clause.
	SORT	GROUP BY	A sort of a result set in order to group them for the GROUP BY CLAUSE.

GUIDELINES FOR USING EXPLAIN PLAN

❏ The plan generated by the EXPLAIN PLAN command depends on
the optimizer goal in force (RULE, COST, FIRST_ROWS,
LAST_ROWS) and the statistics present for the tables in question. Be

very cautious if you are using explain plan in a different environment (for instance, development or test) and trying to apply the results to a different environment (such as, production). Differences in table statistics will quite likely lead to different execution plans in the two environments.

❑ Take care not to insert duplicate rows into your plan table. Either use a unique statement_id for each EXPLAIN PLAN statement, or ensure that you clear the plan table before use. Both the explain utility and plantree script will take care of this for you.

EXPLAIN PLAN UTILITIES

Using the EXPLAIN PLAN command is an awkward multi-step operation. Typically, you need to perform the following steps:

❑ Create the plan_table if it doesn't exist.

❑ Delete existing rows from the plan_table if it does exist.

❑ Run the EXPLAIN PLAN command.

❑ Execute a query to format explain plan output.

❑ Clear or drop the plan table.

Because the procedure for running explain plan is so awkward, many Oracle users write scripts to automate the process. In addition, there are a number of commercial and shareware products which can display explain plans and perform additional analysis of your SQL statement. Demonstrations for some of these products can be found on the companion CD-ROM.

The tuning toolkit contained on the companion CD-ROM includes free utilities which can assist in the generation and interpretation of execution plans. You can use these tools to quickly compare the execution plans for variations of SQL statements, to reveal parallel and distributed query information and to illustrate execution plans in a graphical format.

THE XPLAIN WINDOWS TOOL

Xplain is a Microsoft Windows-based tool which displays execution plans (and optionally, execution statistics) for SQL statements provided. Xplain allows you to make changes to SQL syntax or hints and to immediately get feedback on the effect on the execution plan. This tool was used to generate many of the examples in this book.

Figure 5.1 shows the Xplain tool displaying an execution plan for our sample SQL statement. More details about the Xplain tool can be found in Appendix G.

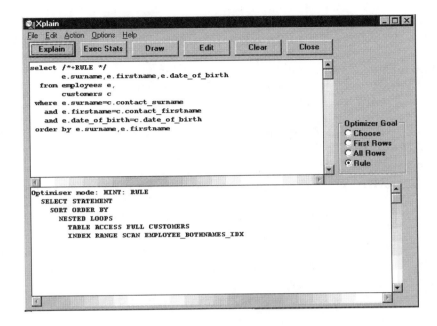

FIGURE 5.1   The Microsoft Windows Xplain tool.

GRAPHICAL REPRESENTATION OF EXECUTION PLANS WITH PLANTREE.SQL

The nested format of traditional execution plans will become familiar and easy to interpret with experience. But for those new to Oracle, the indented layout of the traditional execution plan is anything but intuitive.

Plantree.sql will generate a tree-structured representation of the execution plan. This can help in interpreting complex execution plans, especially for those new to SQL tuning.

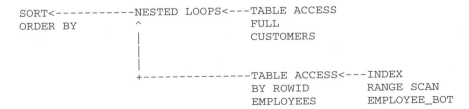

FIGURE 5.2   Example of *plantree.sql* output.

Figure 5.2 shows the output that *plantree.sql* would generate for the SQL statement we have used in previous examples. To interpret this tree-structure output, we simply start at the upper right hand corner—this step is the first step to be executed. Follow the arrows until you come to a step at which another line of execution merges and then follow that line of execution.

For instance, in the case of the *plantree.sql* output shown in Figure 5.2, we would follow this logic:

1. First, we start with the upper, rightmost execution step—the full table scan of CUSTOMERS. This is the first and therefore *driving* step.

2. Following the arrow along, we find that the next step is nested loops. The nested loops operation involves executing an operation for every row returned by the first operation. In this case, it means that for every row from the full table scan of CUSTOMERS, the operation "below" is performed.

3. The operation "below" is an index lookup of the EMPLOYEES table using the EMPLOYEE_BOTHNAMES_IDX index (the name is truncated in the display).

4. The joined result set of EMPLOYEE and CUSTOMERS is passed to the SORT operation.

USING SQL TRACE

The EXPLAIN PLAN statement is extremely useful, but is not a complete SQL tuning tool. For instance, EXPLAIN PLAN cannot tell you which of two execution plans is the more efficient—it provides no information about the resources required to execute a particular SQL statement.

Luckily, Oracle does provide a facility for tracing SQL statement execution, which can provide all of the information provided by EXPLAIN PLAN together with details of CPU and I/O requirements and even the number of rows processed by each step in the execution plan.

This facility essentially consists of two components:

❑ The ALTER SESSION SET SQL_TRACE TRUE SQL statement allows SQL tracing to be initiated.

❑ The *tkprof* command allows the trace files generated to be formatted in a meaningful way.

The SQL tracing facility and *tkprof* utility are a powerful tuning combination, but they are somewhat awkward to use and the output is sometimes difficult to interpret. Consequently, these tools are not used as widely as they should be. However, the SQL tracing facility is one of the most powerful and widely available tools for tuning SQL statements.

OVERVIEW OF THE SQL TRACING PROCESS

The usual tuning cycle when using SQL_TRACE/*tkprof* is:

1. Enable SQL_TRACE for the instance or sessions in question.
2. Locate the trace files(s) of interest.
3. Use *tkprof* to generate trace output.
4. Interpret the formatted trace file.
5. Tune SQL and repeat.

This process is essentially the one outlined in Chapter 1. We'll cover each of these steps in detail.

PREPARING TO USE SQL_TRACE

You may find that you have difficulty using SQL_TRACE unless your database is set up appropriately. Guidelines for setting up Oracle for SQL_TRACE can be found in Appendix D. In particular you should ensure that the TIMED_STATISTICS option is set to "true."

ENABLING SQL_TRACE WITHIN A SESSION

From within a session, SQL_TRACE is activated with the following statement:

```
ALTER SESSION SET SQL_TRACE TRUE;
```

Because PL/SQL cannot issue the alter session statement directly, a special function call can be used to switch on SQL_TRACE in PL/SQL blocks:

```
dbms_session.set_sql_trace(TRUE)
```

Table 5.3 gives examples of initiating SQL_TRACE from various client tools.

TABLE 5.3 Enabling SQL_TRACE from various client tools.

Development Tool	Syntax for enabling SQL_TRACE
SQL*PLUS	`alter session set sql_trace true;`
PRO*C	`EXEC SQL ALTER SESSION SET SQL_TRACE TRUE;`
Oracle FORMS	Use `statistics=YES` on the command line.
SQL*Windows	`call sqlPrepareAndExecute(hSql,"alter session set sql_trace true")`
Oracle Power Obects	`EXEC SQL ALTER SESSION SET SQL_TRACE TRUE;`
Powerbuilder	`EXECUTE IMMEDIATE ALTER SESSION SET SQL_TRACE TRUE;`
Stored procedures	`dbms_session.set_sql_trace(TRUE)`

It is useful to build the ability to turn on SQL tracing from within your programs, perhaps by a command line argument. This will allow you to easily generate traces as required without turning SQL_TRACE on for the entire database.

SWITCHING ON SQL TRACING FROM ANOTHER SESSION

Sometimes, you can't easily turn SQL_TRACE on for the session in which you are interested (for instance, if you didn't have the source code). To overcome this difficulty, Oracle provides a facility to invoke SQL tracing from a different session. The DBMS_SYSTEM.SET_TRACE_IN_SESSION package provides this functionality. The syntax is:

```
dbms_system.set_sql_trace_in_session(sid,serial#,TRUE|FALSE)
```

where *sid* and *serial* are the session identifier and serial number for the session you wish to trace. You can get these values from the V$SESSION pseudo-table. For instance, the following PL/SQL block enables tracing for all sessions matching a given username:

```
begin
    for sess_rec in (select sid,serial#
                        from v$session
                        where username like upper('&user_mask'))
```

```
loop
    sys.dbms_system.set_sql_trace_in_session
        (sess_rec.sid, sess_rec.serial#,TRUE);
        end loop;
end;
```

To use this facility, you or your DBA must ensure the *dbms_system* package is installed and grant execute on this package to users who require access to it.

FINDING THE TRACE FILE

Having enabled SQL_TRACE, your next challenge is often to find the trace file which has been generated. The trace file is written to the location defined by the Oracle configuration parameter USER_DUMP_DEST. The name of the trace file is port specific, but in UNIX and many other operating systems it will be:

```
header_pid.trc
```

where *header* is usually "ora" but sometimes "*oracle_sid*_ora," and *pid* is the process identifier for the Oracle server process.

You can determine your USER_DUMP_DEST with the following query (providing you have access to the V$PARAMETER pseudo-table—see your DBA if you don't):

```
select value
    from v$parameter
  where name='user_dump_dest'
```

However, there might be numerous trace files in the USER_DUMP_DEST directory and typically they will all be owned by the Oracle account. Some of the ways you can determine which trace is yours are:

❑ Examine timestamps of the files.

❑ Search for a particular SQL statement. A handy way of "tagging" your trace file is by issuing a statement such as "select 'Catherines trace file' from dual;"—then you can search among trace files for the string "Catherines trace file."

❑ Have your program tell you where the trace will be written. For instance, the following PL/SQL block enables SQL_TRACE, determines the location of the trace file and stores it in the bind variable *trace_file_name*. The calling program could display the trace file name and location in a log file or on the screen:

```
declare
   cursor udd_csr is
           select value
             from sys.v_$parameter
            where name='user_dump_dest';

   cursor my_pid_csr is
           select spid
             from sys.v_$process
            where addr=(select paddr
                          from sys.v_$session
                         where audsid=userenv('sessionid'));

      l_user_dump_dest  varchar2(256);
      l_pid             varchar2(20);
begin
   -- set trace on
   dbms_session.set_sql_trace(TRUE);
   -- Get user_dump_dest
   open  udd_csr;
   fetch udd_csr into l_user_dump_dest;
   close udd_csr;
   -- Get process id for the shadow
   open my_pid_csr;
   fetch my_pid_csr into l_pid;
   close my_pid_csr;
   -- Return the name of the trace file

:trace_file_name:=l_user_dump_dest||'/ora_'||l_pid||'.trc');
end;
```

USING THE *TKPROF* TRACE FILE FORMATTER

Once the trace file is found, the *tkprof* utility is used to render it into a usable form.
The basic syntax for *tkprof* is:

```
tkprof trace_file output_file explain=username/password sort=(sort options)
```

where:

trace_file   is the raw trace file generated by the
                                    SQL_TRACE facility.

output_file   is the file to which formatted trace informa-
                                    tion will be written.

explain=username/password   specifies the connection which will be used
                                    to generate SQL execution plans. If you
                                    don't specify the explain keyword, no exe-
                                    cution plans will be generated.

sort=(sort keys)   Displays the SQL statements in descending values of the sort keys. The sort keys "(prsela,exeela,fchela)" sort the SQL statements in descending order of elapsed time and are a common choice.

A typical *tkprof* invocation would be:

```
tkprof ora_12345.trc trace1.prf explain=/
        sort='( prsela,exeela,fchela)'
```

which processes the raw trace file *ora_12345.trc* and writes the output file *trace1.prf*, generating execution plans using your default ("OPS$") account and sorting SQL statements by elapsed time. Note that because this example was under the UNIX operating system, the parentheses were enclosed in quotes.

Tkprof sort options

Tkprof sort keys consist of two parts: the first part indicates the type of calls which are to be sorted, the second part indicates the values to be sorted. So *exedsk* indicates statements are to be sorted on disk reads during execute calls. Adding options together causes statements to be sorted by the sum of the options specified: so *prsdsk,exedsk,fchdisk* causes statements to be sorted by overall physical disk reads. A few combinations are not valid: *mis* can only be applied to *prs*, and *row* can only applied to *exe* or *fch*. Table 5.4 outlines the components of the sort options.

TABLE 5.4   *Tkprof* sort keys.

First part		Second part	
prs	Sort on values during parse calls	**cnt**	Sort on number of calls
exe	Sort on values during execute calls (equivalent to open cursor for a query)	**cpu**	Sort on CPU consumption
fch	Sort on values during fetch calls (queries only)	**ela**	Sort on elapsed time
		dsk	Sort on disk reads
		qry	Sort on consistent reads
		cu	Sort on current reads
		mis	Sort on library cache misses
		row	Sort on rows processed

Other tkprof options

Mostly, the *tkprof* options used in the previous examples will give you output which contains all the information needed to tune your SQL. Table 5.5 details the other *tkprof* options which may be useful in specific circumstances.

TABLE 5.5 "Other" options for *tkprof*.

Option	Comments
table=owner.tablename	By default, *tkprof* creates a plan_table in your account to generate the execution plans. If you don't have privileges to create the table, or your site likes to use a central plan table, you can specify it with this option.
print=number_of_statements	Restricts the number of SQL statements printed.
aggregate=yes/no	If set to "yes" (the default), SQL statements in the trace file which are identical will be reported only once and execution statistics will be summed. If set to "no," each time an SQL statement is parsed, a separate entry will be written to the *tkprof* output, even if the statements are identical to one encountered previously.
sys=no	If set to "no," statements executed as the SYS user will not be included in the trace output. These statements are usually recursive SQL which, in some cases, might not be of interest.
record=filename	Generates a file containing all the SQL statements (aside from recursive SQL) in the trace file.
insert=filename	Generates a file which can be run under SQL*PLUS to keep a record of the SQL statements in the trace file and their execution statistics. This facility was introduced to allow you to set and compare SQL statement execution over time, perhaps to establish the effect of increasing data volumes or user load.
verbose=yes	In early versions of Oracle 7, the verbose flag could generate an analysis of wait information contained in the trace file. In current releases, its only effect seems to be to cause a summary of recursive SQL execution statistics to be generated.

"PROBLEM" TRACE FILES

You may encounter one of the following problems when trying to format your trace file:

1. "I can't read my trace file." Oracle usually generates trace files as read-only to the Oracle user or DBAs in case they contain sensitive information (such as passwords for roles or hardcoded data values such as account numbers). If you can't read the trace file and are confident that there are no security implications, have your DBA set the undocumented initialization parameter _TRACE_FILES_PUBLIC=TRUE. This should result in trace files being created with public read permission.

2. "My SQL_TRACE is spread across multiple files." This can happen if you are connected to multi-threaded servers. Since each SQL statement might be executed by a different server, the trace information ends up in files associated with each server. The workaround is to use a dedicated server connection.[1]

INTERPRETING *TKPROF* OUTPUT

When you first encounter *tkprof* output, there appears to be a lot of information and very little guidance on how to interpret it. Figure 5.3 shows some sample *tkprof* output. Some highlighted superscripts have been added, which are mentioned in the commentary.

```
********************************************************************
select /*+RULE */1
       e.surname,e.firstname,e.date_of_birth
  from employees e
 where exists (select 1
                 from customers c
                where upper(e.surname)=upper(c.contact_surname)
                  and upper(e.firstname)=upper(c.contact_firstname)
                  and e.date_of_birth=c.date_of_birth)
 order by e.surname,e.firstname
```

---

[1]For instance, in your *tnsnames.ora* file, insert the keyword (SERVER=DEDICATED) in the CONNECT_DATA section. If using network manager, create an alias for the server in question and tick "Dedicated server" on the Options page. See your DBA if unable to establish a dedicated server connection.

call	count[2]	cpu[3]	elapsed[4]	disk[5]	query[6]	current[7]	rows[8]
Parse[a]	1[d]	0.00	0.43	0	0	0	0
Execute[b]	1[e]	0.00	0.00	0	0	0	0
Fetch[c]	11[j]	0.00	323.74	204161	212083	2400	151[i]
Total	13	0.00	324.17	204161	212083[f]	2400[g]	151[h]

```
Misses in library cache during parse: 0
Optimizer hint: RULE
Parsing user id: 12   (SQLTUNE)
```

Rows[1]	Execution Plan[m]
0	SELECT STATEMENT HINT: RULE
800	FILTER
800	TABLE ACCESS (BY ROWID) OF 'EMPLOYEES'
801	INDEX (RANGE SCAN) OF 'EMPLOYEE_BOTHNAMES_IDX' (NON-UNIQUE)
4109475	TABLE ACCESS HINT: ANALYZED (FULL) OF 'CUSTOMERS'

FIGURE 5.3   Sample *tkprof* output—before optimization.

Tkprof execution statistics

First, let's look at the top half of the output. Letters in brackets refer to super-scripts in Figure 5.3:

1. The SQL text is displayed (1).

2. Next is a table containing the execution statistics. Working across the top of the table:

   ❏ The number of times each category of call was issued (2).

   ❏ The CPU time required (3).

   ❏ The elapsed time required (4).

   ❏ Number of disk reads required (5)

   ❏ Number of buffers read in query (consistent) (6) or current (7) mode. Blocks read in query mode are usually for consistent read queries. Blocks read in current mode are often for modifications to existing blocks. I don't believe the distinction is particularly important when tuning SQL, so I usually add them together and call them "logical reads."

   ❏ The number of rows processed (8).

3. Working down the table, we see that each measurement is broken down by the category of Oracle call. The three categories are:

❑ Parse(a), in which the SQL statement is checked for syntax, valid objects and security, and in which an execution plan is determined by the optimizer.

❑ Execute(b), in which an SQL statement is executed, or in the case of a query, prepared for fetching.

❑ Fetch(c), in which rows are returned from a query. Note that in the case of a query which contains an ORDER BY or a FOR UPDATE, rows may actually have to be accessed during the execute stage.

We can tell a great deal about the efficiency of the SQL statement by deriving some ratios from this output. Some of the important ratios are:

1. Blocks read (f+g) to rows processed (h). This is a rough indication of the relative expense of the query. The more blocks that have to be accessed relative to the number of rows returned, the more "expensive" each row is. A similar ratio is blocks read (f+g) to executions (e). In our example, the blocks-to-rows ratio is about 1,420—which means that each row "cost" about 1,420 block I/Os. Ratios above 10 to 20 (or lower for simple index lookups) may indicate room for improvement.

2. Parse count (d) over execute count (e). Ideally, the parse count should be close to one. If it is high in relation to execute count, then the statement has been needlessly re-parsed. We discussed the problems and causes of excessive parsing—lack of bind variables or poor cursor reuse—in Chapter 3. Guidelines for minimizing parsing in client tools is in Appendix C.

3. Rows fetched (i) to fetches (j). This indicates the level to which the *array fetch* facility has been exercised (see Chapters 3 and 6 for a discussion of array processing). In our example the ratio is about 14, which indicates that rows were fetched 14 at a time. A ratio close to one indicates no array processing—which may indicate a significant opportunity for optimization.

4. Disk reads (k) to logical reads (f+g). This is a measurement of the "miss rate" within the data buffer cache. We usually aim to get this ratio less than about 10%. In our case, we had 204,161 disk reads and therefore a miss rate of 204161/(212083+2400) = 95%—very high. Configuring the database to reduce this miss ratio is discussed in Chapter 16.

The tkprof execution plan

If the "explain=" command line option has been used, the SQL statement's execution plan is displayed in the familiar "nested" display format. A significant enhancement to the *tkprof* execution plan is the presence of both the step (m) and also the number of rows processed by each step (l). The row count (l) can indicate which step did the most work and hence might be most effectively tuned.

These execution step row counts provided by SQL_TRACE/*tkprof* cannot be obtained by any other method and are an invaluable aid to SQL tuning. All other things being equal, the more rows processed, the more computer resources required. Therefore, the step with the highest execution count is usually the step which is most in need of optimization.

USING *TKPROF* TO TUNE SQL

When looking at *tkprof* output, you should consider:

❑ How efficient is the statement as indicated by block gets per row returned?

❑ How was the data retrieved? In other words, what does the execution plan mean?

❑ Which steps in the execution plan processed the most rows? How can I improve or avoid these steps?

Applying these principles to the output in Figure 5.3, you could conclude:

❑ The ratio of blocks read to rows returned is very high (1,420). The statement is very inefficient by this criteria and you might hope for a substantial improvement.

❑ The execution plan reveals that the EMPLOYEE_BOTHNAMES_IDX index was used to retrieve every row in EMPLOYEES (800). The rule based optimizer uses the index to retrieve the rows in the order requested in the ORDER BY clause.

❑ For each employee row retrieved, a full table scan of the CUSTOMERS table was undertaken.

❑ The step with the most rows processed—by a substantial margin—is the full table scan of CUSTOMERS. This is, therefore, a logical place to start tuning.

Over four million rows were processed in the step involving the full table scan of CUSTOMERS. Since CUSTOMERS contains only 5,150 rows, it's obvious that this table scan must have occurred more than once. In fact, we can see both from our earlier interpretation of the execution plan, and from simple mathematics, that the full table scan happened once for every row in EMPLOYEES (800 employee rows times 5,150 customer rows equals 4.1 million rows).

At this point, we might consider the following:

❏ Can we use an index instead of a full table scan of CUSTOMERS?

❏ If not, can't we at least perform a full table scan of CUSTOMERS only once?

To answer the first question, we can't use indexes because of the UPPER functions surrounding the SURNAME and FIRSTNAME columns. These are presumably there in case there is a difference in capitalization between the CUSTOMERS and EMPLOYEES table.

To answer the second question, it is possible to resolve this query with only a single table scan of the CUSTOMERS table. The problem with the SQL statement is its use of the EXISTS operator. The EXISTS operator executes its subquery once for each row in the outer query—so you need to avoid full table scans in the subquery. An alternative is to formulate the query using the IN clause or as a join of the two tables. By rewording the statement to use the IN operator, we obtain the execution plan shown in Figure 5.4.

```
select /*+RULE */
       e.surname,e.firstname,e.date_of_birth
  from employees e,
       customers c
 where upper(e.surname)=upper(c.contact_surname)
   and upper(e.firstname)=upper(c.contact_firstname)
   and e.date_of_birth=c.date_of_birth
 order by e.surname,e.firstname
```

call	count	cpu	elapsed	disk	query	current	rows
Parse	1	0.00	0.12	0	0	0	0
Execute	2	0.00	0.96	0	0	1	0
Fetch	11	0.00	9.82	278	364	370	151
Total	14	0.00	10.90	278	364	371	151

```
Misses in library cache during parse: 0
Optimizer hint: RULE
Parsing user id: 12   (SQLTUNE)
```

Rows	Execution Plan
0	SELECT STATEMENT HINT: RULE
151	SORT (ORDER BY)
151	MERGE JOIN
5151	SORT (JOIN)
5151	TABLE ACCESS HINT: ANALYZED (FULL) OF 'CUSTOMERS'
800	SORT (JOIN)
800	TABLE ACCESS (FULL) OF 'EMPLOYEES'

FIGURE 5.4   This shows *tkprof* output after optimization.

We are now doing only one table scan of each table. Our blocks to row ratio has dropped to 4.8 and the overall I/O requirement for the query is now only 0.3% of the original I/O requirement—a considerable improvement!

TKPROF RULES, OK?

We've just seen an example of how *tkprof* can be used to tune SQL. In the example, we reduced I/O requirements by 99.7%—an impressive improvement.

Now it's perfectly true that this SQL statement was written with the intention of demonstrating poor performance characteristics. However, it's not at all uncommon to see impressive improvements to SQL statement execution as shown in the above example.

It would, of course, be possible to get such an improvement without *tkprof*. But think of how much harder it would be. *Tkprof* told us exactly how I/O requirements changed as we tuned the SQL. Also, *tkprof* led us directly to the execution step responsible for the poor performance. No other tool can do this, and that is why you should master *tkprof* and use it as your primary tool in your pursuit of high performance SQL.

USING THE AUTOTRACE FACILITY IN SQL*PLUS

As we've seen, SQL_TRACE and *tkprof* are powerful tools. But they are not always easy to use. Each time you use SQL_TRACE, you have to find the trace file (which, in a client server environment, will often be on a different machine) then format and interpret the *tkprof* output. Finding and interpreting the trace files can be time-consuming and you might wish that you could get *tkprof*-like feedback immediately after executing a new SQL statement.

Starting with SQL*Plus version 3.3 (the version released with Oracle 7.3), Oracle moved part of the way towards providing such a facility. The facility is enabled with the SET AUTOTRACE command within SQL*PLUS.

AUTOTRACE can generate execution plans and execution statistics for SQL statements executed from SQL*PLUS. However, it doesn't provide all the facilities of *tkprof*—in particular, it doesn't show rows processed for each step in the execution plan.

REQUIREMENTS FOR USING AUTOTRACE

Your DBA should grant the PLUSTRACE role to users who are required to use the AUTOTRACE utility.

You must have a plan table called PLAN_TABLE in your account. Creating a plan table was discussed earlier in this chapter.

INITIATING AUTOTRACE

This command has the following options:

OFF	Normal behavior, generate no trace output.
ON EXPLAIN	Following each SQL statement execution, display the execution plan in the normal "nested" format.
ON STATISTICS	Following each SQL statement execution, print a report detailing I/O, CPU and other resource utilization.
ON	After SQL statement execution, display both the execution plan and the execution statistics.
TRACEONLY	Same as the "ON" setting, but suppresses the display of data from an SQL statement, so that only the execution plan and statistics are shown.

For instance, to have the execution plan displayed after each SQL statement, use the statement:

```
SET AUTOTRACE ON EXPLAIN
```

To show both the execution plan and the execution statistics, but to suppress the display of rows returned by queries, use the following statement:

```
SET AUTOTRACE TRACEONLY
```

AUTOTRACE OUTPUT

Figure 5.5 shows some output from a sample autotrace session.

```
SQL> set autotrace traceonly explain statistics
SQL> @qry1

SQL> l
  1  select /*+ ORDERED USE_HASH(C) */
  2         c.contact_surname,c.contact_firstname,c.date_of_birth
  3    from
  4         employees e,
  5         customers c
  6   where e.surname=c.contact_surname
  7     and e.firstname=c.contact_firstname
  8*    and e.date_of_birth=c.date_of_birth
SQL>
SQL> /
```

```
no rows selected


Execution Plan
-----------------------------------------------------------
   0          SELECT STATEMENT Cost=77 Optimizer=CHOOSE
   1    0      HASH JOIN
   2    1       TABLE ACCESS (FULL) OF 'EMPLOYEES'
   3    1       INDEX (FULL SCAN) OF 'SURNAME_FIRSTNAME_DOB_PHONENO'


Statistics
-----------------------------------------------------------
    1361   recursive calls
      13   db block gets
     768   consistent gets
     618   physical reads
       0   redo size
     245   bytes sent via SQL*Net to client
     523   bytes received via SQL*Net from client
       3   SQL*Net roundtrips to/from client
       0   sorts (memory)
       0   sorts (disk)
       0   rows processed
```

FIGURE 5.5   AUTOTRACE Output.

AUTOTRACE COMPARED TO TKPROF

The AUTOTRACE facility can be extremely useful, but it has the following deficiencies when compared to SQL_TRACE and *tkprof*:

❑ Row counts are not assigned to individual execution steps. We have seen that the SQL_TRACE/*tkprof* facility can show the number of rows processed by each stage of execution. This capability is one of *tkprof*'s greatest strengths because it allows you to quickly focus in on a particular stage of the execution plan. This often shows up an inappropriate index or other weakness. The AUTOTRACE facility cannot produce this information and is accordingly less powerful.

❑ SQL_TRACE can be turned on from within any Oracle session, but AUTOTRACE only works from within SQL*PLUS.

❑ AUTOTRACE statistics do not include CPU or elapsed times and also do not break execution down by parse, execute and fetch.

❑ So *tkprof* output is definitely more useful than AUTOTRACE output—but you shouldn't write off AUTOTRACE. You can use AUTOTRACE under the following circumstances:

    • AUTOTRACE is easy to use, and you get the results more quickly than if you have to find and format a trace file. Therefore, you may wish to use AUTOTRACE to rapidly compare multiple approaches to an SQL statement (e.g., changing hints, wordings, perhaps even indexes). When the SQL statement seems to be close to optimal, you may use SQL_TRACE and *tkprof* to confirm this.

- Some client-server developers may not have access to the server platform. Therefore, they won't have access to the trace files produced by SQL_TRACE. In this case, the AUTOTRACE facility may be the best option for tuning available.

CHAPTER SUMMARY

In this chapter, we've looked at the tools provided by Oracle for tuning SQL statements. These tools allow you to determine the steps which Oracle will undertake to execute your SQL statement and can measure the resources required.

The EXPLAIN PLAN command can be used to determine the execution plan for an SQL statement. To use EXPLAIN PLAN, you must first create a "plan table." The EXPLAIN PLAN command will insert the details of your SQL statement's execution plan into this table. You can then use SQL queries to retrieve and format the execution plan.

Because the procedure for retrieving execution plans using EXPLAIN PLAN is cumbersome, most SQL programmers use scripts to simplify the process. There are also commercial and shareware products available to simplify the process. Some of these tools can be found on the companion CD-ROM.

The SQL_TRACE facility provides a more powerful way of generating tuning information for SQL statements. SQL_TRACE generates a trace file containing details of the SQL statements executed and the resources required. The *tkprof* program can be used to format these trace files and can also generate execution plans for each statement included.

SQL_TRACE is usually enabled by issuing the ALTER SESSION SET SQL_TRACE TRUE statement. The location of the trace file is dependent on the operating system and database configuration and is defined by the configuration parameter USER_DUMP_DEST.

Tkprof includes a number of command line options. A common usage, which sorts SQL statements by elapsed time and which shows the execution plan for each statement is:

```
tkprof trace_file output_file sort='(prsela,exeela,fchela)' explain=username/password
```

Tkprof generates details of I/O and CPU requirements for each stage (parse, execute, fetch) of SQL statement execution. It also shows the number of rows processed by each stage of the execution plan. *Tkprof* output can be complex, but the following guidelines for interpretation are always useful:

❑ The ratio of "query" and "current" to "rows" gives a measure of the cost (number of I/Os) required to fetch each row.

❑ The execution steps with the highest row counts are often the best candidates for tuning.

❑ Low ratios of "parse" to "execute" for statements which are frequently executed may indicate unnecessary parsing of SQL statements.

❑ The ratio of "rows" to "fetch" gives an indication of the use of the array fetch facility. Values close to one indicate that array processing was not enabled.

The SET AUTOTRACE option can be used to generate execution plans and statistics directly from SQL*PLUS. This facility is easier to use than SQL_TRACE and *tkprof,* but provides less detailed output.

Chapter 6

TUNING TABLE ACCESS

INTRODUCTION

In this chapter, we look at ways of improving the performance of SQL statements which access a single table. The single table query is one of the building blocks of more complex SQL queries; and understanding how to optimize the single table access is a prerequisite for improving the performance of more elaborate queries.

There are usually a number of possible access methods for any given query. A full table scan is always an option and, depending on the indexes which have been created on the table, there may be a number of index retrieval options. Storing your data in a hash cluster provides another option.

The optimizer will not always choose the best access and you will need to be able to evaluate the optimizer's choice and encourage the use of a different access path, if appropriate.

Further, you need to make access paths available by creating appropriate indexes or hash clusters.

The topics we will cover in this chapter are:

❑ Full table scans compared with other access paths.

❑ Using column histograms to improve optimization.

❑ "Accidental" full table scans and how to avoid them.

❑ Creating and optimizing indexes.

❏ Optimizing range scans.

❏ Optimizing queries which include "OR."

❏ Optimizing the configuration of hash clusters.

❏ Configuring tables to maximize scan performance.

FULL TABLE SCANS AND INDEX LOOKUPS

The two most commonly used methods to retrieve rows from a table are:

❏ Full table scan, in which all rows from the table are read and compared against the selection criteria.

❏ Index lookup, in which an index is used to determine the rows to be processed.

Initially, SQL programmers are often taught to avoid the full table scan. However, table scans will sometimes consume less resources than the equivalent index lookup. This will be true when the selection criteria accesses a large proportion of the table data. An index retrieval will require reading both the index blocks and the table blocks. Furthermore, Oracle will have to alternate between index blocks and table blocks and will quite possibly read an individual index block many times. If a large portion of the table is being accessed, the overhead of using the index may be greater than the overhead of scanning the entire table.

At what point does an index retrieval outperform the table access?

Rules of thumb which help the SQL programmer decide whether to use a full table scan or an index lookup are commonplace. Here are some of the rules of thumb which you might encounter:

❏ Use a full table scan if accessing more than 25% of the table data.

❏ Use a full table scan if accessing more than 8 or 16 (or some other number) of data blocks.

❏ Use a full table scan if accessing more than five percent of the table data.

❏ Use a full table scan if it is faster than an index lookup.

The reason why the "rules of thumb" vary so much is because it is not possible to generalize across all types of SQL statements, hardware platforms and data distributions. However, the following statements are indisputable:

❏ If all rows, or a large proportion of rows in the table need to be accessed, then a full table scan will be the quickest way to do this.

❏ If a single row is to be retrieved from a large table, then an index based on that column will offer the quicker retrieval path.

❏ Between these two extremes, it may be difficult to predict which access path will be quicker.

In many cases, you are either selecting a small number of rows from a table to satisfy a transaction processing (OLTP) type query, or selecting a large number of rows to satisfy a decision support (OLAP) type query. In these circumstances, your decision will be an easy one—use the index or hash for the OLTP query and use a full table scan for the OLAP query.

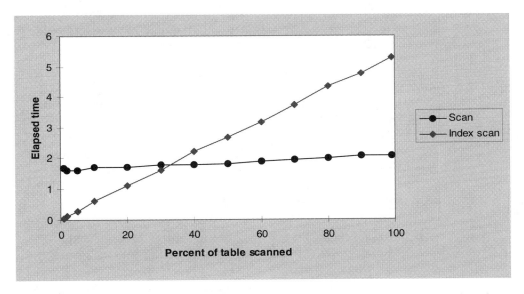

FIGURE 6.1 Elapsed time for full table scan versus elapsed time for index retrieval against percentage of table rows accessed.

When accessing between 5 and 20% of the table, you will probably want to test the query using each access path and analyze the results using SQL_TRACE and *tkprof*. Below the five percent threshold, an index lookup will probably be fastest; above 20%, the full table scan will perform best.

> **When retrieving a substantial proportion of a table's data, full table scans are likely to offer the best performance. When retrieving small numbers of rows, avoid full table scans.**

HOW THE OPTIMIZER CHOOSES BETWEEN
TABLE SCANS AND INDEXES

The rule based optimizer will almost always favor an access path involving an index to one involving a full table scan. This is because in the absence of any information about the sizes of tables, the index based access path is the safer choice. A full table scan might be faster than an index lookup in some circumstances—say 50% faster. However, a full table scan could be 10,000% slower—depending on the size of the table. So the rule based optimizer plays it safe and favors the index based path.

The cost based optimizer knows more—or thinks it knows more—about the distribution of data in the tables. As a result, it will often choose a full table scan even where an index is available, if it calculates that the full table scan will be less expensive. This decision can sometimes be misplaced if:

❏ A candidate index has only a few distinct values, but the value being queried is quite selective. Unless you have created a histogram on the column, discussed later in this section, *and* explicitly coded the value being selected into the SQL, the cost based optimizer will probably ignore the index.

❏ The optimizer goal is set to ALL_ROWS or CHOOSE, but the requirement is really for response time. A full table scan might result in the best response time to retrieve all the rows, but an index will usually be quicker when retrieving just the first row.

❏ If you haven't kept your optimizer statistics up-to-date (by using the ANALYZE command), the cost based optimizer may think that the table is smaller than it really is. This might lead it to incorrectly choose the full table scan.

❏ The cost based optimizer is heavily biased in terms of reducing I/O. CPU overheads, such as that involved in sorting rows for a merge join, are not always accurately estimated. On some systems, these overheads can be substantial.

To encourage the cost based optimizer to use suitable indexes, you should therefore do the following:

❏ Create histograms on indexed columns where there are only a few distinct values, but where the values are very rare. Hardcode these values in the SQL statement (e.g., don't use bind variables) to allow the histogram information to be used.

❏ Specify the FIRST_ROWS optimizer goal if interactive response time is your aim. This can be specified as a hint, in an ALTER SESSION statement or in the database configuration.

❏ Use hints to direct the optimizer towards specific indexes.

> Help the cost based optimizer choose between indexes and table scans by keeping your tables analyzed, specifying the correct optimizer goal, using histograms where appropriate and using hints.

USING COLUMN HISTOGRAMS

Column histograms, introduced in Chapter 3, provide the cost based optimizer with details of the distribution of data within a column. By creating a histogram, you provide the cost based optimizer with more information about column data and help it to make a more informed choice. In particular, the presence of a histogram can help the optimizer decide between an index retrieval and a full table scan. This is especially true when the access involved is on a column with a small number of values and some of the values are particularly selective (because they appear relatively rarely). Histograms also help the cost based optimizer make the right decision during range scans. For instance, without a histogram, the cost based optimizer would probably resolve the following query with a full table scan, since it would not know the proportion of persons over 90:

```
select *
  from people
 where age>90
```

Creating a histogram on the age column would allow the optimizer to determine that only a small proportion of people are over 90, and that an index based execution plan was therefore to be preferred.

We create a histogram for a column by specifying the column name in the ANALYZE command. For instance, the following command creates histograms for date_of_birth, contact_surname and customer_status:

```
analyze table customers estimate statistics sample 20 percent for columns
    date_of_birth          size 50,
    contact_surname        size 200,
    customer_status        size 3;
```

The size parameter specifies the number of "buckets" in the histogram. Each bucket specifies a range of values. Where there are only a few distinct values in a column, a small size can be specified. For columns with a larger number of values, a higher size will increase the accuracy of the histogram.

We'll see examples of histograms applied to various types of queries in subsequent sections.

Histograms and bind variables

Histograms can dramatically improve the quality of the cost based optimizer's decisions for certain queries.

Unfortunately, there is a catch. The cost based optimizer cannot take advantage of a histogram if the column values are specified with bind variables. You may recall from Chapter 3 that bind variables are a way of "hiding" the actual value of a variable from the optimizer until after the statement has been parsed. This allows SQL statements which have different search criteria to be recognized as the same statement and allows Oracle to avoid re-parsing the statement.

Because the value of the bind variable is evaluated after the statement has been parsed, the cost based optimizer cannot take the value of a bind variable into account and can therefore not take advantage of a column histogram.

This leads us to a dilemma—bind variables reduce parsing, and histograms improve cost based optimizer decisions, but you can't have both!

You need to weigh a number of factors when deciding upon bind variables versus histograms. Table 6.1 shows some of these considerations.

TABLE 6.1   Deciding between bind variables and histograms.

Situation	Use bind variables?	Use histograms?
The value of the search variable never changes.	No need, since the value doesn't change, the SQL statement will always match.	Maybe, if other criteria suggest it.
The SQL statement is performing a range scan.	Not unless strongly indicated by other factors.	Yes, if the range scan varies in the amount of rows picked up (so that sometimes a scan will be preferred, sometimes an index).
The SQL statement is performing an exact lookup, but some of the values are common and some are rare.	Not unless strongly indicated by other factors.	Yes, since the histogram will help the cost based optimizer decide between a full table scan and an index lookup.
The SQL statement is executed very frequently and is expected to complete quickly.	Yes. For an inexpensive statement executed very frequently, the cost of parsing can be significant.	No. Bind variables are indicated here. Use a hint if the optimizer makes the wrong decision.
The SQL statement is executed infrequently and takes a long time to run.	Probably not. Parse overhead will be a small component of overall requirements, so using bind variables will probably not help much.	If indicated by other factors.

TABLE 6.1 Deciding between bind variables and histograms. *(Continued)*

Situation	Use bind variables?	Use histograms?
The SQL is ad hoc and user driven. It alternates between the specific and the general or uses range conditions.	Probably not. End users are unlikely to use bind variables, and the statement probably wouldn't find a match in the shared pool anyway.	Yes. Allow the optimizer to make the most informed choice.
The SQL is being generated by some third-party product (perhaps a query tool).	You probably don't get a choice.	Probably, since you can't control the SQL, you're dependent on the cost based optimizer—so give it all the information you can.

The conditions in which histograms are favored are typical of decision support or data warehousing applications, while the conditions in which bind variables are favored are typical of transaction processing applications.

> **Histograms can improve the optimization of range scans or lookups on unevenly distributed data. However, bind variables should usually be used to reduce parsing in transaction processing environments, and histograms can't be used in conjunction with bind variables.**

ALTERNATIVES TO FULL TABLE SCANS

In Chapter 4, we introduced Oracle's indexing and clustering offerings. Table 6.2 summarizes these options. To briefly review:

❑ The default Oracle index type, the B*-tree, offers good performance for a wide range of query and data distribution types.

❑ Hash clusters can outperform the B*-tree index for lookups of small numbers of rows matching a single value. However, if the structure of the hash cluster is not carefully configured, or if the table is subject to growth, then the performance of the hash cluster can degrade—both for the single value lookup and for table scans.

❑ Bitmap indexes can improve performance when selecting against multiple columns of low selectivity in very large tables.

TABLE 6.2   Features of the various table access paths.

Access type	Use
Full table scan	Use when reading more than 10 to 20% of the rows in the table OR the table is very small.
B*-tree index lookup	Use for flexible retrieval, looking up ranges or direct lookups. Also good for returning rows in sorted order.
hash cluster	Use when you will only be accessing the key by direct comparisons (e.g., "=") and you rarely expect to scan the table. The table should be static in size, or you should be prepared to rebuild it regularly.
bitmap index	Use when you need to generate summary information from large tables where your selection criteria is based on several columns, each with few unique values. Tables should not be subject to heavy updates.

AVOIDING "ACCIDENTAL" TABLE SCANS

Even if there is an appropriate index or hash retrieval available, the optimizer may not be able to take advantage of the access because of the wording of the SQL statement. Some of the query types which prevent indexes being used are:

❑ Queries involving a != NOT EQUALS condition.

❑ Searching for NULL values.

❑ Accidentally disabling an index with a function.

Using not equals

Oracle will not employ an index if the NOT EQUALS operator (!=) is employed. This is generally sensible, because when retrieving all rows except for those matching a single value, a full table scan will usually be the fastest way of retrieving the data. However, if the value in question accounts for the majority of the rows in the database, then an index based retrieval of the minority of rows (which don't match the value) might be preferable.

For example, let's suppose that the valid values for the CUSTOMER_STATUS column in the CUSTOMERS table is "VALID," "OVERDUE" or "CANCELED" and that the vast majority of customers (more than 95%) are "VALID." If we want to get all customers who aren't "VALID," we might issue the following query:

```
SQL> select customer_id
  2    from customers
  3    where customer_status != 'VALID'
  4    /

204 rows selected.

Execution Plan
-----------------------------------------------------------
SELECT STATEMENT Optimizer=CHOOSE
    TABLE ACCESS (FULL) OF 'CUSTOMERS'
```

As expected, a full table scan was required—even though there is an index on STATUS. Oracle won't use an index where the search condition is NOT EQUALS.

If we reword the query to match on "OVERDUE" and "CANCELED," the cost based optimizer still chooses not to use the index. Because there are only three distinct values, the cost based optimizer calculates that by fetching two of these three values, two-thirds of the table will need to be retrieved and a full table scan is most appropriate:

```
SQL> select customer_id
  2    from customers
  3    where customer_status IN ('CANCELED','OVERDUE')
  4    /

204 rows selected.


Execution Plan
-----------------------------------------------------------
SELECT STATEMENT Optimizer=CHOOSE
    TABLE ACCESS (FULL) OF 'CUSTOMERS'
```

Since we know that the two values actually comprise only a small proportion of rows, we can use a hint to force an index scan:

```
SQL> select /*+ USE_CONCAT INDEX(C CUSTOMER_STATUS_IDX) */
customer_id
  2    from customers C
  3    where customer_status IN ('CANCELED','OVERDUE')
  4    /

204 rows selected.


Execution Plan
-----------------------------------------------------------
0       SELECT STATEMENT Optimizer=CHOOSE
1    0    CONCATENATION
2    1      TABLE ACCESS (BY ROWID) OF 'CUSTOMERS'
```

```
3    2        INDEX (RANGE SCAN) OF 'CUSTOMER_STATUS_IDX' (NON-UNIQUE)
4    1        TABLE ACCESS (BY ROWID) OF 'CUSTOMERS'
5    4        INDEX (RANGE SCAN) OF 'CUSTOMER_STATUS_IDX' (NON-UNIQUE)
```

If we create a histogram on the STATUS column, we get the desired execution plan without a hint:

```
SQL> select customer_id
  2    from customers
  3   where customer_status IN ('CANCELED','OVERDUE')
  4  /

204 rows selected.


Execution Plan
----------------------------------------------------------
0        SELECT STATEMENT Optimizer=CHOOSE
1    0   CONCATENATION
2    1      TABLE ACCESS (BY ROWID) OF 'CUSTOMERS'
3    2     INDEX (RANGE SCAN) OF 'CUSTOMER_STATUS_IDX' (NON-UNIQUE)
4    1      TABLE ACCESS (BY ROWID) OF 'CUSTOMERS'
5    4     INDEX (RANGE SCAN) OF 'CUSTOMER_STATUS_IDX' (NON-UNIQUE)
```

But even if a column histogram exists, Oracle will not use an index if the search condition is not equals.

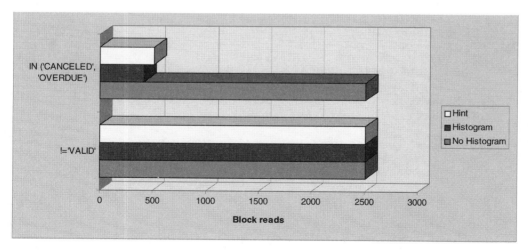

FIGURE 6.2 Performance of a != query compared with the performance of the alternative IN based query.

> Oracle will not use an index if the query condition is "not equals" (!=). If you think the query could benefit from an indexed approach, reword the query using IN, OR or ">." You may still need to use hints or a column histogram to encourage Oracle to use the appropriate index.

Searching for NULLS

As we discovered in Chapter 4, index entries are not created when all the columns in the index have the NULL value. As a result, you can't use an index on a column to search for a NULL value. For instance, let's suppose the CUSTOMERS.STATUS column may contain NULL values (perhaps prior to the customer being fully registered). We might have a query to find these customers, as follows:

```
select customer_name
from
 customers where status is null

Rows      Execution Plan
-------   --------------------------------------------------
      0   SELECT STATEMENT    HINT: CHOOSE
   5151   TABLE ACCESS    HINT: ANALYZED (FULL) OF 'CUSTOMERS'
```

To find customers with the NULL status, we must perform a full table scan. If we redefine the column so that it is not NULL and has a default value of unknown:

```
alter table customers modify status  default 'UNKNOWN';
```

we can then use the index to find these NULL values:

```
select /*+ INDEX(CUSTOMERS CUSTOMER_STATUS_INDEX) */
       customer_name
from
 customers where status='UNKNOWN'
```

In this example, using the index reduced I/O requirements from 275 block reads to 33. For bigger tables, the improvement is even more pronounced. Note that, as in the previous value, it may be necessary to use a hint or define a histogram if the number of unique values is low.

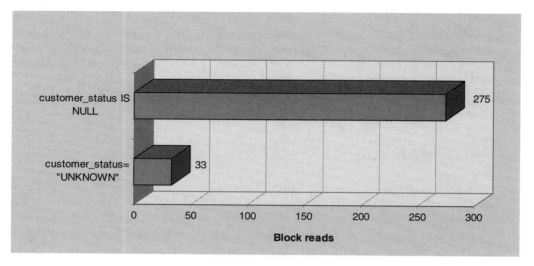

FIGURE 6.3 Searching for NULL values versus searching for a default value.

Avoid searching for NULL values in an indexed column. Instead, define the column as NOT NULL with a default value.

Searching for values which are NOT NULL

Although Oracle cannot use an index to search for NULL values, it can use the index to find values which are NOT NULL. The cost based optimizer will choose to do this only if it calculates that the combined cost of accessing the table and the relevant index will be less than the cost of performing a full table scan.

In many circumstances, the cost based optimizer will determine that the full table scan is the cheaper cost and will perform a full table scan, as in the following example:

```
SQL> select *
  2    from customers
  3   where process_flag IS NOT NULL
  4  /

Execution Plan
----------------------------------------------------------
   0        SELECT STATEMENT Optimizer=CHOOSE
   1  0       TABLE ACCESS (FULL) OF 'CUSTOMERS'
```

The cost based optimizer may favor a full index scan to identify the NOT NULL rows if most of the rows are NULL or if the query can be resolved by the use of the index alone. For instance, in the following example, the cost based optimizer used a full index scan without a table access:

```
SQL> select count(*)
  2     from customers
  3     where process_flag is not null
  4  /

Execution Plan
----------------------------------------------------------
   0  SELECT STATEMENT Optimizer=CHOOSE
  10    SORT (AGGREGATE)
  21      INDEX (FULL SCAN) OF 'CUSTOMERS_PROCESS_FLAG_IDX'
```

You can encourage Oracle to use an index-based retrieval with the INDEX hint:

```
SQL> select /*+ INDEX(CUSTOMERS) */
  2        *
  3     from customers
  4     where process_flag IS NOT NULL
  5  /

Execution Plan
----------------------------------------------------------
   0  SELECT STATEMENT Optimizer=CHOOSE
  10    TABLE ACCESS (BY ROWID) OF 'CUSTOMERS'
  21      INDEX (FULL SCAN) OF 'CUSTOMERS_PROCESS_FLAG_IDX' (NON-UNIQUE)
```

Creating indexes on nullable columns

It's usually wise to define columns referenced in the where clause as NOT NULL, so that indexing these columns can be effective. However, it can be worthwhile using NULL values in an indexed column if the following conditions apply:

❏ The column is almost always NULL.

❏ We never want to find rows where the column is NULL.

❏ We do want to search for rows where the column is NOT NULL.

❏ We want to minimize the space required by the index.

Since NULLS are not stored in an index, an index created when the above conditions are true will be very compact and can be used to quickly locate rows where the column contains a value. Ensure that the cost based optimizer makes use of the appropriate index and uses a hint, if necessary.

Searching for a selective value in an unselective column

If the column is of marginal selectivity, it may be difficult for Oracle to determine whether the full table scan or the index retrieval is preferable. If the column has only a few values, but you know that the values concerned are rare, then you could force an index lookup using a hint.

For instance, only a handful of customers have the status of "INVALID." Nevertheless, the cost based optimizer will decline to use an index on status for the following statement, since there are only three values for CUSTOMER_STATUS:

```
select count(distinct contact_surname)
  from customers
 where customer_status='INVALID'

Rows        Execution Plan
-------     ---------------------------------------------------------
      0     SELECT STATEMENT    GOAL: CHOOSE
    204       SORT (GROUP BY)
 100000         TABLE ACCESS   GOAL: ANALYZED (FULL) OF 'CUSTOMERS'
```

The INDEX hint can be used to encourage the cost based optimizer to perform the more efficient index scan:

```
select /*+ INDEX(CUSTOMERS CUSTOMER_STATUS_IDX) */
       count(distinct contact_surname)
  from customers
 where customer_status='INVALID'


Rows        Execution Plan
-------     ---------------------------------------------------
      0     SELECT STATEMENT    GOAL: CHOOSE
    204       SORT (GROUP BY)
    204         TABLE ACCESS   GOAL: ANALYZED (BY ROWID) OF 'CUSTOMERS'
    205           INDEX   GOAL: ANALYZED (RANGE SCAN) OF
                      'CUSTOMER_STATUS_IDX'
                    (NON-UNIQUE)
```

If you don't know in advance whether the value to be selected will be INVALID (< 1% of rows, or "VALID" (>90% of rows), it may be a mistake to force the use of an index in all cases. A column histogram might be a better solution. Providing bind variables were not being used, you could use a column histogram to promote the use of the index for searches on "INVALID," while retaining full table scans when searching for "VALID" rows.

Use hints or column histograms to avoid full table scans when searching for a rare value in an otherwise non-selective index.

Unintentionally disabling the index with a function

We saw in Chapter 3 how we can influence the rule based optimizer by disabling certain indexes. The "trick" is to apply an operator or a function to the column in question. If a column is subjected to any modification, then an index on that column cannot be used.

In the past, this was a useful way to influence the rule based optimizer. Nowadays, hints provide a much more powerful and self-documenting method.

Obviously, if index paths can be intentionally disabled, they can also be unintentionally disabled. For instance, consider the following query to get customer details:.

```
select
        customer_id,customer_name
   from customers
  where contact_surname=:1
    and contact_firstname=:2
```

We can use an index on surname and firstname to satisfy this query with only a couple of I/Os. However, let's suppose that the query is issued from an on-line inquiry screen. It might be decided to make the search ignore distinctions between upper and lowercase by rewording the query as follows:

```
select
        customer_id,customer_name
   from customers
  where upper(contact_surname)=upper(:1)
    and upper(contact_firstname)=upper(:2)
```

By surrounding the columns in a function, we prevent the use of an index. The previously efficient index lookup has now been replaced by an onerous full table scan. It's therefore important to avoid using functions on indexed columns. When possible, apply the inverse function to the search criteria.

Avoid applying functions to an indexed column as this will disable the index. If possible, apply a reciprocal function to the search values.

OPTIMIZING INDEX LOOKUPS

The inexperienced SQL programmer will often use EXPLAIN PLAN to determine that a full table scan has been avoided. If there is no full table scan, then this person will conclude that the plan is a good one. In fact, there are often a wide variety of index based retrievals possible and merely ensuring that one of these indexes is used does not mean that the SQL statement is optimized. Selecting the best of all actual and potential indexes, and ensuring that the indexes are being used to their full potential, is at least as important as avoiding a full table scan.

TYPES OF INDEX RETRIEVALS

Some of the types of index retrievals which can occur are:

1. Finding a single row by lookup of a unique index.
2. Finding multiple rows matching a single value in a non-unique index.
3. Finding rows matching all the values in a concatenated index.
4. Finding rows matching some of the values in a concatenated index.
5. Finding rows matching a range of values in a concatenated index.
6. Using multiple indexes to find matching values.

For all but the first type of index retrieval, some sort of optimization is possible. For instance:

❑ If the index is not unique, are all the columns used in the selection criteria used in the index? If not, perhaps adding the missing columns to a *concatenated index* will improve the index's efficiency.

❑ If multiple indexes are being merged, you can be almost certain that the use of a concatenated index would improve performance.

❑ If only using some of the columns in the concatenated index, are the additional columns in the index used by other queries?

❑ Even if the columns in the concatenated index match the columns in the WHERE clause, is the order of the columns in the index optimal?

❑ If searching on a range, have we restricted the range correctly? Is Oracle performing the range scan efficiently?

The primary techniques for improving index lookups are:

❑ Create new indexes.
❑ Add or remove columns from a concatenated index.
❑ Use alternative techniques, such as hash clustering or bitmap indexing.
❑ Create column histograms.
❑ Use hints.

FINE-TUNING CONCATENATED INDEXES

If we are querying against multiple column values in a table, then a concatenated index on all of those values will usually offer the most efficient retrieval.

A concatenated index is optimized if:

❑ It contains *all* columns referenced for that table in the WHERE clause.

❑ The order of columns in the concatenated index supports the widest range of queries.

❑ The most selective columns come first in the column list.

❑ If possible, the concatenated index contains the columns in the SELECT list as well as the columns in the WHERE clause. This may improve query performance by allowing the query to be satisfied from the index lookup alone.

Make sure all columns are in the concatenated index

Usually, the more columns specified in the concatenated index, the more selective the index will be and the better your query performance will be. Figure 6.4 provides an example of typical improvements gained by adding columns to the concatenated index for the following query:

```
select
       contact_surname,contact_firstname,date_of_birth,phoneno
  from customers
 where contact_surname='SMITH'
   and contact_firstname='JOHN'
   and date_of_birth='15-SEP-50'
```

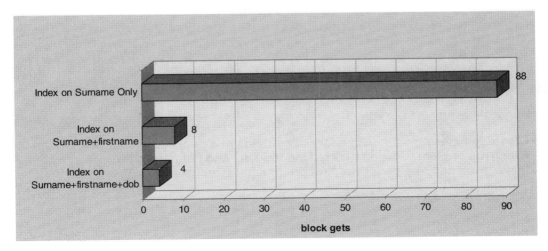

FIGURE 6.4   Improvements from adding columns to a concatenated index.

Where possible, optimize a query by including all of the columns contained in the WHERE clause within a concatenated index.

Optimize the order of the columns in the index

Changing the column order can have the least significant improvement and can have the biggest negative effect on other queries. For instance, it might make good sense to create a concatenated index on the CUSTOMERS table on the following columns:

```
contact_surname, contact_firstname, date_of_birth
```

This allows us to search on contact_surname alone, contact_surname+contact_firstname or the three columns combined. Putting the surname first in the index seems a sensible choice, since there might be other queries which specify only the surname—and these can use the index if the surname is the first column.

However, if we ignore the effect on other queries, what is this optimal order when all three columns are specified?

The optimal order for columns in a concatenated index is that in which the most selective column—that is the one with the most distinct values—is specified first in the index. In this case, the following index would be slightly more efficient for a query on all three columns (see Figure 6.5):

```
date_of_birth ,contact_surname, contact_firstname
```

In general, the flexibility gained by creating the index with surname first will overcome the increased efficiency gained by specifying date of birth first. The ultimate decision will be based on your individual requirements. Remember, you can always create both indexes, although there will be a storage cost and a performance penalty during inserts, updates and deletes.

Carefully determine the best order of columns in a concatenated index. Columns which are subject to being queried individually and columns with high selectivity make good candidates for the first column in the index.

Adding columns in the select list to the index

Sometimes, we only want to select a small number of columns from a table. For instance, in the following example, we know surname, first name and date of birth, but want to retrieve the phone number:

```
select contact_surname,contact_firstname,date_of_birth,phoneno
  from customers
 where contact_surname='SMITH'
   and contact_firstname='JOHN'
   and date_of_birth='15-SEP-50'
```

With our index on the surname, first name and date of birth, we can satisfy this query very effectively. Oracle will access the head index block, one or two branch index blocks and the appropriate index leaf block. This leaf block will contain the ROWID for the row in question, which will then be retrieved from the table block. A total of four or five block I/Os will be required.

If we still want to speed up this query, we can add the phone number to the index. If we do this, we can resolve the query without having to access the table at all—since all the data required is contained in the index. This usually saves a single I/O—not very noticeable for a single lookup, but a 20 to 25% savings which could be a significant improvement if the query is being executed very frequently (perhaps in an OLTP environment). Figure 6.5 illustrates the reduction in I/O when we fine-tune a concatenated index.

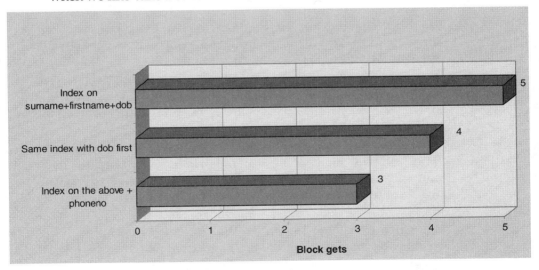

FIGURE 6.5 Effect of fine-tuning concatenated indexing on retrieval of the phoneno column using a selection criteria involving surname, first name and date of birth.

> **Supercharge queries by adding columns which appear in the SELECT list to a concatenated index. If a query can be satisfied by accessing an index alone, performance will be improved.**

SEARCHING FOR RANGES

Using indexes to select rows matching a range of data is a very common operation. We can identify the following types of range scans:

- ❏ *Unbounded range scan*. This involves getting all rows with a column value greater or less than a particular value.
- ❏ *Bounded range scan*. This involves getting all rows with column values *between* two values.
- ❏ *Range lookup*. Find a row in a table where one column is less than the specified value and the other column is greater. In other words, the table has a "high" value column and a "low" value column.

From the optimizer's point of view, range scans present particular problems:

- ❏ Unless a column histogram is present, the cost based optimizer cannot calculate the cost of the range lookup—since it does not know the extent of the range.
- ❏ Regardless of the optimizer mode (e.g., RULE, FIRST_ROWS, ALL_ROWS) Oracle will almost always perform an index range scan to resolve a query containing a bounded range condition (if an appropriate index exists).
- ❏ The rule based optimizer and cost based optimizer in "FIRST_ROWS" mode will use an index to resolve a bounded range scan. The cost based optimizer in "ALL_ROWS" mode will usually perform a full table scan to resolve an unbounded range query.
- ❏ Both optimizers prefer exact value lookups to range lookups. If an alternative path involving an equality condition exists, then it will probably be used in preference to a range condition.
- ❏ Range lookups tend to be fairly inefficient by default, since Oracle doesn't know that the high value is always higher than the low value and also cannot assume that there are no overlaps.

Unbounded range scan

The cost based optimizer will not use an index for an unbounded range scan unless you instruct it to do so or there is a histogram on the relevant column. For instance, the following query retrieves details for all customers born after 1975 (a definite minority):

```
select count(contact_surname)
  from customers
 where date_of_birth > '01-JAN-75'

Rows        Execution Plan
-------     ---------------------------------------------------------
      0     SELECT STATEMENT    GOAL: CHOOSE
   3473       SORT (AGGREGATE)
 100000         TABLE ACCESS    GOAL: ANALYZED (FULL) OF 'CUSTOMERS'
```

The cost based optimizer chooses to perform a full table scan unless a hint is specified. You could specify the INDEX hint as above, or use the RULE or FIRST_ROWS hint.

Creating a histogram on a column subjected to range scans is a very good idea—unless the ranges are specified by bind variables. Otherwise, if you know that the ranges specified will be small, you can specify the INDEX or FIRST_ROWS hint.

Bounded range scan

The cost based optimizer has the same problem with the bounded range scan as with the unbounded range scan. That is, it doesn't know the extent of the range (in the absence of a histogram) and so can't accurately compute the cost. Its strategy is to use an index if the optimizer goal is FIRST_ROWS and to use a full table scan if the optimizer goal is ALL_ROWS. For instance, unless we use a FIRST_ROWS goal, or a RULE or INDEX hint, the cost based optimizer will resolve the following statement via a full table scan:

```
select
       customer_name
  from customers
 where date_of_birth > to_date('1-JAN-60')
   and date_of_birth < to_date('1-JAN-61')

Rows        Execution Plan
-------     ---------------------------------------------------------
      0     SELECT STATEMENT    HINT: CHOOSE
   5151       TABLE ACCESS      HINT: ANALYZED (FULL) OF 'CUSTOMERS'
```

If you know that the range to be scanned is short, force the optimizer to use an index range scan by using the FIRST_ROWS or INDEX hint. If you know that the range will be wide, then the default behavior (full table scan) will be optimal. If you don't know in advance how wide the range to be searched is going to be (perhaps the parameters to the query are fed in from an interactive application), consider creating a histogram on the column in question.

Consider using histograms for range scans so that the cost based optimizer can accurately estimate costs. If a histogram is not possible (when using bind variables, for instance), consider specifying a hint to force a table scan or an index lookup if you believe these will be more efficient.

Range lookup

In a range lookup, we are trying to find a particular value in a table which is keyed on a low value–high value pair of columns. For instance, in the sample database, the SALESREGION defines each region in terms of a range of phone numbers which exist in that region. To find the region for any given phone number, you might enter a query like this:

```
select /*+FIRST_ROWS */ * from salesregion
where '500000015' between lowphoneno and highphoneno
```

```
Rows        Execution Plan
-------     -------------------------------------------------------
     0      SELECT STATEMENT    HINT: FIRST_ROWS
     1        TABLE ACCESS   HINT: ANALYZED (BY ROWID) OF 'SALESREGION'
 40002         INDEX (RANGE SCAN) OF 'SALESREGION_HINUMBER' (NON-UNIQUE)
```

Instead of using the index to go directly to the matching row, we see that Oracle scans a very large number of index rows. What's going on?

To understand why Oracle's retrieval plan seems so poor, we have to recognize the hidden assumptions we make when formulating our "mental" execution plan. For instance, Oracle does not know that LOWPHONENO is always higher than HIGHPHONENO, whereas we know this intuitively from the names of the columns. Furthermore, we assume that there are no overlaps between rows (i.e., that any given phone number only matches a single SALESREGION)—Oracle cannot assume this.

Without knowing what we know about the data, the optimizer must perform the following steps:

1. Search the index to find a row where the lowphoneno is less than the phone number specified. This will be the first (i.e., lowest) matching entry in the index.

2. Checks to see if the highphoneno is greater than the number specified.

3. If it is not, check the next index entry.

4. Continue performing a range scan of this nature until it finds an entry where lowphoneno is higher than the phone number provided. The entry just prior to this entry will be the correct entry.

So in essence, the optimizer must perform a range scan from the lowest range in the index until the row after the range for which we're looking. On average, then, half of the index will be scanned.

How then can we improve this query? If we know that a match will be found, we can specify a "rownum=1" condition to prevent Oracle from continuing the scan once a match has been found:

```
select * from salesregion
where '500000015' between lowphoneno and highphoneno
  and rownum=1
```

This works, but only when there is a valid matching row. If there is no matching row, then Oracle will again continue the scan until the end of the table.

A better solution can be achieved by employing PL/SQL (or another procedural language). By using an index on the "high" value (highphoneno, in this case), we can position ourselves at the first row in the lookup table which has a high value greater than our search value. If the low value is less than our lookup value, then we have found a match. The following PL/SQL block illustrates the technique:

```
declare
   cursor salesregion_csr(cp_phone_no varchar2) is
          select *
            from salesregion
           where cp_phone_no < highphoneno
           order by highphoneno;
   salesregion_row salesregion_csr%ROWTYPE;
begin
   open salesregion_csr('500000015');
   fetch salesregion_csr into salesregion_row;
   if salesregion_csr%NOTFOUND then
      -- No match found;
      null;
   elsif salesregion_row.lowphoneno > '500000015' then
      -- Still no match
      null;
```

```
else
   -- The row in salesregion_row is the matching row
   dbms_output.put_line(salesregion_row.lowphoneno||' '||
                        salesregion_row.highphoneno);
end if;
close salesregion_csr;
end;
```

An example of resolving a range lookup using a PL/SQL procedure can be found in Chapter 13.

If performing a range lookup where you will almost always find a matching range, add "and rownum=1" to prevent Oracle from searching too many rows. If you don't know if there will be a matching range, consider coding the range lookup in PL/SQL.

USING THE LIKE OPERATOR

You can use the LIKE operator to search for rows columns which match a wild-card. For instance, the following query selects all customers with a surname that starts with "HARD:"

```
select count(*)
  from customers
 where contact_surname like 'HARD%'
```

This query makes good use of our index on surname and requires only a few I/Os to satisfy. However, if we use a wildcard to match the starting portion of a column, we cannot use the index directly. For instance, we can search for all sur-names ending in "RDY" using the following query:

```
select count(*)
  from customers
 where contact_surname like '%RDY'
```

The optimizer will resolve the above query using a full table scan. This is because it cannot find an appropriate index entry unless the first characters of the entry are known.

Interestingly enough, we can sometimes improve on the full table scan solution by forcing the optimizer to use an index. Since the index is physically smaller than the table (it contains only the surname and a ROWID, while the table contains all columns), it takes less reads to scan the entire index than to scan the entire table.

To force an index retrieval, you can use the following statement:

```
select /*+ INDEX(CUSTOMERS SURNAME_ONLY) */ count(*)
  from customers
where contact_surname like '%RDY'
```

Figure 6.6 illustrates the I/O required to retrieve rows based on a LIKE condition with a wildcard. Although using an index was most efficient where the leading portion of the index was used, substantial improvements were still observed when using the index to find the trailing parts of a column.

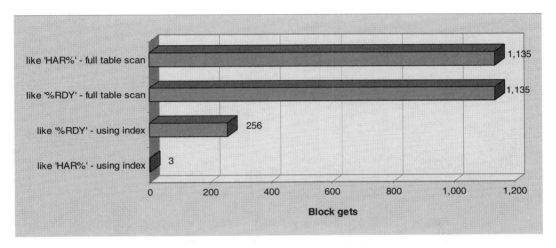

FIGURE 6.6   Using indexes with the LIKE operator.

Wildcard searches will usually benefit substantially from an index if the leading portion of the column is specified (e.g., SMI%). However, queries specifying the trailing portion (e.g., %ITH) may still gain some benefit from using the index—but you will need to use a hint.

QUERIES INVOLVING OR CONDITIONS

When a query on a single table contains an OR clause on a single column (or the equivalent IN clause), it can be processed in one of the following ways:

❏ Perform a full table scan and check each row against the selection criteria (which shows up as a filter in the execution plan).

❏ Perform multiple index based lookups of the table. Perform a UNION of all the results obtained (which show up as a concatenation). This is roughly equivalent to issuing a separate query for each of the OR conditions.

The cost based optimizer tries to estimate when the cost of performing multiple index lookups will be higher than the cost of a full table scan. If the column values are not evenly distributed, the cost based optimizer's calculations will be improved by the presence of a histogram on the relevant column.

For instance, consider the following query:

```
SQL> select customer_id
  2     from customers
  3   where contact_surname='ZIRBEL'
  4   or contact_surname='ZIRBELL'
  5   or contact_surname='ZIRRBEL'
  6   or contact_surname='ZIRRBELL'
  7   /

94 rows selected.

Execution Plan
-----------------------------------------------------------
0       SELECT STATEMENT Optimizer=CHOOSE
1    0     TABLE ACCESS (FULL) OF 'CUSTOMERS'
```

Because four OR conditions were specified, the cost based optimizer calculated that the effort of performing four index lookups will outweigh the effort of performing a full table scan and so concludes that the full table scan is the best path.

However, we can see that the query is looking for a few variations in spelling on a fairly uncommon name. If we decide that we'd like to try an index based retrieval plan, then we can provide a hint as follows:

```
SQL> select /*+ USE_CONCAT INDEX(CUSTOMERS CUSTOMERS_SURNAME_IDX) */
customer_id
  2     from customers
  3   where contact_surname='ZIRBEL'
  4      or contact_surname='ZIRBELL'
  5      or contact_surname='ZIRRBEL'
  6      or contact_surname='ZIRRBELL'
  7   /

94 rows selected.


Execution Plan
-----------------------------------------------------------
0       SELECT STATEMENT Optimizer=CHOOSE
1    0     CONCATENATION
2    1       TABLE ACCESS (BY ROWID) OF 'CUSTOMERS'
3    2         INDEX (RANGE SCAN) OF 'CUSTOMERS_SURNAME_IDX' (NON-UNIQUE)
```

```
4    1        TABLE ACCESS (BY ROWID) OF 'CUSTOMERS'
5    4          INDEX (RANGE SCAN) OF 'CUSTOMERS_SURNAME_IDX' (NON-UNIQUE)
6    1        TABLE ACCESS (BY ROWID) OF 'CUSTOMERS'
7    6          INDEX (RANGE SCAN) OF 'CUSTOMERS_SURNAME_IDX' (NON-UNIQUE)
8    1        TABLE ACCESS (BY ROWID) OF 'CUSTOMERS'
9    8          INDEX (RANGE SCAN) OF 'CUSTOMERS_SURNAME_IDX' (NON-UNIQUE)
```

The concatenation execution step shown above is typical of index retrievals of OR queries. The concatenation step indicates that the steps below were executed independently and the result sets concatenated in much the same manner as for the UNION operator. To influence the optimizer to perform such a retrieval, it's usually not sufficient to use the INDEX hint on its own. You must also specify the USE_CONCAT hint.

We can understand that Oracle doesn't correctly determine that an index lookup is the best plan, since without a histogram it doesn't know that "ZIRBEL" is a rare surname. So perhaps a histogram would improve its decision? Unfortunately not. The cost based optimizer still chooses a full table scan, even if a histogram exists on the column in question.

The optimizer can also incorrectly choose to perform concatenated index scans where a full table scan would have been faster. For instance, the following query searches for the two most common surnames in the CUSTOMER table:

```
SQL> select customer_id
  2    from customers
  3    where contact_surname='SMITH'
  4      or contact_surname='JONES'
  5    /

1682 rows selected.

Execution Plan
-----------------------------------------------------------
0        SELECT STATEMENT Optimizer=CHOOSE
1    0   CONCATENATION
2    1    TABLE ACCESS (BY ROWID) OF 'CUSTOMERS'
3    2      INDEX (RANGE SCAN) OF 'CUSTOMER_SURNAME_IDX' (NON-UNIQUE)
4    1    TABLE ACCESS (BY ROWID) OF 'CUSTOMERS'
5    4      INDEX (RANGE SCAN) OF 'CUSTOMER_SURNAME_IDX' (NON-UNIQUE)
```

Because only two surnames were specified this time, the cost based optimizer estimated that an index lookup would be more efficient. But because the two surnames are so common, a full table scan is actually the best path. We can use a hint to ensure that a full table scan is performed:

```
SQL> select /*+ FULL(CUSTOMERS) */ customer_id
  2    from customers
  3    where contact_surname='SMITH'
  4    or contact_surname='JONES'
  5    /

1682 rows selected.
```

```
Execution Plan
----------------------------------------------------------
0          SELECT STATEMENT Optimizer=CHOOSE
1     0    TABLE ACCESS (FULL) OF 'CUSTOMERS'
```

Interestingly, in this case, the presence of a histogram did cause the cost based optimizer to choose the more efficient table scan. Histograms don't actually contain the number of rows matching every distinct value, so the cost based optimizer still has to do some guesswork when choosing between the index based retrieval and a full table scan. It's up to you to monitor its decisions and amend them when it seems warranted.

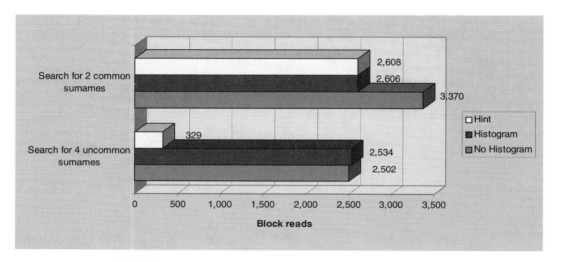

FIGURE 6.7   Effect of hints and histograms on an OR query.

In the case of the search for two common surnames, a FULL hint was used. In the case of the four uncommon surnames, the USE_CONCAT and INDEX hints were used.

Queries involving OR conditions can be difficult for the cost based optimizer to resolve efficiently. Sometimes (but not always) a histogram can help. Otherwise, FULL or USE_CONCAT and INDEX hints can be used to select the best execution plan.

USE OF THE FOR UPDATE CLAUSE

The FOR UPDATE clause can be used to lock the rows selected. This is useful when intending to update or delete the rows you are selecting, since it prevents another session from updating the row between the time it is selected and the time it is updated.

The FOR UPDATE clause requires that all eligible rows be locked before the first row can be returned, and consequently, Oracle must retrieve *all* the rows before the first row can be fetched. This has the following consequences:

❑ FOR UPDATE queries can only be optimized for throughput. Attempts to optimize for response time will be ineffective because no rows will be available until all have been accessed.

❑ Because all eligible rows are locked, even if only a few rows are fetched, an excessive number of row locks may be created. Contention for these locks may lead to poor performance.

> Be aware that the FOR UPDATE clause locks *all* rows before the first row can be returned. This can defeat attempts to optimize for response time and can lead to lock contention.

INDEX MERGES FOR QUERIES INVOLVING AND

If you have selection criteria for multiple columns, and each column has a separate index, Oracle may perform an *index merge*. When performing an index merge, Oracle retrieves rows from each index matching the appropriate condition. Rows which are common to both "lists" are returned. For instance, in the following query:

```
select /*+ RULE */ *
  from customers
 where contact_surname='SMITH'
   and  date_of_birth='19-JAN=66'

Rows     Execution Plan
-------  --------------------------------------------------
      0  SELECT STATEMENT   HINT: RULE
      1   TABLE ACCESS   HINT: ANALYZED (BY ROWID) OF 'CUSTOMERS'
     39    AND-EQUAL    ← Index merge
     38     INDEX (RANGE SCAN) OF 'CUSTOMER_SURNAME_INDEX' (NON-UNIQUE)
      2     INDEX   HINT: ANALYZED (RANGE SCAN) OF 'CUSTOMERS_DOB_INDEX'
```

Oracle scanned 38 CUSTOMER_SURNAME_INDEX entries to obtain all customers with the surname of "SMITH," Oracle also scanned two CUSTOMERS_DOB_INDEX entries to find all those with date-of-birth of 19-JAN-66. The list of matching surnames and the list of matching date-of-births are merged, and only entries found in both returned. Total I/O required was eight blocks.

The rule based optimizer often resorts to index merges because it doesn't know how selective any of the indexes are. Since the cost based optimizer does know about index selectivity, it can be smarter and will usually pick one index or another rather than resorting to a merge. Using cost based optimizer, we received the following execution plan (4 block gets):

```
Rows     Execution Plan
-------  --------------------------------------------------
     0   SELECT STATEMENT   HINT: CHOOSE
     1    TABLE ACCESS   HINT: ANALYZED (BY ROWID) OF 'CUSTOMERS'
     2      INDEX   HINT: ANALYZED (RANGE SCAN) OF 'CUSTOMERS_DOB_INDEX'
                    (NON-UNIQUE)
```

The cost based optimizer picked the most selective index and avoided the needless scan of customer surnames.

Index merges (as indicated by the AND-EQUALS step) are generally undesirable. If you see an index merge in your execution plan, consider the following:

❏ Are you missing a concatenated index which would allow all column conditions to be satisfied by a single index? If so, consider creating the index.

❏ If using rule based optimization, is one of the indexes much more selective than the other? If so, use a hint to force the optimizer to use this index.

If Oracle performs an index merge (AND-EQUALS in the execution plan), it may indicate that an appropriate concatenated index is missing. Avoid index merges— especially if using the rule based optimizer.

DETECTING INEFFICIENT INDEXES WITH *TKPROF*

One of the useful features of *tkprof* output is that it highlights the number of rows processed by each step of the execution plan. In the case of an index, these row counts indicate how many rows were picked up by the index. If there's a big discrepancy between these counts and the number of rows processed by the query or in subsequent steps, then the index probably isn't as efficient as it could be.

For instance, consider the following *tkprof* output:

```
select contact_surname,contact_firstname
  from customers c
where contact_surname='SMITH'
  and contact_firstname='STEPHEN'
order by contact_surname,contact_firstname
```

call	count	cpu	elapsed	disk	query	current	rows
Parse	1	0.00	0.06	0	0	0	0
Execute	1	0.00	0.00	0	0	0	0
Fetch	1	0.00	0.03	0	88	0	3
Total	3	0.00	0.09	0	88	0	**3**

```
Rows     Execution Plan
-------  ------------------------------------------------------
     0   SELECT STATEMENT    HINT: CHOOSE
    43     TABLE ACCESS    HINT: ANALYZED (BY ROWID) OF 'CUSTOMERS'
    44       INDEX (RANGE SCAN) OF 'CUSTOMER_FOO_INDEX' (NON-UNIQUE)
```

Although only three rows are returned from the query, the index is processing 44 rows. Perhaps the index could be improved? Sure enough, the index was on SURNAME only. Replacing this index with one on SURNAME and FIRSTNAME, we get the following output:

call	count	cpu	elapsed	disk	query	current	rows
Parse	1	0.00	0.08	0	0	0	0
Execute	1	0.00	0.00	0	0	0	0
Fetch	1	0.00	0.07	0	2	0	3
Total	3	0.00	0.15	0	2	0	**3**

```
Rows     Execution Plan
-------  ------------------------------------------------------
     0   SELECT STATEMENT    HINT: CHOOSE
     4     INDEX (RANGE SCAN) OF 'CUSTOMER_FOO_INDEX' (NON-UNIQUE)
```

Now the number of rows processed by the index more closely matches the number of rows retrieved by the query. We can therefore conclude that the index is efficient.

Use the row count column of *tkprof* output to highlight indexes which are inefficient. A higher than expected value in the row count column may indicate that not all columns in a concatenated index are being used.

CASE INSENSITIVE INDEX LOOKUPS

SQL programmers often accidentally disable an otherwise appropriate index by applying some function to the indexed column. Earlier, we discussed the case where we need to perform a case-insensitive query against a case-sensitive column. For instance, if we store customer details in mixed case within our database, but want to ensure that queries will ignore difference in case, we would need a query such as:

```
select
        customer_id,customer_name
   from customers
  where upper(contact_surname)=upper(:1)
    and upper(contact_firstname)=upper(:2)
```

Since the use of the UPPER function disables the index, how can we implement this sort of operation efficiently?

One way is to store the uppercase surname and firstname in alternate columns within the table, index these and query from them. We can use a trigger to ensure that the columns are automatically kept up-to-date. The following script implements such an arrangement.

```
alter table customers add upper_contact_surname varchar2(30);
alter table customers add upper_contact_firstname varchar2(30);

create or replace trigger customers_upper_name_trg
  before insert or update of contact_surname,contact_firstname
  on customers
  for each row
begin
    :NEW.upper_contact_firstname:=upper(:NEW.contact_firstname);
    :NEW.upper_contact_surname:=upper(:NEW.contact_surname);
end;
.
/
update customers
   set upper_contact_surname=contact_surname,
       upper_contact_firstname=contact_firstname
/
create index customer_uppername_index on customers
       (upper_contact_surname,upper_contact_firstname);
```

Once this script is run, we have two new columns which contain uppercase representations of the contact surname and first name. The columns are indexed and will be maintained automatically by the trigger. We can use these columns to perform case insensitive queries on customer names and avoid a full table scan:

```
select
        customer_id,customer_name
  from customers
 where upper_contact_surname=upper(:1)
   and upper_contact_firstname=upper(:2)
```

We'll look more closely at the use of triggers to *denormalize* table data in Chapter 10.

If a column to be queried must be subjected to a function, consider using a trigger to apply the function to a copy of the original column. You can then use an index on the modified copy and avoid a table scan.

OPTIMIZING HASH CLUSTER LOOKUPS

We first encountered hash clusters in Chapter 4. In a hash cluster, the value of the *cluster key* is transformed mathematically to a *hash key* which can be used to determine the physical location of rows matching that key, therefore avoiding the I/O overhead of traversing an index structure.

In Chapter 4 we saw that hash clusters could be subject to a number of problems, for instance:

❏ If the amount of space reserved for individual hash keys was insufficient, then blocks would be chained, resulting in additional I/O requirements to retrieve the row.

❏ At the other extreme, if too much space is allocated to the hash cluster, then the hash cluster will be sparsely populated and full table scans will be degraded.

Two clauses of the create cluster are of critical significance to the performance of a hash cluster:

HASHKEYS   -which specifies the expected number of hash values.

SIZE   -which specifies the amount of storage required to store all rows associated with a hash value.

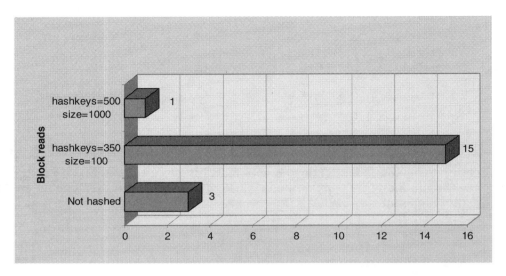

FIGURE 6.8 Number of blocks required to fetch a single key value for an unclustered (but indexed) table and for two differently configured hash clusters. The hash cluster can provide better performance, but only if properly configured.

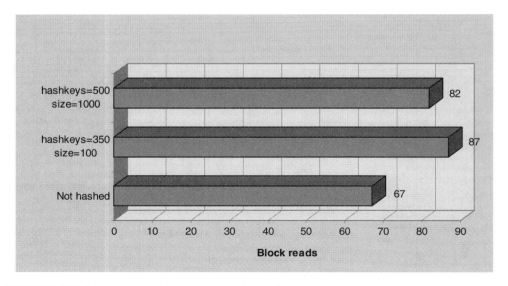

FIGURE 6.9 Blocks required for full table scans of the tables/hash clusters shown in Figure 6.8. Hash clusters tend to require more reads for a full table scan, although this depends on how well the hash cluster storage is configured.

Figures 6.8 and 6.9 illustrate the I/O requirements for key lookups and full table scans for an indexed table and for two differently configured hash clusters based on the same table. The hash cluster can offer better performance for a key lookup, but only if the hash cluster is appropriately configured. Table scans of the hash clusters tended to require some additional I/O, but again, this can depend on the configuration of the hash cluster.

The major consideration in optimizing the hash cluster is to accurately determine the SIZE and HASHKEYS settings. There are three pieces of information you need before you can calculate accurate values for these parameters:

❏ The number of rows in the hash cluster.

❏ The number of distinct hash keys (for a unique index, equal to the number of rows in the cluster).

❏ The average length of a row in the hash cluster.

Once this information is obtained, you can calculate the values of HASH-KEYS and SIZE as follows:

$$HASHKEYS = number\_of\_distinct\_hash\_keys\_values$$

$$SIZE = \frac{total\_rows}{HASHKEYS} \times average\_row\_length \times 1.1$$

In the case of a unique key, set HASHKEYS to the number of rows in the table and size to the average row length plus 10% to allow for variation in row sizes (this is the "1.1" ratio in the above formula).

If the data to be included in the hash table is already in a non-clustered table and the table has been analyzed, you can get an estimate of the average row length and the number of rows in the table with a query like this one:

```
SQL> select avg_row_len, num_rows
  2    from user_tables
  3    where table_name='CUSTOMERS'
  4  /

AVG_ROW_LEN  NUM_ROWS
-----------  ---------
         90       5150
```

You can get the number of distinct values for a column with a query such as this:

```
SQL> select num_distinct
  2    from user_tab_columns
  3    where table_name='CUSTOMERS'
  4      and column_name='CONTACT_SURNAME'
  5  /
```

```
NUM_DISTINCT
------------
         670
```

So, if we wanted to move the CUSTOMERS table into a hash cluster with CONTACT_SURNAME as the hash key (not that this would necessarily be a good choice for a cluster key), we could set HASHKEYS to a value of about 670 (the number of distinct key values) and use the formula above to estimate SIZE:

$$SIZE = \frac{5150}{670} \times 50 \times 1.1 = 423$$

If the number of rows in the table increases, then the calculations above will cease to be valid and the hash cluster may become de-optimized. Oracle will run out of space in the hash cluster for new rows, and blocks will need to be chained. Rows in these chained blocks will require extra I/Os to retrieve, and hence, the hash cluster will lose its advantage over a B*-tree index. Figure 6.8 shows the effect on I/O when this occurs.

On the other hand, if we overconfigure the SIZE parameter, we risk wasting database space and degrading the performance of full table scans (as shown in Figure 6.9).

Ensure that you only use hash clusters for static tables, or be prepared to rebuild the hash cluster periodically. When deciding on a hash cluster, ensure that the SIZE and HASHKEYS parameters are correctly configured.

The approach to sizing a hash cluster outlined above assumes that hash keys will be distributed evenly throughout the hash cluster. This assumption is usually a safe one, since Oracle's internal hashing algorithm has been designed to evenly distribute values across a wide range of data types and distributions. However, if you know that Oracle's hash function will lead to unevenly distributed hash keys, you can use the HASH IS syntax of the CREATE CLUSTER command to specify the hash function. There are two ways to do this.

❏ First, if you know that your cluster key will be evenly distributed, then you can specify the cluster key. This only works if the cluster key is an integer.

❏ Specify your own hash function, written in PL/SQL.

OPTIMIZING TABLE SCANS

If a full table scan is the only practical way of retrieving the required data there are still options for improving the performance of your query. Two ways of optimizing full table scans are:

❑ Reduce the number of block reads required for the scan.

❑ Assign more resources to the scan by using the parallel query option.

REDUCING NUMBER OF BLOCKS TO BE SCANNED

The amount of work required to complete a full table scan is essentially defined by the number of blocks to be scanned. There are a number of ways to reduce this number:

❑ Lower the *high water mark* by rebuilding the table.

❑ Squeeze more rows into each block by reducing PCTFREE and increasing PCTUSED.

❑ Moving large, infrequently accessed columns to a separate sub-table.

❑ Encouraging Oracle to keep table scanned blocks in memory with the *cache* hint.

Lowering the high water mark

Oracle does not have to scan every block which is allocated to the table. For instance, when we first create a table with a large storage allocation, Oracle knows that none of the blocks have data in them and so a full table scan will be almost instantaneous—no matter how many blocks have been allocated to the table.

When a full table scan is required, Oracle reads every block from the first block allocated to the highest block which has ever contained data. This "highest" block is called the *high water mark*. For instance, if we insert enough rows into a table to cause 100 blocks to be populated, then a full table scan will read approximately 100 block reads. Even if we delete every row in the table, the high water mark will still be at 100 blocks and the table scan will still need to read about 100 blocks.

It should therefore be apparent that if a table is subject to a large number of deletes, then the high water mark will be higher than it would otherwise be. The average number of rows per block decreases, and the I/O "cost" to retrieve each row increases.

Unfortunately, Oracle doesn't provide a way to reset the high water mark other than to truncate the table—which deletes all the data. To really reset the high water mark to its "true" value—without losing data—we have to rebuild the table. This can be achieved by exporting the table data, truncating the table and re-importing the data. Another, very fast way to rebuild a table is to use a parallel, unrecoverable, create table as SELECT (see Chapter 9). If you find that a table is smaller than it has been in the past and seems to be taking too long to scan, consider rebuilding it to adjust the high water mark.

Tables which contain substantially fewer rows than they did in the past may require a rebuild in order to reset the high water mark. This will reduce the number of blocks required for a full table scan.

OPTIMIZING TABLE STORAGE WITH PCTFREE AND PCTUSED

If you do decide to recreate a table in order to improve scan performance, you should carefully consider the storage characteristics of the table. Aim to configure the table to maximize the average number of rows stored in each block. The two relevant parameters are:

❑ *PCTFREE*, which controls the amount of space reserved in the block for updates that increase the row length. When there is only PCT-FREE% free space in the block, no more rows will be inserted.

❑ *PCTUSED*, which determines the point where a block that has reached PCTFREE will become re-eligible for inserts when DELETEs reduce the number of rows in the block. When the block is only PCTUSED% full, new rows can once more be inserted into the block.

If a table is subject to both inserts and deletes, then the amount of space actually used up by data in a block is going to oscillate between PCTUSED and 100-PCTFREE. We might suspect that, on average, the block would be:[1]

$$PCTUSED + \frac{(100 - PCTFREE) - PCTUSED}{2} \text{ full.}$$

The default values for PCTFREE and PCTUSED are 10 and 40, respectively. This means that we might expect that, on average, each block will be about 65% full:

---

[1] Actually, it might well be less, since some blocks will not yet have reached 100-PCTFREE.

$$40 + \frac{(100 - 10) - 40}{2} = 65\%$$

This means that the number of blocks required for a full table scan defaults to about 150% of that required if the rows were fully packed into the blocks. While achieving a 100% block fill is not practical, it is often possible to get a better fill than that provided by the defaults. In particular, if a table is subject to inserts and deletes but never updates, or if the updates never increase the row length, then you can set PCTFREE to near 0. You can also increase PCTUSED. For instance, if we set PCTFREE to 0 and PCTUSED to 70, then blocks would be 85% full on average. This could result in a reduction in full table scan I/O of more than 20%.

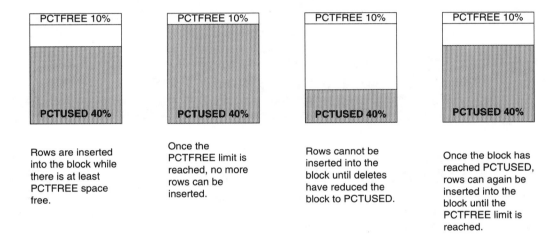

Rows are inserted into the block while there is at least PCTFREE space free.

Once the PCTFREE limit is reached, no more rows can be inserted.

Rows cannot be inserted into the block until deletes have reduced the block to PCTUSED.

Once the block has reached PCTUSED, rows can again be inserted into the block until the PCTFREE limit is reached.

FIGURE 6.10 Effect of PCTUSED and PCTFREE on block fill.

Although amending PCTFREE and PCTUSED can increase the number of rows per block—and hence improve full table scan performance—you should use care when adjusting these settings.

❑ If PCTFREE is set too low and the table is subject to heavy update activity, then *row fragmentation* (or *row chaining*) can occur. This happens when an update causes a row to increase in length. If this increase cannot be accommodated by free space within the block, then the row will be relocated to a new block and a pointer to the new block will remain in the original block. Index entries will still contain the address of the original row. This means that an index lookup of the row will incur an additional I/O as Oracle accesses the original row, only to find that it must jump to the new row location. Excessive row fragmentation is generally a result of setting PCTFREE too low. Detection of these *chained rows* is discussed in Chapter 16.

❏ If you set PCTFREE very low, consider increasing the value of the INITRANS setting in the CREATE TABLE statement. This parameter controls the initial number of *transaction slots* within an Oracle data block and defaults to only one. When additional transaction slots are required, they are allocated from free space within the block. If PCT-FREE is 0, it's possible that the block will become completely full before an additional transaction slot is required. If this occurs, then multiple sessions will be unable to update the block concurrently and *row level locking* will effectively break down to *block level locking*.

❏ Setting PCTUSED too high can degrade performance of DML operations. If PCTUSED is high, then blocks which become eligible for inserts will contain a smaller amount of free space. This means that blocks will move on and off the list of free blocks (the *freelist*) more rapidly. This might increase the contention for free blocks.

❏ If the difference between PCTUSED and PCTFREE is less that the size of an average row, then blocks may be placed on the free list even though there is insufficient space for a new row. This will severely degrade insert performance.

If a table is subject to frequent table scans, ensure that PCTFREE is no higher than necessary—especially if the table is not updated. Also consider increasing PCTUSED—especially if there are not high rates of concurrent inserts.

BLOCK SIZE

The size of the Oracle block can have an influence on the efficiency of full table scans. Larger block sizes can often improve scan performance. Every table in the database will have the same block size, which is set when the database is created. A further discussion on determining an appropriate block size is contained in Chapter 15.

TABLE DESIGN

If a table is often subjected to a full table scan and contains large, infrequently accessed columns, you may be able to reduce the number of blocks to be scanned by moving these columns to another table. A good example of this technique is to move LONG columns to a subtable.

For instance, let's imagine that we stored a bitmap image of every customer in the CUSTOMERS table, but that we only accessed these bitmaps when we performed an index lookup of a single row (perhaps from a "customer details" screen). The average row length of the CUSTOMERS table is 86 bytes and it uses 264 2K blocks. If each bitmap consumed 20K on average, then we would require at least a further 96,000 blocks and a full table scans would take several hundred times longer.

The solution to this problem is to move these long columns to a separate table with the same primary key. If you wish to retrieve the bitmap together with customer details, you will have to perform a join; this might slow the retrieval down somewhat, but the small cost when viewing the bitmap will probably be justified by the large improvement in table scan performance.

Putting LONG columns in a separate table is almost always a good idea if full table scans are common, because the LONG column will often have a greater length than the rest of all the columns combined. You can also consider this technique for tables with infrequently accessed VARCHAR2 or CHAR columns. However, when you do need to access these columns, you will have to perform an otherwise unnecessary join. Consequently, it's not a good idea to move columns which are frequently accessed.

Consider moving large, infrequently accessed columns into a subtable to improve table scan performance.

USING THE CACHE HINT

When Oracle reads data from the database files on disk, it stores the data in a shared memory cache—technically, the *buffer cache* within the *System Global Area (SGA)*. Storing data in the cache avoids disk I/O if data in the cache is required by a subsequent SQL statement. Sizing this cache appropriately is one of the fundamental server tuning procedures—see Chapter 16 for details.

If this cache is full, the blocks which were accessed least recently will be discarded to make room for new blocks. This algorithm is called the *Least Recently Used (LRU)* algorithm. Oracle makes an exception to the normal LRU algorithm in the case of full table scans. Because Oracle expects that large full table scans will be infrequent and that the blocks read will probably not be required again in the near future, blocks read from a large scan will be placed at the least recently used end of the LRU chain. This means that they will be discarded from the cache almost immediately. This strategy prevents large table scans from pushing out blocks retrieved by index lookups.

A drawback of this approach is that if you perform two table scans of a large table within a short time period, the second scan will probably not find the blocks retrieved from the first scan in the cache. The second scan will therefore have to re-access these blocks from disk. If you know that the blocks requested by the full table scan are likely to be requested again soon, you can keep the blocks in the cache by using the CACHE hint. The CACHE hint tells Oracle to put the blocks retrieved from the full table scan at the *most recently used* end of the cache—exactly like blocks retrieved from index lookups and short table scans. This increases the probability that the blocks will still be in cache when you repeat your table scan and will reduce the amount of disk I/O required for the scan.

```
select /*+ CACHE(EMPLOYEES) */ *
  from employees;
```

You can also specify the CACHE keyword in the CREATE TABLE statement or associate it with the table using an ALTER TABLE statement. If the CACHE keyword is associated with a table, then Oracle will always leave blocks from a full table scan of the table at the most recently used end of the cache.

You can override the CACHE table setting using the NOCACHE hint.

It's usually bad practice to use the CACHE hint for very large tables. In a full table scan of a huge table, it's possible that you will push all blocks out of the cache except those from the table you are scanning—and this will degrade the performance of other queries. The CACHE hint is best used when the table in question is not very large, it will be accessed again soon and there is not a high degree of concurrent query activity.

Consider using the CACHE hint to reduce the disk I/O of frequently scanned, moderately big tables. But beware of the effect on other queries.

USING THE PARALLEL QUERY OPTION

One way to significantly improve the performance of any statement which involves a full table scan is to take advantage of the parallel query option introduced in Oracle 7.1. Because of the importance and complexity of this topic, it is addressed in detail in Chapter 12. To briefly summarize, however, you can get very significant improvements in full table scan performance if any or all of the following are true:

❏ There are multiple CPUs on your host computer.

❏ There is spare CPU capacity.

❏ The data in your table is spread across multiple disk drives.

If these conditions are met, you can expect to get moderate to large improvements in the performance of full table scans through parallel query technology. Refer to Chapter 12 for more details.

ARRAY FETCH

Oracle can either retrieve rows from the database one at a time, or can retrieve rows in *batches* or *arrays*. The *array fetch* is the mechanism by which Oracle can retrieve multiple rows in one operation. Fetching rows in batches reduces the number of calls issued to the database server, and can also reduce network traffic.

In some tools, it's necessary to explicitly define the arrays to receive the data. In other tools, the array processing is performed transparently and the size of the array is established by a configuration parameter. Guidelines for implementing array processing in popular client tools are contained in Appendix C.

Figure 6.11 shows the relationship between the size of the fetch array and the response time for a 10,000 row query. We can see that even relatively small array sizes (less than 20 rows per fetch) can result in very significant reductions in processing time. In this example, higher array sizes had only a minimal effect on response time.

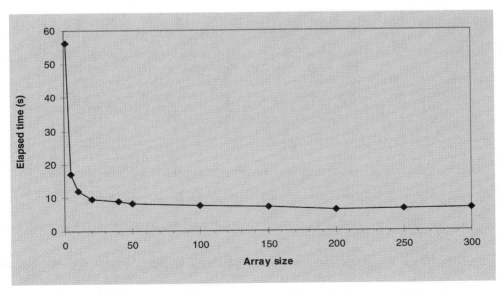

FIGURE 6.11 Response time improvements gained by fetching into an array of various sizes.

> **Use array fetches to retrieve batches of rows from the database in a single call. This will reduce both database and network overhead.**

USING HINTS TO INFLUENCE AN ACCESS PATH

In this chapter, we've seen numerous examples in which a hint was used to force a particular execution plan. Some of the hints we can use to influence the execution for an individual table are shown in Table 6.3.

TABLE 6.3   Hints which affect single table access.

Hint	Usage
ALL_ROWS	Instructs the cost based optimizer to optimize for throughput, minimizing the time taken to retrieve all the rows. This approach tends to favor full table scans over index based retrieval plans.
AND_EQUAL	Merges the specified indexes. This involves retrieving matching rows from each index and then selecting rows which are common to all. The use of an index merge is usually a poor substitute for a concatenated index.
BITMAP	Uses the nominated bitmap index.
CACHE	Retains the rows retrieved from the full table scan in Oracle's cache. See "Using the CACHE hint" in this chapter.
FIRST_ROWS	Instructs the cost based optimizer to optimize for response time, minimizing the time taken to retrieve the first row. This approach tends to favor index lookups over table scans.
FULL	Performs a full table scan to retrieve rows from the nominated table.
HASH	Uses a hash key lookup to retrieve the specified rows.
INDEX	Uses the nominated index to retrieve rows from the table.
INDEX_DESC	Scans the nominated index in descending order to retrieve rows from the table.
NOCACHE	Avoids storing rows from the table in Oracle's cache. This hint is used to override the effect of the CACHE clause in the table's CREATE TABLE statement. See "Using the CACHE hint" in this chapter.

TABLE 6.3 Hints which affect single table access. *(Continued)*

Hint	Usage
NOPARALLEL	Don't use the parallel query option to retrieve rows from this table.
NO_EXPAND	Normally, the optimizer will expand a query with an OR clause into unions of SQL statements—one for each condition. This hint prevents this expansion from occurring.
PARALLEL	Use the parallel query option to retrieve rows from this table.

CHAPTER SUMMARY

In this chapter, we examined ways of optimizing retrieval of data from a single table—one of the building blocks of more complex queries.

One of the principal decisions to be made when retrieving data from a table is whether to use a full table scan or an index or hash based lookup. Index based lookups are appropriate when a small proportion of the table data is being accessed—usually less than 10%. Otherwise, a full table scan is likely to be more efficient.

The cost based optimizer will attempt to decide between full table scans and index based retrieval based on estimates of the number of rows to be returned by the query. These estimates can be very inaccurate if the data is unevenly distributed. You can improve the cost based optimizer's decisions by creating histograms on columns to be searched. But remember that histograms cannot be used in conjunction with bind variables and are therefore usually not used in an OLTP environment.

Certain types of query operations cannot take advantage of indexes. These operations can lead to unintentional table scans and are a common cause of poor application performance. Some of the things to look out for are:

❑ Searching for NULL values in an indexed column.

❑ Performing a NOT EQUALS (!=) operation on an indexed column when only a small proportion of rows satisfy the NOT EQUALS operation.

❑ Using a function on an indexed column.

When using indexes, make sure that the indexes are selective. For instance, don't index a column which has only a few distinct values, unless some of the values are very rare (and then, use hints or histograms to encourage the use of the index).

Take advantage of concatenated indexes, which are indexes created against more than one column. A query will perform best if all the columns in the WHERE clause appear in the concatenated index. Remember that the leading columns in the concatenated index can be used to resolve queries which don't refer to all the concatenated index columns, but trailing columns cannot. Try to create concatenated indexes which can be used in a wide range of queries. Where possible, place the column with the most unique values first in the concatenated index.

The cost based optimizer won't always be able to calculate the best execution plan, so be prepared to use hints when necessary to ensure that the best plan is chosen. Some of the circumstances in which hints are particularly useful are:

❑ Columns do not have histograms or the use of bind variables prevents histograms from being used.

❑ Data values are unevenly distributed in the table.

❑ Range scans are being performed.

❑ The query contains OR conditions.

Hash clusters are an alternative to the use of traditional B*-tree indexes for exact value lookups and a primary key may be a particularly suitable cluster key. However, if not configured correctly, hash clusters can result in either degraded full table scans or hash key lookup performance. Tables which are subject to constant growth or are subject to frequent table scans are probably poor candidates for hash clusters.

If a table is subject to frequent table scans, you can improve the performance of these scans by:

❑ Increasing the number of rows stored in each data block by reducing PCTFREE and increasing PCTUSED—but not so far as to cause row chaining or degrade DML performance.

❑ Resetting the high water mark by rebuilding the table after bulk deletes.

❑ Moving large, infrequently queried columns—especially LONG or VARCHAR2 columns—to a subtable.

❑ Keeping moderate to small tables which are frequently scanned in memory with the CACHE hint or table parameter.

❑ Using the parallel query option. The parallel query option has the greatest potential for speeding up full table scans—but your host computer must be suitably configured and you need to assess the impact on other concurrent operations.

Chapter 7

OPTIMIZING JOINS AND SUBQUERIES

INTRODUCTION

In this chapter, we will discuss ways of improving performance when two or more tables are joined. Most non-trivial SQL statements contain joins, and ensuring that the tables involved are joined in the most effective manner is key to tuning Oracle SQL.

The Oracle optimizer will, of course, do its best to ensure that the types of joins and the order in which tables are joined is the best possible. Sometimes, the optimizer will be unable to determine the best join plan because of limitations in its algorithms and its understanding of your data. It's then up to you to enforce the optimal join approach through hints or other means.

Subqueries are close relatives to joins. Subqueries allow an SQL query to be embedded in an SQL statement and can often perform similar operations to joins—possibly more efficiently. Subqueries can also be used to express the reverse of a join by retrieving rows from one table without a match in a second table.

Subqueries can be used to formulate very complex queries; and the more complex the query, the greater the likelihood that the optimizer will fail to reach the best solution. In this chapter, we'll discuss when to use subqueries, which sort of subquery to use and ways of improving the performance of subqueries.

The topics we shall cover are:

❏ Choosing between the various join methods—nested loops, sort merge and hash join.

❏ Choosing the optimum join order.

❏ Clustering tables to improve join performance.

❏ Improving the performance of special joins, such as outer joins, star joins and hierarchical self joins.

❏ Using and optimizing subqueries.

❏ Optimizing "anti-joins."

CHOOSING THE BEST JOIN METHOD

As we saw in Chapter 3, Oracle can perform joins using the following methods:

❏ In a nested loops join, Oracle performs a search of the *inner table* for each row found in the *outer table*. This type of access is most often seen when there is an index on the inner table—since, otherwise, multiple "nested" table scans may result.

❏ When performing a sort merge join, Oracle must sort each table (or result set) by the value of the join columns. Once sorted, the two sets of data are merged, much as you might merge two sorted piles of numbered pages.

❏ When performing a hash join, Oracle builds a hash table for the smaller of the two tables. This hash table is then used to find matching rows in a somewhat similar fashion to the way an index is used in a nested loops join.

SORT MERGE/HASH VERSUS NESTED LOOPS

In a sense, the sort merge join and the hash join can be considered as the same "family" of joins—they provide good performance under similar conditions. On the other hand, the nested loops join suits a very different category of queries. So when determining the optimal join type, you might first decide if a nested loops join is appropriate.

The decision between the sort merge/hash and nested loops approach should be based on:

❏ The need for throughput versus the need for response time. Nested loops usually offer better response time, but sort merge can often offer better throughput.

❏ The proportion of the tables which are being joined. The larger the subset of rows being processed, the more likely that a sort merge or hash join will be faster.

❏ Indexes available to support the join. A nested loops approach is usually only effective when an index can be used to join the tables.

❏ Memory and CPU available for sorting. Large sorts can consume significant resources and can slow execution. Sort merge involves two sorts, while nested loops usually involves no sorting. Hash joins also require memory to build the hash table.

❏ Sort merge and hash joins may get greater benefit from parallel execution—although nested loop joins can be parallelized.

Table 7.1 provides general guidelines for deciding between the two join techniques. In borderline cases, you need to try both methods and use SQL_TRACE to determine which is superior.

TABLE 7.1 Deciding between sort merge and nested loops joins.

When joining A to B (in that order)	Consider sort merge or hash join?	Consider nested loops using an index on B?
Both A and B are small	Yes.	Maybe—depending how small the tables are.
Only selecting a small subset of rows from B	No—performing a table scan of B will be cost-inefficient.	Yes—the index will reduce the number of I/Os on B.
Want the first row as quickly as possible	No—the first row won't be returned until both A and B are scanned, sorted and merged or until the hash table has been built.	Yes—rows can be returned as soon as they are fetched using the index.
Want to get all rows as quickly as possible.	Maybe.	Maybe—nested loops may still get all rows before sort merge if other conditions apply.
Doing a full table scan of A, and want to use parallel query	Yes.	Yes—nested loops can be resolved in parallel if the outer (first) table in the join is retrieved via a full table scan.
Getting rows from A by an index lookup and want to use parallel query	Yes—sort merge and hash joins can proceed in parallel, even if one result set was retrieved by an index lookup.	No—nested loops cannot be resolved in parallel unless the outer (first) table in the join was retrieved via a full table scan.

TABLE 7.1 Deciding between sort merge and nested loops joins. *(Continued)*

When joining A to B (in that order)	Consider sort merge or hash join?	Consider nested loops using an index on B?
Memory is limited and SORT_AREA_SIZE is low.	Maybe not—large sorts can be a significant overhead, especially if memory for sorts is limited. A hash join may be preferable to a sort merge.	Yes—the nested loops join avoids sorting and is therefore less affected by memory limitations.

EXAMPLES OF NESTED LOOPS AND SORT MERGE JOINS

A nested loops plan can be specified using the USE_NL hint. Remember that the table specified in the USE_NL hint is the inner table in the join: the table which comes second in the join order. In the case of nested loops, this is usually a table which contains an index to support the join. The following example illustrates the hint and shows the execution plan which would result:

```
select /*+ ORDERED USE_NL(E) */
  count(*)
  from customers c,
       employees e
 where c.sales_rep_id=e.employee_id
```

```
Rows        Execution Plan
-------     -------------------------------------------------------
      0     SELECT STATEMENT    GOAL: CHOOSE
      0      SORT (AGGREGATE)  ← The sort is for the COUNT(*)
  99500       NESTED LOOPS
 100000        TABLE ACCESS    GOAL: ANALYZED (FULL) OF 'CUSTOMERS'
 100000        INDEX    GOAL: ANALYZED (UNIQUE SCAN) OF 'PK_EMPLOYEES'
               (UNIQUE)  ← Joined to the index rather than to the table
```

The next example shows the same query with a USE_MERGE hint to force a sort merge join. The execution plan shows full table scans and sorts of each of the tables in the join.

```
select /*+ ORDERED USE_MERGE(E) */
  count(*)
  from customers c,
       employees e
 where c.sales_rep_id=e.employee_id
```

```
Rows        Execution Plan
-------     -------------------------------------------------------
      0     SELECT STATEMENT   GOAL: CHOOSE
      0      SORT (AGGREGATE)       ← This sort is for the COUNT(*)
  99500       MERGE JOIN
```

```
100000       SORT (JOIN)       ← This sort is for the join
100000          TABLE ACCESS   GOAL: ANALYZED (FULL) OF 'CUSTOMERS'
   800       SORT (JOIN)       ← This sort is for the join
   800          TABLE ACCESS   GOAL: ANALYZED (FULL) OF 'EMPLOYEES'
```

USING HASH JOINS

If the conditions favor a sort merge join over a nested loops join, it's possible that using a hash join may provide further performance improvements. A hash join should match the performance of a sort merge join in most circumstances, and should outperform sort merge joins for large tables when one table is much larger than the other. Depending on your database configuration, a hash join may be performed automatically when the cost based optimizer determines it is appropriate. Otherwise, you may need to use the USE_HASH hint, as in the following example (it's a good idea to use the ORDERED hint with the USE_HASH hint, to ensure the correct hash join order):

```
select /*+ ORDERED USE_HASH(E) */
  count(*)
  from customers c,
       employees e
 where c.sales_rep_id=e.employee_id
```

This statement generates the following execution plan. If we compare this with the execution plan for sort merge, we note that the tables do not need to be sorted—the sort shown is for calculating the COUNT(*).

```
Rows       Execution Plan
-------    -------------------------------------------------------
      0    SELECT STATEMENT   GOAL: CHOOSE
      0      SORT (AGGREGATE)  ← This sort is for the count(*)
 100000     HASH JOIN
 100000        TABLE ACCESS   GOAL: ANALYZED (FULL) OF 'CUSTOMERS'
    800        TABLE ACCESS   GOAL: ANALYZED (FULL) OF 'EMPLOYEES'
```

If a sort merge join is appropriate, a hash join will usually perform as well or better than the sort merge. The hash join requires no sorting and, if the table is too large to be sorted in memory, but not so large that the hash table won't fit in memory, then the performance improvement should be dramatic.

Hash joins will be performed by the cost based optimizer unless disabled with the initialization parameter HASH_JOIN_ENABLED=FALSE.

Leave hash joins enabled (don't set HASH_JOIN_ENABLED=FALSE) unless you are sure that the hash join is the wrong choice. Consider using hash joins in place of sort merge, especially if reducing sorts is your objective.

COMPARISON OF JOIN PERFORMANCE

Figure 7.1 shows the elapsed time for executing the following statement using the three join techniques available:

```
select count(*)
  from customers c,
       employees e
 where c.sales_rep_id=e.employee_id
```

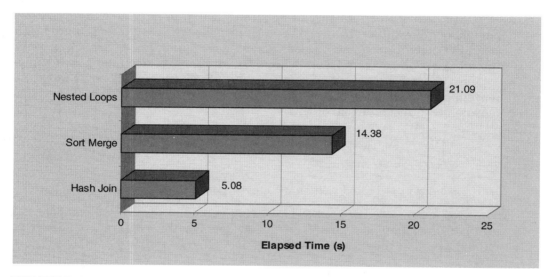

FIGURE 7.1   Comparison of join techniques for a join of all rows in CUSTOMERS and EMPLOYEES.

As the results displayed in Figure 7.1 indicate, nested loops provides the worst performance for a join of all rows in the two tables. Sort merge provides better performance, and the hash join provides even better performance.

Don't use nested loops if joining all or most of the rows in two tables: use sort merge or hash join instead.

Nested loops may be a poor choice for joining all rows in multiple tables, but is much more suitable when a small subset of rows is being processed. For instance, in the following example, we join customer and employee data only for sales representative Colin James:

```
select /*+ ORDERED USE_NL(C) */ c.customer_name
  from
        employees e,
        customers c
 where c.sales_rep_id=e.employee_id
   and e.surname='JAMES'
   and e.firstname='COLIN'
```

Figure 7.2 shows the results obtained using each join method for the above examples. The nested loops join is vastly superior to other methods, providing that there is an appropriate index to support the join. Sort merge and hash joins perform less efficiently, although hash join significantly outperforms sort merge.

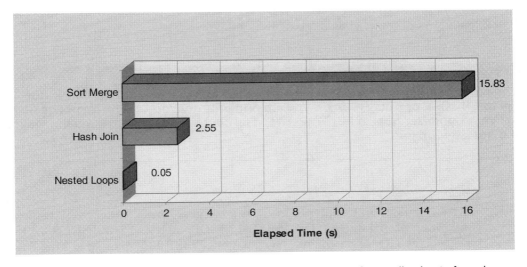

FIGURE 7.2 Performance of various join methods for a join of a small subset of employees with related customer rows.

Use nested loops when joining a small subset of the tables involved and where an index is available to support the join.

OPTIMIZER GOAL AND JOINS

We've seen that the sort merge join is most efficient when all rows are being returned and that nested loops is best when a small number of rows are being returned. In a similar way, sort merge is favored when throughput is the goal and nested loops is favored when response time is the goal. As a result, the cost based optimizer is strongly biased towards sort merge and hash join techniques when the optimizer goal is set to ALL_ROWS (the default) and biased towards nested loops when the goal is set to FIRST_ROWS.

The rule based optimizer will almost always prefer an index based nested loops join to a sort merge join and is unable to perform a hash join. When users first shift from rule based optimization to the cost based optimization, they often notice reduced response time. Upon examination, they discover that SQL statements previously resolved using nested loops are now being resolved by the cost based optimizer using sort merge. The problem is that the default goal of the cost based optimizer is throughput (ALL_ROWS) and this default setting results in an increase in sort merge joins. It's especially important when optimizing joins that the optimizer goal be set appropriately. If your aim is response time, make sure that your optimizer goal is set to FIRST_ROWS.

The cost based optimizer will favor sort merge joins when your optimizer goal is set to CHOOSE or ALL_ROWS. If you are primarily concerned with response time, set your optimizer goal to FIRST_ROWS. The cost based optimizer will then favor the nested-loop join.

As discussed in Chapter 3, the optimizer goal can be adjusted by using the configuration parameter OPTIMIZER_MODE, the ALTER SESSION SET OPTIMIZER_GOAL statement or by using the FIRST_ROWS or ALL_ROWS hint.

OPTIMIZING THE JOIN

There are a few things which you can do to optimize the join of your choice:

❏ For a nested loops join, ensure that the index used for the join contains as many columns as possible from the WHERE clause. If the index can also contain the columns in the SELECT list (if there are not too many), so much the better.

❏ For sort merge, optimize your database sort parameters (see Appendix D for details). Make sure that you eliminate any rows not needed in the result set before you perform the sort (perhaps an index will help here). If performing full table scans, see Chapter 6 for guidelines on optimizing these scans.

❑ If performing hash joins, the configuration of your database is also important. See Appendix D for details of the configuration parameters which affect hash joins.

CHOOSING THE BEST JOIN ORDER

Determining the best possible join order can be complex. There are often a large number of potential access methods, join methods and join orders. For the mathematically inclined, the number of possible join orders is the factorial of the number of tables in the FROM clause. For instance, if there are five tables in the FROM clause, then the number of possible join orders is:

$$5! = 5 * 4 * 3 * 2 * 1 = 120$$

The cost based optimizer tries to work out the cost of a range of join orders and methods. It has to make a lot of assumptions—for instance, the cost of sorting, the number of rows to retrieve from an index lookup and so on. The rule based optimizer uses a simpler set of "rules of thumb" to guess the best approach. Both optimizers make mistakes, so it's up to you to try various join approaches.

It's not possible to predict which join approach will be the best for your query, but the following are a good set of principles for your "first try":

❑ The driving table—the first table in the join order—should be the one which returns the least rows. That is, it should be the smallest table, or if there is a WHERE condition on the table, that condition should return the least number of rows.

❑ Unless you expect to be accessing a substantial subset of the tables, try to use nested loops for each subsequent join. If you are accessing a sizable portion of the tables, try a sort merge or hash join approach.

❑ Make sure the indexes supporting the nested loops join contain all of the columns in the WHERE clause for the table being joined.

When determining the best join order, try to start with the table which will return the fewest rows, providing that subsequent tables can be joined efficiently.

CONTROLLING THE JOIN WITH HINTS

If you feel that the optimizer has decided on a join order which is less than per-fect—and you have an alternative in mind—-you can use the following hints to influence the optimizer:

❑ The ORDERED hint instructs the optimizer to join the tables in the exact order in which they appear in the FROM clause.

❑ You can use the hints which determine access paths—such as FULL, INDEX and HASH—to force the access required on the driving table.

❑ The hints USE_NL, USE_MERGE or USE_HASH can force a particu-lar join method.

When using USE_NL or USE_MERGE, it's important to remember that the table specified in the hint is the *second* (or inner) table in the join. For instance, if the join order is A,B,C, then the hint USE_NL(B) results in a nested loops join between A and B; USE_NL(C) results in a nested loops of B and C, and USE_NL(A) is meaningless, since A is the driving table.

The following example illustrates the use of these hints. ORDERED ensures that the tables are joined in the same order in which they appear in the FROM clause. The INDEX hint ensures we use an index to get the relevant product entry. USE_NL ensures that SALES is joined to PRODUCTS using the nested loops method and USE_MERGE ensures that CUSTOMERS is joined with that result set using a sort merge.

The following example shows how to use hints to force a particular execution plan:

```
select /*+ ORDERED INDEX(P PK_PRODUCTS) USE_NL(S)
        USE_MERGE(C) */
      p.product_description,
      s.sale_date ,
      c.customer_name
  from products p,
      sales s,
      customers c
 where p.product_id=s.product_id
   and s.customer_id=c.customer_id
   and c.customer_name='SMITH and sons'
   and p.product_id=1

Execution Plan:
```

```
MERGE JOIN              ← From the USE_MERGE hint
   SORT JOIN
      NESTED LOOPS     ← From the USE_NL hint
         TABLE ACCESS BY ROWID PRODUCTS
            INDEX UNIQUE SCAN PK_PRODUCTS  ← From the INDEX hint
         TABLE ACCESS FULL SALES
   SORT JOIN
      TABLE ACCESS FULL CUSTOMERS
```

OPTIMIZING JOINS WITH INDEX CLUSTERS

Index clusters—introduced in Chapter 3—allow rows from two or more tables
which share a common key value to be stored within the same data blocks. In a
sense, the index cluster is a way of "pre-joining" two or more tables. Not surprisingly, clusters do improve the performance of joins. For instance, to improve the
performance of the following query, we could create an index cluster for
EMPLOYEES and CUSTOMERS based on the sales_rep_id/employee_id column.

```
select e.surname,c.contact_surname
  from employee_clus e,
       customer_clus c
 where e.employee_id=c.sales_rep_id
   and e.employee_id=20

Rows      Execution Plan
-------   ------------------------------------------------------
      0   SELECT STATEMENT    HINT: CHOOSE
   3333   NESTED LOOPS
      1     TABLE ACCESS (BY ROWID) OF 'EMPLOYEE_CLUS'
      1       INDEX (UNIQUE SCAN) OF 'EMPLOYEE_CLUS_I0' (UNIQUE)
   3333     TABLE ACCESS (CLUSTER) OF 'CUSTOMER_CLUS'
```

Figure 7.3 shows the improvement gained by clustering the two tables
involved. Clustering the tables significantly improves join performance.

Despite the improvement to join performance provided by clustering, index
clusters are rarely used in real world applications and have a poor reputation in
the Oracle community. While the use of index clusters can improve joins, other
operations show a severe performance degradation. As with hash clusters, a poor
setting for the SIZE parameter can negate the benefits of clustering. Further, when
scanning individual tables in the cluster, all blocks in the cluster will need to be
accessed.

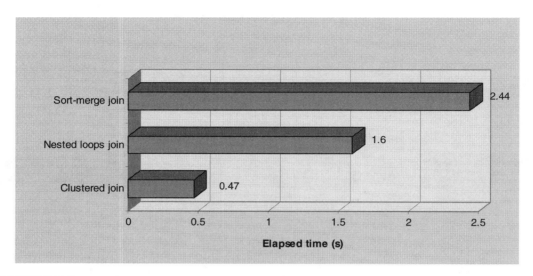

FIGURE 7.3   Join performance improvements gained by clustering EMPLOYEES and CUSTOMERS.

Figure 7.4 shows how clustering the tables affects full table scan performance for the EMPLOYEES table.

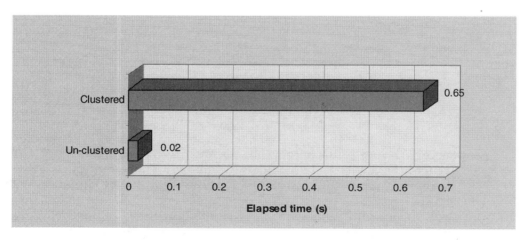

FIGURE 7.4   Elapsed time for the full table scan of EMPLOYEES when clustered with EMPLOYEES and when un-clustered.

Because of the drawbacks of clustering tables, most Oracle specialists choose not to cluster tables unless the tables are always accessed as joined. If these conditions are met then denormalizing the tables (see Chapter 14) may be a valid alternative.

> Clustering tables can improve performance when the tables are joined—but can degrade the performance of many other operations on the tables. Only consider clustering tables if they are almost always accessed together. Even then, consider alternatives such as denormalization.

OUTER JOINS

You may recall from Chapter 2 that an outer join is one in which a row is returned from the outer table, even if there is no matching row in the inner table. The performance of an outer join is usually equivalent to that of the corresponding inner join, and all join methods are available. However, an outer join does impose a particular join order. If we perform an outer join of A to B (returning rows in B even if there are no matches in A), then the join order *must* be A,B; it cannot be B,A.

For instance, the following query joins departments to employees using an index and nested loops join:

```
select /*+RULE*/ d.department_name,e.surname
  from departments d,employees e
 where d.department_id=e.department_id

Execution Plan:

NESTED LOOPS
    TABLE ACCESS FULL EMPLOYEES
    TABLE ACCESS BY ROWID DEPARTMENTS
        INDEX UNIQUE SCAN PK_DEPARTMENTS
```

If we transform this query to an outer join, so that departments without employees are included, we get the following result:

```
select /*+RULE*/ d.department_name,e.surname
  from departments d,employees e
 where d.department_id=e.department_id(+)
```

Execution Plan:

```
MERGE JOIN OUTER
    SORT JOIN
      TABLE ACCESS FULL DEPARTMENTS
    SORT JOIN
      TABLE ACCESS FULL EMPLOYEES
```

We can see that as a result of the outer join, not only has the join order changed, but the join method has also changed. We can use a nested loops join when employees are joined to departments because there is an index on department_id in the departments table. When we change this join into an outer join, we must join in the opposite order—from departments to employees. There is no index on department_id in employees, so the only option is to use a sort merge join.

You may encounter queries which specify the outer join operator incorrectly. For instance, in the following query, the outer join is meaningless, because the outer join might return rows where surname is NULL. Since we've specified that surname must be equal to 'SMITH,' these rows will be eliminated anyway:

```
select /*+RULE*/ d.department_name,e.surname
  from departments d,employees e
 where d.department_id=e.department_id(+)
   and surname = 'SMITH'
```

The query will return the same rows as the equivalent inner join, but because the outer join is specified, the join order must be departments, employees and cannot be employees, departments. This could limit the range of join and access methods and consequently degrade the query. Oracle (starting with version 7.3) can sometimes recognize such meaningless outer joins and eliminate them.

The outer join operation limits the join orders which the optimizer can consider. Don't perform outer joins needlessly.

STAR JOINS

The STAR schema is a way of organizing relational data which is very popular in data warehouses. In a STAR schema, business data is stored in one or more tables, referred to as *fact tables*. These tables can be joined to multiple *dimension tables* which contain the more static details. For instance, Figure 7.5 displays a very simple STAR schema.

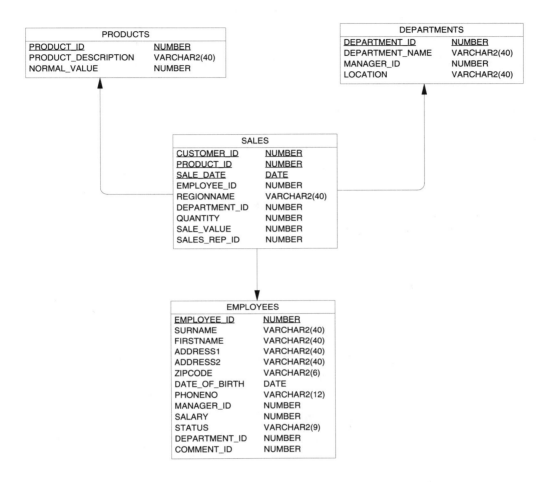

FIGURE 7.5 Simple STAR schema.

Note that there is no relationship between the dimension tables themselves, only between dimension tables and the fact table. Also, data in the fact table is not meaningful unless joined with data in the dimension tables.

These types of queries have typically been resolved very poorly—especially by the rule based optimizer. For instance, the rule based optimizer resolves the following query with a full table scan of the relatively large sales table followed by a series of joins to the dimension tables:

```
select /*+RULE */ sum(sale_value)
  from departments d,
       employees e,
       products p,
       sales s                               ← Fact table
 where p.product_description='Oracle Tune Tool mk 2'
   and e.surname='MCLOUGHLIN'
   and e.firstname='FREDERICK'
   and d.department_name='Database Products'
   and p.product_id=s.product_id
   and e.employee_id=s.sales_rep_id
   and d.department_id=s.department_id
```

```
Rows      Execution Plan
-------   -------------------------------------------------------
      0   SELECT STATEMENT    GOAL: HINT: RULE
      8    SORT (AGGREGATE)
      8     NESTED LOOPS
      9      NESTED LOOPS
   1212      NESTED LOOPS
 200000      TABLE ACCESS   GOAL: ANALYZED (FULL) OF 'SALES' ← Full table scan
 200000       TABLE ACCESS (BY ROWID) OF 'PRODUCTS'
 200000        INDEX (UNIQUE SCAN) OF 'PK_PRODUCTS'  (UNIQUE)
   1212       TABLE ACCESS (BY ROWID) OF 'EMPLOYEES'
   1212        INDEX (UNIQUE SCAN) OF 'PK_EMPLOYEES'  (UNIQUE)
      9      TABLE ACCESS (BY ROWID) OF 'DEPARTMENTS'
      9       INDEX (UNIQUE SCAN) OF 'PK_DEPARTMENTS'  (UNIQUE)
```

The Oracle cost based optimizer can recognize STAR queries and will employ a special method to resolve them. Oracle's approach to implementing STAR queries is:

❑ Identify the table with the most rows: this must be the fact table.

❑ Get result sets for all the dimension tables (usually, they will be subject to selection criteria in the WHERE clause, as in our example above).

❑ Create a Cartesian product of the dimension result sets. A Cartesian product is the result of joining every row in one table with every row in another table. Usually our dimension tables are small and perhaps only a few values satisfy the WHERE clause, so these Cartesian joins are hopefully not too expensive.

❑ Use a concatenated index to retrieve rows from the fact table for each row in the Cartesian product.

The rationale for this approach is based on the assumption that Cartesian joins, although inefficient in principle, allow us to delay querying the huge fact table until the last possible moment and allow us to use a concatenated index on the fact table matching the keys of the dimension tables.

The cost based optimizer will sometimes recognize the STAR schema and perform this optimization automatically. In the case of our example query, the cost based optimizer did not use the STAR algorithm and still performed a full table scan on sales (although it used a more efficient algorithm than the rule based optimizer):

```
Rows        Execution Plan
-------     --------------------------------------------------
      0     SELECT STATEMENT    GOAL: CHOOSE
      8       SORT (AGGREGATE)
      8        HASH JOIN
    180         TABLE ACCESS (FULL) OF 'PRODUCTS'
     22         HASH JOIN
     50          TABLE ACCESS (FULL) OF 'DEPARTMENTS'
    312          NESTED LOOPS
      1           TABLE ACCESS (BY ROWID) OF 'EMPLOYEES'
      2           INDEX (RANGE SCAN) OF 'EMPLOYEES_SURNAME' (NON-UNIQUE)
 200000         TABLE ACCESS   GOAL: ANALYZED (FULL) OF 'SALES'← Full table scan
```

Oracle provides a special hint to force Oracle to use the STAR join method. This hint is called (not surprisingly) STAR. The STAR hint forces Oracle to consider a STAR join methodology in preference to other techniques. Using the STAR hint, we see that the dimension tables are subject to a Cartesian join and the fact table is accessed via the concatenated index:

```
Rows      Execution Plan
-------   --------------------------------------------------
    0     SELECT STATEMENT    GOAL: CHOOSE
    8       SORT (AGGREGATE)
    8        NESTED LOOPS
    1         MERGE JOIN (CARTESIAN)
    1          MERGE JOIN (CARTESIAN)← Cartesian product of EMPLOYEES and DEPARTMENTS
    1           TABLE ACCESS (BY ROWID) OF 'EMPLOYEES'
    2            INDEX (RANGE SCAN) OF 'EMPLOYEES_SURNAME' (NON-UNIQUE)

    1           SORT (JOIN)
   50            TABLE ACCESS (FULL) OF 'DEPARTMENTS'
    1          SORT (JOIN)
  180           TABLE ACCESS (FULL) OF 'PRODUCTS'
    8         TABLE ACCESS   GOAL: ANALYZED (BY ROWID) OF 'SALES'
    9          INDEX   GOAL: ANALYZED (RANGE SCAN) OF
                 'SALES_REP_DEPT_PRODUCT_IDX' (NON-UNIQUE) ← index lookup on SALES
```

Figure 7.6 compares the performance of the rule based optimizer, the cost based optimizer and the STAR hint. We can see that the STAR hint can lead to great improvements for suitable queries. The improvements will be even more marked for very large fact tables (since the bigger the table, the greater the incentive to avoid a full table scan).

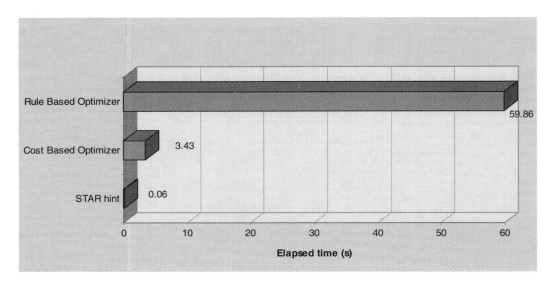

FIGURE 7.6   Optimization of a STAR query.

> **Consider using Oracle's STAR query optimization when joining a very large "fact" table to smaller, unrelated "dimension" tables. You will need a concatenated index on the fact table and may need to specify the STAR hint.**

Oracle's approach to STAR queries may fail for more complex schemas. For instance:

❑ If the number of rows called from the dimension tables are large, then the Cartesian products may become huge.

❑ Concatenated indexes which support all possible combinations of dimension keys will be required; this might not be practical.

❑ Multiple fact tables are not directly supported.

HIERARCHICAL QUERIES

We introduced the hierarchical query using Oracle's CONNECT BY operator in Chapter 2. A hierarchical query, sometimes referred to as an "explosion of parts," is a special case of self join. In the hierarchical query, a column in the table points to the primary key of another row in the same table. This row in turn points to a further row and so on until the head of the hierarchy is reached. In our sample database, the manager_id and employee_id columns of the employee table form such a hierarchy. The manager_id column points to the employee_id of the rows manager. If we want to print the full organizational hierarchy, we can use the following query:

```
select rpad(' ',level*3)||surname employee
  from employees
 start with manager_id=0
connect by prior employee_id=manager_id;
```

For a hierarchical query of a large table to be efficient, you need an index to support the START WITH and CONNECT BY clauses. In the case of the above query, this means an index on manager_id. The index on manager_id is required to position at manager_id=0 initially and to find employees with a particular manager_id. Without the index on manager_id, we get the following execution plan for the hierarchical query above:

```
Rows      Execution Plan
-------   -------------------------------------------------
      0   SELECT STATEMENT    HINT: CHOOSE
    800    CONNECT BY
    800     TABLE ACCESS    HINT: ANALYZED (FULL) OF 'EMPLOYEES'
      1     TABLE ACCESS    HINT: ANALYZED (BY ROWID) OF 'EMPLOYEES'
 640000     TABLE ACCESS    HINT: ANALYZED (FULL) OF 'EMPLOYEES'  ← Nested Scans
```

Note the 640,000 rows processed in the second full table scan of EMPLOYEES. Since EMPLOYEES is an 800 row table, how can we process 640,000 rows? 640,000 just happens to be the square of 800 (800 x 800 = 640,000). For every row in the EMPLOYEES table, we have to perform a further scan of EMPLOYEES to find the matching manager_ids. Therefore, for each of 800 rows, we perform a table scan of 800 rows; hence 800 x 800 = 640,000—a classic "nested table scans" solution and a real performance problem.

Creating an index on manager_id leads to the following plan, a much more palatable execution plan:

```
Rows      Execution Plan
-------   -------------------------------------------------
      0   SELECT STATEMENT    HINT: CHOOSE
    800    CONNECT BY
      2     INDEX (RANGE SCAN) OF 'EMPLOYEES_MANAGER_IDX' (NON-UNIQUE)
      1     TABLE ACCESS    HINT: ANALYZED (BY ROWID) OF 'EMPLOYEES'
    799     TABLE ACCESS    HINT: ANALYZED (BY ROWID) OF 'EMPLOYEES'
   1599     INDEX (RANGE SCAN) OF 'EMPLOYEES_MANAGER_IDX' (NON-UNIQUE)
```

Figure 7.7 shows the improvement in performance obtained by creating the index on manager_id.

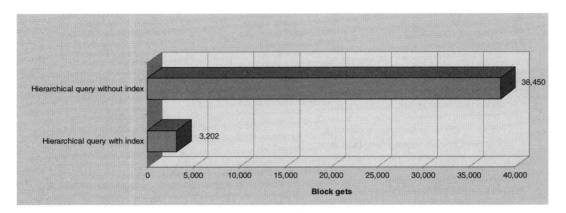

FIGURE 7.7 Performance improvement gained by creating indexes to support a hierarchical query.

> **When performing a hierarchical query using the CONNECT BY operator, ensure that both the START WITH and CONNECT BY clauses can be resolved using an index.**

We may often wish to retrieve a subset of a hierarchy. For instance, to print the employee hierarchy only for a specific department, we might add a WHERE condition:

```
select rpad(' ',level*3)||surname employee
  from employees
 where department_id=(select department_id
                         from departments
                        where department_name='Compiler products')
 start with manager_id=0
connect by prior employee_id=manager_id
```

Unfortunately, Oracle builds the hierarchy before eliminating rows using the WHERE clause. In other words, the START WITH and CONNECT BY clauses are processed before the WHERE clause.

Providing that employees don't manage people outside their own department, we can get the same results, at a much reduced cost, by changing the START WITH clause so that we begin our join with the manager of the appropriate department:

```
select rpad(' ',level*3)||surname employee
   from employees
start with manager_id=(select manager_id
                          from departments
                        where department_name='Compiler products')
connect by prior employee_id=manager_id
```

The WHERE clause eliminates rows only after the entire hierarchy has been built and is less efficient than the START WITH clause.

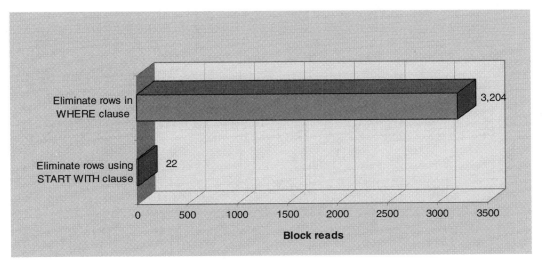

FIGURE 7.8 Improve the performance of a hierarchical query by moving the selection criteria from the WHERE clause to the START WITH clause.

If selecting only part of a hierarchy, eliminate rows using the START WITH clause rather than the WHERE clause. The WHERE clause will be processed only after the entire hierarchy has been built.

Although the tuning of a simple hierarchical query is relatively straightforward, hierarchical queries have certain limitations which can affect the performance of any complex queries involving a hierarchical query.

A SELECT statement which includes a hierarchical query cannot include a join, nor can it include a subquery. As a result, if you try to include a hierarchical query within a more complex query, your options for tuning such a query become very limited. You should therefore avoid placing hierarchical queries within subqueries and remember that they cannot themselves include subqueries or joins.

SIMPLE SUBQUERIES

As described in Chapter 2, a subquery is a SELECT statement contained within another SQL statement. The other SQL statement, sometimes called the *outer* or *parent* statement, can be another SELECT statement, a DML statement (DELETE, INSERT or UPDATE) or a DDL statement (such as CREATE TABLE).

A simple subquery is one which makes no reference to the parent query. In the case of a simple subquery, both the parent and child query are complete in themselves and could actually be executed independently.

For instance, the following query returns the number of employees who share the honor of having the lowest salary in the firm:

```
select count(*)
  from employees
 where salary=(select min(salary)
                 from employees)
```

Such a query could easily be executed using the parent and the subquery separately:

```
select min(salary)
   into :minsal
   from employees

select count(*)
  from employees
 where salary=:minsal
```

It follows that since each subquery is executed independently, each can be optimized independently. For example, we would optimize the join query above by first optimizing the query to find the minimum salary, and then optimizing the query to find the count of a given salary. The obvious way to optimize each would be to create an index on the salary column.

The optimization of simple subqueries is therefore relatively straightforward—optimize parent and child statements separately.

Although subqueries are often the best or only way of formulating a specific operation within a single SQL statement, they often require more resources than are absolutely necessary. For instance, our example subquery results in the following execution plan:

```
Rows     Execution Plan
-------  ----------------------------------------------------
      0  SELECT STATEMENT    HINT: CHOOSE
      0   SORT (AGGREGATE) ← Count the employees
    800    FILTER← Find employees with that salary
    800     TABLE ACCESS (FULL) OF 'EMPLOYEES'
    800      SORT (AGGREGATE) ← Get the lowest salary
    800       TABLE ACCESS (FULL) OF 'EMPLOYEES'
```

As we might expect, two full table scans of the employees table are required: one to find the maximum salary and another to get those employees with that salary.

Without adding an index, it's hard to avoid these full table scans using a single SQL statement. However, using PL/SQL, we can query the table only once:

```
DECLARE
        -- Query to retrieve employees in order of salary
        cursor emp_csr is
          SELECT employee_id,surname,firstname,date_of_birth,salary
            FROM employees
           ORDER by salary;

    last_salary  employees.salary%TYPE;  -- Keep track of previous salary
    counter      number:=0;-- Count the number of rows
BEGIN
        FOR emp_row in emp_csr LOOP
          --
    -- Exit the loop if the salary is greater than the previous salary
        --
            exit when counter>0 and emp_row.salary > last_salary;

            -- Update the counter
            counter:=counter+1;

            -- save the salary
            last_salary:=emp_row.salary;
        END LOOP;
        :min_salary_count:=counter; -- Count of the lowest paid employees
END;
```

With this approach, we scan the employees table only once. Furthermore, we stop fetching rows once we hit an employee on more than the minimum wage. This further reduces I/O and network traffic. Figure 7.9 shows the substantial improvement gained by using the PL/SQL approach.

Although the PL/SQL approach is a substantial improvement, the best results can be obtained if we create an index on salary. This changes the execution plan to two relatively inexpensive index lookups:

```
Rows       Execution Plan
-------    ---------------------------------------------------
    0      SELECT STATEMENT    HINT: CHOOSE
    0       SORT (AGGREGATE)
    2        INDEX (RANGE SCAN) OF 'EMPLOYEE_SAL_IDX' (NON-UNIQUE)
    1         SORT (AGGREGATE)
    1          INDEX (RANGE SCAN) OF 'EMPLOYEE_SAL_IDX' (NON-UNIQUE)
```

Using an index on salary also improves the performance of the PL/SQL approach. As Figure 7.9 shows, the PL/SQL approach requires only 3 I/Os, while the indexed SQL query requires 4 I/Os.

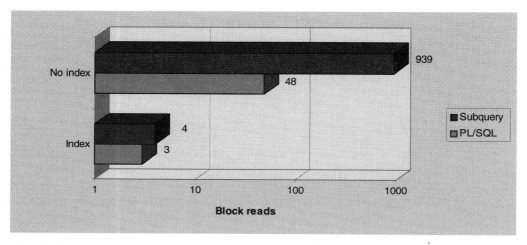

FIGURE 7.9 Performance of a correlated subquery and a PL/SQL alternative, with and without an index (note logarithmic scale: Each axis mark is 10 times the previous mark).

SUBQUERIES INVOLVING THE IN OPERATOR

Subqueries involving the IN operator are very common. They allow a result set to be returned from the child query and joined to the parent query. For instance, the following query returns the count of all customers who appear to be employees:

```
select count(*)
  from customers
 where (contact_surname,contact_firstname,date_of_birth) in
    (select surname,firstname,date_of_birth
       from employees)
```

Most subqueries using the IN clause can be reformulated as a join. For instance, the following join will return the same rows as the previous example:

```
select count(*)
  from customers c,
       employees e
 where c.contact_surname=e.surname
   and c.contact_firstname=e.firstname
   and c.date_of_birth=e.date_of_birth
```

Oracle will sometimes automatically transform a subquery containing the IN clause to the corresponding join statement—particularly if the "join" columns correspond to a unique or primary key.

If an IN subquery is not transformed to a join, Oracle will execute the subquery and create a temporary table based on the subquery. This temporary table will then be joined to the parent query—probably using a sort merge join. For instance, our subquery above resulted in the following execution plan:

```
Rows        Execution Plan
-------     ---------------------------------------------------
      0     SELECT STATEMENT    GOAL: CHOOSE
      0      SORT (AGGREGATE)  ← Count the rows
      0      MERGE JOIN           ← Join customers to the temporary table
  99928       INDEX    GOAL: ANALYZED (FULL SCAN) OF
                  'SURNAME_FIRSTNAME_DOB' (NON-UNIQUE) ← Get customers
    800       SORT (JOIN)
    800        VIEW       ← Temporary table created
    800         SORT (UNIQUE) ← Eliminate duplicate employees
    800          TABLE ACCESS (FULL) OF 'EMPLOYEES'    ← Start here
```

If you re-code the same query as a join—or if Oracle transforms it into a join—then it is possible to use any indexes which may exist on the table referenced in the subquery. Remember that in the subquery approach, a temporary table is created and this temporary table will have no indexes. As a join, we also have access to the efficient hash join algorithm.

When our query was reformulated as nested loops join, we had the following execution plan:

```
Rows        Execution Plan
-------     ----------------------------------------------------
      0     SELECT STATEMENT    GOAL: CHOOSE
      0      SORT (AGGREGATE)
      0      NESTED LOOPS
    800       TABLE ACCESS (FULL) OF 'EMPLOYEES'       ← For each employee
    800       INDEX    GOAL: ANALYZED (RANGE SCAN) OF
                  'SURNAME_FIRSTNAME_DOB' (NON-UNIQUE)  ← Look in the index for a
                                                          matching customer
```

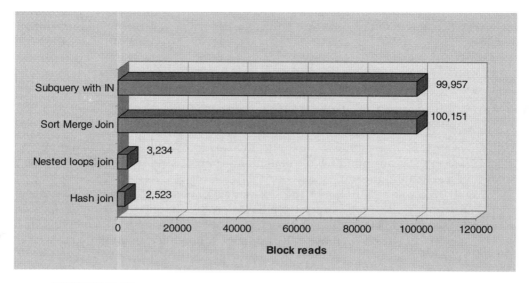

FIGURE 7.10   Subquery using IN compared with equivalent join alternatives.

Although a join won't always outperform an IN subquery, the join formulation gives the optimizer more choices. The optimizer can take advantage of indexes or the hash join facility. For these reasons, a join will often outperform an IN subquery. Figure 7.10 illustrates the superiority of the nested-loop and hash join approaches to the IN subquery approach.

> **Most subqueries involving an IN can be re-coded as a join and Oracle will sometimes do this automatically. Joins allow the optimizer to take advantage of indexes or the hash join technique. Try to re-code IN subqueries as joins where possible.**

CORRELATED SUBQUERIES

A correlated subquery is one in which the child query is executed once for every row returned by the parent query. For instance, the following subquery finds employees with the highest salary within each department. To do this, it executes the subquery (get highest salary for a department) for every row in the parent query:

```
select department_id,employee_id,surname,firstname
  from employees e1          ← Note alias "e1"
 where salary=(
        select max(salary)← This subquery executed once per employee
          from employees
         where department_id=e1.department_id) ← "e1" alias refers to parent query
```

Because the subquery must be executed many times, it is essential that it be able to execute efficiently. This almost always means creating an appropriate index to support the subquery. With the default indexes on the EMPLOYEES table, we get the following execution plan:

```
Rows      Execution Plan
-------   ----------------------------------------------------
      0   SELECT STATEMENT   HINT: CHOOSE
    800    FILTER
    800     TABLE ACCESS (FULL) OF 'EMPLOYEES'
  97789    SORT (AGGREGATE)
 497600     TABLE ACCESS (FULL) OF 'EMPLOYEES'  ← Nested table scan
```

We can see that the execution plan is very expensive. We process almost 500,000 employee rows—although the table only contains approximately 800 rows. The high row count is because we are executing the subquery 800 times, performing a full table scan of the table each time.

Clearly, we need to try and avoid the full table scan within the subquery. If we create an index on department_id, we get the following execution plan:

```
Rows      Execution Plan
-------   ----------------------------------------------------
      0   SELECT STATEMENT   HINT: CHOOSE
    800    FILTER
    800     TABLE ACCESS (FULL) OF 'EMPLOYEES'
  97789    SORT (AGGREGATE)
  97789     TABLE ACCESS (BY ROWID) OF 'EMPLOYEES'
  98410      INDEX (RANGE SCAN) OF 'DEPARTMENT_IDX' (NON-UNIQUE)
```

We now use an index to retrieve employees for the appropriate department, but still have to read each matching table row to retrieve the maximum salary. As a result, we've actually made matters worse (see Figure 7.11). However, if we create an index on department_id *and* salary, we get the following execution plan:

```
Rows      Execution Plan
-------   ----------------------------------------------------
      0   SELECT STATEMENT   HINT: CHOOSE
    800    FILTER
    800     TABLE ACCESS (FULL) OF 'EMPLOYEES'
  97789    SORT (AGGREGATE)
  98410     INDEX (RANGE SCAN) OF 'DEPARTMENT_SAL_IDX' (NON-UNIQUE)
```

We can now satisfy the subquery by index alone. Figure 7.11 shows the substantial improvement in I/O obtained.

> For a correlated subquery, ensure that the subquery is completely optimized. If possible, allow the subquery to be resolved by a direct index lookup without a table access.

We probably can't improve this query any further using a single SQL statement, but it is possible to retrieve these rows even faster using PL/SQL. The approach is similar to that used for the simple subquery which found the employees with the minimum salary:

```
declare
      -- Cursor to retrieve employees in department and
      -- descending salary order
      cursor emp_csr is
              select department_id,surname
                from employees
               order by department_id,salary desc;

      last_department_id   employees.department_id%TYPE;
      counter         number:=0;
begin
      for emp_row in emp_csr loop
          if counter=0 or emp_row.department_id != last_department_id then
              -- The department id has changed,  so output the employee name
              -- This will be the highest paid employee in the department
              dbms_output.put_line(to_char(emp_row.department_id)||' '||
                                    emp_row.surname);
          end if;

          -- Remember the last department_id
          last_department_id:=emp_row.department_id;

          counter:=counter+1;
      end loop;
end;
```

Using this approach, we simply move once through the employees table in department and descending salary order. The first row for any department will be the employee with the highest salary for that department. Note that the PL/SQL doesn't cope with the case when two employees in a department both have the highest salary, but could easily be amended to do so.

Using this approach, our I/O is down to its theoretical minimum—and we didn't need to use the index!

```
Rows      Execution Plan
-------   -------------------------------------------------------
      0   SELECT STATEMENT    HINT: CHOOSE
    800     SORT (ORDER BY)
    800       TABLE ACCESS (FULL) OF 'EMPLOYEES'
```

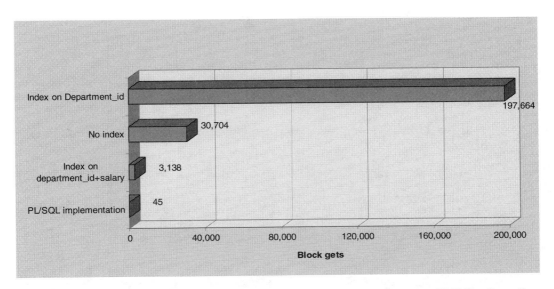

FIGURE 7.11 The effect of various indexes on a correlated subquery and a PL/SQL alternative.

> **Correlated subqueries can often be more efficiently executed using a procedural approach—perhaps by using PL/SQL.**

CORRELATED SUBQUERIES USING EXISTS

EXISTS is a special operator used only in subqueries—and almost always in correlated subqueries. The EXISTS operator returns TRUE if the subquery returns one or more rows and FALSE otherwise. For instance, the following query uses the EXISTS operator to return department details only for departments with employees:

```
select * from departments where exists
(select * from employees where department_id=departments.department_id)
```

The principles for optimizing an SQL statement containing an EXISTS subquery are fundamentally the same as that for any correlated subquery—optimize the execution of the subquery's SQL. As with previous examples, this optimization usually involves creating an appropriate index on the columns referenced in the subquery.

Without an index on EMPLOYEES.DEPARTMENT_ID, we get the following execution plan:

```
Rows        Execution Plan
------      ----------------------------------------------------
     0      SELECT STATEMENT    HINT: CHOOSE
    51       FILTER
    51        TABLE ACCESS    HINT: ANALYZED (FULL) OF 'DEPARTMENTS'
 15700        TABLE ACCESS    HINT: ANALYZED (FULL) OF 'EMPLOYEES'  ← Nested scans
                                                                       of the employ-
                                                                       ees table
```

If an index on employees.department_id is created, the execution plan changes:

```
Rows        Execution Plan
------      -----------------------------------------------------
     0      SELECT STATEMENT    HINT: CHOOSE
    51       FILTER
    51        TABLE ACCESS    HINT: ANALYZED (FULL) OF 'DEPARTMENTS'
    51        INDEX (RANGE SCAN) OF 'EMPLOYEE_DEPT_IDX' (NON-UNIQUE)
```

> **When using EXISTS, ensure that the subquery can be executed efficiently. Ideally, the subquery should be able to be satisfied using an index lookup only.**

WHEN TO USE EXISTS

Sometimes, using the EXISTS operator is the only way to express a complex query. However, most other queries using EXISTS can be reformulated as either a subquery using IN or a join. For instance, the following two statements are equivalent to our previous EXISTS example:

```
select * from departments where department_id in
  (select distinct department_id from employees);

select distinct d.*
  from departments d, employees e
 where d.department_id=e.department_id;
```

When deciding between basing your query on an EXISTS subquery or an IN subquery, consider the fundamental differences between the two approaches:

❑ An IN subquery is only executed once, while an EXISTS subquery is executed once per row of parent query.

❑ An IN subquery might not be able to take advantage of indexes on the subquery table, while EXISTS can.

❏ An EXISTS subquery can't take advantage of indexes in the parent query, while IN can.

❏ The optimizer will sometimes automatically translate IN-based subqueries into joins.

Table 7.2 compares the costs and benefits of the EXISTS and IN approaches some typical scenarios.

TABLE 7.2   Deciding between IN and EXISTS subqueries.

Situation	Use EXISTS?	Use IN?
There is an index available to support the execution of the subquery.	Yes.	Yes.
There is no index available to support the subquery.	No. Each execution of the subquery will require a table scan.	Yes. The subquery is only executed once, so a scan may be acceptable.
The subquery returns a large number of rows.	Possibly not. EXISTS will retrieve these rows once for every row in the parent query.	Yes. The subquery is only executed once, so retrieving large numbers of rows may be acceptable.
The subquery returns only one or a few rows.	Yes, the smaller the result set and subquery overhead, the more suitable EXISTS will be.	Yes, if indicated by other factors.
Most of the parent rows are eliminated by the subquery.	Possibly not. Since EXISTS will execute for every row in the parent query, the overhead will be high if only a minority of rows are eventually returned.	Yes. Since the subquery is executed only once, the parent rows will be eliminated efficiently.
There is an index in the parent column(s) which matches the subquery column(s).	Possibly not. EXISTS won't be able to take advantage of the index.	Yes. The IN subquery can use the index.

Our example query is a good candidate for using EXISTS. The full table scan of DEPARTMENTS is acceptable and unavoidable; and the department_id lookup in employees is supported by an index. The EXISTS formulation outperforms our alternative IN and join solutions, as shown in Figure 7.12. However, many queries which work well with the IN operator will suffer drastic performance degradation if re-coded with EXISTS—so use EXISTS with caution.

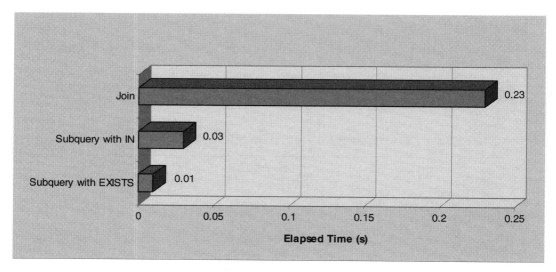

FIGURE 7.12 Performance of an EXISTS subquery versus an equivalent IN subquery and a join.

> **Only use a subquery with EXISTS if the subquery can execute quickly and if the overhead of processing all rows in the parent query is acceptable or unavoidable. In other circumstances, consider an IN subquery or a join.**

THE ANTI-JOIN

An anti-join is a query which returns rows in one table which do not match some set of rows from another table. Since this is effectively the opposite of normal join behavior, the term anti-join has been used to describe this operation. Anti-joins are usually expressed using a subquery, although there are alternative formulations, as we will see.

ANTI-JOIN WITH NOT IN

Perhaps the most natural and commonly used method for expressing the anti-join is to use the IN operator together with the NOT operator. For instance, the following query returns all employees who are not customers:

```
select surname,firstname,date_of_birth
  from employees
 where (surname,firstname,date_of_birth) not in
              (select
 contact_surname,contact_firstname,date_of_birth
                from customers)
```

Although it is natural to express the anti-join using NOT IN, this type of query is executed very inefficiently by the rule based optimizer. In our example, the rule based optimizer will undertake a full table scan of customers for each row in employees. If a matching row is not found, then the employee row is returned. The rule based optimizer doesn't use any indexes on CUSTOMERS because there is no WHERE clause in the subquery. The execution plan looks like this:

```
Rows        Execution Plan
-------     ------------------------------------------------------
      0     SELECT STATEMENT    GOAL: HINT: RULE
    800      FILTER
    800       TABLE ACCESS   GOAL: ANALYZED (FULL) OF 'EMPLOYEES'
80000000       TABLE ACCESS   GOAL: ANALYZED (FULL) OF 'CUSTOMERS' ← Nested table
                                                                        scans
```

Since there are 800 rows in employees and over 100,000 rows in customers, we end up processing 80 million (800*100,000) customer rows.

Luckily, the cost based optimizer is clever enough to take advantage of indexes on the CUSTOMERS table and can avoid the unacceptable nested table scans. The cost based optimizer's execution of the above query looks like this:

```
Rows        Execution Plan
-------     ----------------------------------------------------
      0     SELECT STATEMENT    GOAL: CHOOSE
    800      FILTER
    800       TABLE ACCESS   GOAL: ANALYZED (FULL) OF 'EMPLOYEES'
    800        INDEX   GOAL: ANALYZED (RANGE SCAN) OF 'SURNAME_FIRSTNAME_DOB'
                 (NON-UNIQUE)
```

This is much more efficient. The rule based optimizer requires almost one million block reads to resolve our example, whereas the cost based optimizer only requires 6,430 block reads. The rule based optimizer does not handle NOT IN subqueries efficiently. If using rule based optimization, use another anti-join method, such as NOT EXISTS—which we'll discuss next.

ANTI-JOIN WITH NOT EXISTS

Our query to return all employees who are not customers could be formulated using NOT EXISTS rather than NOT IN:

```
select surname,firstname,date_of_birth
  from employees
 where not exists
               (select *
                  from customers
                 where contact_surname=employees.surname
                   and contact_firstname=employees.firstname
                   and date_of_birth=employees.date_of_birth)
```

Using this style of query, we tell the optimizer to search for a matching row in customers for each row in employees. Since there is a WHERE clause in the subquery, even the rule based optimizer can use available indexes. Both optimizers choose a plan like the following (although the rule based optimizer may choose a different index if there is more than one available):

```
Rows        Execution Plan
-------     --------------------------------------------------
      0     SELECT STATEMENT    GOAL: CHOOSE
    800      FILTER
    800       TABLE ACCESS   GOAL: ANALYZED (FULL) OF 'EMPLOYEES'
    800       INDEX    GOAL: ANALYZED (RANGE SCAN) OF 'SURNAME_FIRSTNAME_DOB'
                 (NON-UNIQUE)
```

We can see that this plan is virtually identical to the cost based optimizer's plan for the NOT IN method. The cost based optimizer treats NOT IN and NOT EXISTS equivalently. However, the rule based optimizer will usually perform NOT EXISTS queries more efficiently than NOT IN queries.

If using rule based optimization, avoid using NOT IN to perform an anti-join. Use NOT EXISTS instead.

ANTI-JOIN USING MINUS

Another less common method of performing an anti-join is to use the MINUS operator. The MINUS operator returns all rows from one result set except those found in another result set. At first glance, MINUS would seem to be tailor-made for the anti-join. However, there is a limitation—each of the result sets must be identical with regard to the number and type of columns in each result set.

In the case of our anti-join example, a MINUS operation will work. For instance, the following query returns the same rows as our NOT IN and NOT EXISTS subqueries:

```
select surname,firstname,date_of_birth
  from employees
 minus
select contact_surname,contact_firstname,date_of_birth
  from customers

Rows       Execution Plan
-------    ----------------------------------------------------
      0    SELECT STATEMENT    GOAL: CHOOSE
 100795    MINUS
    800      SORT (UNIQUE)
    800       TABLE ACCESS    GOAL: ANALYZED (FULL) OF 'EMPLOYEES'
 100000      SORT (UNIQUE)
 100000       TABLE ACCESS    GOAL: ANALYZED (FULL) OF 'CUSTOMERS'
```

Although the MINUS operation does not use an index, it actually gives us the best result of all the examples we have considered so far (see Figure 7.13). Of course, the optimal approach depends on the nature of the query and of the data, but the MINUS approach is worth considering if the number and types of columns are suitable. Remember, we could not use the MINUS method to retrieve employee_id because the number and types of columns in each query would not match:

```
select surname,firstname,date_of_birth,employee_id ← Wrong number of columns
  from employees
 minus
select contact_surname,contact_firstname,date_of_birth
  from customers
```

The MINUS operator can be used to efficiently perform an anti-join. However, there are restrictions on the columns which can be returned in the query.

ANTI-JOIN USING OUTER JOIN

Yet another way of implementing the anti-join operation is as an outer join. An outer join includes NULL for rows in the inner table which have no match in the outer table. We can use this feature to include only rows which have no match in the inner table. We could express our anti-join as an outer join as follows:

```
select e.surname,e.firstname,e.date_of_birth
  from employees e, customers c
 where c.contact_surname(+)=e.surname
   and c.contact_firstname(+)=e.firstname
   and c.date_of_birth(+)=e.date_of_birth
   and c.contact_surname is null
```

This approach leads to an execution profile very similar to that of the MINUS method and slightly more efficient than the not exists and not in methods.

```
Rows        Execution Plan
-------     ----------------------------------------------------
      0     SELECT STATEMENT    GOAL: CHOOSE
    800      FILTER
      0       NESTED LOOPS (OUTER)
    800        TABLE ACCESS    GOAL: ANALYZED (FULL) OF 'EMPLOYEES'
    800        INDEX   GOAL: ANALYZED (RANGE SCAN) OF
                        'SURNAME_FIRSTNAME_DOB' (NON-UNIQUE)
```

USING THE ANTI-JOIN HINTS

Because anti-joins were frequently causes of poor performance, and because there was such a bewildering number of alternative measures for optimizing the anti-join, Oracle introduced specific hints for the anti-join in Oracle 7.3. These hints allow an anti-join using the NOT IN format to be performed using either sort merge or hash join techniques. The hints involved are HASH_AJ or MERGE_AJ and they must appear in a NOT IN subquery. For instance, the following query will use a hash join based anti-join:

```
select surname,firstname,date_of_birth
  from employees
 where (surname,firstname,date_of_birth) not in
              (select /*+ HASH_AJ */
  contact_surname,contact_firstname,date_of_birth
                from customers)
```

The hASH_AJ hint resulted in the following execution plan:

```
Rows        Execution Plan
-------     ----------------------------------------------------
      0     SELECT STATEMENT    GOAL: CHOOSE
  28009      HASH JOIN (ANTI)
    800       TABLE ACCESS    GOAL: ANALYZED (FULL) OF 'EMPLOYEES'
 100000       VIEW
 100000        TABLE ACCESS    GOAL: ANALYZED (FULL) OF 'CUSTOMERS'
```

Performance from the hash anti-join was dramatically better than that for any other method we have tried. On the other hand, the MERGE_AJ hint resulted in performance which was only slightly better than the cost based optimizer's default behavior. Figure 7.13 compares all the techniques.

To use the Oracle 7.3 anti-join methods, the following must be true:

❑ Cost based optimization must be enabled.

❑ The anti-join columns used must not be NULL. This either means that they are not NULL in the table definition, or an IS NOT NULL clause appears in the query for all the relevant columns.

❑ The subquery is not correlated.

❑ The parent query does not contain an OR clause.

❑ The database parameter ALWAYS_ANTI_JOIN is set to either MERGE or HASH *or* a MERGE_AJ or HASH_AJ hint appears within the subquery.

COMPARISON OF ANTI-JOIN TECHNIQUES

Figure 7.13 compares the performance of the anti-join methods we have discussed. Note that the scale of the chart is logarithmic, which means that each mark on the axis is 10 times the value of the previous mark.

The clear winner—at least for our example—is the hash anti-join. The clear loser is the NOT IN anti-join using rule based optimization.

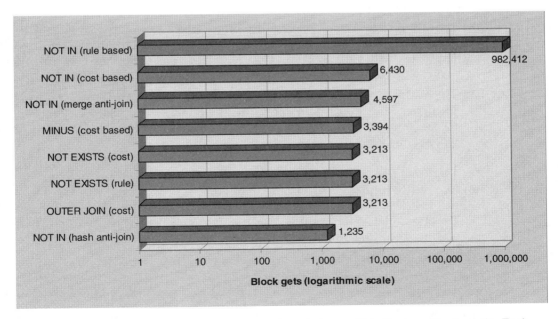

FIGURE 7.13 Comparison of various anti-join techniques. Note the logarithmic scale. Each point on the axis is ten times the previous point.

When wanting to retrieve all rows in a table except those not found in another table (an anti-join), try to take advantage of Oracle's anti-join hints. Otherwise (if using rule based optimization or prior to Oracle 7.3), use NOT EXISTS subqueries in preference to NOT IN subqueries.

CHAPTER SUMMARY

Joins are a fundamental operation which must be efficient if your SQL is to perform to requirements.

Oracle provides three types of join operations:

❑ The nested loops join, which is suitable for joins of small subsets of tables where there is a supporting index. The cost based optimizer will tend to favor this join when the optimizer goal is "FIRST_ROWS."

❑ The merge join, which sorts and merges result sets and is suitable when larger subsets of table data are being joined. The cost based optimizer will tend to favor this join when the optimizer goal is "ALL_ROWS."

❑ The hash join, which requires the cost based optimizer and Oracle 7.3 or higher. This join is suitable in most circumstances where a sort merge join can be used, and is particularly efficient for large tables where one table is larger than the other.

The optimal join order can be difficult to determine when many tables are involved, but two fundamental considerations are:

❑ Pick the smallest table, or the table with the most selective WHERE clause, as the first or driving table.

❑ Ensure that all subsequent joins are efficient.

You can use the hints USE_MERGE, USE_NL, USE_HASH and ORDERED to force the optimizer to use a particular join approach.

Index clusters allow more rows from two or more tables to be stored together based on a common key. Such tables can be thought of as "pre-joined." Using clusters does improve join performance but other operations, such as full table scans, can be severely degraded.

STAR queries are common in data warehouses and involve a large central "fact" table joined to a number of unrelated "dimension" tables. The rule based optimizer will generally perform STAR queries very poorly. Although the cost based optimizer does a better job, using the STAR hint can improve the performance of these types of queries remarkably.

Hierarchical self joins using the CONNECT BY operator may perform poorly unless there are indexes to support the CONNECT BY and START WITH clauses. If wishing to extract only a subset of the hierarchy, try to do this by placing a condition in the START WITH, rather than the WHERE, clause.

Subqueries are related to joins in that they too can relate rows from multiple tables. Simple, uncorrelated subqueries can be enhanced by optimizing each of the component queries independently.

Subqueries using the IN and EXISTS operators provide similar functionality to the join operation. Some queries can be expressed using either an IN subquery, an EXISTS subquery or a join. Specific categories of queries and data distributions may benefit from different approaches. You may need to try each approach for individual queries.

Subqueries which are correlated to the parent query tend to be executed many times during statement execution. It is therefore important that these subqueries be able to execute quickly—preferably through a direct index lookup with no table access.

A subquery combined with the NOT operator can perform the reverse logic of a join—returning only those rows from the parent query without a match in the subquery. Such anti-joins are a definite problem for the rule based optimizer if the IN operator is used. If using the rule based optimizer, ensure that you create anti-joins with the EXISTS operator. Introduced in Oracle 7.3, the MERGE_AJ and HASH_AJ hints can be used to enhance anti-join performance. Using these hints can result in substantially improved anti-join performance.

Chapter 8

OPTIMIZING SORTING AND GROUPING

INTRODUCTION

In this chapter, we look at improving the performance of SQL operations which require Oracle to order or group data.

Oracle may need to sort data as a result of an explicit request to return data in order (for instance, ORDER BY) or as a result of an internal intermediate operation which requires the data to be in sorted order (for instance, INTERSECT). Sorts can consume significant computer resources and have a substantial effect on query performance. Knowing when Oracle performs sorts, ways of avoiding sorts, and how to optimize sorts is therefore useful when tuning SQL.

The GROUP BY operator aggregates rows with common values and returns a summary row for each group. Aggregate operations almost always involve sorting and have specific tuning requirements.

The set operations, UNION, INTERSECT and MINUS, combine two or more result sets with the same number and types of columns into a single result set. Set operators usually involve sorts and are also discussed in this chapter.

Some of the topics we will cover are:

❏ How and when Oracle performs sorts.

❏ Performance problems which can be caused by sorts.

❏ Avoiding accidental or unnecessary sorts.

❏ Using and optimizing the GROUP BY clause and group function to aggregate data.

❏ Using the set operators to combine or compare two result sets.

❏ Alternatives to the MINUS and INTERSECT operators.

SORT OPERATIONS

Sorting is one of the most common operations undertaken by computers, especially in the field of data retrieval—and Oracle is no exception. The operations which may require Oracle to sort data are:

❏ Creating an index.

❏ Grouping or aggregating data via the GROUP BY or DISTINCT keywords.

❏ Returning data in sorted order as a result of the ORDER BY clause.

❏ Joining tables or result sets using the sort merge method.

❏ Using the set operators UNION, INTERSECT or MINUS.

❏ Performing certain subqueries.

Sorting can require significant resources:

❏ CPU will always be consumed. The amount of CPU required is proportional to the size of the result set to be sorted.

❏ Oracle allocates an area of memory for the sort (primarily determined by the SORT_AREA_SIZE configuration parameter).

❏ If the area of memory is not sufficient for the sort to complete, Oracle allocates a temporary segment within a temporary tablespace. This is known as a "disk sort." If a disk sort is required, there is the additional overhead of allocating space in the temporary segment and I/O to write and read back blocks from the temporary tablespace.

The impact of a disk sort is much higher than the impact of memory sorts. Avoiding disk sorts may require that you or your DBA adjust the configuration of your database. See Chapter 16 for guidance on detecting the extent of disk sorting, and see Appendix D for a brief overview of the database configuration parameters which affect sorting.

PROBLEMS WITH SORTS

Because sort operations consume significant memory and CPU resources as well as database I/O, the cost based optimizer has to make certain assumptions about the relative cost of these resources. For instance, the optimizer may have to perform a trade-off between I/O consumption and CPU consumption. The assumptions made by the cost based optimizer may not be appropriate for your system and you will therefore sometimes need to override the cost based optimizer's decisions.

If a sort is required to satisfy an ORDER BY clause, then all the rows must be accessed and sorted before the first row can be returned. Consequently, sort operations tend to result in poor response time, even if they deliver good throughput. For instance, imagine you want to return all the rows from a 100,000 row table in sorted order. You might be very pleased if the rows were sorted in ten seconds. However, if you are sitting in front of a customer inquiry screen, ten seconds might be totally unacceptable! For these reasons, the cost based optimizer tries to avoid sorts when the optimizer goal is set to FIRST_ROWS, but favors sorts when the optimizer goal is set to ALL_ROWS. In other words, if there is an alternative to performing a sort (we'll consider some alternatives shortly) and the optimizer goal is FIRST_ROWS, Oracle is likely to choose the alternative path.

The cost based optimizer will try to avoid sorting if the optimizer_mode= FIRST_ROWS.

UNNECESSARY SORTS

It's possible to inadvertently cause Oracle to perform a sort which you don't really require. This can happen for two reasons:

❏ **Unnecessary use of the DISTINCT clause.** The DISTINCT clause will almost always require a sort to eliminate duplicate rows. Some programmers like the DISTINCT clause so much that they use it in every select. Sadly, many client-server tools will also throw in a DISTINCT for good measure. Sometimes the DISTINCT clause is necessary and unavoidable, but bear in mind that it does have a sort overhead so use it only when necessary.

❏ **Using UNION instead of UNION ALL.** The UNION operator sorts the result set to eliminate any rows which are duplicated within the subqueries. UNION ALL includes duplicate rows and, as such, does not require a sort. Unless you require that these duplicate rows be eliminated, use UNION ALL.

Don't use the DISTINCT operator unless you are sure that you need it. DISTINCT will usually perform a sort. Use UNION ALL in preference to UNION unless you really need to eliminate duplicates.

AVOIDING SORTS WITH AN INDEX

If an index exists with some or all of the columns in the ORDER BY clause, Oracle may use the index to fetch the rows in the required order and hence eliminate the sort operation. This can happen where:

❏ There is no WHERE clause which results in the use of a conflicting index.

❏ The columns to be sorted are not nullable (since NULL values won't appear in the index).

Although the use of an index may eliminate the need to perform a sort, the overhead of reading all the index blocks *and* all the table blocks may be greater than the overhead of performing the sort. However, using the index should result in a quicker retrieval of the first row since as soon as the row is retrieved it may be returned, whereas the sort approach will require that all rows be retrieved before the first row is returned. As a result, the cost based optimizer will tend to use the index if the optimizer goal is FIRST_ROWS, but will choose a full table scan if the goal is ALL_ROWS.

A way of avoiding both sort and table lookup overhead is to create an index which contains all the columns in the select list as well as the columns in the ORDER BY clause. Oracle can then resolve the query via an index lookup alone. For instance, the following query will be optimized if there is an index on contact_surname, contact_firstname, date_of_birth and phoneno.

```
select contact_surname,contact_firstname,date_of_birth,phoneno
    from customers c1
    order by contact_surname,contact_firstname,date_of_birth;
```

Performance of the various methods are compared in Figure 8.1. Using an index with all the select columns is faster than other methods both for first row lookup and for full table lookup. Otherwise, full table scan is best when retrieving all rows and an index/table lookup is better for the first row lookup.

An index which contains the columns in the ORDER BY clause and the columns in the select list will provide good performance for both first row and all row retrievals. An index on ORDER BY columns alone will speed retrieval of the first row, but will usually be slower than a full table scan when retrieving all rows.

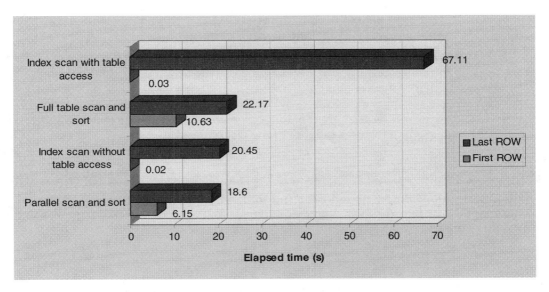

FIGURE 8.1 Performance comparison of various sort techniques.

EXPLOITING PARALLELISM

If rows have been retrieved from a full table scan, Oracle can use the parallel query option to improve sort performance. Using the parallel query option effectively requires that certain conditions be met and that your database configuration is appropriate. We'll discuss these requirements and the parallel query option in detail in Chapter 12.

An operation which requires a sort may benefit from the parallel query option if:

❏ The host has multiple CPUs.

❏ There is spare CPU capacity on the host.

❏ Data files are located on multiple physical disk devices (otherwise, the query may become I/O bound).

We'll discuss configuration and optimization of the parallel query option in Chapter 12. For now, bear the following in mind when contemplating parallelizing a sort operation:

❏ Each sort process can allocate its own SORT_AREA_SIZE. This means that a query which normally requires a disk sort may avoid a disk sort when performed in parallel. There may, however, be an increase in memory requirements.

❏ If a disk sort is required, each sort process will allocate its own temporary segment in the temporary tablespace. This could result in contention—especially in early versions of Oracle 7 (prior to 7.3).

❏ When using parallel query, there is a higher risk of degrading the performance of the entire system with a single statement—since a single statement may now use a greater proportion of CPU resources. Implement parallel query with care. Adjust the number of parallel query servers so that parallel operations are optimized without degrading the performance of the rest of the system.

When performing a sort based on a full table scan, consider using the parallel query option to improve scan and sort performance—but watch for increased system overhead.

WHICH APPROACH TO USE FOR ORDERING DATA?

We've seen that we can use an index to avoid a sort, and that this is usually only effective when trying to optimize response time rather than throughput. We've also seen that the parallel query option can be employed when the sort results from a full table scan. Figure 8.1 compares response times for the various approaches. The times recorded were for queries of the form:

```
SELECT CONTACT_SURNAME,CONTACT_FIRSTNAME,DATE_OF_BIRTH,
       PHONENO
  FROM CUSTOMERS C
ORDER BY CONTACT_SURNAME,CONTACT_FIRSTNAME,DATE_OF_BIRTH
```

Hints were used as follows to force a particular execution plan:

Index and table lookup /*+INDEX(CSURNAME_FIRSTNAME_DOB)*/	Uses an index on surname, first name and date of birth to return the rows in the required order. This avoids a sort, but since phone number is not in the index, both the index and table must be accessed.
Full table scan /*+ FULL(C) */	Performs a sequential scan of the table and sorts the rows returned.
Index alone /*+ INDEX(C SURNAME_FIRSTNAME_DOB_PHONENO) */	Uses an index containing all the rows in the SELECT clause, allowing the rows to be returned in the correct order without performing a sort and without accessing the table itself.
Full table scan in parallel /*+ PARALLEL(C,2) */	Performs a parallel table scan feeding into a parallel sort. Two processes will scan the table, feeding rows to two sort processes.

We can draw the following conclusions from the results shown in Figure 8.1:

❏ If it's possible to use an index which can avoid both a sort and a table access—and it often won't be possible—then this index will offer good performance both for the retrieval of all rows (throughput) and for the retrieval of the first row (response time).

❏ If an index is available which allows a sort to be avoided, but still requires that the table be accessed to get the row data, then this index can offer significant improvements for response time. But it should not be used if maximizing throughput is your goal.

❏ Full table scans can give good performance for the retrieval of all rows, but offers poor performance when response time is required.

❏ Sorts involving full table scans can be improved by using the parallel query option. In our example, this improvement is marginal; but in a larger table, and for a database optimized for parallel processing, the improvement could be very substantial.

As always, your mileage will vary depending on your data, database configuration and specific SQL statement. Usually, the cost based optimizer can be expected to make a reasonably good decision providing you ensure that appropriate indexes and table statistics are available. When the cost based optimizer fails, know your options and test alternate plans.

AGGREGATE OPERATIONS

Aggregate operations are those which use the GROUP BY clause or the group functions. Examples of the group functions are MAX, MIN, SUM, AVG and COUNT. Each row returned by an aggregate operation summarizes data from multiple rows in the source data.

COUNTING THE NUMBER OF ROWS IN A TABLE

One of the most common uses of an aggregate operation is the use of the COUNT function to count all the rows in a table. It's also subject to much rumor and misconception. Here are a few of the claims regarding row counting:

❑ When counting the number of rows in a table, use an index on a
 · unique column. This will be faster since you can count the rows of the (usually) smaller index.

❑ When counting the number of rows in a table, use count(*). Oracle has some special optimizations for count(*).

❑ When counting the number of rows in a table, use count(0). By using a constant, you avoid having to read all the columns in the table.

Which is correct? It turns out that both the first and second suggestions have merit. If the size of a unique index is substantially smaller than the size of the table, then it can be quicker to count the rows using the index. In addition, Oracle does perform an optimization if the "count(*)" expression is encountered.

Consider counting all rows in the customers table using "count(0)," *tkprof* shows the following execution plan:

```
Rows      Execution Plan
-------   -------------------------------------------------
      0   SELECT STATEMENT    HINT: CHOOSE
   5151   SORT (AGGREGATE)          ← sort performed
   5151     TABLE ACCESS    HINT: ANALYZED (FULL) OF 'CUSTOMERS'
```

When using count(customer_id) and using the primary key index, we get the following execution plan:

```
Rows       Execution Plan
-------    ----------------------------------------------------
     0     SELECT STATEMENT    HINT: CHOOSE
  5151       SORT (AGGREGATE)            ← sort performed
  5152        INDEX   HINT: ANALYZED (RANGE SCAN) OF 'PK_CUSTOMERS' (UNIQUE)
```

When we use "count(*)" and a full table scan, we get the following plan:

```
Rows       Execution Plan
-------    ----------------------------------------------------
     0     SELECT STATEMENT    HINT: CHOOSE
     0       SORT (AGGREGATE)            ← No rows sorted!
  5151        TABLE ACCESS   HINT: ANALYZED (FULL) OF 'CUSTOMERS'
```

Note that although each execution plan shows a SORT (AGGREGATE) step, no rows are actually processed by the SORT associated with the count(*) method. This is the "special optimization"—Oracle will avoid a sort when you specify count(*).

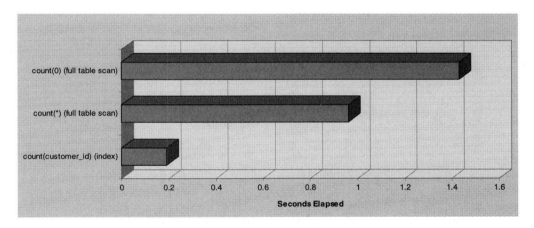

FIGURE 8.2   Counting all rows in the customer table.

Figure 8.2 shows the response times for each of the approaches we've discussed. Counting using an index is usually a very efficient way of counting the rows in the table—but the index should be on a NOT NULL column. Count(*) outperforms count(*constant*) because it avoids a sort.

When counting all the rows in a table, use an index on a non-NULL column if possible. Otherwise use count(*) in preference to count(0), count(column) or some similar variation.

MAXIMUMS AND MINIMUMS

Finding a maximum or minimum value for a particular column is another common operation. You might expect that an index on the column in question would allow rapid retrieval of the maximum or minimum value. Unfortunately, Oracle doesn't use the index to resolve this sort of lookup very efficiently. For instance, to find the maximum HIGHPHONENO in the SALESREGION table, we could issue the following statement:

```
select max(highphoneno)
   from salesregion
```

Without an index on HIGHPHONENO, we expect and require a full table scan and a sort:

```
Rows      Execution Plan
-------   --------------------------------------------------
      0   SELECT STATEMENT    HINT: CHOOSE
  90000    SORT (AGGREGATE)
  90000      TABLE ACCESS   HINT: ANALYZED (FULL) OF 'SALESREGION'
```

When there is an index on HIGHPHONENO, we hope to be able to use the index to get the lowest or highest row directly. Unfortunately, it doesn't work the way we expect. Oracle reads every row in the index to find the highest value:

```
Rows      Execution Plan
-------   --------------------------------------------------
      0   SELECT STATEMENT    HINT: CHOOSE
  90000    SORT (AGGREGATE)
  90001      INDEX   HINT: ANALYZED (RANGE SCAN) OF 'SALESREGION_HINUMBER'
               (NON-UNIQUE)
```

Because the index is smaller than the table, this approach does reduce the amount of I/O required. Additionally, the sort operation is significantly enhanced because the rows are already in sorted order. However, the index doesn't allow us to go directly to the maximum or minimum.

We encountered a similar situation in Chapter 7 and used a PL/SQL block to find a minimum value. In a similar fashion, the following PL/SQL block finds the maximum value with only three block reads:

```
declare
   cursor c1 is
   select /*+INDEX_DESC(SALESREGION_HINUMBER)*/
          highphoneno
     from salesregion
    order by highphoneno desc;
begin
   open c1;
   fetch c1 into :max_number;
   close c1;
end;
```

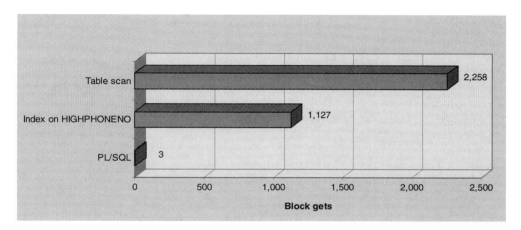

FIGURE 8.3 Finding the maximum HIGHPHONENO in SALESREGIONS.

Figure 8.3 compares the I/O requirements for the various approaches. Although using an index on the column in question can reduce I/O requirements—simply because the index will be smaller than the table—finding a maximum or minimum value using PL/SQL is vastly superior.

Consider using PL/SQL—or other procedural language—to find the maximum or minimum value in a table as this can avoid both a full scan and a sort.

GROUPING

The GROUP BY clause can be used to return aggregate values for each value in the columns in the GROUP BY clause. For instance, the following statement returns the number of employees together with maximum, minimum and average salary for each department:

```
select department_id,count(*),min(salary),avg(salary),max(salary)
  from employees
 group by department_id
```

By default, this query requires a full table scan of employees and a sort to collate the data into groups—44 block reads are required. The execution plan is:

```
Rows        Execution Plan
------      -------------------------------------------------
     0      SELECT STATEMENT    HINT: CHOOSE
   800      SORT (GROUP BY)
   800       TABLE ACCESS    HINT: ANALYZED (FULL) OF 'EMPLOYEES'
```

An index on department_id does not help, and Oracle will not use one—even if prompted by a hint. However, if an index on department_id + salary exists, Oracle can use this index to resolve the query at a cost of only 11 blocks (you may need to use an INDEX hint to encourage the optimizer to use the index):

```
Rows        Execution Plan
------      -------------------------------------------------
     0      SELECT STATEMENT    HINT: CHOOSE
   800      SORT (GROUP BY)
   801       INDEX (RANGE SCAN) OF 'EMPLOYEE_DEPT_SAL_IDX' (NON-UNIQUE)
```

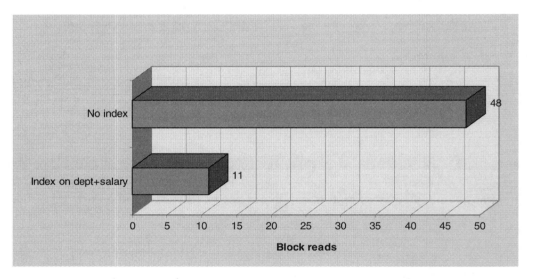

FIGURE 8.4 Using an index to enhance the performance of a GROUP BY. The index contains all the columns referred to in the query.

As with our use of indexes to get maximum and minimum values, the use of the index does not avoid a sort. The index is smaller than the table and takes less I/O to scan. Although there is a sort operation in the execution plan, the index retrieves the rows in sorted order—significantly reducing the overhead of the sort.

> **You can use an index to resolve a GROUP BY, if the index contains the columns in the GROUP BY list, and all the columns aggregated in the SELECT list.**

THE HAVING CLAUSE

The HAVING clause can be used to eliminate rows from a GROUP BY after they have been aggregated. For instance, the following query eliminates departments with less than five employees:

```
select department_id,count(*),min(salary),avg(salary),max(salary)
  from employees
 group by department_id
 having count(*) > 4
```

This is a valid use of HAVING, and merely adds a filter condition after the aggregation. However, you should never use HAVING in place of WHERE. If rows can be eliminated by WHERE, then they will be eliminated *before* the aggregation, whereas HAVING eliminates rows *after* the aggregation. The less rows to be aggregated the better, and WHERE is therefore preferable to HAVING.

For instance, the following generates salary statistics only for departments in Hobart using the HAVING clause:

```
select d.department_name,d.location,max(e.salary)
  from departments d,
       employees e
 where d.department_id=e.department_id
 group by department_name,d.location
 having d.location='HOBART'
```

```
Rows      Execution Plan
-------   --------------------------------------------------------
      0   SELECT STATEMENT    HINT: CHOOSE
     50   FILTER              ← Remove non-Hobart departments
    799    SORT (GROUP BY)
    799     MERGE JOIN
    801      INDEX (RANGE SCAN) OF 'EMPLOYEE_DEPT_SAL_IDX' (NON-UNIQUE)
     51      SORT (JOIN)
     51       TABLE ACCESS   HINT: ANALYZED (FULL) OF 'DEPARTMENTS'
```

We can see from the execution plan that all rows from EMPLOYEES must be merged and sorted before the FILTER step removes all non-Hobart locations.

On the other hand, using WHERE resulted in this plan:

```
select d.department_name,d.location,max(e.salary)
  from departments d,
       employees e
 where d.department_id=e.department_id
   and d.location='HOBART'
 group by department_name,d.location
```

```
Rows      Execution Plan
-------   --------------------------------------------------------
      0   SELECT STATEMENT    HINT: CHOOSE
    100    SORT (GROUP BY)
    100     NESTED LOOPS
```

```
51      TABLE ACCESS    HINT: ANALYZED (FULL) OF 'DEPARTMENTS'  ← Non-Hobart
                                                                  departments removed here
100     TABLE ACCESS    HINT: ANALYZED (BY ROWID) OF 'EMPLOYEES'
102      INDEX (RANGE SCAN) OF 'EMPLOYEE_DEPT_IDX' (NON-UNIQUE)
```

Using WHERE allowed non-Hobart departments to be eliminated in the first execution step. As a result, fewer rows needed to be joined and to be sorted. Figure 8.5 shows the performance improvement obtained.

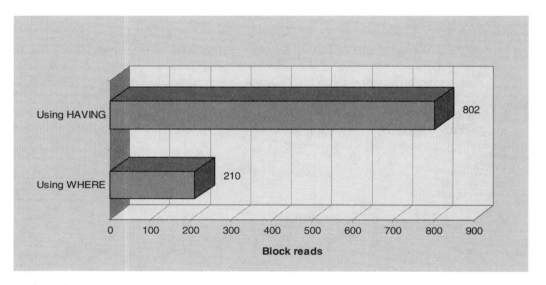

FIGURE 8.5   Using WHERE in place of HAVING (where possible) reduces I/O requirements.

> **Where possible, use the WHERE clause in place of the HAVING clause to eliminate rows before they are grouped. Use the HAVING clause with group functions only.**

SET OPERATIONS

The set operators, UNION, MINUS and INTERSECT allow multiple result sets with the same number and type of columns to be combined into a single result set.

Oracle usually resolves a set operation as follows:

❏ The query defined by each component query is executed.

❏ The results of the combined queries are sorted by the entire select list.

❏ Depending on the type of set operation, the results are either combined, intersected or subtracted.

An exception is the UNION ALL operation, which does not require that the component result sets be sorted.

The general procedure for optimizing a set operation is as follows:

❏ Optimize each component query, using principles already discussed.

❏ Optimize your database for sort operations—see Appendix D.

❏ Consider an index on the columns in the select list. Such an index will be cheaper to scan than the table and will already be in sorted order.

As well as following these general principles, you can often improve performance by employing alternatives to set operations.

UNION AND UNION ALL

The UNION operator is undoubtedly the most commonly used set operation. UNION differs from UNION ALL in that UNION will eliminate any duplicate rows across the two results sets, whereas UNION ALL returns all rows, even if duplicated. For instance, the following query returns all customers and all employees, but if a customer and employee have the same name and date of birth, they are only reported once (perhaps they are the same person and we don't want them reported twice):

```
select contact_surname,contact_firstname,date_of_birth
  from customers
union
select surname,firstname,date_of_birth
  from employees

Rows     Execution Plan
-------  ---------------------------------------------------------
      0  SELECT STATEMENT    GOAL: CHOOSE
 100800    SORT (UNIQUE)    ← Sort required to eliminate duplicates
 100800    UNION-ALL
 100000      TABLE ACCESS    GOAL: ANALYZED (FULL) OF 'CUSTOMERS'
    800      TABLE ACCESS    GOAL: ANALYZED (FULL) OF 'EMPLOYEES'
```

The corresponding UNION ALL query returns the same result set, but if a matching row exists in both CUSTOMERS and EMPLOYEES, it will be reported twice:

```
select contact_surname,contact_firstname,date_of_birth
  from customers
union all
select surname,firstname,date_of_birth
  from employees

Rows      Execution Plan
-------   -------------------------------------------------
      0   SELECT STATEMENT    GOAL: CHOOSE
 100800     UNION-ALL
 100000       TABLE ACCESS    GOAL: ANALYZED (FULL) OF 'CUSTOMERS'
    800       TABLE ACCESS    GOAL: ANALYZED (FULL) OF 'EMPLOYEES'
```

You may notice that the execution plan for the UNION statement is almost exactly identical to that of the UNION ALL statement, except that the SORT(UNIQUE) step is absent in the UNION ALL version. Removing the sort from a large UNION can substantially speed up the query. In the case of the above example, UNION ALL took only 12.34 seconds, while UNION took 22.74 seconds (see Figure 8.6).

If you don't need to eliminate duplicate rows in a UNION operation, use UNION ALL instead of UNION. This will avoid a potentially expensive sort.

As with most of the sort and aggregate operations we've looked at in this chapter, the query can be improved by an index on all the relevant columns. When a surname, firstname and date of birth index was available on CUSTOMERS, the time taken to perform a UNION was reduced from 22.74 seconds to only 15.75 seconds.

INTERSECT

The INTERSECT operation returns rows which are common to both tables or result sets. For instance, the following INTERSECT statement returns all customers who are also employees (or who at least have the same name and date of birth):

```
select contact_surname,contact_firstname,date_of_birth
  from customers
 intersect
```

```
select surname,firstname,date_of_birth
  from employees

Rows        Execution Plan
-------     ---------------------------------------------------
      0     SELECT STATEMENT    GOAL: CHOOSE
 100795      INTERSECTION
 100000       SORT (UNIQUE)
 100001        INDEX (FULL SCAN) OF 'SURNAME_FIRSTNAME_DOB_PHONENO'
                  (NON-UNIQUE)
    800       SORT (UNIQUE)
    800        TABLE ACCESS   GOAL: ANALYZED (FULL) OF 'EMPLOYEES'
```

You can alternately express an INTERSECT query as a join. If a sort merge join is performed, you can expect the performance to be very similar to that of the INTERSECT—since Oracle has to perform a sort and merge for both methods. However, using a join allows you to employ the nested loops or hash join methods. Depending on the data being intersected, this can lead to substantial performance improvements. If one result set is a small subset of an entire table, and the other result set has an index on join columns, then the nested loops join might be more effective than the INTERSECT. On the other hand, if the tables are large and/or we are scanning all rows of the tables, then a hash join is a viable alternative. For instance, our previous INTERSECT example is re-coded as follows:

```
select /*+ ORDERED USE_HASH(C) */
         c.contact_surname,c.contact_firstname,c.date_of_birth
  from
         employees e,
         customers c
 where e.surname=c.contact_surname
   and e.firstname=c.contact_firstname
   and e.date_of_birth=c.date_of_birth

Rows        Execution Plan
-------     ---------------------------------------------------
      0     SELECT STATEMENT    GOAL: CHOOSE
  28009      HASH JOIN
    800       TABLE ACCESS   GOAL: ANALYZED (FULL) OF 'EMPLOYEES'
 100001       INDEX (FULL SCAN) OF 'SURNAME_FIRSTNAME_DOB_PHONENO'
                  (NON-UNIQUE)
```

The elapsed time reduces from 7.79 to 1.69 seconds (see Figure 8.6).

When performing an intersect, consider re-coding the statement to a join—using either a nested loops or hash join method.

MINUS

We saw in Chapter 7 how the MINUS operator can be used in place of an anti-join (for instance, a subquery using NOT IN). MINUS outperformed the anti-join, except in the case where a hash anti-join was performed. For instance, a MINUS statement like this:

```
select contact_surname,contact_firstname,date_of_birth
  from customers
minus
select surname,firstname,date_of_birth
  from employees

Rows       Execution Plan
-------    --------------------------------------------------------
      0    SELECT STATEMENT     GOAL: CHOOSE
 100795    MINUS
 100000     SORT (UNIQUE)
 100000      TABLE ACCESS     GOAL: ANALYZED (FULL) OF 'CUSTOMERS'
    800     SORT (UNIQUE)
    800      TABLE ACCESS     GOAL: ANALYZED (FULL) OF 'EMPLOYEES'
```

can be expressed as a hash anti-join like this:

```
select /*+ FULL(CUSTOMERS) */
       contact_surname,contact_firstname,date_of_birth
  from customers
 where (contact_surname,contact_firstname,date_of_birth) not in
       (select /*+HASH_AJ */
               surname,firstname,date_of_birth
          from employees)


Rows       Execution Plan
-------    --------------------------------------------------------
      0    SELECT STATEMENT     GOAL: CHOOSE
   2398    HASH JOIN (ANTI)
 100000     TABLE ACCESS     GOAL: ANALYZED (FULL) OF 'CUSTOMERS'
    800     VIEW
    800      TABLE ACCESS     GOAL: ANALYZED (FULL) OF 'EMPLOYEES'
```

If conditions are right, the hash anti-join can significantly outperform the MINUS operation. In our example, elapsed time reduced from 22.38 to 14.64.

When performing a MINUS operation, consider re-coding the statement into an ANTI-JOIN using the HASH_AJ hint.

SET OPERATIONS AND THEIR ALTERNATIVES

Figure 8.6 shows elapsed times for the set operations and alternatives for our examples. Keep the following points in mind:

❑ The alternatives do not always return exactly the same result set. Set operations (aside from UNION ALL) return distinct rows only and return rows in sorted order. If eliminating duplicates or returning rows in order is essential, you could modify the alternatives with the DISTINCT or ORDER BY clause, or you may wish to stick with the set operators.

❑ In the examples, CUSTOMERS is much bigger than EMPLOYEES. This is the ideal situation for the hash join, and consequently, hash join alternatives did very well in our examples. Different data might give different results. As always, it's up to you to try the alternatives and choose the solution most appropriate for your application.

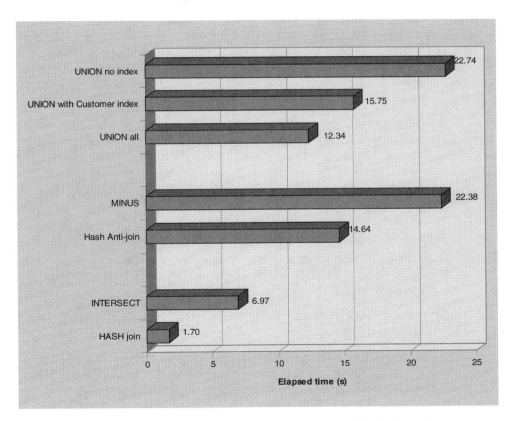

FIGURE 8.6 Performance of the SET operators and their alternatives.

CHAPTER SUMMARY

Many Oracle procedures require sort operations. Sorts can be expensive and avoiding sorting can result in significant improvements to query performance. The most common cause of Oracle sorts are:

❏ Using the ORDER BY clause to return rows in sorted order.

❏ Using the GROUP BY clause to return aggregated information.

❏ Table joins using the sort merge method.

❏ Set operations such as UNION, MINUS and INTERSECT.

It's not uncommon to inadvertently cause Oracle to perform unnecessary sorts. This often occurs through unnecessary use of the DISTINCT keyword or the use of UNION in preference to UNION ALL.

An index can be used to perform an ORDER BY without a sort. This will be effective if you are optimizing for response time, rather than throughput, or when the query can be resolved entirely from the index. Oracle may use indexes to avoid sorts if the optimizer goal is FIRST_ROWS.

The GROUP BY clause returns one row for each unique combination of columns specified. The group functions can report on maximums, minimums, counts, averages and other statistics for each group. Some ways of optimizing group operations are:

❏ Operations which group data can show strong improvements when an index-only solution is possible. This will be possible if an index exists on all of the columns in both the GROUP BY and SELECT clauses. An index on the GROUP BY columns alone will not be helpful.

❏ Counting the number of rows in a table can be enhanced by counting the rows in an indexed column which is not nullable. Alternately, use "count(*)" in preference to counting a constant or column because Oracle transparently avoids a sort in this circumstance.

❏ Finding a maximum or minimum value can often be performed more effectively by a PL/SQL block—especially if an index on the column in question exists.

The set operators UNION, INTERSECT and MINUS allow multiple result sets to be combined or compared.

❏ The frequently used UNION operator is less efficient than UNION ALL, since UNION ALL doesn't require a sort to eliminate duplicates. Use UNION ALL in preference to UNION unless you need these duplicates eliminated.

❏ The set operators INTERSECT and MINUS can often be more efficiently expressed as a join or a hash anti-join.

Chapter 9

OPTIMIZING DATA MANIPULATION STATEMENTS

INTRODUCTION

In this chapter, we look at issues relating to the performance of Data Manipulation Language (DML) statements. These statements (INSERT, UPDATE and DELETE) alter the information contained within your Oracle database.

Even in transaction processing environments, most database activity is related to data retrieval. This is partially because updates and deletes must first retrieve the rows before they can be processed. Because DML operations usually have a query component, you can often tune DML statements using query optimization techniques.

One of the key features of relational databases is the ability to group multiple DML statements into a group of statements which must succeed or fail as a unit. These groups of statements are known as transactions. Transactions have distinct performance problems and tuning opportunities.

Some of the topics covered in this chapter are:

❏ Optimizing individual DML statements through the optimization of the WHERE clause and subqueries.

❏ Optimizing correlated updates using PL/SQL alternatives.

❏ Using TRUNCATE to delete all rows in a table.

❏ The effect of indexes on DML performance.

❏ Using array processing to enhance bulk DML performance.

❏ Using discrete transactions.

❏ Improving bulk DML by adjusting the COMMIT frequency.

❏ Locking issues.

❏ The effect of referential integrity constraints and triggers.

OPTIMIZING INDIVIDUAL DML STATEMENTS

WHERE CLAUSES AND SUBQUERIES IN DML

Much of the overhead involved in UPDATE and DELETE rows is incurred when locating the rows to be processed. DELETE and UPDATE statements usually contain a WHERE clause which defines the rows to be deleted or updated. INSERT and UPDATE statements can contain subqueries, which define either the data to be inserted or the updated row values. The obvious first step in optimizing the performance of these statements is to optimize the WHERE clauses or subqueries.

These subqueries and WHERE clauses can be optimized using the same principles discussed in previous chapters. For instance:

❏ Creating indexes on columns in the WHERE clause.

❏ Using anti-join hints to improve performance of NOT IN subqueries.

❏ Ensuring that correlated subqueries are very efficient.

> **If a DML statement contains a WHERE clause or a subquery, ensure that the subquery or WHERE clause is optimized using the standard query optimization principles.**

CORRELATED UPDATES

Updates often contain a subquery in the WHERE or the SET clause. When the same table is referenced in both the WHERE and in the SET clauses, duplicate processing and inefficient processing can occur. For example, the following update references the employee table in both the SET clause and the WHERE clause:

```
update customers c
   set sales_rep_id=(select manager_id
                      from employees
                     where surname=c.contact_surname
                       and firstname=c.contact_firstname
                       and date_of_birth=c.date_of_birth)
 where (contact_surname,contact_firstname,date_of_birth) in
       (select surname,firstname,date_of_birth
          from employees)
```

```
Rows      Execution Plan
-------   -------------------------------------------------------
      0   UPDATE STATEMENT    GOAL: CHOOSE
  28009   HASH JOIN
    800    VIEW
    800     SORT (UNIQUE)
    800      TABLE ACCESS (FULL) OF 'EMPLOYEES'  ← Get manager_id
 100000    TABLE ACCESS   GOAL: ANALYZED (FULL) OF 'CUSTOMERS'
      0    TABLE ACCESS (FULL) OF 'EMPLOYEES'    ← From WHERE clause
```

Although the subquery in the WHERE clause can use an index to find rows to be processed, a second access of the EMPLOYEES table must be made to obtain the relevant manager_id column. At best, this will result in unnecessary index lookups; at worst, no index will be available and multiple table scans will be performed.

There is often no alternative to this format for the UPDATE statement, because there is simply no way to reference the employee rows to which the WHERE clause refers from the SET subquery.

Logically, we could perform the update more efficiently by using procedural logic, as in this PL/SQL block:

```
DECLARE
   CURSOR cust_csr is
           select c.rowid crowid,e.manager_id
             from customers c,
                  employees e
            where e.surname=c.contact_surname
              and e.firstname=c.contact_firstname
              and e.date_of_birth=c.date_of_birth;
BEGIN
   FOR cust_row in cust_csr LOOP
        update customers
           set sales_rep_id=cust_row.manager_id
         where rowid=cust_row.crowid;
   END LOOP;
END;
```

In the case where an index is not available to support the SET clause, the PL/SQL approach requires only a single scan of EMPLOYEES and reduces block gets from 8,033 blocks to 1,089 blocks.

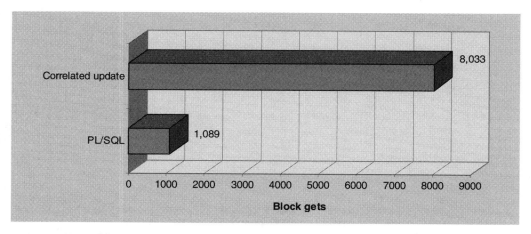

FIGURE 9.1 Comparison of correlated update and PL/SQL equivalents when no index exists to support the SET subquery.

> **Consider replacing a correlated update with a PL/SQL approach where matching tables appear in the SET and WHERE clauses, or where there are no indexes to support the SET subquery.**

TRUNCATE TABLE VERSUS DELETE

The TRUNCATE TABLE command allows all rows to be removed from a table with minimal overhead. Emptying a table using the DELETE command results in a high overhead in rollback segment and redo log entries. Additionally, using TRUNCATE resets the table's *high water mark* which will improve subsequent full table scans.

Strictly speaking, the TRUNCATE command is a Data Definition Language (DDL) statement rather than a Data Manipulation Language (DML) statement. This means that it cannot be rolled back, and it issues an implicit COMMIT (so any preceding statements will be committed and also will become permanent).

Remember that TRUNCATE can only be used to remove *all* rows from a table.

> **When removing all rows from a table, use TRUNCATE in preference to DELETE.**

INDEXES AND DML PERFORMANCE

In previous chapters, we have made extensive use of indexes to improve the performance of queries. Usually, when we have been able to improve query performance by adding an index, we have done so. Although indexes can considerably improve query performance, they do reduce the performance of DML. All of a table's indexes must be updated when a row is inserted or deleted and an index must also be amended when an update changes any column which appears in the index.

It is therefore important that all our indexes contribute to query performance,[1] since these indexes will otherwise needlessly degrade DML performance. In particular, you should be especially careful when creating indexes on frequently updated columns. A row can only be inserted or deleted once, but may be updated many times. Indexes on heavily updated columns or on tables which have a very high insert/delete rate will therefore exact a particularly high cost.

> **Indexes always add to the overhead of INSERT and DELETE statements, and may add to the overhead of UPDATE statements. Avoid over-indexing, especially on columns which are frequently updated.**

Inserts and deletes will be significantly slower for tables with a large number of indexes. If you are regularly inserting large numbers of rows into such a table during a batch window which has no associated query activity, then it may be worth dropping the indexes before the data load and recreating them later. This will be especially effective if you use the UNRECOVERABLE clause (see Chapter 11) and PARALLEL INDEX CREATION option (see Chapter 12).

To reduce the overhead of deleting from heavily indexed tables, you should consider "logically" deleting the rows using a status column. Queries against the table would have a WHERE clause condition which eliminated the "logically" deleted rows. During a regular batch window the rows could either be deleted or the table could be rebuilt without the unwanted rows. You can rebuild a large table surprisingly quickly using CREATE TABLE AS SELECT with the UNRECOVERABLE and PARALLEL options. See Chapter 11 for details on the UNRECOVERABLE option and Chapter 12 for details of parallel table creation.

---

[1] An exception can be made for foreign key indexes—which reduce lock contention and unique constraint indexes. We may wish to keep these even if they don't contribute to query performance.

ARRAY INSERTS

Array INSERT refers to the Oracle feature which allows more than one row to be inserted into a table in a single operation. This reduces communication traffic between your client program and the Oracle server. It also reduces the number of SQL calls executed. In many environments, array processing is provided transparently. Appendix C contains some guidelines for implementing array processing in commonly used development tools.

Array processing can have a dramatic effect on insert performance.

Figure 9.2 shows the effect of varying the array size on the performance of a bulk insert.

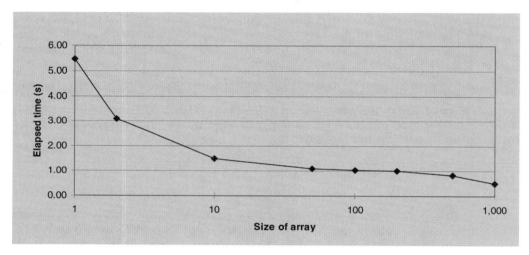

FIGURE 9.2   Effect of varying the array size on bulk insert performance.

Use the array INSERT facility whenever possible to improve bulk insert performance.

OPTIMIZING TRANSACTIONS

A *transaction* is a set of DML statements which will succeed or fail as a unit. In Oracle (and in the ANSI standard), a transaction implicitly commences when a DML statement is issued, and completes with a COMMIT or ROLLBACK statement or when a program terminates.

DISCRETE TRANSACTIONS

Oracle includes a feature which is designed to speed up certain categories of transactions. This feature is known as *discrete transaction* and improves performance of transactions by eliminating some of the overhead of DML statements.

To understand how a discrete transaction works, let's review how Oracle processes DML statements in a normal transaction. For instance, consider the following statement:

```
update customer_account
   set balance=balance-20
 where customer_id=3
```

When this statement is issued, Oracle performs the following activities:

❏ The data block containing the relevant CUSTOMER_ACCOUNT row is retrieved. If the block is not in memory (in the *SGA*) then Oracle will retrieve the block from disk.

❏ An image of the row as it was before the update is copied to an Oracle *rollback segment*. This "before image" of the row can be used to revert the row to its original state in the event that a ROLLBACK is issued. The copy will also be used by other sessions which must access the old customer balance until a COMMIT is issued.

❏ The value of the BALANCE column is changed in the "current" version of the data block.

❏ An entry recording the changed values is written to the *redo log*. The redo log contains details of transaction information which can be used to reconstruct the transaction in the event of a system failure.

❏ If a COMMIT is issued, then the contents of the redo log are written to disk—making the changes permanent.

❏ If a ROLLBACK is issued, then the copy of the relevant blocks in the rollback segment are used to revert the block to its previous value.

In the case of a discrete transaction, changes to the data block and redo log are deferred until the last possible moment—when the transaction commits. No entries are made to the rollback segment because no changes are made until a COMMIT is issued; therefore rollback information is not required.

As a result of this methodology, discrete transactions have the following restrictions and consequences:

❏ If a discrete transaction queries a row which it has modified, it will see the unmodified value of the row, since the row is not truly changed until the commit is issued.

❏ Discrete transactions cannot be distributed transactions—that is, a discrete transaction cannot alter data in another database.

❏ Tables which contain referential integrity constraints may cause problems for discrete transactions. For instance, if we added a new department, and then tried to add an employee to this department within the same discrete transaction, the operation may fail since the new department row has not yet "really" been added.

❏ Discrete transactions cannot change the same block twice.

❏ Discrete transactions can cause errors in queries which attempt to read the changed blocks while discrete transactions are in progress. For instance, suppose we attempt to issue a "sum(balance)" on customer accounts. If a discrete transaction alters a block after the query commences, but before we encounter the block, we will encounter a problem when we come to read the changed block. Oracle will detect that the block has been changed since the query began and will attempt to find an older version of the row in the rollback segment. Since discrete transactions don't generate rollback segment information, we won't find a previous block and a *Snapshot too old* error will result.

These restrictions are fairly severe and violate ANSI standards and some commonsense expectations. Oracle received some fairly harsh criticism when discrete transactions were introduced on the grounds that they were a "benchmark special": introduced to improve performance in standard industry benchmark tests, but not useful in the real world. As a result, discrete transactions have a fairly poor reputation and are not often used in production systems.

However, if the circumstances favor discrete transactions, then significant performance improvements can be realized. For instance, on average, the following discrete transaction shown in Figure 9.3 completed in 80% of the time of its non-discrete equivalent:

```
dbms_transaction.begin_discrete_transaction;

    insert into sales ( CUSTOMER_ID,
                        PRODUCT_ID ,
                        SALE_DATE  ,
                        QUANTITY   ,
                        SALE_VALUE )
        values (p_customer_id,
                p_product_id,
                sysdate,
                p_quantity,
                p_value);
```

```
update customer_balance
    set balance=balance-p_value
  where customer_id=p_customer_id;

commit;
```

If you can tolerate the limitations of discrete transactions and need to improve the performance of some update intensive operations, you may wish to consider using them. They suit small transactions in update intensive environments where long running queries do not occur.

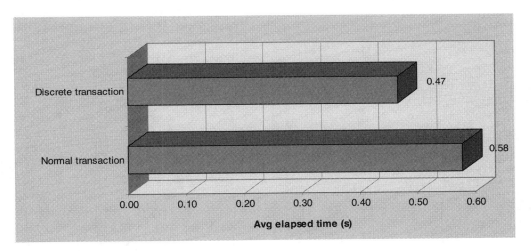

FIGURE 9.3 Comparison of execution time for a discrete transaction and a normal transaction.

Discrete transactions can improve the performance of certain small transactions in very specific circumstances. However, they can prevent successful execution of long running queries.

USING SET TRANSACTION OPTIONS

The SET TRANSACTION command allows you to control characteristics of your transaction. Some of these options have performance implications.

SET TRANSACTION option	Usage notes
USE ROLLBACK SEGMENT segment_name	This option allows you to specify the *rollback segment* to be used by your transaction. Oracle will usually assign a rollback segment to your transaction using load balancing algorithms and it's generally not helpful to force the use of a particular segment. However, if you know that your transaction will affect a large number of rows (a bulk update, for instance) you may wish to explicitly choose a larger rollback segment. Performance will be improved, since dynamic growth of the rollback segment during your transaction will be avoided.
READ ONLY	This option prevents your transaction from seeing changes to rows which were made after your transaction began. This can be useful for reports comprising multiple SQL statements which need a consistent view of the data. However, enabling this option in a long running set of queries unnecessarily may reduce the performance of your report. This is because additional visits to rollback segments will be required to obtain "before images" of rows. Accessing the rollback segments involves additional I/Os.

COMMITING TRANSACTIONS

A transaction is successfully terminated when a COMMIT statement is issued or when a COMMIT is issued implicitly, such as when a program successfully terminates. Committing a transaction causes the following events to occur:

❑ The transaction is marked as committed in the relevant rollback segment.

❑ The transaction is marked as complete in the redo log.

❑ The redo log entries are written to the redo log file on disk.

While the first two events occur in memory, the third event—writing to the redo log—always requires a write to disk. This is so your transaction is not lost if the system should crash and the information in memory is lost.

Since a COMMIT always requires some disk I/O, it follows that the more frequently a program commits, the more I/O overhead it will incur.

Usually, the determination of when to COMMIT a transaction is driven by application design or user requirements rather than by performance considerations. For instance, if users press a *SAVE* button in an on-line application, they have a reasonable expectation that the transaction is now saved—and this would require a COMMIT.

On the other hand, when coding bulk load or maintenance jobs, you may have some options as to how often to COMMIT. For instance, in the following PL/SQL code, we can adjust how often we COMMIT by altering the value of the *commitf* variable:

```
DECLARE
    counter_1 number:=0;
    status_1  varchar2(10);
    commitf   number:=1000;  -- ← Commit frequency
BEGIN
    FOR customer_row in (select * from customer_balance) LOOP
        counter_1:=counter_1+1;
        IF customer_row.balance < 0 THEN
            status_1:='DEBIT';
        ELSE
            status_1:='CREDIT';
        END IF;

        UPDATE customers
           SET status=status_1
         WHERE customer_id=customer_row.customer_id;
        IF counter_1 > commitf THEN
            -- Commit every "commitf" rows
            commit;
            counter_1:=0;
        END IF;
    END LOOP;
    commit;
END;
```

Figure 9.4 shows elapsed times for various COMMIT frequencies. By reducing the COMMIT frequency, we reduced elapsed times for the job by more than 75%.

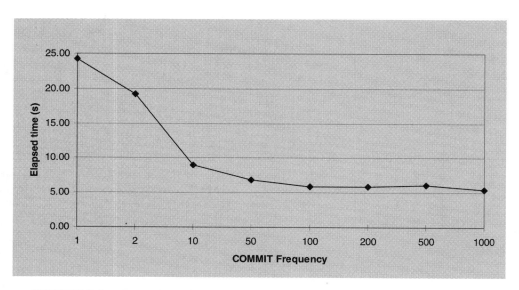

FIGURE 9.4 Effect of changing the COMMIT frequency for a bulk update program.

> **Since committing a transaction involves an I/O overhead, COMMIT infrequently during bulk updates.**

LOCKING

Oracle applies a *row-level lock* to each row affected by a DML statement. This lock prevents other DML statements from affecting the row in question without hindering any queries on that row. The locks are released when a transaction terminates—usually as the result of a COMMIT or ROLLBACK statement.

Contention for locks can severely impact the throughput of concurrent transactions. You can reduce the impact of locking on your application using the following guidelines:

❑ COMMIT transactions as soon as is logically possible in a transaction-processing environment.

❑ Avoid holding locks during interaction with a user. Some applications allow a user to hold a lock pending the hit of an "OK" button.

This can result in long delays for other users—especially if the user holding the lock goes to lunch!

❏ Carefully consider your locking strategy. An *optimistic locking strategy*—in which rows are locked at the last minute and an error is generated if another user changes the row—can result in less contention than the pessimistic locking strategy, in which the row is locked as it is fetched from the database. See Chapter 14 for a more detailed comparison of the two strategies.

❏ Ensure that columns with foreign key constraints are indexed if the parent table is subject to updates. Missing foreign key indexes can cause Oracle to lock the entire parent table against updates when a child table is updated (prior to Oracle 7.2, it was the child table which was locked).

Ensure that you minimize your locking contention by COMMITING transactions appropriately, avoiding user interaction while locks are held and carefully considering your locking strategy.

OTHER DML PERFORMANCE ISSUES

REFERENTIAL INTEGRITY

Referential integrity constraints prevent a foreign key column from referring to non-existent primary keys. For instance, the following constraint prevents the department_id column in SALES referring to a non-existent customer:

```
alter table SALES
    add constraint fk1_sales foreign key (CUSTOMER_ID)
        references CUSTOMERS (CUSTOMER_ID);
```

The presence of the foreign key constraint forces Oracle to check the CUSTOMER table for every row inserted into the SALES table. Not surprisingly, this slows down inserts into SALES (see Figure 9.5). Using referential integrity constraints helps ensure self-consistency within your database and is generally recommended. However, be aware of the impact during INSERTs (and UPDATEs of the foreign key).

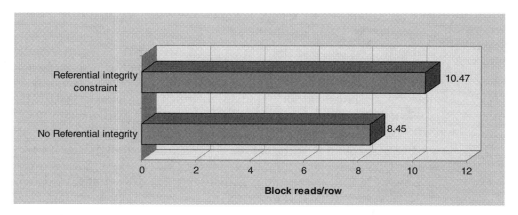

FIGURE 9.5 The effect of a foreign key constraint on inserts into the SALES table.

Also remember that referential integrity constraints can result in Oracle locking the entire parent table (or the child table prior to Oracle 7.2) during an update to the child table if a foreign key index does not exist. In our example, the CUSTOMER table would be subject to a full table lock unless there was an index on the CUSTOMER_ID column in the SALES table. These full table locks could cause severe performance problems for sessions trying to perform DML against the CUSTOMER table.

> **Use referential integrity constraints to maintain self-consistency in your data, but be aware of the performance impact for DML statements. Ensure that you have an index on the foreign key columns to avoid costly full table locks.**

TRIGGERS

Triggers are PL/SQL blocks which execute when specified DML operations occur. The overhead of executing the PL/SQL is going to depend on the contents of the trigger and the rate of DML on the table involved, but there will be an overhead. We will discuss the optimization of triggers in Chapter 10.

FREE LISTS

When an Oracle session wants to INSERT a new row into a table, it is necessary for that session to find a block with enough free space available for the row to be INSERTed. A block will be eligible for INSERTs depending on the values of PCT-

FREE and PCTUSED—as explained in Chapter 6. Oracle maintains a list of blocks eligible for INSERTs which is called the *freelist*. If there are a large number of sessions concurrently inserting into a table, then there may be contention for these free lists.

We will see how to detect contention for freelists in Chapter 16. It's not easy to detect freelist contention or to determine which tables are experiencing freelist contention. If you suspect that many concurrent sessions will INSERT into one table, it may be wise to create this table with multiple freelists using the FREELISTS clause of the CREATE TABLE statement:

```
CREATE TABLE table_name
    (column specifications)
    STORAGE (FREELISTS number_of_freelists)
```

Use the FREELISTS clause of the CREATE TABLE statement to create multiple freelists for tables which experience heavy concurrent insert activity.

PARALLEL DML

Oracle 8 allows you to use parallel processing for UPDATE statements. This subject is covered in detail in Chapter 12. As an example, we could give all employees a ten percent pay increase using four processes in parallel with the following SQL:

```
alter session enable parallel_dml;

update /*+ parallel(e,4) */ employees e
    set salary=salary*1.1;
```

By allocating multiple processes to the DML statement, we can potentially improve its performance very substantially.

CHAPTER SUMMARY

In this chapter, we've discussed ways of improving the performance of DML statements—UPDATE, DELETE and INSERT—and of improving the performance of DML statements grouped in transactions.

The major principles for optimizing DML are:

❑ Optimize the subqueries and WHERE clauses of the DML statements as you would optimize the performance of queries.

❏ Indexes slow down INSERTs, UPDATEs and DELETEs. Ensure that all indexes "pay their way" in terms of improving query performance and especially watch out for indexes on heavily updated columns.

❏ UPDATEs which contain subqueries within the SET clause may be more efficiently executed if re-coded in PL/SQL.

❏ When deleting all rows in a table, TRUNCATE will be much faster than DELETE.

❏ An array INSERT can significantly improve performance when inserting many rows.

❏ Tables which must sustain high rates of INSERTs from multiple sessions may benefit from multiple *freelists*.

❏ Triggers and referential integrity may reduce the performance of DML statements.

❏ In Oracle version 8, parallel DML can be used to improve the performance of DML statements which process large numbers of rows.

Groups of DML statements which are combined in transactions can be subject to special optimizations:

❏ Discrete transactions can improve the performance of short transactions which meet specific guidelines.

❏ Although in many circumstances, frequent COMMITS are required by application design, less frequent transactions can improve performance, especially for jobs which INSERT, UPDATE or DELETE very large quantities of data. On the other hand, committing frequently in a transaction-processing environment can reduce lock contention. Choose the COMMIT frequency which best suits your application.

Chapter 10

USING AND TUNING PL/SQL

INTRODUCTION

In this chapter, we will see how PL/SQL can be used to improve performance of "traditional" SQL statements, and how PL/SQL programs themselves can be tuned.

Many SQL statements—especially DML statements or queries which return only a small result set—can be more efficiently implemented using PL/SQL.

As a procedural language, PL/SQL is subject to the standard techniques of code optimization. We will see how procedural code optimization can improve the performance of PL/SQL. We'll also discuss other ways of improving the performance of PL/SQL programs.

This chapter will cover the following topics:

❑ Using PL/SQL in place of standard SQL.

❑ Disadvantages of a PL/SQL approach.

❑ Using PL/SQL to implement denormalization.

❑ Using PL/SQL functions in standard SQL.

❑ Principles of code optimization applied to PL/SQL.

❑ Using and optimizing packages and procedures.

❑ Optimizing PL/SQL cursors.

❑ Using PL/SQL tables to cache frequently accessed values.

REVIEW OF PL/SQL

PL/SQL is Oracle's proprietary set of procedural extensions to the SQL language. PL/SQL adds standard procedural constructs (conditionals [IF..THEN], looping, recursion, and subroutines) and advanced language capabilities (overloading and exception handling) to Oracle's implementation of SQL.

The basic building block of Oracle PL/SQL is the *PL/SQL block*. A PL/SQL block contains a single declaration section, a code section and an exception handling section. PL/SQL blocks may be nested; that is, a PL/SQL block may itself contain a PL/SQL block within the statement body.

A PL/SQL block can be submitted to the database "as is." In this case it is known as an *anonymous block*. Anonymous blocks may be contained within 3GL code or within a development tool (developer/2000, for instance).

More usefully, a PL/SQL block can be contained within a *stored subprogram* within the Oracle server. Stored subprograms come in the following flavors:

❏ A stored *procedure* or *function* consists of a single PL/SQL program (which may, however, contain multiple or nested PL/SQL blocks).

❏ A stored *package* consists of a number of stored subprograms. A package may contain public and private procedures, variables and cursors. Most non-trivial PL/SQL stored programs would usually be contained within a package.

❏ A database trigger is a stored subprogram which is invoked as a result of a DML operation (INSERT, UPDATE or DELETE) against a table. The trigger consists of a PL/SQL block, but may contain nested blocks or calls to stored subprograms.

PERFORMANCE CHARACTERISTICS OF PL/SQL

PL/SQL can often add to program functionality and programmer efficiency, and there are certainly many cases where the use of a procedural language, such as PL/SQL, is essential for delivering required functionality. However, there are also a number of reasons why a PL/SQL approach may offer performance improvements over a traditional SQL approach.

REDUCTION IN PARSING

Stored procedures and packages are held within the database in a compiled form. This means that all the SQL within the stored procedure has already been parsed. When the SQL statement is executed, there is no need to check the statement for syntax, object references or to determine the execution plan.

If the same set of statements were executed from a client tool, there would be a need to search for each statement in the shared pool. If not found, the statements would require syntax and semantic checking and would need to be optimized. The overhead of parsing can be very significant—especially in an OLTP environment where I/O requirements for each SQL statement are typically low and the relative cost of parsing is consequently high.

REDUCTION IN CLIENT–SERVER TRAFFIC

In a traditional SQL-based application, SQL statements and data flow back and forth between the client and the server. This traffic can cause delays even when both client and server programs are on the same machine. If the client and server are on different machines, then the overhead is even higher.

Using PL/SQL stored programs eliminates this overhead. A succinct message is sent from the client to the server (the stored procedure execution request) and a minimal response is sent from the server to the client (perhaps only a return code).

The reduction in network traffic can significantly enhance performance—especially in a client-server environment.

USING PL/SQL TO DEFINE PROCESSING LOGIC

As we discussed in Chapter 2, SQL is a *non-procedural* language: you specify the data you want and not how to retrieve it. While this simplifies the task for the programmer, it sometimes limits the potential for tuning.

When using PL/SQL, you have the option of specifying exactly how you want the data retrieved. You can break complex SQL into multiple steps and process data one row at a time. For certain operations, this can lead to substantial performance improvements.

DRAWBACKS OF PL/SQL

Although there are certain circumstances in which a PL/SQL approach will yield large gains in performance terms, a PL/SQL approach is not always the best approach. You should bear the following drawbacks in mind:

❑ The procedural nature of PL/SQL can exact a higher demand on the programmer than does "straight" SQL. The PL/SQL can be harder to code than the equivalent SQL statement.

❑ Although PL/SQL procedures and functions can return values, they cannot return *result sets* as such. A procedure can return a cursor variable and a package can include a globally accessible cursor definition, but these can't be used effectively in most development environments. When you need a set of data, a SELECT statement is usually still the most appropriate approach.

❏ Although individual SQL statements within a PL/SQL program may be executed using the parallel query option (see Chapter 12 for more details of the parallel query option), the logic within the PL/SQL block can usually only be executed in *serial*. This may defeat attempts to fully leverage Oracle's parallel capabilities.

USING PL/SQL IN PLACE OF "STANDARD" SQL

In previous chapters, we've seen examples of how PL/SQL can be used in place of standard SQL to improve performance. Although it's not possible to exhaustively categorize all the situations in which PL/SQL can be used in place of standard SQL, it's possible that PL/SQL is a valid alternative when:

❏ There is little or no requirement to return large quantities of data. For instance, for UPDATE transactions or when retrieving a single value or row.

❏ Standard SQL requires more resources than seems logically required and no combination of hints seem to work. This is particularly likely if there are some implicit characteristics of the data which the optimizer cannot "understand" or where the SQL is particularly complex.

❏ You have a clear idea of how the data should be retrieved and processed, but can't implement your algorithm using standard SQL.

FINDING MAXIMUMS AND MINIMUMS

In previous chapters, we've seen examples of how PL/SQL can be used to enhance the retrieval of data based on maximum or minimum conditions:

❏ In Chapter 7, we examined a PL/SQL alternative to a correlated subquery (retrieving the highest paid employees in each department) which executed in under two percent of the time taken by the standard SQL approach.

❏ In Chapter 8, we saw how PL/SQL (with appropriate indexes) can retrieve a maximum or minimum value in a fraction of the time taken by standard SQL—a 99% reduction in I/O requirements.

Both these examples used PL/SQL to move through a table in index order and retrieve only those rows which are of interest. Standard SQL is less efficient when processing these types of requests, because it insists on processing all the rows and it sorts the results. For instance, consider the query: "Who is the second highest paid employee?" In standard SQL, the following query might be required:

```
select surname, firstname, salary
  from employees
 where salary=(select max(salary)
                 from employees
                where salary!=(select max(salary)
                                 from employees))
```

```
Rows      Execution Plan
-------   --------------------------------------------------
      0   SELECT STATEMENT    HINT: CHOOSE
    800    FILTER
    800     TABLE ACCESS (FULL) OF 'EMPLOYEES' ← Get employee with second
                                                        highest salary
    799     SORT (AGGREGATE)  ← Get second highest salary
    800      FILTER
    800       TABLE ACCESS (FULL) OF 'EMPLOYEES'
    800       SORT (AGGREGATE)    ← Get highest salary
    800        TABLE ACCESS (FULL) OF 'EMPLOYEES'
```

Alternately, a short PL/SQL block could be used.

```
DECLARE
    CURSOR emp_csr is
                select rownum, e.* from employees e
                order by salary desc;
        second_high_sal    number:=0;
        prev_sal        number;
BEGIN
  FOR emp_row in emp_csr LOOP
    IF emp_row.rownum > 1 THEN
       IF emp_row.salary < prev_sal and second_high_sal=0 THEN
          -- Found second highest!
          second_high_sal:=emp_row.salary;
          dbms_output.put_line(
            emp_row.surname||' '||
            to_char(emp_row.salary));
       ELSIF emp_row.salary=second_high_sal THEN
          -- Another person earning second highest!
          dbms_output.put_line(
            emp_row.surname||' '||
            to_char(emp_row.salary));
       ELSIF emp_row.salary < prev_sal and second_high_sal>0 THEN
          -- Gone below second highest,  so exit;
          exit;
       END IF;
    END IF;
    prev_sal:=emp_row.salary;
  END LOOP;
END;
```

The PL/SQL block requires only one scan of the EMPLOYEES table and 13 I/Os to complete, whereas the standard SQL consumes 1631 blocks and requires three scans of the EMPLOYEES table. For an indexed column on a large table, the effect can be even more pronounced since PL/SQL can use the index to move through the table in the correct order without requiring a sort.

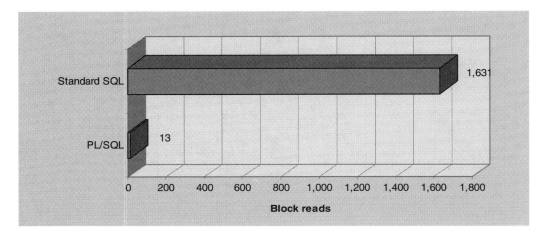

FIGURE 10.1   I/O requirements for finding the employee with the second highest salary.

Consider PL/SQL for queries which ask for maximums or minimums—especially on indexed columns.

USING PL/SQL FOR DE-NORMALIZATION

In Chapter 6, we saw how a database trigger written in PL/SQL could be used to automatically maintain capitalized versions of the surname and first name. Using PL/SQL in this way can allow you to effectively maintain an index on a function.

You can also use triggers to *de-normalize* your tables. For instance, a trigger could be used to maintain a copy of the department_name in the EMPLOYEES table. In the infrequent event that the department name changed, the trigger would update all matching rows in the EMPLOYEES table. This might avoid the most common reason for joining employees to customers. The following SQL implements this sort of de-normalization:

```
CREATE or replace trigger cutomer_insUpd1
  before insert or update of department_id on employees
  for each row
DECLARE
```

```
CURSOR dept_csr (cp_dept_id number) is
     SELECT department_name
        FROM departments
        WHERE department_id=cp_dept_id;

BEGIN
  OPEN dept_csr(:NEW.DEPARTMENT_ID);
  FETCH dept_csr into :NEW.DEPARTMENT_NAME;
  CLOSE dept_csr;
END;
.
/


CREATE or replace trigger department_insUpd1
 before insert or update of department_name on departments
 for each row
BEGIN
  UPDATE employees
    SET department_name=:NEW.DEPARTMENT_NAME
    WHERE department_id=:NEW.DEPARTMENT_ID;

end;
.
```

Implementing this sort of de-normalization can lead to tremendous improvements if a join is avoided as a result. For example, for a query which returns all employees and the name of their departments, I/O requirements are reduced from 2,414 block reads to just 67 block reads.

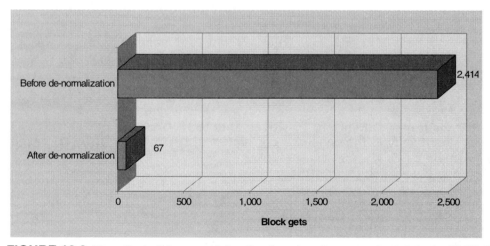

FIGURE 10.2 The effect of de-normalizing the department name column into the EMPLOYEES table on a query which returns department and employee names.

De-normalizing a table is not something which should be done thoughtlessly and we'll discuss the pros and cons of de-normalizing your tables in Chapter 14. However, by using PL/SQL triggers, you can automate the maintenance of the de-normalized data and reduce the application overhead of de-normalization.

> **Consider using PL/SQL triggers to de-normalize your tables. De-normalization can reduce join requirements and can effectively allow indexed lookups on functions.**

OPTIMIZING DML WITH PL/SQL

We saw in Chapter 9 how PL/SQL could be used in place of a correlated update with great effect (I/O reduced to 13%). Correlated updates can perform poorly, especially when the same table is referenced in the SET and WHERE clauses or when there is not an index to support the subqueries.

DML (UPDATE, INSERT or DELETE) statements are often good candidates for conversion to PL/SQL:

❏ DML statements do not return result sets which PL/SQL would find difficult to display or pass back to the calling program.

❏ It's often tricky to formulate a DML operation which is based on a join query. DML statements do not support a FROM clause (except in a subquery). Using PL/SQL allows you to move through a join query issuing DML statements where appropriate.

❏ For DML statements which affect a large number of rows, PL/SQL can allow you to COMMIT at regular intervals, reducing the *rollback segment* overhead.

> **PL/SQL can offer substantial improvements to UPDATE and DELETE transactions, specifically in the case of a correlated UPDATE or an UPDATE based on a join query.**

USING PL/SQL FUNCTIONS IN SQL

PL/SQL functions, providing that they do no database manipulation, can be called from within standard SQL. Using PL/SQL functions in this way can add to the functionality of Oracle SQL by allowing SQL to perform tasks which would otherwise be awkward or impossible.

Embedded stored functions can also be used to improve performance when the selection criteria are so complex that they cannot be included within the WHERE clause of the query. For example, let's say that a CPU intensive function defines some complex process which returns "1" if the row is eligible for further processing and "0" otherwise. We could then formulate our SQL query as follows:

```
select * from customers
  where cpu_intensive_function(address1)=1;
```

By using a PL/SQL function in the WHERE clause, we avoid having to evaluate the rows in our application. This saves resources at the server and at the client and reduces the network traffic between the two. We can also take advantage of parallel query, if appropriate.

Consider encapsulating CPU intensive PL/SQL into functions which can be called from the WHERE clause to implement selection criteria which would otherwise need to be implemented in the client application.

OPTIMIZING PL/SQL

Having decided to implement some processing in PL/SQL, whether as a replacement for standard SQL or to implement some complex application logic, we have some opportunities for improving the performance of that PL/SQL:

❏ The procedural constructs in PL/SQL (loops, branches, etc.) are subject to many of the same optimization techniques appropriate for other procedural languages.

❏ Storing PL/SQL routines in the database as a stored program reduces the overhead of parsing PL/SQL.

❏ There are some PL/SQL specific techniques which can be used to improve database access (for instance, explicit cursors, CURRENT OF CURSOR and PL/SQL tables).

CODE OPTIMIZATION

Usually, we think of PL/SQL as a database access language and concentrate on optimizing the SQL within the PL/SQL program. But as a procedural language, PL/SQL is subject to many of the same principles of optimization as other languages. There are circumstances in which PL/SQL itself—without any database accesses—can consume CPU resources at an excessive rate. Some of the basic principles for optimizing PL/SQL code (and indeed other languages) are:

❏ Optimize or minimize loop processing.

❏ Optimize conditional statements (such as IF).

❏ Avoid recursion.

Optimize loop processing

The LOOP–END LOOP clauses are used to execute the statements within the loop repeatedly. A badly constructed loop can have a drastic effect on performance. Two important principles in the optimization of loops are:

❏ Try to minimize the number of iterations in the loop. Each iteration will consume CPU, so if you are finished in the loop, use the EXIT statement to move out of the loop.

❏ Make sure that there are no statements inside the loop which could be located outside of the loop. If a statement doesn't reference a loop variable, it's possible that it could execute outside the loop—and perhaps execute only once, rather than many times.

The following code fragment illustrates a poorly designed loop:

```
FOR counter1 in 1..500 LOOP

 FOR counter2 in 1..500 LOOP

    modcounter1:=mod(counter1,10);    -- will execute 250,000 times
    modcounter2:=mod(counter2,10);
    sqrt1:=sqrt(counter1);    -- Could be located outside of this loop
    sqrt2:=sqrt(counter2);
    IF modcounter1=0 THEN

      IF modcounter2=0 THEN
        -- DO something with sqrts
      END IF;
    END IF;

  END LOOP;
END LOOP;
```

Some of the problems with this piece of code are:

❏ Although we only want to process numbers divisible by ten (the MOD function specifies that only multiples of ten get processed), we are actually looping though every value from 1 to 500. The FOR statement in PL/SQL doesn't allow you to iterate in multiples of ten, so it's pretty easy to make this mistake. However, by using FOR, we've actually executed the statements inside each loop ten times more often than necessary.

❏ The SQRT and MOD functions for counter1 are included within the second (inner) loop. This means that they are executed once for every iteration of the inner loop—even though the value of counter1 does not change. This means it must be executed 500 times more often than necessary.

The following code fragment implements the same logic as the previous example, but with optimized loop processing:

```
WHILE counter1 <= 500 LOOP
   sqrt1:=sqrt(counter1);-- Executed 50 times
   WHILE counter2 <=500 LOOP
         sqrt2:=sqrt(counter2);
               -- DO something....
         counter2:=counter2+10;-- increment by 10s
   END LOOP;
   counter1:=counter1+10;
END LOOP;
```

In this example, we use the WHILE clause and manually increment the loop counter by ten. Consequently, we execute the inner loop only 50 times, rather than 500. The *modulus* calculations (MOD functions) are no longer necessary and the square root calculation on counter1 (SQRT function) has been moved out of the inner loop to the outer loop. This reduces executions of this from 250,000 executions in the first example to only 50 executions in this example.

The second example greatly outperforms the first example. The first example took 111 seconds to execute—almost two minutes. The second example takes only .02 seconds to execute—almost instantaneous! So we can see that optimizing loop processing can lead to large improvements.

When possible, reduce the number of iterations of a loop. Each loop consumes CPU, so EXIT the loop if there is no need to continue. Also reduce processing within the loop by moving statements outside of the loop if possible.

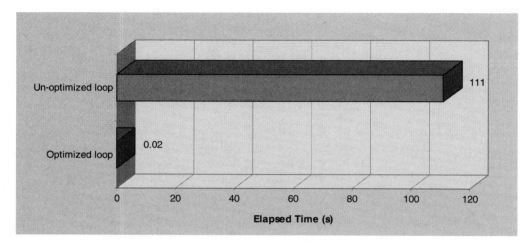

FIGURE 10.3 Elapsed time for a PL/SQL block with de-optimized loops and for an optimized equivalent.

Optimize IF statements

When processing an IF statement with multiple conditions, PL/SQL will consider each condition specified in turn until a match is found. Once the match is found, PL/SQL doesn't have to evaluate any of the subsequent conditions. It therefore follows that if the most likely condition comes first in the IF block, then the average amount of processing that PL/SQL will have to do is reduced.

The following code fragment illustrates a de-optimized IF statement. The first condition will be true only 9 times out of 10,000 loops. The final ELSE condition will be true for 9,910 of the 10,000 loops, but the preceding nine comparisons will be needlessly evaluated for each of these iterations.

```
FOR counter1 in 1..10000 LOOP
        IF counter1 < 10 THEN
                -- Do some processing;
        ELSIF counter1 <20 THEN
                -- Do some processing;
        ELSIF counter1 <30 THEN
                -- Do some processing;
        ELSIF counter1 <40 THEN
                -- Do some processing;
        ELSIF counter1 <50 THEN
                -- Do some processing;
        ELSIF counter1 <60 THEN
                -- Do some processing;
```

```
        ELSIF counter1 <70 THEN
                -- Do some processing;
        ELSIF counter1 <80 THEN
                -- Do some processing;
        ELSIF counter1 <90 THEN
                -- Do some processing;
        ELSE    -- counter above 91
                -- Do some processing;
        END IF;
    END LOOP;
```

The next example shows the IF block optimized. Now the most commonly satisfied expression is first in the IF structure. For most iterations, this first evaluation is the only one that needs to be performed:

```
FOR counter1 in 1..10000 LOOP
        IF counter1 >90 THEN
                -- Do some processing;
        ELSIF counter1 <10 THEN
                -- Do some processing;
        ELSIF counter1 <20 then
                -- Do some processing;
        ELSIF counter1 <30 THEN
                -- Do some processing;
        ELSIF counter1 <40 THEN
                -- Do some processing;
        ELSIF counter1 <50 THEN
                -- Do some processing;
        ELSIF counter1 <60 THEN
                -- Do some processing;
        ELSIF counter1 <70 THEN
                -- Do some processing;
        ELSIF counter1 <80 THEN
                -- Do some processing;
        ELSIF counter1 <90 THEN
                -- Do some processing;
        END IF;
    END LOOP;
```

Optimizing the IF statement reduced execution time from 1.22 seconds to .21 seconds.

When constructing a PL/SQL IF block with multiple conditions, place the conditions in decreasing order of probability. Make sure that the condition most likely to be satisfied is the first condition tested in the block.

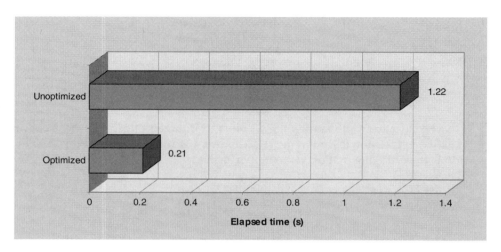

FIGURE 10.4   Execution times for optimized and un-optimized IF statements.

Recursion

A recursive routine is one that invokes itself. Recursive routines often offer elegant solutions to complex programming problems but tend to consume large amounts of memory and tend to be less efficient than a non-recursive alternative.

Many recursive algorithms can be re-formulated using non-recursive techniques. Where possible, use non-recursive solutions to improve performance.

USE STORED PROCEDURES INSTEAD OF ANONYMOUS BLOCKS

A PL/SQL block which is not contained in a procedure or function is referred to as an *anonymous block*. When submitted, anonymous blocks go through much the same parsing process as standalone SQL statements. A search of the shared pool is performed for a matching PL/SQL block and, if not found, the block is parsed and stored in the shared pool. Parsing PL/SQL blocks is typically a more expensive operation than parsing an SQL statement, since SQL statements contained within the PL/SQL must also be parsed.

Parsing PL/SQL blocks is therefore a time-consuming process and one that we want to avoid where possible. Because stored procedures and functions are stored in the database in compiled form, they normally do not need to be compiled when executed, only when created.

For instance, the following anonymous PL/SQL block executes in 0.19 seconds:

```
DECLARE
   CURSOR get_dept_csr(cp_dept_id number) is
   SELECT department_name
     FROM departments
     WHERE department_id=cp_dept_id;
BEGIN
   OPEN get_dept_csr(3);
   FETCH get_dept_csr into :dept_name;
   CLOSE get_dept_csr;
END;
```

When converted to a stored function, execution time reduces to 0.12 seconds. Although this is a reduction of only .07 seconds, it does represent 37%, which could be very significant if the procedure were being executed frequently in an OLTP environment.

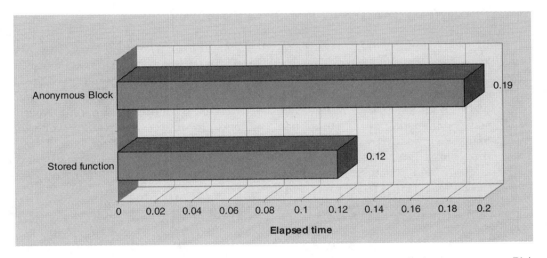

FIGURE 10.5   Execution times for a stored procedure and for an equivalent anonymous PL/ SQL block.

Use PL/SQL stored programs in preference to anonymous PL/SQL blocks. Stored programs are stored in compiled form and can be executed without parse overhead.

Using packages

A PL/SQL package allows related procedures, functions, cursor and variable definitions to be stored together. Packages are useful from a programming point of view, since they allow related program units to be grouped and allow encapsulation of local variables and subroutines. In an application which contains a complex of interrelated procedures, using packages can also reduce *dynamic recompilation*.

Dynamic recompilation occurs when a PL/SQL program refers to another PL/SQL program which has changed. Oracle keeps track of dependencies between PL/SQL programs and other objects and will automatically mark dependent objects as needing recompilation when a PL/SQL program changes. PL/SQL packages consist of a package header and a body. Providing the package header remains constant, the package body can be changed without requiring recompilation of dependent programs.

PINNING PACKAGES IN THE SHARED POOL

PL/SQL stored programs are stored within the Oracle shared memory area known as the *shared pool*. The shared pool contains a number of other objects, including standard SQL statements, object definitions and sometimes private session objects. When the shared pool memory is exhausted, objects are "aged out" of the pool using a "Least Recently Used" (*LRU*) algorithm. In some circumstances, the aging out of stored packages and procedures may result in a performance degradation when the package is next executed. You can prevent PL/SQL programs from being aged out of the shared pool by using the *dbms_sharedpool* package. For instance, the following command (from SQL*PLUS) keeps the COMPLEX_FUNCTION pinned in the shared pool:

```
SQL> exec sys.dbms_shared_pool.keep('COMPLEX_FUNCTION','P')
```

Your DBA will need to install the *dbms_shared_pool* package (using the *dbmspool.sql* script). If you want to use the package as a non-DBA, your DBA will need to grant execute permission on the package.

Take advantage of PL/SQL packages to reduce dynamic recompilation of sorted subprograms. Consider pinning large or performance critical packages in the shared pool.

TRIGGERS VERSUS STORED PROCEDURES

In earlier versions of Oracle7 (prior to 7.3), database triggers were stored in the database in un-compiled format. Consequently, the trigger would need to be parsed when first executed by an Oracle session. It therefore makes sense in these versions of Oracle to move as much code as possible from the trigger into a stored procedure and call the stored procedure from the trigger. The parse requirements for the trigger will then be reduced.

> If using a version of PL/SQL prior to 2.3 (Oracle 7.3), minimize the amount of code in database triggers since triggers are not stored in compiled format. Put the program code in a stored procedure and call it from the trigger.

Using the UPDATE OF and WHEN clauses in triggers

The UPDATE OF clause of the CREATE TRIGGER statement allows a FOR UPDATE trigger to fire only when the nominated columns are updated. In a similar fashion, the WHEN clause can be used to prevent the execution of the trigger unless a logical condition is met.

These clauses help to prevent the trigger from executing unnecessarily and can improve performance of DML operations on the table on which the trigger is based.

For example, the following trigger fires whenever any column in the EMPLOYEES table is updated:

```
CREATE or replace trigger employee_upd
  before update
     or insert
   on employees
   for each row
BEGIN
   IF :new.salary > 100000 THEN
       :new.adjusted_salary:=complex_function(:new.salary);
   END IF;
END;
```

The following trigger is more efficient because it only fires when the SALARY column is updated, and only when the new value of SALARY is greater than $100,000:

```
CREATE or replace trigger employee_upd
 before update of salary
     or insert
     on employees
   for each row
 when (new.salary > 100000)
BEGIN
     :new.adjusted_salary:=complex_function(:new.salary);
END;
```

The optimized trigger only fires when the salary column is updated. This will improve the performance of updates which don't update the salary clause.

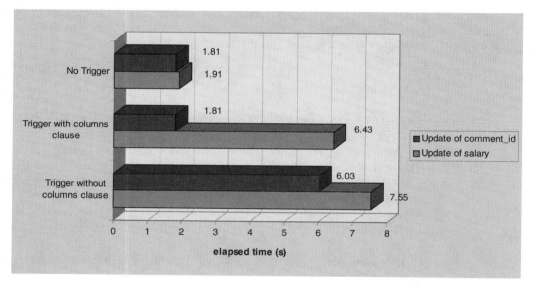

FIGURE 10.6   Using the WHEN and UPDATE OF trigger clauses to reduce trigger overhead.

Make use of the OF COLUMNS and WHEN clauses of the CREATE TRIGGER statement to ensure that your trigger only fires when necessary.

USING EXPLICIT CURSORS

PL/SQL allows an SQL statement to be included in a block without being explicitly associated with a cursor. For instance, the following block is legal:

```
begin
  select contact_firstname
    into :firstname
    from customers
   where contact_surname='SMITH'
     and contact_firstname='STEPHEN'
     and date_of_birth='26-MAR-44';
end;
```

A cursor is in fact associated with such a statement, but is created automatically by PL/SQL. Such a cursor is referred to as an *implicit* cursor.

Although implicit cursors can be convenient when programming, they can impose some execution overhead. Implicit cursors may only return a single row and Oracle must check to make sure that only one row is returned.

If the retrieval is based on an index, then the check can be done with a single additional I/O. Typically, this increases the number of reads required from three to four—which may still be significant if the procedure is executed frequently. If the retrieval is based on a table scan, then Oracle continues scanning until it finds an eligible row or reaches the end of the table. On average, this will result in twice as many block reads.

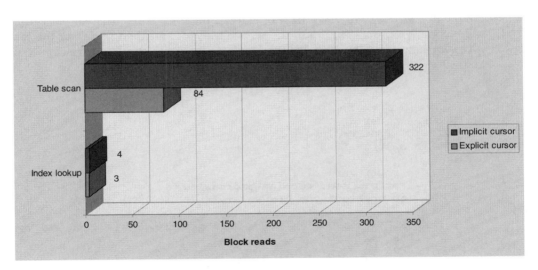

FIGURE 10.7 I/O requirements for returning a single row or table scan in PL/SQL using implicit and explicit cursors.

Using an explicit cursor—as in the code fragment below—avoids the overhead involved in the implicit cursor processing and is therefore the more efficient approach.

```
DECLARE
   CURSOR get_cust_csr is
   SELECT contact_firstname
     from customers
    WHERE contact_surname='SMITH'
      AND contact_firstname='STEPHEN'
      AND date_of_birth='26-MAR-44';
BEGIN
   OPEN get_cust_csr ;
   FETCH get_cust_csr into :firstname;
   CLOSE get_cust_csr;
END;
```

Implicit cursors in PL/SQL involve additional processing overheads. Explicit cursors will usually provide better performance.

THE WHERE CURRENT OF CLAUSE

Frequently, you will find yourself opening a cursor against a table, performing some complex processing upon the data retrieved, and then updating the table row in question. For instance, the following fragment illustrates such a processing loop:

```
DECLARE
    l_newsal number;
   CURSOR emp_csr is
    SELECT * from employees
     WHERE salary >50000;
BEGIN
    FOR emp_row in emp_csr LOOP
        -- Perform some complex processing
        -- to work out the new salary
        l_newsal:=complex_function(emp_row.salary);
        UPDATE employees          -- Use primary key to find employee
           SET salary=l_newsal
          WHERE employee_id=emp_row.employee_id;
   END LOOP;
END;
```

The UPDATE statement within the loop uses the primary key of the table, and is therefore a reasonably efficient index lookup. However, since we just fetched the row in question, why should we need to perform an index lookup? Shouldn't we already know where the row is?

In fact, the second index lookup IS unnecessary. PL/SQL (and the programmatic interfaces) can refer to the current row selected by the cursor using the clause WHERE CURRENT OF *cursor_name*. Using this notation, PL/SQL can use the row address (ROWID) stored in the cursor structure to locate the row without an index lookup. Using this method, our example now looks like this:

```
DECLARE
    l_newsal number;
    CURSOR emp_csr is
    SELECT * from employees
     where salary >50000
       for update;    -- Need FOR UPDATE since using
                      -- WHERE CURRENT OF
BEGIN
    FOR emp_row in emp_csr LOOP
        -- Perform some complex processing
        -- to work out the new salary
        l_newsal:=complex_function(emp_row.salary);
        UPDATE employees
            set salary=l_newsal
         where current of emp_csr;
    END LOOP;
END;
```

The WHERE CURRENT OF clause eliminates the I/Os involved with an index lookup and does improve the performance of the UPDATE statement. However, to use the WHERE CURRENT OF notation, you must first lock the rows involved using the FOR UPDATE clause in the cursor's SELECT statement. The FOR UPDATE clause has the following side effects:

❏ All rows selected by the query must be locked before the first row can be returned. If you only intend to process a subset of rows, or if response time for the first row is your primary concern, then you probably don't want to use FOR UPDATE.

❏ Locking the rows requires a transaction entry to be made in every block to be updated. This involves a considerable I/O overhead and is another reason why you may not want to use the FOR UPDATE clause.

If you want to optimize the UPDATE statement by avoiding the unnecessary index read but don't wish to endure the locking overhead of the FOR UPDATE clause, you can keep track of the ROWID yourself and use it in subsequent updates. The following PL/SQL block illustrates this technique:

```
DECLARE
    l_newsal number;
    CURSOR emp_csr is
      SELECT e.rowid employee_rowid, -- Give the ROWID an alias
             e.*
       from employees e
      where salary >50000 ;
BEGIN
    FOR emp_row in emp_csr LOOP
        -- Perform some complex processing
        -- to work out the new salary
        l_newsal:=complex_function(emp_row.salary);
        UPDATE employees
          SET salary=l_newsal
          WHERE rowid=emp_row.employee_rowid; -- Refer to the ROWID by alias
    END LOOP;
END;
```

By using this technique, we avoid both the overhead of locking rows and the overhead of the needless index lookup.

Figure 10.8 compares I/O requirements for the three approaches. Using the WHERE CURRENT OF cursor technique reduces the I/Os required for the UPDATE statement, but imposes an additional I/O requirement because rows had to be locked by the FOR UPDATE clause. Fetching the rows' ROWID and specifying this in the WHERE clause give a "best of both worlds" solution.

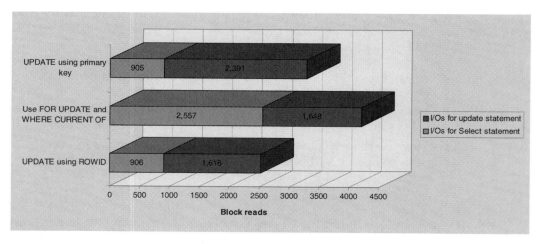

FIGURE 10.8 I/O requirements for an update within a cursor loop using various lookup techniques.

A word of caution: Although the FOR UPDATE clause imposes a processing overhead, it does prevent another user from updating the row between the time you open the cursor and the time you issue your update. If there is any chance that such an event may render your update invalid or that you will overwrite another session's update, you should do one of the following:

❏ Use the FOR UPDATE clause and accept the performance conse-quences. This is referred to as the *pessimistic locking strategy*.

❏ Check that the row has not changed by including a check in the WHERE clause of the UPDATE statement. For instance, adding the condition "SAL=EMP_ROW.SAL" to the UPDATE statement might be sufficient. This is the *optimistic locking strategy*.

❏ If you are processing all or most of the rows in the table, you might consider issuing a LOCK TABLE statement to lock the entire table. This has less overhead than locking each row individually, but will prevent any concurrent updates—even of rows not being accessed by our procedure.

Make use of the WHERE CURRENT OF CURSOR clause to update a row fetched from a cursor. If you don't want to lock the rows, store and use the ROWID column to speed up the update.

CACHING WITH PL/SQL TABLES

PL/SQL tables are analogous to arrays in other languages. Like arrays, PL/SQL tables can be used to remember, or to *cache*, frequently accessed codes or values. Using this technique, we can minimize our database accesses.

The following example illustrates the technique. A PL/SQL table is used to hold the normal value for a product with a given product id. Only if the normal value is not found in the table will it be necessary to query the PRODUCTS table.

```
CREATE or replace package body demo is

    -- Declare a PL/SQL table to hold product values.
    type product_val_tab_typ is table of products.normal_value%TYPE
             index by binary_integer;
    product_val_table product_val_tab_typ;

PROCEDURE make_sale(p_customer_id number,
                    p_product_id number,
                    p_quantity number ) is

        -- Cursor to get the normal value for a product
        CURSOR product_csr(cp_product_id number) is
            SELECT normal_value
              from products
             where product_id=cp_product_id;
```

```
        l_product_normal_value        products.normal_value%TYPE;
BEGIN
        -- Look in the PL/SQL table for the product_id in question
        BEGIN
            l_product_normal_value:=product_val_table(p_product_id);
        EXCEPTION
         WHEN no_data_found THEN
                -- Not found in the PL/SQL table,  so fetch from
                -- the database and add to the table
                OPEN  product_csr(p_product_id);
                FETCH product_csr into l_product_normal_value;
                CLOSE product_csr;
                product_val_table(p_product_id):=l_product_normal_value;
            END;

        INSERT into sales(customer_id,product_id,sale_date,
                        quantity,sale_value)
            values (p_customer_id,p_product_id,SYSDATE,
                    p_quantity, p_quantity*l_product_normal_value);
        COMMIT;
    END;
END;
```

Figure 10.9 shows the improvement which results from implementing the PL/SQL cache table for 400 executions of our function. The PL/SQL cache table is especially effective when the same PL/SQL function will be executed many times within a session. Because the cache table is destroyed when you disconnect from Oracle, you won't see much improvement if you execute the function only a couple of times in each session.

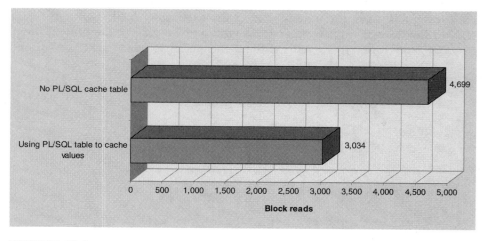

FIGURE 10.9 Using a PL/SQL table to cache frequently accessed data reduces I/O requirements.

Since Oracle caches recently accessed data values within its shared memory (the *buffer cache* within the *SGA*) it might occur to you to wonder if it's wasteful to maintain a cache within your program's memory. In fact, caching data within a program does yield substantial performance improvements even if the data is held within Oracle's shared memory. Issuing SQL to retrieve data from Oracle requires that parse and execute calls be issued to Oracle. The overhead of issuing these calls will be greater than the overhead of examining the cache table. If you implement some caching mechanism in a client-server environment then the local cache will be even more effective, since it will reduce network traffic.

> **Consider using PL/SQL tables to cache frequently accessed values and reduce unnecessary database I/O.**

CHAPTER SUMMARY

In this chapter, we've seen how PL/SQL can be used in place of standard SQL to improve performance of certain operations. PL/SQL has the following advantages over ANSI SQL;

❏ It can be stored in compiled form within the database. This reduces parse overhead.

❏ It operates completely within the server environment, eliminating or reducing client-server traffic.

❏ It allows the programmer to fully specify the processing logic and to implement data access paths which might not be possible using standard SQL.

PL/SQL is often more efficient than standard SQL for:

❏ Operations which return very limited amounts of data to the calling program.

❏ Operations which seek maximum or minimum values via an index.

❏ Correlated updates.

PL/SQL can also be used in triggers to maintain de-normalized or pre-processed data to assist in query performance.

There are a number of measures we can take to improve the performance of PL/SQL code:

❑ Use normal code optimization techniques. In particular, avoid unnecessary loops and place the more frequently satisfied conditions first in IF clauses.

❑ Take advantage of stored procedures and functions. Storing PL/SQL in the database avoids parsing overhead.

❑ Use explicit cursors in PL/SQL. An implicit cursor will often perform additional fetches.

❑ Use the WHERE CURRENT OF CURSOR clause to quickly access a row currently open in a cursor. Alternately, fetch and use the ROWID column if you want to avoid the overhead of the FOR UPDATE statement.

❑ Cache frequently accessed data values in PL/SQL tables.

MISCELLANEOUS TOPICS

INTRODUCTION

In previous chapters, we have discussed methods of optimizing SQL operations which are found in commonly occurring SQL. These operations, such as table access, joins and ordering, appear frequently in SQL statements in a wide variety of situations.

In this chapter, we will look at an assortment of specific or unusual SQL statement types and optimization techniques. The topics which we will consider are:

❏ Optimizing SQL statements which include views, and using views to improve the performance of ad hoc queries.

❏ Partitioning tables using Oracle7 partition views or Oracle8 partition tables.

❏ Using snapshots to maintain summary information.

❏ Optimizing snapshot refresh performance.

❏ Optimizing distributed SQL.

❏ Using Oracle sequence numbers.

❏ Using the DECODE statement to avoid multiple table accesses.

❏ Optimizing Data Definition Language statements (DDL).

OPTIMIZING VIEWS

A view can be thought of as a "virtual table" or as a "stored query." A view's definition consists of a standard SQL query. When a view is accessed, the view's query is retrieved and any additional WHERE conditions merged into the final query. For instance, suppose we create a view like this:

```
create view department_summ_view as
select d.department_name,
       count(e.salary) employee_count,
       sum(e.salary)   total_salary
  from departments d,
       employees e
 where e.department_id=d.department_id
 group by d.department_name
```

We can get summary information for a department by issuing the following query:

```
select * from department_summ_view
 where department_name='Database development'
```

Oracle will "push" the WHERE clause from this query into the view definition so that the query that is finally executed will be equivalent to this:

```
select d.department_name,
       count(e.salary) employee_count,
       sum(e.salary)   total_salary
  from departments d,
       employees e
 where e.department_id=d.department_id
   and d.department_name='Database development' ←Added to the view definition
 group by d.department_name
```

When optimizing views, it's most important to optimize the query upon which the view is based. In the case of our example view, we would need to ensure that the join between departments and employees was optimized. In the case of the join in the view, a sort merge or hash join would be appropriate, since all rows in each table participate in the join.

However, when we issue a query against the view which includes some additional selection criteria, the optimal plan for the view changes. For instance, once we query against a particular department using the DEPARTMENT_SUMM_VIEW, the join of choice becomes nested loops and an index on EMPLOYEES.DEPARTMENT_ID becomes desirable.

> **When optimizing a view, consider not only optimizing the query which defines the view but also queries which result from merging of additional selection criteria into the view. Create indexes, histograms or take other means to optimize the queries which are likely to be generated when resolving queries on the review.**

USING HINTS IN VIEWS

Hints can be embedded into a view definition. This can be useful when optimizing the execution of the view and can be useful to influence the performance of SQL over which you have little or no control.

For instance, some client-server development or ad-hoc query tools may generate SQL which is generated dynamically and which can't be amended by the user. We can hope that the cost based optimizer generates effective plans in these cases, but we may find that the SQL generated is performing badly and we don't have the option to use hints. In these circumstances, we could create a view which contains the hint we wish to use and ensure that it is the view which is referenced by the client tool.

> **Embed hints in views to influence SQL generated by third party query or development tools which generate SQL over which you have no control.**

This technique can be particularly valuable where a client tool attempts to join two tables at the client end. For instance, it's easy in many query tools to set up links to multiple tables and join these two tables graphically. Unfortunately, these tools will often fetch all rows separately from the tables and join the rows within the client environment. This will be expensive in terms of network overhead, will disallow the use of Oracle indexes, hash joins, and the superior processing power available on the server. In this case, a view which performs the join will force the processing to remain on the server side, with a very positive impact on performance.

> **Consider creating join views to avoid costly client-side joining of tables in ad hoc query and PC development tools.**

PARTITION VIEWS

A partition view allows you to split a logical table into multiple tables, each of which contains a specific range of data. A *check constraint* ensures that each table contains data only for the appropriate range. The partition view itself is a UNION ALL of each partition table.

A partition view can help performance when a large subset of a table is being accessed. If the proportion of the table being queried is too large to make an index retrieval practical, you may be able to use partition view to avoid a full table scan.

In our sample database, we might be tempted to partition the SALES table in this way. For instance, we could partition the SALES table on calendar years using the following SQL:

```
create table sales1 as
      select * from sales
       where sale_date < '01-JAN-93';

alter table sales1 add (constraint s1_partition_chk
      check (sale_date < '01-JAN-93'));

create table sales2 as
      select * from sales
       where sale_date between '01-JAN-94' and '31-DEC-94';

alter table sales2 add (constraint s2_partition_chk
          check (sale_date between '01-JAN-94' and '31-DEC-94'));

-- Create additional tables for other years

create or replace view partitioned_sales as
  select * from sales1
   union all
  select * from sales2
   union all
  select * from sales3
   union all
  select * from sales4
   union all
  select * from sales5
```

The constraints allow the cost based optimizer to work out which of the component tables need to be accessed to satisfy a query. *Tkprof* output for the following query shows that only the appropriate table is accessed:

```
select sum(sale_value)
  from partitioned_sales
 where sale_date between '01-JAN-96' and '31-JUL-96'
```

```
Rows        Execution Plan
-------     ---------------------------------------------------
      0     SELECT STATEMENT    GOAL: CHOOSE
  23120      SORT (AGGREGATE)
  23120       VIEW OF 'PARTITIONED_SALES'
  23120        UNION-ALL (PARTITION)
  23120         TABLE ACCESS    GOAL: ANALYZED (FULL) OF 'SALES1'
      0          TABLE ACCESS   GOAL: ANALYZED (FULL) OF 'SALES2'
      0          TABLE ACCESS   GOAL: ANALYZED (FULL) OF 'SALES3'
      0          TABLE ACCESS   GOAL: ANALYZED (FULL) OF 'SALES4'
      0          TABLE ACCESS   GOAL: ANALYZED (FULL) OF 'SALES5'
```

Figure 11.1 compares I/O requirements for the above query for the SALES table and the partition view based on SALES. By avoiding the full table scan, the query was able to complete in only a fraction of the time. Where too great a proportion of the table is being scanned to allow for effective indexed retrieval, and a full table scan still requires more I/O than is acceptable, a partition view can be very useful.

Partition views can complicate application logic, however. In the case of our partitioned SALES table, we need to alter our INSERT statements to ensure that the rows are inserted into the appropriate partition. An UPDATE which would result in the row belonging in another partition would fail on a check constraint violation—we would have to DELETE the row and INSERT into a separate partition. You may be able to use synonyms to overcome some of these problems (for instance, creating a synonym CURRENT_SALES which points to the table containing this year's sales).

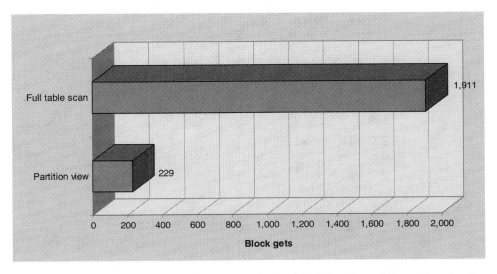

FIGURE 11.1 Comparison of I/O requirements for the SALES table and a partition view based on SALES.

Partition views can be useful if the percentage of rows which you are retrieving is too high to allow an index to be helpful, but you are retrieving substantially less than the entire table. However, partition views can add significantly to application complexity and administrative overheads.

PARTITION TABLES

Oracle8 introduces the partition table. A partition table is similar to a partition view, but instead of multiple tables concatenated by a view, the partition table is a single table in which rows for specific ranges are stored within partitions contained within the table. Unlike the partition view, rows inserted into the table will be directed automatically to the appropriate partition. Like the partitioned view, the cost based optimizer has the option of limiting scans to the relevant partitions only and thus avoiding a costly full table scan. Partition tables, therefore, have the performance advantages of partition views without the INSERT or UPDATE complexities.

We could create a partition table for SALES with a statement such as this:

```
create table sales_partition
      (column definitions for SALES)
      partition by range (sale_date)
      (partition s1 values less than ('01-JAN-93'),
      partition s2 values less than ('01-JAN-94')
       -- Other years
      partition s5 values greater than ('01-JAN-98'));
```

Partition tables have some additional benefits over partition views:

❑ During INSERTs or UPDATEs, rows will be allocated automatically to the appropriate partition.

❑ If a partition gets too large, it can be split into two partitions using an ALTER TABLE statement.

```
alter table sales_partition
      split partition s5
      at ('30-JUN-97')
      into ( partition s5a,
                  partition s5b);
```

❑ You can limit SQL operations to individual partitions using a PARTITION clause:

```
update sales_partition partition(s1)
   set purge_ind='Y'
   where sale_value < 10000
```

❏ DELETE and UPDATE statements can be processed in parallel on partitioned tables.

❏ You can create indexes which span the entire partitioned table (global indexes) or indexes which apply only to a specific partition (local indexes).

Consider Oracle8 partitions to improve scan performance and maintainability of large tables. Use partition tables in preference to partition views.

USING SNAPSHOTS

If views can be considered "stored queries," then snapshots can be considered "stored results." Like a view, a snapshot is based on a query. When a view is accessed, the underlying query is executed. The query underlying a snapshot is executed at regular intervals—perhaps overnight. As a result, snapshots can return results more quickly than a view or a query, but the results returned by a snapshot may not be totally up-to-date.

If it's not essential that a query returns results which are totally up-to-date, then using a snapshot can result in performance improvements over an equivalent query or view. For instance, in our sample database, we may frequently require a sum of sales totals for a particular customer. We might implement this by creating a view:

```
create or replace view sales_by_customer_v as
  select s.customer_id,c.customer_name,sum(s.sale_value)
sale_value
    from sales s ,
         customers c
  where s.customer_id(+)=c.customer_id
  group by s.customer_id,c.customer_name
```

We could query against this view to find details for a particular customer:

```
select *
  from sales_by_customer_v
where customer_id=747
```

This approach is not particularly efficient since it requires a join of CUSTOMER and SALES tables whenever the query is issued. If we don't mind if our query returns results which are not totally up-to-date, we could create a snapshot based on the same query as the view. The snapshot could be refreshed nightly:

```
create snapshot sales_by_customer_snp as
  select s.customer_id,c.customer_name,sum(s.sale_value)
sale_value
    from sales s ,
         customers c
  where s.customer_id(+)=c.customer_id
  group by s.customer_id,c.customer_name
```

Not surprisingly, a query against the snapshot requires much less I/O than the query against the view. The I/O overhead of joining and finding the relevant rows occurred when the snapshot was last refreshed (probably during some off-peak period) and so we don't have to experience that overhead when querying from the snapshot.

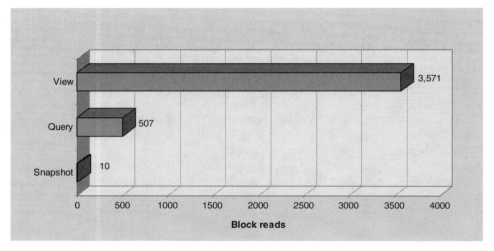

FIGURE 11.2 Obtaining summarized sales information for a customer via a view, an explicit query and a snapshot.

Figure 11.2 illustrates the performance characteristics of a snapshot compared to an equivalently configured view and to an explicit query. In this case, the explicit query outperformed the view because Oracle chose to perform a sort merge join when the view was queried, but used a nested loops join for the explicit query. The snapshot substantially outperformed both the view query and explicit query. If we weren't concerned that the results returned by the view might not be totally current, then using the snapshot would be a good decision.

Consider using snapshots to facilitate complex queries on large tables where the results do not have to be absolutely current.

SNAPSHOT LOGS

Snapshot logs can be used to optimize refreshing of snapshots based on "simple" queries. These "simple" snapshots are based on queries which return every row from the source table without modification (for instance, select * from sales). Once a snapshot log is created, any changes to the source table will be recorded in the log. When it is time to refresh the snapshot, this log can be examined to determine which rows in the snapshot need to be amended.

The use of a snapshot log can slow down DML operations on the source table, since each DML will result in an additional insert into the snapshot log. If there is heavy activity on the source table, contention for inserts into the snapshot log can result. In this case, it may be worthwhile creating the snapshot log with multiple *freelists* (see Chapter 16 for more information on freelists).

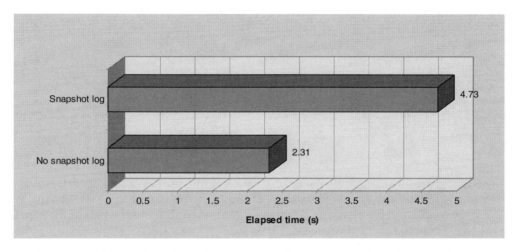

FIGURE 11.3   Effect of creating a snapshot log on update times (1000 updates).

The enhanced performance of the snapshot refresh may justify the diminished UPDATE performance resulting the snapshot log. The key considerations here are:

❑ The higher the DML rate on the source table, the higher the overall overhead of maintaining the snapshot log.

❑ The larger the source table, the greater the incentive for maintaining the snapshot log, since the complete refresh will require a full table scan. On the other hand, creating snapshot logs on small tables is usually not required, since the overhead of a complete refresh will be small.

❏ As the proportion of rows in the source table which need to be refreshed in the snapshot increases, the performance of complete and fast refreshes will converge. If a source table is subject to very high UPDATE activity, or refreshes are scheduled far apart, the performance of the "fast" refresh may be no better than that of the full refresh.

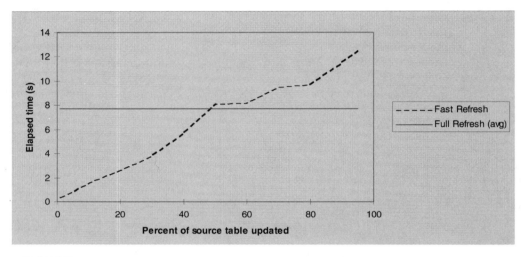

FIGURE 11.4 Performance of complete and fast snapshot refreshes against the percent of the source table which has been updated.

Figure 11.4 compares the performance of full and fast snapshot refreshes plotted against the percentage of rows changed in the parent table. In this example, the complete refresh was more efficient than the full refresh when more than 50% of the source table's rows were altered.

> **Use snapshot logs and the fast refresh mechanism when a minority of rows in the source table are changed. If a majority of rows are changed, avoid the overhead of the snapshot log and use complete refreshes—which will be faster than "fast" refreshes anyway.**

If a source table for a simple snapshot is usually a good candidate for the fast refresh mechanism, but is occasionally subject to bulk loads or complete rebuilds, you can use the following guidelines to avoid the overhead of the fast refresh:

❑ Drop the snapshot log before the bulk load. This will avoid the over-head of inserting rows into the snapshot log.

❑ Consider dropping and recreating the snapshot rather than executing a full refresh. A full refresh will often take longer than a snapshot rebuild because any indexes on the snapshot will have to be updated, which will be slower than rebuilding the indexes after the creation of the snapshot.

DISTRIBUTED SQL

A *distributed* SQL statement is one which accesses tables which reside in more than one Oracle database. Distributed SQL is made possible by Oracle's SQL*NET product, which allows tables located in separate instances of Oracle, possibly on different server computers, to be accessed as if they were local.

You can formulate a distributed query by including a *database link* referencing a foreign database in the WHERE clause:

```
select e.surname, e.employee_id, e.firstname
  from employees@node2 e   ← "node2" refers to a remote database
 where e.surname='SMITH'
   and e.firstname='DAVID'
```

HOW ORACLE PROCESSES DISTRIBUTED SQL

Oracle resolves a distributed query as follows:

❑ If all of the tables exist within the same remote database, then the entire statement is sent to that database for execution.

❑ If tables which are referenced in the distributed SQL exist within multiple databases, then the optimizer will determine an execution plan in much the same way as it would for non-distributed SQL. The optimizer will take into account the available indexes and the cost based optimizer will obtain table statistics for remote tables. The cost based optimizer will also try to estimate the additional network costs involved in a distributed table access, although these estimates may be little better than guesses (the cost based optimizer won't know how fast or how busy network connections to other databases may be).

❏ For each table involved in a multiple database distributed SQL, Oracle will issue SQL to the remote database to retrieve the data. Sorts, joins and other operations will be performed at the site executing the query (the *driving site*).

The execution plan shows that Oracle resolves a simple remote query such as our previous example by sending the entire query to the remote database. The query is optimized by the remote database's optimizer and a result set is passed back to the calling database:

```
select e.surname,e.employee_id,e.firstname
  from employees@node2 e
 where e.surname='SMITH'
   and e.firstname='DAVID'

Rows     Execution Plan
-------  ----------------------------------------------------
      0  SELECT STATEMENT   HINT: CHOOSE (REMOTE) ← Entire SELECT statement is remote
      0    TABLE ACCESS   HINT: ANALYZED (BY ROWID) OF 'EMPLOYEES'
              [NODE2.WORLD]
      0      INDEX   HINT: ANALYZED (RANGE SCAN) OF 'EMPLOYEES_SURNAME'
              (NON-UNIQUE) [NODE2.WORLD]
```

EXPLAINING DISTRIBUTED SQL

When a distributed SQL statement is explained, the plan table will contain some special information:

TABLE 11.1   PLAN_TABLE columns for a distributed SQL statement.

Column Name	Description
OPERATION	If "REMOTE", then this step will be executed at the remote node.
OBJECT_NODE	Contains the identifier of the remote node.
OTHER_TAG	Will contain the tag (SERIAL_FROM_REMOTE) if the OTHER column contains the text of an SQL statement being executed at a remote node.
OTHER	Contains the text of the SQL text executed at the remote site.

These columns aren't always reported by "traditional" queries against the plan table and it's difficult to produce a well-formatted plan using the OTHER column because of the restrictions on LONG columns. *Tkprof* will produce well-formatted EXPLAIN PLANs automatically and the *eplan.sql* and Windows based Xplain tools on the companion disks will also produce suitably formatted output.

PROBLEMS WITH DISTRIBUTED SQL

Distributed SQL presents unique problems for the Oracle optimizer and the SQL programmer. Distributed SQL statements often perform poorly and can be difficult to optimize. Some of the reasons are:

❏ The databases involved in the distributed SQL may have very different performance characteristics. For instance, the version of Oracle or the host configuration (number of CPUs, memory and operating system) may differ. The optimizer may not be able to take all of these factors into account.

❏ Although the cost based optimizer will factor in some network overhead when formulating a distributed execution plan, it has no knowledge of the capacity or utilization of the network between two databases.

❏ Oracle's approach of generating a separate SQL statement for each table participating in a distributed join sometimes results in tables which reside on the same database being joined across the network.

❏ It's harder for the SQL programmer to tune distributed SQL since EXPLAIN PLAN and *tkprof* output will only show the SQL sent to the remote node, not the execution plan at the remote node. In complex cases, it may be necessary to manually obtain execution plans from the remote node using EXPLAIN PLAN.

DISTRIBUTED JOINS

One of the more common distributed SQL operations is the distributed join. The following example illustrates a three-way join involving two remote databases:

```
select
      dp.department_name,e.surname,c.customer_name
  from employees@node2   e,
       departments@node1 dp,
       customers@node2 c
 where dp.department_id=e.department_id
   and c.sales_rep_id=e.employee_id
   and dp.department_name='Database Products'

Rows    Execution Plan
-------  -------------------------------------------------------
      0  SELECT STATEMENT    HINT: CHOOSE
   6646   MERGE JOIN
     66    SORT (JOIN)
     66     NESTED LOOPS
      1      REMOTE [NODE1.WORLD]
               SELECT "DEPARTMENT_ID","DEPARTMENT_NAME" FROM "DEPARTMENTS"
               DP WHERE "DEPARTMENT_NAME"='Database Products'
```

```
    66        REMOTE [NODE2.WORLD]
                 SELECT "EMPLOYEE_ID","SURNAME","DEPARTMENT_ID" FROM
                 "EMPLOYEES" E WHERE :1="DEPARTMENT_ID"
 100000     SORT (JOIN)
 100000     REMOTE [NODE2.WORLD]
                 SELECT "CUSTOMER_NAME","SALES_REP_ID" FROM "CUSTOMERS" C
```

We can interpret this execution plan as follows:

1. Oracle starts by issuing an SQL statement to node1 which will retrieve the department ID for the department "Database Products."

2. For each row returned (only one in this case), Oracle issues an SQL statement to NODE2 to get the employee details for all employees in matching departments using the nested loops join method.

3. Oracle then issues a query to NODE2 to retrieve all customers. The customers are then sort merged with the result set from step 2.

This execution plan is the same as the plan that would be generated if the tables were all local. Oracle accesses table statistics and index details at the remote node and determines that appropriate indexes exist to support a nested loop join.

A potential problem with this approach is Oracle's strategy of performing each table access with a separate SQL statement, even when multiple tables reside on the same node. This strategy can increase the number of requests to the remote node and can lead to tables being joined across the network.

Improving distributed joins with views

If you determine that a distributed query is joining two tables from the same remote database locally and you suspect that the join would be more efficient if performed at the remote site, you can create a view at the remote site which pre-joins the tables involved.

For instance, in the previous example, we joined EMPLOYEES and CUSTOM-ERS locally, even though they were both located on the same remote node. If we create a view which joins the two tables on node2:

```
create view employees_and_customers
  as select  e.surname,e.employee_id,e.firstname,e.department_id,c.customer_name
       from employees e,
            customers c
     where c.sales_rep_id=e.employee_id
```

We can now issue a query which refers to the remote view. This results in the two tables being joined at the remote node:

```
select
       d.department_name,e.surname,e.customer_name
  from employees_and_customers@node2   e,
       departments@node1 d
 where d.department_id=e.department_id
   and d.department_name='Database Products'
```

```
Rows      Execution Plan
-------   -------------------------------------------------------
      0   SELECT STATEMENT   HINT: CHOOSE
   6646     NESTED LOOPS
      1       REMOTE [NODE1.WORLD]
                SELECT "DEPARTMENT_ID","DEPARTMENT_NAME" FROM "DEPARTMENTS" D
                  WHERE "DEPARTMENT_NAME"='Database Products'
   6646       REMOTE [NODE2.WORLD]   ← View is accessed at the remote node
                SELECT "SURNAME","DEPARTMENT_ID","CUSTOMER_NAME" FROM
                  "EMPLOYEES_AND_CUSTOMERS" E WHERE :1="DEPARTMENT_ID"
```

For this example, performing the join at the remote node results in a very substantial performance gain, since otherwise we would have to retrieve all the customer details across the network. In this example, the remote node was also on a more powerful computer, so the SORT operation could be performed more efficiently.

The technique of using a remote view is useful, but will only result in improved performance if the conditions are suitable. In particular, this technique is probably not useful in earlier versions of Oracle (7.1 or earlier). These versions may execute the view remotely without forwarding the WHERE clause, leading to an increased overhead.

Also note that you may not be able to use an *in-line view* to obtain this effect. The in-line view will evaluated locally, not at the remote node.

> **Creating a view of a table join at a remote node can cause the join to be executed at the remote node rather than at the driving site. This may improve performance if conditions are suitable.**

Choosing the best "driving site"

The driving site is the site at which the SQL is optimized and at which non-remote operations such as joins and sorts are performed. The driving site will usually be the site at which the SQL is executed, unless one of the following conditions are true:

❏ If all the tables referenced in the SQL exist on the same remote node, then Oracle will send the entire SQL to the remote node and the remote node will be the driving site. For instance:

```
select  dp.department_name,e.surname
 from employees@node3     e,
      departments@node3 dp
where dp.department_id=e.department_id

Execution Plan:


SELECT STATEMENT REMOTE  ← Entire statement executed remotely
     NESTED LOOPS
       TABLE ACCESS FULL DEPARTMENTS
       TABLE ACCESS BY ROWID EMPLOYEES
       INDEX RANGE SCAN EMPLOYEE_DEPT_ID
```

❏ If you INSERT, UPDATE or DELETE from a remote table, the optimizer may send the query to the remote site for execution. For instance, the following INSERT will be executed from NODE1:

```
insert into junk@node1
 select e.surname,d.department_name
   from employees e,
        departments d
  where e.department_id=d.department_id

  INSERT STATEMENT REMOTE  ← Executed at node1
     MERGE JOIN
       SORT JOIN
         REMOTE(!): SELECT "DEPARTMENT_ID","DEPARTMENT_NAME"
                    FROM "DEPARTMENTS" A2  ← Sent back to the
                                              orginating node
       SORT JOIN
         REMOTE(!): SELECT "SURNAME","DEPARTMENT_ID" FROM "EMPLOYEES" A3
```

❏ An undocumented hint "DRIVING_SITE(*table_alias)*" will cause the driving site to be the node at which the nominated table is located. Use this hint with caution as it has been known to be unstable in some versions of Oracle. The following example shows the effect of the DRIVING_SITE hint:

```
select /*+ driving_site(E) execute the query at node1*/
    dp.department_name,e.surname,c.customer_name
  from employees@node1  E,
       departments@node1 dp,
       customers c
 where dp.department_id=e.department_id
   and e.surname='SMITH'
   and e.firstname='DAVID'
   and c.sales_rep_id=e.employee_id

Execution plan:

  SELECT STATEMENT REMOTE  ← Entire statement sent to remote node
    NESTED LOOPS
      NESTED LOOPS
```

```
      TABLE ACCESS BY ROWID EMPLOYEES
          INDEX RANGE SCAN EMPLOYEES_SURNAME
      TABLE ACCESS BY ROWID DEPARTMENTS
          INDEX UNIQUE SCAN PK_DEPARTMENTS
      REMOTE (!)                      ← Send back to originating node
SELECT "CUSTOMER_NAME","SALES_REP_ID" FROM "CUSTOMERS" A1 WHERE
"SALES_REP_ID"=:1
```

The choice of the driving site for a distributed query can have a tremendous effect on the performance of distributed SQL. Consider the following when deciding on a driving site:

❑ The driving site is usually the site which performs CPU intensive operations such as joins and sorts. Therefore, the driving site will ideally be on the most powerful computer involved in the distributed SQL.

❑ Network overhead is a major factor in the performance of distributed SQL. Therefore, the site with the most local data is a good candidate for the driving site.

❑ Since the driving site performs the query optimization and joins, using the site with the most recent version of Oracle installed may improve performance. For instance, in a distributed join between databases running Oracle 8.0, 7.2 and 7.1, the Oracle8 site would be a good candidate for the driving site since it would have superior optimization facilities and would be able to take advantage of hash joins and other features.

Choose the driving site for your distributed SQL carefully. The ideal driving site is the site with the most powerful processing capabilities with the most local data and the most recent version of Oracle.

Improving distributed queries with snapshots

Earlier in this chapter, we discussed the use of snapshots to improve the performance of complex queries which aren't required to produce information which is absolutely current. While this is a useful and valid utilization of snapshots, snapshots were primarily designed to replicate data across the network and thus affect the performance of distributed queries.

If we query against a snapshot which is based on a remote table, we are avoiding the overhead of network operations and may also get the added advantage of reduced join or sort overheads (if using complex snapshots).

Of course, snapshots are only as current as their most recent refresh. Only use snapshots when obtaining potentially out-of-date information is acceptable.

Using snapshots as an alternative to distributed queries can reduce your query time remarkably. But remember that data returned from snapshot queries may be out-of-date.

Comparison of distributed join performance

Figure 11.5 compares the elapsed time for a distributed join, a distributed join using a remote view and a local join using snapshots. For our example, using a remote view almost halved execution time; but remember that your results may vary—make sure you try alternate approaches. Using local snapshots reduced execution time by 90%. You will almost always realize improvements on distributed joins if you use snapshots, but remember that the improvement is at the possible expense of the accuracy of your results.

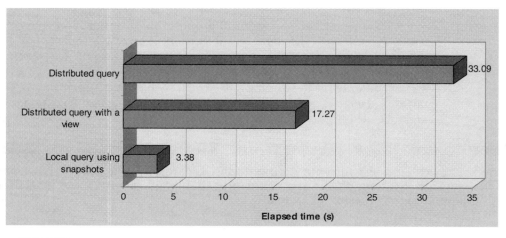

FIGURE 11.5 Comparison of distributed join, distributed join with remote view and local join using snapshots.

SEQUENCES

Sequences (or sequence number generators) efficiently generate unique sequential numbers. Sequences are primarily intended to speed up the process of acquiring a unique primary key value. Obtaining a unique primary key value without a sequence would usually involve selecting the next key value from a sequence number table. The following PL/SQL procedure illustrates the sequence table technique:

```
CREATE or replace procedure get_seq_table(nbr number) as
   cursor get_seq_csr is
           select last_sequence+1
             from sequence_table
               for update;
   i number;
   new_sequence number;
BEGIN
   FOR i in 1..nbr LOOP
      OPEN get_seq_csr;
      FETCH get_seq_csr into new_sequence;
      CLOSE get_seq_csr;
      -- Do something with the sequence
      UPDATE sequence_table
         SET last_sequence=new_sequence;
      -- Commit to release locks
      COMMIT;
   END LOOP;
END;
```

Obtaining a unique key value in this way has the following problems:

❏ The FOR UPDATE clause locks the sequence number table to ensure that no two users get the same sequence number. This can lead to lock contention.

❏ I/O is required to fetch the sequence number, lock the row, UPDATE the row and COMMIT the change. This can become a substantial overhead in a transaction processing environment.

Using a sequence generator avoids most of these overheads. In particular, sequences involve no locks and there is no contention between sessions which are obtaining sequence numbers. However, sequence numbers can only be accessed from within an SQL statement and you may sometimes SELECT a sequence number from the DUAL table, as in the following example:

```
CREATE or replace procedure get_seq_1(nbr number) as
   i number;
   new_sequence number;
      CURSOR get_seq_csr is
          SELECT seq_1.nextval from dual;
BEGIN
   FOR i in 1..nbr LOOP
       OPEN· get_seq_csr;
       FETCH get_seq_csr into new_sequence;
       CLOSE get_seq_csr;
       -- Do something with the sequence number
   END LOOP;
END;
```

Although the accesses of the DUAL table are not in themselves resource intensive, they can add up in a transaction processing environment. You can reduce the impact of these lookups by specifying that the sequence increment by some higher number. For instance, we can define a sequence with increments of 500:

```
create sequence seq_500 increment by 500
```

We are now effectively fetching the sequence number in "batches" of 500 and we can alter our program to fetch a new batch only every 500th number:

```
CREATE or replace procedure get_seq_500(nbr number) as
    i number;
    new_sequence number;
    CURSOR get_seq_csr is
            SELECT seq_500.nextval from dual;
BEGIN
    FOR i in 1..nbr LOOP
        -- every 500 iterations, get a new sequence number
        IF mod(i,500)=0 or i=1 THEN
            OPEN get_seq_csr;
            FETCH get_seq_csr into new_sequence;
            CLOSE get_seq_csr;
        ELSE
            new_sequence:=new_sequence+1;
        END IF;
    END LOOP;
END;
```

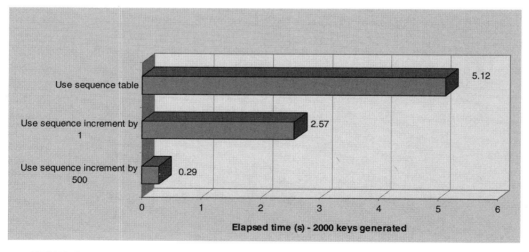

FIGURE 11.6 Time taken to generate 2,000 unique keys using a sequence table, a default sequence generator and a sequence generator with a 500 increment.

Figure 11.6 compares the performance of the sequence number table, a default sequence generator and fetching sequences in batches of 500. The sequence generator outperforms the sequence table and the performance is further enhanced by fetching sequences in batches of 500.

CACHING SEQUENCE NUMBERS

One of the reasons sequence numbers are efficient is that the numbers are cached in Oracle's shared memory area—the *SGA*. By default, 20 sequence numbers are cached. Once the 20 numbers are allocated, Oracle must fetch a further 20 from the database. If sequence numbers are being allocated at a very high rate, you can improve the performance by increasing the cache size when you create the sequence:

```
create sequence seq_cached cache 100
```

The CREATE SEQUENCE command also includes an ORDER clause, which if used, guarantees that sequence numbers will be generated in sequential order. This option is intended for use with the *Oracle Parallel Server* (OPS) option.[1] In a non-OPS system, sequence numbers are always generated in sequential order. Users sometimes specify the ORDER option in the mistaken belief that doing so is necessary to avoid generating sequence numbers in a random order. Specifying ORDER in the CREATE SEQUENCE command can have dire consequences for sequence performance as it effectively disables the sequence cache mechanism. You should not specify the ORDER clause unless you are in a parallel server environment and even then, only if you absolutely require that sequence numbers be generated in sequential order.

When creating sequences, specify a cache value which reflects the frequency with which the sequence will be accessed. Do not specify the ORDER option unless you are in a parallel server environment.

---

[1] Don't confuse parallel server with parallel query. Parallel server is a special version of Oracle used for clustered computers which allows multiple hosts to share a single Oracle instance.

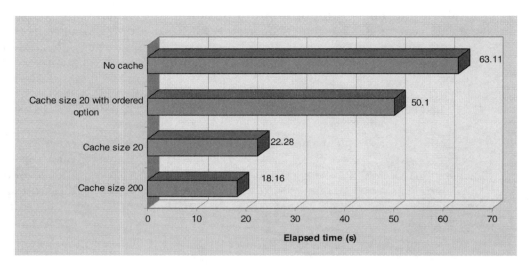

FIGURE 11.7 Effect of the CACHE and ORDER clauses on sequence performance.

"MISSING" SEQUENCE NUMBERS

Although sequences are an efficient way of allocating unique key values, they have one feature which is sometimes regarded as undesirable: sequence numbers can be skipped. Sequence numbers can be skipped in the following circumstances:

❏ A transaction obtains a sequence number, but for some reason the transaction fails and a ROLLBACK is issued. The sequence number issued will not be reallocated.

❏ If the Oracle server fails, then all numbers in the sequence cache will be lost.

❏ If the amount of space reserved for sequence numbers (by the database parameter *SEQUENCE_CACHE_ENTRIES*) in the SGA is insufficient for the sequences in use, the sequence numbers in the cache may be discarded.

Normally the skipping of sequence numbers is inconsequential. After all, the numbers by themselves mean nothing. However, there is sometimes an application requirement that primary key values not be skipped. In this case, if a transaction INSERTing a new row is ROLLBACKed, then the sequence number should be made available to the next transaction. If such a requirement exists, then the use of a sequence generator is not appropriate, and you may be forced to use a sequence table.

Before implementing a sequence table in preference to a sequence generator, try to ensure that the requirement for contiguous number ranges is unavoidable. Using a sequence table will not only increase the I/O overhead of obtaining a sequence number, but could also lead to lock contention for the sequence table in a transaction processing environment. If you must use a sequence table lookup, try to defer locking the sequence table until the last possible stage in your transaction. This will reduce the duration of any locks.

> **Use sequence generators in preference to sequence tables unless there is a definite requirement that no unique key values be skipped. When using a sequence generator, ensure that the CACHE value is appropriate and consider fetching sequence numbers in batches in busy transaction processing environments.**

USING DECODE

The DECODE operator is a powerful but underutilized extension to ANSI standard SQL. DECODE allows an expression to be replaced (or decoded) with an alternate value. In some respects, it's similar to an embedded IF statement.

Decodes are useful when aggregating data based on some complex condition which can't be expressed using standard SQL. Without DECODE, these queries can often only be resolved through multiple table scans.

For example, suppose we wanted to count the number of customers in the under 25, 25-40 and over 40 age groups. Using standard SQL, we would probably issue a query similar to this ("f_age" is a user PL/SQL function which simply returns age in years):

```
select '< 25 ' age,count(*)
  from customers
 where f_age(date_of_birth) <25
 union
 select '25-40' age,count(*)
  from customers
 where f_age(date_of_birth) between 25 and 40
 union
 select '> 40' age,count(*)
  from customers
 where f_age(date_of_birth) >40
```

This example returns the required rows, but requires three table scans to do so. If we increase the number of categories, we will require more scans and performance will degrade further.

Using the DECODE and SIGN operators, we can retrieve the same results with a single scan of the CUSTOMERS table:

```
select  sum(decode(sign(f_age(date_of_birth)-25),-1,1,0)) under_25,
        sum(decode(sign(f_age(date_of_birth)-25),-1,0,
                   decode(sign(f_age(date_of_birth)-40),-1,1,0)))
                   "25_to_40",
        sum(decode(sign(f_age(date_of_birth)-40),1,1,0)) over_40
from customers
```

The SQL is somewhat more complex. Let's consider each nesting of functions in the first expression (the under 25 expression):

❏ The f_age variable returns the age of the customer in years. By subtracting 25 from that age, we return a negative number if the customer is under 25.

❏ The SIGN function returns "-1" if its argument is less than "0" and "1" if the argument is greater than "0."

❏ The DECODE function returns "1" if the SIGN returns "-1" and "0" otherwise. In other words, the DECODE function returns "1" if the customer is under 25 and "0" otherwise.

❏ The sum function adds the results of the decode function. Since the decode returned "1" only if the customer is under 25, the sum function returns the number of customers under 25.

A similar technique was employed to count customers between 25 and 40. Two decodes were used: one to test if the customer was under 25 and one to test if the customer was over 40. If neither test succeeded, then a "1" was returned by the DECODE.

Not surprisingly, using the DECODE required only a third of the block reads required by the UNION solution. If the number of categories was increased, the difference would have been even more marked.

Consider using DECODE to compile aggregate statistics for expressions which are too complex for a GROUP BY clause. You can aggregate ranges by using the SIGN function.

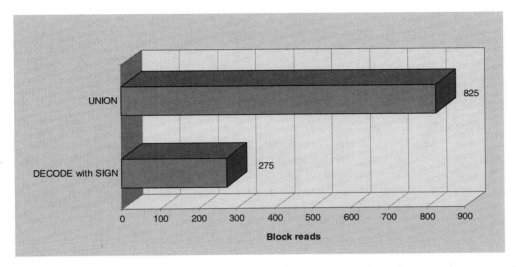

FIGURE 11.8 Aggregating CUSTOMERS using a UNION query compared with the use of DECODE and SIGN.

DATA DEFINITION LANGUAGE

Data Definition Language (DDL) is the component of SQL which allows you to CREATE, ALTER or DROP schema objects (tables, views, indexes, etc.). Generally, we create schema objects once only and don't need to be too concerned about execution time. In any case, schema objects which are created as empty objects usually don't take too long to create.

However, there are times the performance of DDL can be very important:

❏ When you CREATE a table as a query, perhaps for temporary processing or in order to rebuild the table to improve table scan performance.

❏ When you CREATE an index, perhaps to enhance the performance of a query.

❏ When you REBUILD an index to improve storage.

The options for improving the performance of these operations are to:

❏ Take advantage of Oracle parallel processing capabilities.

❏ Take advantage of UNRECOVERABLE and no-logging options.

❏ Use the REBUILD clause of the ALTER INDEX statement.

THE UNRECOVERABLE OPTION

The CREATE TABLE statement allows a table to be CREATEd from a query. This can be used to CREATE a temporary table as a subset of the source table, to CREATE a new permanent table for some purpose or to REBUILD the source table to improve scan performance or to change storage characteristics.

The query used to create the new table should be tuned using the principles outlined earlier. That is, to optimize table accesses, joins, sorts and other mechanisms.

Oracle provides a special keyword which can be used to improve the performance of the CREATE TABLE AS SELECT statement. The UNRECOVERABLE clause instructs Oracle not to create *redo log* entries for the new table. This can significantly improve the performance of the table creation. However, in the event that the database is recovered from a backup taken *before* the table was created and rolled forward using archived redo logs, then the new table will not be recovered. The table will be included in any subsequent backups.

You can also use the UNRECOVERABLE option when creating an index.

Consider using the UNRECOVERABLE option when creating temporary tables or indexes. Be aware that objects created with the UNRECOVERABLE option will not be restorable until they are included in a backup.

THE INDEX REBUILD OPTION

The REBUILD clause of the ALTER INDEX statement allows an index to be rebuilt using the index itself as the source of data. This is substantially faster than using the table as the source of data since the index is smaller and the data is already presorted.

PARALLEL OPTIONS

Indexes and tables created with subqueries can take advantage of Oracle's parallel processing capabilities. Using parallel DDL can result in tremendous performance improvements if the prerequisites are met. Using the unrecoverable and parallel options together can result in even faster index of table builds. Parallel DDL is discussed in detail in Chapter 12.

CHAPTER SUMMARY

In this chapter, we've looked at some miscellaneous techniques for improving SQL performance.

❏ Optimizing the performance of views involves optimizing the SQL statement upon which the view is based and also the SQL which is likely to result when selection criteria are "pushed up" into the view.

❏ Creating views which contain hints can be a useful technique for optimizing ad hoc queries and SQL generated by query tools.

❏ In Oracle7, partition views can be created which reduce the overhead of scanning a substantive range of large tables. In Oracle8, the partition table provides the same functionality but with reduced administration overhead and additional functionality.

❏ Snapshots can be used to store the results of complex queries and allow the rapid retrieval of results which may, however, be somewhat out-of-date.

❏ The performance of simple snapshot refreshes is improved by the creation of a snapshot log providing that only a small proportion of the source table has been changed.

❏ Distributed SQL can require careful optimization. The choice of the driving site can have a big influence on overall performance. Views can be useful to encourage tables at remote sites to be joined on their home host rather than at the driving site. Snapshots can reduce the overhead of SQL dramatically for static tables.

❏ Oracle sequences are an efficient mechanism of generating primary key values and should be used in preference to sequence tables or other mechanisms. The performance of sequences can be improved by setting an appropriate cache value and by fetching sequences in batches.

❏ The DECODE operator can be used to perform complex aggregations which might otherwise need to be performed via multiple queries.

❏ Oracle provides special facilities to enhance the creation of tables and indexes. The UNRECOVERABLE option can be used to suppress the logging of the CREATE INDEX and CREATE TABLE AS SELECT operations. Parallel processing can also be employed for these statement types. Existing indexes can be rebuilt efficiently using the REBUILD option.

PARALLEL SQL

In this chapter, we will consider the use of Oracle's parallel capabilities to improve the performance of your SQL statements.

In a *serial* (i.e., non-parallel) execution environment, the operations required to act upon your SQL statement are undertaken by a single *process* and each action must complete before the succeeding action can commence. This single process may only leverage the power of a single CPU and, because most modern hardware platforms include more than a single *CPU*, serial SQL execution is unable to take advantage of all of the available processing power.

Parallel processing allows SQL execution to be broken down into multiple tasks, each of which can be undertaken by a different process. Each of these processes can use a different CPU and so can make more effective use of computer resources.

Parallel processing can improve the performance of suitable SQL statements to a degree which is often not possible by any other method. However, not all SQL statements can use parallel processing and not all application environments are suitable.

In this chapter, we'll see how parallel SQL works, the circumstances under which parallel SQL can or should be used and ways of getting the greatest benefit from this powerful facility. The topics we'll cover include:

❑ How parallel SQL works.

❑ The performance improvements which can be achieved.

❑ When to use parallel SQL.

❑ How to use parallel SQL.

❑ Explaining and optimizing parallel SQL.

❑ Examples of parallel queries.

❑ Using parallel DML and parallel DDL.

UNDERSTANDING PARALLEL SQL

Parallel processing allows SQL execution to be divided into a number of separate tasks. Each of these tasks can be executed at the same time—in parallel—allowing full use of multiple CPUs available on mid-range and high-end computers.

For example, consider executing the following statement:

```
SELECT CONTACT_SURNAME,CONTACT_FIRSTNAME,DATE_OF_BIRTH,
       PHONENO
  FROM CUSTOMERS C1
ORDER BY CONTACT_SURNAME,CONTACT_FIRSTNAME,DATE_OF_BIRTH
```

If executing without the parallel query option, a single process would be responsible for fetching all the rows in the CUSTOMERS table. The same process would be responsible for sorting the rows to satisfy the ORDER BY clause.

Process A

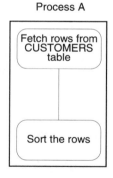

FIGURE 12.1   Serial execution of an SQL statement.

We can request that Oracle execute this statement in parallel, in this case by using a hint:

```
SELECT /*+ PARALLEL(C1,2)  */
       CONTACT_SURNAME,CONTACT_FIRSTNAME,DATE_OF_BIRTH,PHONENO
  FROM CUSTOMERS C1
 ORDER BY CONTACT_SURNAME,CONTACT_FIRSTNAME,DATE_OF_BIRTH
```

If parallel processing is available, the statement will now be executed by two streams in parallel. Further, the fetch component and the sort component will be executed by separate processes. A total of five processes will now be involved in the query, as shown in Figure 12.2.

WHAT SORT OF STATEMENTS CAN BE PARALLELIZED?

Parallel processing is only available to SQL statements which process an entire table or partition. These statements include:

❏ SQL queries which contain at least one full table scan.

❏ Building or rebuilding an index.

❏ Creating a table from a SELECT statement, providing that the SELECT statement performs a full table scan.

❏ An UPDATE or DELETE statement which is based on a full table scan of a partitioned table (in Oracle8 only).

❏ An INSERT into a partitioned table based on a parallel subquery (in Oracle8).

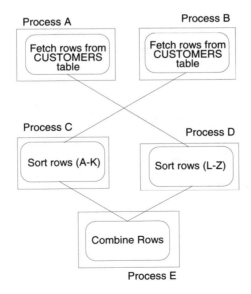

FIGURE 12.2   Parallel processing of an SQL statement.

WHAT SORT OF PERFORMANCE IMPROVEMENTS CAN BE ACHIEVED?

The performance improvements which you can expect to obtain from parallel SQL depends on the suitability of your host computer, Oracle configuration and SQL statement. If all the conditions for parallel processing are met, you can expect to get performance improvements in line with the *degree of parallelism* (the number of concurrent streams of processing). For instance, if your degree of parallelism is three and all preconditions for parallel processing are met, then you could expect that your SQL statement might run up to three times faster.

Figure 12.3 shows the improvement gains obtained by increasing the degree of parallelism for a statement performing a full table scan. The host computer was configured with eight CPUs and a high performance disk array. The performance improvements gained for initial degrees of parallelism were very substantial. As the degree of parallelism was increased, performance improvements diminished and no real improvement was obtained once the degree of parallelism exceeded the number of CPUs.

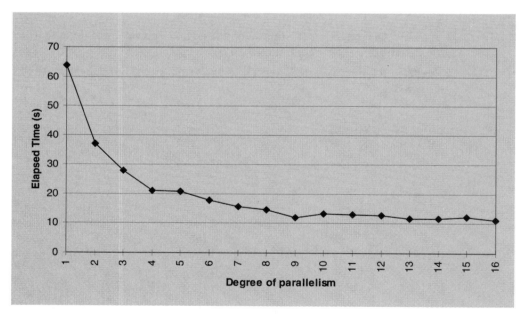

FIGURE 12.3   Performance improvements gained with various degrees of parallelism.

WHEN TO USE PARALLEL PROCESSING

Here are some of the circumstances under which you can effectively use parallel SQL:

Your server computer has multiple CPUs

Parallel processing will usually be most effective if the computer which hosts your Oracle database has multiple CPUs. This is because most operations performed by the Oracle server (accessing the Oracle shared memory, performing sorts, disk accesses) require CPU. If the host computer has only one CPU, then the parallel processes may contend for this CPU and performance might actually decrease.

The data to be accessed is on multiple disk drives

Many SQL statements can be resolved with few or no disk accesses due to Oracle's *buffer cache* in the SGA shared memory area. However, full table scans of larger tables—a typical operation to be parallelized—will tend to require significant physical disk reads. If the data to be accessed resides on a single disk, then the parallel processes will tend to line up for this disk and the advantages of parallel processing might not be realized.

It's usually up to your DBA to ensure that the data files which comprise your database are located across multiple devices, either by operating system *striping* or by manual creation of files across the devices. Guidelines for striping are contained in Chapter 15. Striping data files across multiple devices will also generally improve the performance of serial SQL in a multi-user environment, since it will reduce the likelihood of a disk bottleneck.

The SQL to be parallelized is long running or resource intensive

Parallel SQL suits long running or resource intensive statements. This is because:

❏ Parallel SQL must be based on a table scan.
❏ Scans of smaller tables can probably be done efficiently by a single process.
❏ There can be an overhead in activating and coordinating the multiple parallel query processes.

Parallel processing is typically used for:

❏ Long-running reports.
❏ Bulk updates of large tables.
❏ Building or rebuilding indexes on large tables.
❏ Creating temporary tables for analytical processing.
❏ Rebuilding a table to improve performance or to purge unwanted rows.

Parallel processing is not usually suitable for transaction processing environments. In these environments, large numbers of users process transactions at a high rate. Full use of available CPUs is already achieved because each concurrent transaction can use a different CPU. Implementing parallel processing might actually degrade overall performance by allowing a single user to monopolize multiple CPUs. In these environments, parallel processing would usually be limited to MIS reporting, bulk loads, index or table rebuilds which would occur at off-peak periods.

The SQL performs at least one full table or partition scan

Parallel processing is only available when an entire table or partition is being processed. For parallel queries, this implies a full table scan, although not *every* table in the query needs to be accessed via a table scan. For instance, a nested loops join which uses an index to join two tables can be fully parallelized providing that the driving table is accessed in parallel.

There is spare capacity on your host

You are not likely to realize the full gains of parallel processing if your server is at full capacity. Parallel processing works well for a single job on an underutilized, multi-CPU machine. If all CPUs on the machine are busy, then your parallel processes will bottleneck on the CPU and performance will be degraded.

THE DEGREE OF PARALLELISM

The *degree of parallelism* defines the number of streams of execution which will be performed in parallel. In the simplest case, this translates to the number of parallel slave processes enlisted to support your SQL's execution. However, the number of parallel processes might actually be twice the degree of parallelism for a multi-stage operation.

Figure 12.4 shows how parallel slaves are allocated for a degree of parallelism of two. For very simple statements, the degree of parallelism controls how many parallel slave processes are allocated. Most statements will consist of more than simply a full table scan, and for these statements, Oracle will allocate a second set of parallel processes. For instance, if the statement includes an ORDER BY and a GROUP BY, then three sets of parallel processes are required—but because Oracle reuses the first set of parallel processes to perform the order by sort, only four parallel processes in total are utilized. Because Oracle reuses the parallel slaves within a statement, the number of parallel slaves allocated should never be more than twice the degree of parallelism.

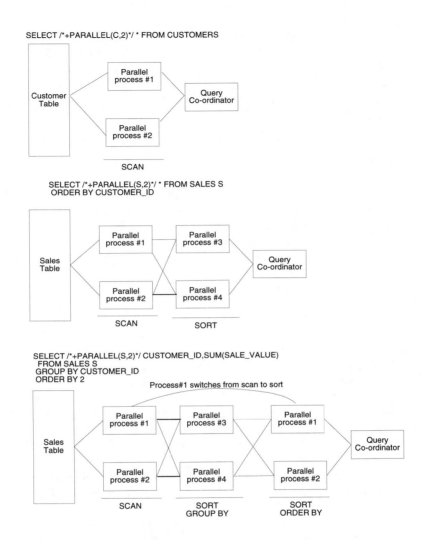

FIGURE 12.4 How processes are allocated for a given degree of parallelism. Note that the number of processes is never more than twice the degree of parallelism (plus the query co-ordinator).

THE DEFAULT DEGREE OF PARALLELISM

The default degree of parallelism, which is used if no explicit degree of parallelism is specified in the PARALLEL hint or table clause, is the number of CPUs available or the number of disk devices upon which the table is stored, whichever is smaller.

Prior to Oracle 7.3, the default degree of parallelism for a table was the number of blocks of the table divided by the database parameter PARALLEL_DEFAULT_SCANSIZE, but limited by PARALLEL_DEFAULT_MAX _SCANS. Thus the larger a table was, the greater the number of query slaves which would be allocated. This approach often led to inappropriate parallelism and relied on the default degree of parallelism, which is not recommended prior to Oracle 7.3.

THE QUERY COORDINATOR

A *query coordinator* process is required whenever any SQL statement—including statements other than queries—is to be processed in parallel. The query coordinator invokes the parallel slaves and is the ultimate recipient of the output of parallel operations. In most environments, the query coordinator is simply the Oracle process which executed the SQL, sometimes called the *server* or *shadow process*. As a result, it is not usually necessary for Oracle to create an additional process to serve as the query coordinator.

THE PARALLEL SLAVE "POOL"

The Oracle server maintains a "pool" of parallel slave processes available for parallel operations. Database configuration parameters determine the initial and maximum size of the pool. If insufficient slaves are currently active but the pool has not reached its maximum value, then Oracle will create more slaves. After a configurable period of inactivity, slave processes will shut down until the pool is again at its minimum size. The configuration parameters controlling the size of the pool are discussed in Appendix D.

If there are insufficient query processes to satisfy the degree of parallelism required by your statement, one of the following outcomes will result:

❏ If there are some parallel query slaves available, but less than requested by your SQL statement, your statement may run at a reduced degree of parallelism.

❏ If there are no parallel query slaves available, your statement will run serially.

❏ Under specific circumstances, you may get an error. This will only occur if the database parameter PARALLEL_MIN_PERCENT has been set to a value which is higher than the percentage of required slaves which are available. For instance, if your query required 8 and only 5 were available (5/8=62%), then your query would execute in parallel if PARALLEL_MIN_PERCENT was below 62. If

PARALLEL_MIN_PERCENT was above 62, your statement would terminate with an error.

PARTITIONING A TABLE FOR THE SLAVE PROCESSES

For all parallel operations, Oracle must split a table or result set into multiple sets of data in order to parallelize each step of a parallel operation.

In the case of a full table scan, Oracle would allocate contiguous sets of blocks to each slave process.

In the case of sort operations, contiguous blocks of sort keys will be allocated to each slave process. For instance, one slave may be assigned to all rows with sort keys starting between A and L, the other slave allocated the sort keys between M and Z.

PARALLEL QUERY OPTION

The parallel query option is the most frequently used of Oracle's parallel facilities. Parallel query option allows a SELECT statement which includes a full table scan to be executed in parallel.

Because the parallel query option is so central to Oracle's parallel strategy, we'll examine parallel query in particular detail. Many parallel query principles also apply to other parallel facilities, such as parallel DML and parallel DDL.

ENABLING PARALLEL QUERY

The parallel query option is invoked if the SQL statement includes a PARALLEL hint or if the PARALLEL clause has been associated with the table definition. In addition, the table to which the PARALLEL clause has been applied must be accessed via a full table scan.

The PARALLEL table clause

The PARALLEL clause of the CREATE or ALTER TABLE statement specifies the default degree of parallelism for the table. The default is NOPARALLEL, which means that the parallel query option will not be invoked unless a PARALLEL hint is used.

For example:

```
ALTER TABLE SALES PARALLEL(DEFAULT)
```

specifies that full table scans of SALES should use the parallel query option with the default degree of parallelism.

```
ALTER TABLE SALES PARALLEL(DEGREE 4)
```

specifies that full table scans of SALES should use the parallel option with four degrees of parallelism.

```
ALTER TABLE SALES NOPARALLEL
```

specifies that full table scans of SALES should not use the parallel query option unless instructed to do so with the PARALLEL hint. This is the default setting.

The PARALLEL hint

The PARALLEL hint instructs the optimizer to use the parallel query option for the nominated table. It takes the form:

```
/*+ PARALLEL(table_name_or_alias[,degree_of_parallelism]) */
```

The hint specifies the table to be processed in parallel and the degree of parallelism to be applied. If no degree of parallelism is specified, then the default degree of parallelism (see above) will be applied. Remember that, as with all hints, if the SQL statement refers to an alias, then it should refer to the same alias in the PARALLEL hint.

Note that although the PARALLEL hint specifies that a table access should be parallel, using it does not guarantee that other operations—such as joins—will be parallelized. Also remember that the PARALLEL hint will be ignored if the table is being processed using an access method other than a full table scan. In some cases, you may wish to force a full table scan using the FULL hint so that parallel execution can occur.

EXPLAINING A PARALLEL SQL STATEMENT

When a parallel SQL statement is EXPLAINED, the OTHER_TAG column of the PLAN_TABLE can be used to determine which of the steps is executed in parallel. Table 12.1 shows the values of the OTHER_TAG column which applies to parallel queries.

The OTHER_TAG column is only available in Oracle7.3. Traditional EXPLAIN queries and some tools which execute EXPLAIN PLANS (including earlier versions of *tkprof*) do not make good use of this column. The *eplan.sql* script and the Xplain tool on the companion disk can be used to produce a well-formatted parallel plan.

TABLE 12.1   Values of the OTHER_TAG column in the PLAN_TABLE.

Value for OTHER_TAG	Meaning
SERIAL (or blank)	The step was executed serially without any parallel processing.
PARALLEL_TO_PARALLEL	This tag denotes parallel processing which passes results to a second set of parallel processes. For instance, a parallel table scan may have passed results to a parallel sort.
PARALLEL_TO_SERIAL	This is the top level of a parallel query. The results were fed in parallel to the query co-ordinator.
PARALLEL_COMBINED_WITH_PARENT PARALLEL_COMBINED_WITH_CHILD	The step was executed in parallel. Either the parent step or the child step was also executed in parallel by the same process. For instance, in a parallel nested loops join, the parallel query process scanned the driving table and also issued index lookups on the joined table.
PARALLEL_FROM_SERIAL	A serial operation which passed results to a set of parallel processes. The presence of this tag indicated a serial bottleneck within a parallel statement, since it suggested that parallel processing might wait on serial processing.

> **Use the OTHER_TAG column of the PLAN_TABLE to determine the parallelism of each step in your SQL. Explain your SQL using a tool which makes good use of this column. Beware of the PARALLEL_FROM_SERIAL tag which may point to a serial bottleneck.**

The OTHER column of the PLAN_TABLE contains the SQL executed by the parallel slave. For the full table scan step, this SQL will show the breakup of the table into parallel partitions. For instance, the following *tkprof* sample uses the OTHER column to show the CUSTOMER table being partitioned by ROWID ranges:

```
TABLE ACCESS   HINT: ANALYZED (FULL) OF 'CUSTOMERS' [:Q33000]
    SELECT /*+ ROWID(A1)*/ A1."CONTACT_SURNAME" C0,
  A1."CONTACT_FIRSTNAME" C1,A1."DATE_OF_BIRTH" C2,A1."PHONENO"
     C3 FROM "CUSTOMERS" A1 WHERE ROWID BETWEEN :1 AND :2
```

For a parallel query, the OBJECT_NODE column contains a tag for the result sets which are output by the parallel query. For instance, in the above *tkprof* sample, the value of the OBJECT_NODE column was :Q33000. The next step of the EXPLAIN PLAN shows the output from that scan step being sorted in parallel:

```
SORT (ORDER BY) [:Q33001]
    SELECT A1.C0 C0,A1.C1 C1,A1.C2 C2,A1.C3 C3 FROM :Q33000 A1 ORDER
      BY A1.C0,A1.C1,A1.C2
```

The contents of the OTHER column can be useful when trying to understand how parallel query works in general, but is of limited use when trying to tune specific queries. The OBJECT_NODE column is more useful, because it can reveal which steps are being executed by the same set of parallel query processes. For instance, in the next execution plan, we can see from the OBJECT_NODE that the sort and sort merge operations are executed by the same set of processes:

```
SELECT STATEMENT
    SORT ORDER BY (PARALLEL_TO_SERIAL) :Q193003
      MERGE JOIN (PARALLEL_TO_PARALLEL) :Q193002
        SORT JOIN (PARALLEL_COMBINED_WITH_PARENT) :Q193002
          TABLE ACCESS FULL SALES (PARALLEL_TO_PARALLEL) :Q193000
        SORT JOIN (PARALLEL_COMBINED_WITH_PARENT) :Q193002
          TABLE ACCESS FULL CUSTOMERS (PARALLEL_TO_PARALLEL) :Q193001
```

TUNING PARALLEL QUERY OPTION

Obtaining the best results often requires careful tuning of SQL statements and database server configuration and the appropriate use of parallelism. To ensure that your parallel SQL is fully tuned, you should:

❏ Tune the Oracle server for parallel SQL.

❏ Use parallel query only when appropriate.

❏ Set an appropriate degree of parallelism.

❏ Analyze your tables.

❏ Ensure that all steps in a complex query are being executed in parallel.

❏ Use query techniques which favor parallelism, such as hash joins.

❏ Optimize your tables for parallel opertaions.

Tuning the Oracle server for parallelism

Unlike most of the tuning techniques outlined previously, the parallel query option can be completely ineffective unless your Oracle server is appropriately configured. Follow the guidelines for configuring the server contained in Chapter 15 and in Appendix D. In particular:

❏ Your database should be configured to support an appropriate number of parallel slave processes.

❏ The data files which comprise your database should be spread across multiple disk devices. This can be done either by operating system striping or through the manual distribution of data files.

> **Configure your database for parallel query. Ensure that your data is spread across multiple disk devices and that there are sufficient slave processes configured.**

Use parallel query option appropriately

The parallel query execution can consume many times the resources of serial query execution. If using the parallel query option doesn't result in a proportionate performance gain, then you may have consumed resources needlessly—resources which may have been required by other users. Avoid using the parallel query option if any of the following are true:

❏ The host computer has only a single CPU or the data to be accessed is not spread over multiple disk devices. You probably won't get a performance gain in these circumstances.

❏ The computer is near full capacity and there are other users competing for resources. If you use parallel query in these circumstances, you may improve your performance marginally, but substantially degrade performance for other users.

> **Don't use parallel query if your host computer is not suitably configured or if you are liable to severely degrade the performance of other users.**

Setting a suitable degree of parallelism

The degree of parallelism determines the resources which will be assigned to your query and thus has a predominate effect on parallel query performance.

Oracle automatically sets the degree of parallelism to either the number of CPUs available on the host computer or the number of disks used to store the table, whichever is smaller. This approach is a good starting point if the query is to be the only significant statement executing within the database.

You may with to change the degree of parallelism if:

❏ You have more disks than CPUs and don't believe that the operation will become CPU bound. In this case, you may wish to set the degree of parallelism to the number of disks.

❏ You want to limit the resources used by your query. If other SQL statements are executing concurrently on your server, it may be considerate to avoid using 100% of CPU resources. In this case, you might want to set the degree of parallelism to less than the number of CPUs.

❏ Earlier versions of Oracle (prior to 7.3) were unable to determine the number of disks used to store a table. They would instead calculate the degree of parallelism from the size of the table and the configuration parameter PARALLEL_DEFAULT_SCANSIZE. In these versions of Oracle, you probably should explicitly set the degree of parallelism using the PARALLEL hint or table clause.

Set a degree of parallelism for your query which will maximize your throughput without having an unacceptable impact on other users.

Analyze your tables

As with most operations which require the cost based optimizer, parallel query execution is very sensitive to table and index statistics generated by the ANALYZE command. The parallel query option option is especially sensitive because it will use table statistics when partitioning blocks for the slave processes involved in full table scans.

Use the ANALYZE command regularly on tables involved in parallel query.

Ensure that all steps in a complex query are being executed in parallel

In a complex parallel SQL statement, it's important to ensure that all significant steps in the query execution are implemented in parallel. If one of the steps in a complex query is performed in serial, then the other parallel steps may have to wait for the serial step to complete and the advantages of parallelism will be lost. The OTHER_TAG column of the PLAN_TABLE will indicate such a step with the PARALLEL_FROM_SERIAL tag.

For instance, in the following query, the SALES table is accessed in parallel but the CUSTOMERS table is accessed in serial. The serial full scan of customers might ruin the overall performance of the query.

```
SELECT STATEMENT
    SORT ORDER BY(PARALLEL_TO_SERIAL)
      HASH JOIN(PARALLEL_TO_PARALLEL)
        TABLE ACCESS FULL SALES(PARALLEL_TO_PARALLEL)      ← Parallel
        TABLE ACCESS FULL CUSTOMERS(PARALLEL_FROM_SERIAL) ← Serial
```

In complex queries, try to parallelize all query execution steps. Use the OTHER_TAG column of the plan table to highlight execution steps which are processed serially.

Using approaches which favor parallelism

Certain operations work particularly well with parallel query. Facilities which work well with parallel execution are:

- ❑ Bitmapped indexes.
- ❑ STAR joins.
- ❑ Hash joins.
- ❑ Anti-joins using the AJ_HASH or AJ_MERGE hint.
- ❑ Partition views and partitioned tables.

> **When using parallel query, try to use operations which work well with parallel query such as hash joins, partitioning, anti-joins, STAR joins and bitmap indexes.**

Optimizing your tables for parallelism

If it is intended that a table will be accessed primarily through parallel operations, you can optimize that table for parallel access:

- ❏ Use the PARALLEL clause in a CREATE or ALTER TABLE statement to ensure that the table is accessed in parallel by default.
- ❏ Consider using partition views or partition tables to improve the performance of scans which access a large subset of table rows.
- ❏ Spread the table across multiple disk devices. Ensure that your DBA has tablespaces which are spread across multiple disks and use these for tables to be accessed in parallel.
- ❏ Optimize your table for table scans, since parallel operations are based on full table access. Use the guidelines outlined in Chapter 6, such as setting PCTFREE/PCTUSED effectively, relocating LONG columns and using the CACHE hint.

> **Optimize your tables for parallel query by optimizing them for table scans, considering partition views or partitioned tables and striping the tables across multiple devices.**

EXAMPLES OF PARALLEL QUERIES

In the following examples, we will see how to make effective use of parallel queries for a range of query types. We'll see how to use hints to invoke parallel query, how to avoid serial bottlenecks in our query and how to indicate which operations can be parallelized.

In the examples which follow, the tables have been created with the default option of NOPARALLEL. The default degree of parallelism is used throughout.

PARALLEL NESTED LOOPS JOIN

Because a nested loops join usually involves an index, it may at first seem surprising that it can be executed in parallel. However, providing that the driving table is based on a parallel full table scan, the index lookups will be performed in parallel by the same processes which perform the full table scan.

The following statement and EXPLAIN PLAN shows a parallel nested loops join between SALES and CUSTOMERS:

```
select /*+ ordered use_nl(c) parallel(s)*/
       c.customer_name,s.sale_date,s.sale_value
  from  sales s,customers c
 where c.customer_id=s.customer_id
   and s.sale_date > sysdate-365
 order by c.customer_name,s.sale_date

Explain Plan:

SELECT STATEMENT
    SORT ORDER BY(PARALLEL_TO_SERIAL)
       NESTED LOOPS(PARALLEL_TO_PARALLEL)    ← Nested loops in parallel
          TABLE ACCESS FULL SALES(PARALLEL_COMBINED_WITH_PARENT)
          TABLE ACCESS BY ROWID CUSTOMERS(PARALLEL_COMBINED_WITH_PARENT)
             INDEX RANGE SCAN PK_CUSTOMERS(PARALLEL_COMBINED_WITH_PARENT)
```

The EXPLAIN PLAN shows us that the nested loops was executed in parallel. The SALES table was scanned in parallel and the processes which scanned SALES also performed index lookups on CUSTOMERS. We can tell that the same processes were involved because of the PARALLEL_COMBINED_WITH_PARENT tag.

A second set of parallel processes sorted the joined rows in order to satisfy the ORDER BY clause.

HASH JOIN

The hash join is very well suited to parallel execution. Providing both tables in the hash join are accessed via a parallel full table scan, then parallelism through the entire join is achieved:

```
select /*+parallel(s) parallel(c)*/
       c.customer_name,s.sale_date,s.sale_value
  from customers c, sales s
 where c.customer_id=s.customer_id
   and s.sale_date > sysdate-365
 order by c.customer_name,s.sale_date

Explain Plan:
```

```
SELECT STATEMENT
   SORT ORDER BY(PARALLEL_TO_SERIAL)
      HASH JOIN(PARALLEL_TO_PARALLEL)
         TABLE ACCESS FULL SALES(PARALLEL_TO_PARALLEL)
         TABLE ACCESS FULL CUSTOMERS(PARALLEL_TO_PARALLEL)
```

However, if only one of the tables in scanned in parallelism, then the PARALLEL_FROM_SERIAL tag indicates a potential bottleneck:

```
select /*+parallel(s)*/
       c.customer_name,s.sale_date,s.sale_value
  from customers c, sales s
 where c.customer_id=s.customer_id
   and s.sale_date > sysdate-365
 order by c.customer_name,s.sale_date
```

Explain Plan:

```
SELECT STATEMENT
   SORT ORDER BY(PARALLEL_TO_SERIAL)
     HASH JOIN(PARALLEL_TO_PARALLEL)
       TABLE ACCESS FULL SALES(PARALLEL_TO_PARALLEL)
       TABLE ACCESS FULL CUSTOMERS(PARALLEL_FROM_SERIAL) ← Serial operation
```

SORT MERGE JOIN

Sort merge joins are also well suited to parallel execution. Providing all of the tables joined are scanned in parallel, then the entire join will proceed in parallel:

```
select /*+ ordered use_merge(c) parallel(s) parallel(c)*/
       c.customer_name,s.sale_date,s.sale_value
  from  sales s,customers c
 where c.customer_id=s.customer_id
   and s.sale_date > sysdate-365
 order by c.customer_name,s.sale_date


Explain Plan:

Optimizer mode: ANALYZED
Optimizer mode: CHOOSE
  SELECT STATEMENT
    SORT ORDER BY(PARALLEL_TO_SERIAL)
      MERGE JOIN(PARALLEL_TO_PARALLEL)
        SORT JOIN(PARALLEL_COMBINED_WITH_PARENT)
          TABLE ACCESS FULL SALES(PARALLEL_TO_PARALLEL)
        SORT JOIN(PARALLEL_COMBINED_WITH_PARENT)
          TABLE ACCESS FULL CUSTOMERS(PARALLEL_TO_PARALLEL)
```

The SALES and CUSTOMERS tables are scanned and sorted in parallel. The parallel sort processes are also responsible for performing the merge. The merged rows are then sorted in parallel.

It's important to ensure that both tables in the sort merge are parallelized. If only one table is parallelized, then the overall parallelism for the statement will be diminished—as we saw in the previous hash join example.

ANTI-JOIN

If we add a NOT IN condition to our query (and ALWAYS_ANTI_JOIN is not set), we can see that the parallel execution breaks down after the join of CUSTOMERS and SALES:

```
select /*+ ordered use_nl(c) parallel(s)*/
       c.customer_name,s.sale_date,s.sale_value
  from   sales s,customers c
 where c.customer_id=s.customer_id
   and s.sale_date > sysdate-365
   and c.customer_id not in (select customer_id
                                 from bad_customers)
 order by c.customer_name,s.sale_date
```

```
Explain Plan:

SELECT STATEMENT
    SORT ORDER BY   ← Sort operation is serial
      FILTER              ← NOT IN operation is serial
        NESTED LOOPS(PARALLEL_TO_SERIAL)
          TABLE ACCESS FULL SALES(PARALLEL_COMBINED_WITH_PARENT)
          TABLE ACCESS BY ROWID CUSTOMERS(PARALLEL_COMBINED_WITH_PARENT)
            INDEX RANGE SCAN PK_CUSTOMERS(PARALLEL_COMBINED_WITH_PARENT)
        TABLE ACCESS FULL BAD_CUSTOMERS
```

Oracle's anti-join facility, which as we saw in Chapter 7, improves performance for serial queries, and also allows the NOT IN operation to be executed in parallel. We might also improve parallelism by scanning the BAD_CUSTOMERS table in parallel:

```
select /*+ ordered use_nl(c) parallel(s)*/
       c.customer_name,s.sale_date,s.sale_value
  from   sales s,customers c
 where c.customer_id=s.customer_id
   and s.sale_date > sysdate-365
   and c.customer_id not in (select /*+hash_aj parallel(bad_customers)*/
                                 customer_id
                               from bad_customers)
 order by c.customer_name,s.sale_date
```

```
Explain Plan:

SELECT STATEMENT
    SORT ORDER BY(PARALLEL_TO_SERIAL)         ← Sort is now parallelized
      HASH JOIN ANTI(PARALLEL_TO_PARALLEL)    ← Anti-join is parallelized
        NESTED LOOPS(PARALLEL_TO_PARALLEL)
          TABLE ACCESS FULL SALES(PARALLEL_COMBINED_WITH_PARENT)
```

```
        TABLE ACCESS BY ROWID CUSTOMERS(PARALLEL_COMBINED_WITH_PARENT)
          INDEX RANGE SCAN PK_CUSTOMERS(PARALLEL_COMBINED_WITH_PARENT)
    VIEW(PARALLEL_TO_PARALLEL)                    ← Parallel execution of the NOT IN
      TABLE ACCESS FULL BAD_CUSTOMERS(PARALLEL_COMBINED_WITH_PARENT)  ← subquery
```

UNION AND SET OPERATORS

The UNION operation can be resolved in parallel, providing all tables in the union are accessed via parallel full table scans:

```
select /*+ parallel(customers) */ contact_surname,contact_firstname
  from customers
union
select /*+parallel(employees) */ surname,firstname
  from employees
```

```
Explain Plan:
SELECT STATEMENT
    SORT UNIQUE(PARALLEL_TO_SERIAL)
      UNION-ALL(PARALLEL_TO_PARALLEL)
        TABLE ACCESS FULL CUSTOMERS(PARALLEL_COMBINED_WITH_PARENT)
        TABLE ACCESS FULL EMPLOYEES(PARALLEL_COMBINED_WITH_PARENT)
```

However, INTERSECT and MINUS operations are not resolved in parallel, even if the tables are scanned in parallel:

```
select /*+ parallel(customers) */ contact_surname,contact_firstname
  from customers
minus
select /*+parallel(employees) */ surname,firstname
  from employees
```

```
Explain Plan:
SELECT STATEMENT
    MINUS                    ← MINUS operation not parallelized
      SORT UNIQUE            ← Sorted serially
        TABLE ACCESS FULL CUSTOMERS(PARALLEL_TO_SERIAL)
      SORT UNIQUE
        TABLE ACCESS FULL EMPLOYEES(PARALLEL_TO_SERIAL)
```

You may recall from Chapter 8 that a MINUS statement can be reformulated using NOT IN and that an INTERSECT can be reworded as a join. We saw that these join and anti-join alternatives could outperform the INTERSECT and

MINUS operations. By using these alternatives to MINUS and INTERSECT, we can also take advantage of the parallel query option, since parallel query can be used for all types of joins and for anti-joins using an anti-join hint.

INTERSECT and MINUS operations do not parallelize—use equivalent join and anti-join alternatives if you wish to parallelize these operations.

AGGREGATE OPERATIONS

Aggregate and sort operations will automatically parallelize if the preceding operations are performed in parallel. For instance, the following example shows ORDER and GROUP BY operations proceding in parallel:

```
select /*+parallel(s) parallel(c)*/ customer_name,sum(sale_value) sale_total
  from sales s,customers c
 where s.customer_id=c.customer_id
 group by c.customer_name
order by 2 desc

Explain Plan:

SELECT STATEMENT
    SORT ORDER BY(PARALLEL_TO_SERIAL)
      SORT GROUP BY(PARALLEL_TO_PARALLEL)
        HASH JOIN(PARALLEL_TO_PARALLEL)
          TABLE ACCESS FULL CUSTOMERS(PARALLEL_TO_PARALLEL)
          TABLE ACCESS FULL SALES(PARALLEL_TO_PARALLEL)
```

PARALLEL QUERY PERFORMANCE

Figure 12.5 shows the performance improvements obtained from implementing the parallel query option for the query types used in our examples. We can see that each category of query responded well to parallel execution, with an average reduction in elapsed time of 75%. Your results will vary depending on your server configuration and characteristics of your query and data.

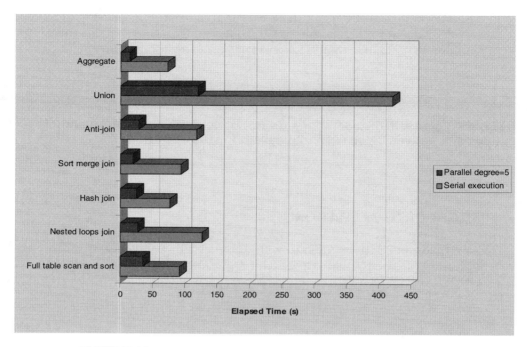

FIGURE 12.5   Performance improvement gained by parallel query.

PARALLEL DDL AND DML

Data Definition Language (DDL) statements such as CREATE TABLE are usually executed infrequently and are relatively inexpensive. However, there are some DDL statements which may be executed more frequently or have very high resource requirements. Oracle allows two categories of DDL statements to be executed in parallel:

❏ The CREATE INDEX statement can take many hours to execute on large tables. We often wish to CREATE new indexes or REBUILD existing indexes to improve performance.

❏ The CREATE TABLE ... AS SELECT statement CREATEs a table and populates it with the results of a query. This statement may be executed to CREATE temporary tables for complex processing, to regularly CREATE summary tables or to REBUILD an existing table.

PARALLEL CREATE INDEX

To CREATE an index requires a full table scan together with a sort of the columns to be indexed. Index builds can therefore benefit substantially from parallel execution.

To create an index in parallel, simply add a PARALLEL clause. For instance:

```
create sales_idx1 on sales(sale_date) parallel(degree 5)
```

This will CREATE an index using a parallel degree of five. Five slaves will scan the table and five will perform sorting and indexing.

Each of the five slaves will create and write to a unique table *extent*. This means that the index will include at least as many extents as the degrees of parallelism used. This is not a bad thing, since large numbers of extents do not usually degrade performance significantly.

However, parallel indexing has a "feature" which may be undesirable. Once the index build is finished, Oracle "trims" free space off the extents which have been created. This is presumably done to avoid wasting space, but it results in index extents which are of uneven sizes. If you are pursuing a *uniform extent sizing policy* (see Chapter 15), you may find this sufficient reason not to use parallel index creation.

Despite this drawback, parallel index creation is the most effective way of improving index build times. The improvement in performance will be similar to the improvement gained in parallel table scan and sorting using the parallel query option.

PARALLEL CREATE TABLE ... AS SELECT

If you issue a CREATE TABLE statement which is based on a parallel query, then the CREATE TABLE itself may also be executed in parallel. This can be very useful for creating a temporary table or to create de-normalized summary tables (as described in Chapter 14).

Oracle will use parallel processing for a CREATE TABLE ... AS SELECT automatically if the underlying query is parallelized. For instance:

```
create table customer_sales_totals
    as
select  /*+parallel(s) parallel(c) */ customer_name,sum(sale_value) sale_total
  from sales s,customers c
 where s.customer_id=c.customer_id
 group by c.customer_name

Explain Plan:
```

```
CREATE TABLE STATEMENT
    CREATE AS SELECT(PARALLEL_TO_SERIAL)      ← The create table is parallelized
        SORT GROUP BY(PARALLEL_TO_PARALLEL)
          HASH JOIN(PARALLEL_TO_PARALLEL)
              TABLE ACCESS FULL CUSTOMERS(PARALLEL_TO_PARALLEL)
              TABLE ACCESS FULL SALES(PARALLEL_TO_PARALLEL)
```

OPTIMIZING PARALLEL DDL

To optimize parallel index and parallel table creation, you should follow the same procedure as for optimizing parallel queries:

- ❏ Choose an appropriate degree of parallelism.
- ❏ Ensure that your host computer is suitably configured.
- ❏ Ensure that your source table is optimized for table scans and is spread across multiple devices.
- ❏ Optimize the underlying query for parallelism (in the case of CREATE TABLE … AS SELECT).
- ❏ Parallel DML operations will benefit very substantially from the UNRECOVERABLE option discussed in Chapter 11. This option disables the generation of redo information and will substantially decrease the build time for indexes or tables.

PARALLEL DML

Oracle8 introduces the capability to perform DML operations in parallel. In Oracle7, only a single process can UPDATE, INSERT or DELETE rows, even if rows to be processed are retrieved in parallel.

In Oracle8 INSERTS based on parallel SELECT statements can be executed in parallel. UPDATES and DELETES can also be executed in parallel providing that the table is partitioned. The parallelism is achieved by applying the UPDATE or DELETE statement to each partition in parallel. It follows, of course, that the degree of parallelism for UPDATES and DELETES cannot be larger than the number of partitions in the table.

For instance, to give all employees a page rise, using four processes in parallel (and assuming that EMPLOYEES is a partitioned table with at least four partitions):

```
update /*+ parallel(e,4) */ employees e
    set salary=salary*1.1;
```

CHAPTER SUMMARY

In this chapter, we've examined Oracle's parallel SQL capabilities. Using parallel SQL is one of the most effective ways of improving the performance of SQL which relies on full table scans.

Parallel SQL works by allocating multiple processes, called *parallel slaves*, to the execution of the SQL statement. The execution of the SQL statement is partitioned into multiple segments and allocated to multiple slave processes. The *degree of parallelism* determines the number of parallel threads of SQL execution. You can set the degree of parallelism yourself, or allow Oracle to use a default value. For most non-trivial SQL statements, Oracle will allocate twice as many parallel slaves as the degree of parallelism.

Parallel SQL is only effective under suitable conditions. These are:

❑ The host computer has multiple CPUs and the database is spread across multiple disk devices.

❑ The SQL statement is based on at least one full table scan of a large table.

❑ There is spare CPU and I/O capacity on the host computer.

Parallel SQL can be used for:

❑ Queries based on a full table scan (parallel query option).

❑ Index builds.

❑ CREATE TABLE statements based on a query.

❑ UPDATEs and DELETEs on partitioned tables (Oracle8 only).

❑ Inserts based on a parallelized select statement (Oracle8 only)

To optimize parallel SQL:

❑ Use EXPLAIN PLAN (or a tool which generates parallel execution plans) to examine the execution plans for your parallel SQL. Use the OTHER_TAG column to establish the parallelism of each step. Steps with an OTHER_TAG of PARALLEL_FROM_SERIAL may indicate a serial bottleneck to parallel execution.

❑ Ensure your server is tuned for parallel SQL. It should have sufficient parallel slaves and data files striped across multiple disk devices.

❏ Set a suitable degree of parallelism.

❏ Analyze your tables.

❏ Use approaches which favor parallelism, such as hash joins, bitmap indexes, anti-joins and partition views or tables

Chapter 13

SQL TUNING CASE STUDIES

In this chapter, we'll look at some real life examples of tuning Oracle SQL.

So far, we've looked at a variety of tuning principles and techniques intended to cover a wide range of circumstances. Wherever possible, we've illustrated each principle using an example based upon the sample database described in Chapter 1. In this chapter, we'll see how the SQL tuning principles we've covered have been used in real world situations to improve the performance of real applications.

Because these examples have been drawn from the actual applications, it has been necessary to change table and column names for privacy and security reasons. In some cases, the SQL statements themselves may have been simplified to make them easier to understand. For instance, a long and complex SELECT list may have been changed to a "*." However, *tkprof* output and other performance related statistics are unchanged.

CASE STUDY 1: USING CONCATENATED INDEXES

In this example, a large marketing database was subject to periodic performance problems and excessive database I/O. Investigation revealed that the cause was a batch job which ran every few hours and which assigned marketing contacts to nominated employees.

By using SQL_TRACE and *tkprof*, it was determined that a single SQL statement which was executed within a loop consumed the majority of CPU and I/O resources. The statement found all appointments for a given employee which had not yet been scheduled. *Tkprof* output for the statement is shown in Figure 13.1. The superscripts in the *tkprof* output are referenced in the commentary which follows.

```
SELECT oa.ContactNo ,
       oa.ContactId ,
       to_char (AppointmentDate ,'dd/mm/yyyy hh24:mi:ss' )
  from Assignments oa
 where oa.EmployeeNo =:e1
   and AppointmentDate is null
   and oa.status ='I'
   and rownum =1⁴
 order by AppointmentDate DESC for update⁵
```

call	count	cpu	elapsed	disk	query	current	rows
Parse	27**5**	0.06	0.10	0	0	0	0
Execute	27**1**	11.37	52.05	617	61282**3**	15	0
Fetch	27	0.01	0.01	0	0	0	5**2**

```
Rows      Execution Plan
-------   -------------------------------------------------------
     0    SELECT STATEMENT
     0      FOR UPDATE
     0        SORT (ORDER BY)
     0⁷         COUNT (STOPKEY)
  1130           TABLE ACCESS (BY ROWID) OF 'ASSIGNMENTS'
  1131⁶            INDEX (RANGE SCAN) OF 'ASSIGNMENTS_I1' (NON-UNIQUE)
```

FIGURE 13.1 *Tkprof* output before optimization. Superscripts in the output are referenced in the commentary.

The first step in tuning the statement is to analyze and interpret the *tkprof* output. What can we tell from this output?

1. Although the statement was executed only 27 times (see [1]) only five rows were returned ([2]).

2. Retrieving these rows cost 61,282 block reads ([3])—a cost of 2,269 block reads per execution or 12,256 blocks per row returned.

3. A ROWNUM clause ([4]) is used to ensure that only one row is returned from each execution of the statement.

4. The statement is parsed once for each execution (5 and 1). This suggests that the execution environment is performing poor cursor handling. Ideally, a statement should be parsed only once even if executed many times.

5. The EXPLAIN PLAN shows that the index ASSIGNMENTS_I1 was used initially to retrieve eligible rows. For the execution used for the EXPLAIN PLAN, 1,131 rows matched on this index's columns but ultimately no rows matched all the selection criteria.

When *tkprof* shows that an index has processed many more rows than are ultimately retrieved from a table, it suggests that an appropriate concatenated index may be missing. The ASSIGNMENTS_I1 index was based on the EmployeeNo column only—not very selective since each employee might have hundreds of assignments.

When the ASSIGNMENTS_I1 index was amended so as to include the columns STATUS and ASSIGNDATE, the execution profile changed to that shown in Figure 13.2.

```
call         count       cpu    elapsed      disk     query current         rows
--------    ------- --------- ---------- --------- -------- ------- ----------
Parse           33      0.11       0.13         4       17       0            0
Execute         33      0.14       0.53        21       92      30            0
Fetch           33      0.01       0.01         0        0       0           10
--------    ------- --------- ---------- --------- -------- ------- ----------
total           99      0.26       0.67        25      109      30           10

Rows        Execution Plan
-------     ------------------------------------------------------
      0     SELECT STATEMENT   OPTIMIZER HINT: RULE
      0       FOR UPDATE
      0         SORT (JOIN)
      0           COUNT (STOPKEY)
      0             TABLE ACCESS (BY ROWID) OF 'ASSIGNMENTS'
      5               INDEX (RANGE SCAN) OF 'ASSIGNMENTS_I1' (NON-UNIQUE)
```

FIGURE 13.2 *Tkprof* output for Case Study 1 after creating a concatenated index.

By adding a concatenated index, block reads per execution were reduced from 2,269 block reads per execution to only four block reads per execution—a reduction of 99.8%. We achieved this result without having to perform any recoding or application redesign.

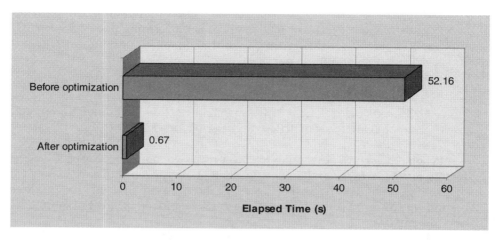

FIGURE 13.3 Performance improvement obtained in Case Study 1 by creating a concatenated index.

There are a few other observations worth making about this case:

❏ The SQL statement contains an ORDER BY clause on Appointment-Date. This ORDER BY is unnecessary for two reasons. First, the WHERE clause requires that AppointmentDate is NULL, so the ordering by AppointmentDate is meaningless. Second, the use of a "rownum=1" clause precludes ordering since the WHERE clause is used before the ORDER BY clause—hence we are only ordering a single row. Although the superfluous ORDER BY is probably causing little or no performance degradation in this case, it should still be removed.

❏ As noted earlier, the SQL statement is being re-parsed at every execution. When I/O requirements were high, parsing contributed only 0.1% to elapsed time. Now that I/O requirements have been optimized, parse requirements are responsible for almost 20% of elapsed time. Almost all of this overhead could be eliminated by parsing the SQL statement only once. Appendix C contains guidelines for reducing parsing in some common development environments.

CASE STUDY 2: THE RULE BASED OPTIMIZER, INDEX MERGES AND BIND VARIABLES

In this example, an on-line inquiry tool required optimization. Very good response time was required and there was a need to fully optimize each SQL statement. One of the SQL statements identified is shown in Figure 13.4.

```
select comment_text
from contacts,comments where contacts.ContactId=906 and contacts.Result code=200
  and contacts.CommentId=comments.CommentId
```

call	count	cpu	elapsed	disk	query	current	rows
Parse	1	0.03	0.05	0	0	0	0
Execute	1	0.00	0.00	0	0	0	0
Fetch	1	0.00	0.04	7	14	0	1

Misses in library cache during parse: 1

```
Rows     Execution Plan
-------  ------------------------------------------------------
    0    SELECT STATEMENT
    1      NESTED LOOPS
    1        TABLE ACCESS (BY ROWID) OF 'CONTACTS'4
    6          AND-EQUAL3
    5            INDEX (RANGE SCAN) OF 'CONTACTS_RESULTCODE_IDX' (NON-UNIQUE)1
    2            INDEX (RANGE SCAN) OF 'CONTACTS_CONTACTID_IDX' (NON-UNIQUE)2
    1        TABLE ACCESS (BY ROWID) OF 'COMMENTS'6
    1          INDEX (UNIQUE SCAN) OF 'COMM_PK_PRIM' (UNIQUE)5
```

FIGURE 13.4 *Tkprof* output for Case Study 2 before optimization.

On first examination, this SQL statement looks to be fairly well tuned. The block get ratio is only 14 blocks per execute and the statement executes in under one-tenth of a second. However, because of the application design, the statement could execute many thousands of times per second across the entire application, so there was a strong incentive to further improve performance if possible.

The EXPLAIN PLAN for this statement can be expressed as follows:

1. First, get all the CONTACTS with a matching RESULTCODE using CONTACTS_RESULTCODE_IDX (see 1).

2. Then, get all the CONTACTS with a matching CONTACTID using CONTACTS_CONTACTID_IDX (2)

3. For each row which is in both lists (3), access the RESULT row and obtain the COMMENTID (4).

4. Use the COMM_PK_PRIM index entry with the matching COMMENTID (5) to access the relevant COMMENT row and get the comment text (6).

5. Two possible improvements come to mind:

   ❏ Using two indexes to obtain a row is almost certainly going to be less efficient than one index, so let's create an index on CONTACTID and RESULTCODE. Index merges such as that used by Oracle in this example (the AND EQUALS step) are usually only performed by the rule based optimizer, which can't determine which of two indexes is most selective. Creating an index on all the keys in the WHERE clause can often improve performance in this case.

❑ We don't actually want any data from CONTACTS, we just want the COMMENTID, so if we added that column to the new index, perhaps we could avoid accessing CONTACTS at all.

The *tkprof* output below shows the improved execution plan. I/O has been halved ([7]) and the COMMENTID has been obtained without accessing the CONTACTS table ([8]).

The use of the INDEX hint was required to force this execution plan ([9]). The rule based optimizer will use an index in which all columns are included in the WHERE clause in preference to an index in which only some of the columns appear in the WHERE clause. Since the COMMENTID column does not appear in the WHERE clause, the rule based optimizer discarded our new index in favor of an existing non-concatenated index. The cost based optimizer would almost certainly have used our new index because it would have determined that the new index was more selective. Unfortunately, converting this application from rule based optimization to cost based optimization was not practical.

```
select /*+ INDEX(CONTACTS CONTACTS_AND_RESULTS_IDX)[9]*/ comment_text
from contacts,comments where contacts.ContactId=906 and contacts.Result-
Code=200[d]
  and contacts.CommentId=comments.CommentId
```

call	count	cpu	elapsed	disk	query	current	rows
Parse	1	0.04	0.04[a]	12	29	0	0
Execute	1	0.00	0.00	0	0	0	0
Fetch	1	0.01	0.01[b]	6	7[7]	0	1

Misses in library cache during parse: 1[c]

```
Rows      Execution Plan
-------   -------------------------------------------------------
     0    SELECT STATEMENT
     1      NESTED LOOPS
     2        INDEX (RANGE SCAN) OF 'CONTACTS_AND_RESULTS_IDX' (NON-UNIQUE)[8]
     1        TABLE ACCESS (BY ROWID) OF 'COMMENTS'
     1          INDEX (UNIQUE SCAN) OF 'COMM_PK_PRIM' (UNIQUE)
```

FIGURE 13.5   *Tkprof* output for Case Study 2 after index optimization.

We can be pretty pleased with the improvements to I/O which we have obtained. However, we can see that 80% of the elapsed time for this statement is now taken up in statement parsing (see [a] and [b]).

The SQL statement has its query parameters hardcoded as literals ("906" and "200") rather than as *bind variables*. We discussed the important role which bind variables play in reducing parse overhead in Chapter 3. Bind variables reduce the effort needed to parse SQL because Oracle needs parse statements with different query parameters once only. In this case, as the values of ContactId and Result-Code change, Oracle will be forced to re-parse the SQL statement on each execution. The inability of Oracle to find a matching statement is indicated by the "Misses in library cache during parse" line (c).

By using bind variables instead of literals to specify the ContactId and Result-Code, we get the execution profile shown in Figure 13.6. Parse time has been reduced by 75% and overall execution time has been reduced by 60%.

```
select /*+ INDEX(CONTACTS CONTACTS_AND_RESULTS_IDX)*/ comment_text
from contacts,comments where contacts.ContactId=:1 and contacts.ResultCode=:2
  and contacts.CommentId=comments.CommentId
```

call	count	cpu	elapsed	disk	query	current	rows
Parse	1	0.00	0.01	0	0	0	0
Execute	1	0.00	0.00	0	0	0	0
Fetch	1	0.01	0.01	6	7	0	1

```
Misses in library cache during parse: 0

Rows     Execution Plan
-------  ----------------------------------------------------
      0  SELECT STATEMENT
      1    NESTED LOOPS
      2      INDEX (RANGE SCAN) OF 'CONTACTS_AND_RESULTS_IDX' (NON-UNIQUE)
      1      TABLE ACCESS (BY ROWID) OF 'COMMENTS'
      1        INDEX (UNIQUE SCAN) OF 'COMM_PK_PRIM' (UNIQUE)
```

FIGURE 13.6 *Tkprof* output for Case Study 2 after parse optimization.

This example illustrates a number of useful tuning principles:

❑ As we saw in the first example, creating concatenated indexes can result in strong performance gains.

❑ Adding columns to an index beyond what is required to satisfy the WHERE clause can further improve performance if it allows a table access to be avoided.

❑ Even when an SQL statement appears to be reasonably efficient, there is often still scope for substantial improvement.

❑ For SQL statements with low I/O requirements, optimizing parsing can be as significant as I/O optimization.

❑ Using bind variables significantly reduces parse overhead.

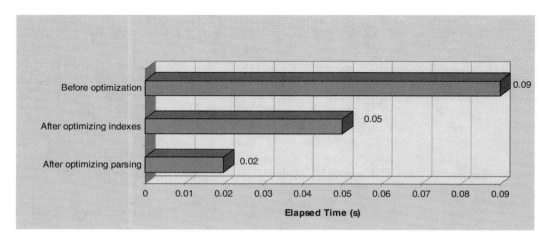

FIGURE 13.7   Effect of indexing and parsing optimizations from Case Study 2.

CASE STUDY 3: THE SLOWLY DEGRADING QUERY

In this case, a JOB_QUEUE table contained details of jobs to be processed by a batch system. Batch programs issue queries against this table in order to select the next job to be processed for a particular job category. Multiple jobs run in parallel and it's important that jobs not be selected by more than one batch program.

Performance of the batch system was disappointing and it was noticed that the greater the backlog of work, the slower the system would become.

Tkprof output for the query which selected jobs for processing is shown in Figure 13.8.

The WHERE clause (see 1) of the query selects all jobs which match the specified job type and status. The ORDER BY clause (2) instructs Oracle to return rows in the order of the job identifier sequence, to ensure that jobs are processed in the correct order. The FOR UPDATE clause (3) locks the rows selected to ensure that they are not accessed by any other batch job. The application issues only a single fetch request to obtain the first eligible job (4).

This approach has a serious flaw. As discussed in Chapter 6, the FOR UPDATE clause requires that all rows be retrieved and locked before the first row can be returned. Consequently, all rows matching the job type and sequence will be retrieved and locked. In the example, 1,537 rows were found in the index (5), accessed in the table (6) and locked (7)—even though only a single row is fetched. Because of the FOR UPDATE clause's locking behavior, 5,058 blocks were accessed in order to retrieve a single row.

```
SELECT *
  FROM JOB_QUEUE A1
 WHERE¹ A1.JOB_TYPE = :b1
   AND A1.JOB_STATUS = :b2
 ORDER² BY A1.JOB_SEQUENCE
   FOR UPDATE³ OF JOB_STATUS
```

call	count	cpu	elapsed	disk	query	current	rows
Parse	1	0.01	0.00	0	0	0	0
Execute	1	0.51	0.52	153	3473	1583	0
Fetch	1⁴	0.00	0.00	0	3	0	1
total	3	0.52	0.52	153	3476	1583	1

```
Rows     Execution Plan
-------  -------------------------------------------------------
     0   SELECT STATEMENT     OPTIMIZER HINT: CHOOSE
 1537⁷      FOR UPDATE
 1538⁶        TABLE ACCESS    OPTIMIZER HINT: ANALYZED (BY ROWID)
                OF 'JOB_QUEUE'
 1539⁵          INDEX (RANGE SCAN) OF 'JOB_QUEUE_1IX' (NON-UNIQUE)
```

FIGURE 13.8   SQL from Case Study 3 before optimization.

We can see that the presence of the FOR UPDATE clause causes a dramatic increase in the I/O overhead of the query. An additional drawback of the approach is the excessive lock contention which is caused by the locking of the 1,500 odd rows. Other batch jobs wishing to obtain a row for processing would be unable to fetch any rows until the session holding the locks had committed.

This query, while logical in construction and supported by appropriate indexes, was obviously not suitable for the task at hand. Unfortunately, there is no simple way to resolve the conflicting aims of good response time and the pre-emptive locking of rows to be processed.

The resolution chosen in this case was to implement a more complex logic along the following lines:

1. Fetch the next row eligible for processing using a fast index lookup, but do not lock the row. Retrieve the ROWID of this row for further processing.

2. Using this ROWID, lock the row in question only if it still meets the selection criteria.

3. There is a small chance that another process may have selected and locked or updated the row in question between step 1 and step 2. For this reason, the procedure must validate that the row is still eligible

when it is locked. If the row is no longer eligible, the procedure will return to step 1 and attempt to lock the next eligible row.

A representation of the technique employed in PL/SQL is shown in Figure 13.9.

```
CREATE or replace function f_get_next_file
        (p_pgm_name     varchar2,
         p_JOB_STATUS varchar2)
  return rowid as

  CURSOR get_nxt_file_csr
        (cp_pgm_name     varchar2,
         cp_JOB_STATUS varchar2) is
        SELECT a.rowid a_rowid
          from JOB_QUEUE a
         where JOB_TYPE=cp_pgm_name
           AND JOB_STATUS=cp_JOB_STATUS
   ORDER BY A.JOB_TYPE, A.JOB_STATUS,A.JOB_SEQUENCE ;

  CURSOR lock_file_csr
        (cp_rowid          rowid,
         cp_pgm_name     varchar2,
         cp_JOB_STATUS varchar2) is
        SELECT *
          FROM JOB_QUEUE
         WHERE rowid=cp_rowid
           AND JOB_TYPE=cp_pgm_name
           AND JOB_STATUS=cp_JOB_STATUS
           FOR update;

  get_nxt_file_row get_nxt_file_csr%ROWTYPE;
  lock_file_row    lock_file_csr%ROWTYPE;
  l_max_retries    number:=5;
  l_attempt_count number:=0;

BEGIN

  WHILE l_attempt_count < l_max_retries LOOP
      --
      -- Find the next eligible row
      --
      OPEN get_nxt_file_csr(p_pgm_name,p_JOB_STATUS);
      FETCH get_nxt_file_csr into get_nxt_file_row;
      IF get_nxt_file_csr%NOTFOUND THEN
         close get_nxt_file_csr;
         return(NULL);                      -- No matching rows found
   END IF;

      CLOSE get_nxt_file_csr;
      --
      -- Lock the selected row,  providing it's still eligible
      --
```

```
          OPEN lock_file_csr(get_nxt_file_row.a_rowid,
                             p_pgm_name,p_JOB_STATUS);
          FETCH lock_file_csr into lock_file_row;

          IF lock_file_csr%NOTFOUND THEN
              --
              -- The row can't be found.  Another process must have
              -- grabbed it and changed its status
              --
              CLOSE lock_file_csr;
              EXIT;                     -- Try again
          ELSE
              close lock_file_csr;
              return(get_nxt_file_row.a_rowid);
          END IF;

    END LOOP;
      -- If we are here,  we've not managed to find an eligible row
      return(NULL);
  END;
```

FIGURE 13.9 PL/SQL is implemented to improve performance of Case Study 3.

Although the new implementation requires two queries rather than one, it is tremendously more efficient than the original approach.

Figure 13.10 shows *tkprof* output for the first of the two queries in the PL/SQL block. We can see that an index alone was sufficient to resolve the query (**8**) and that only two block gets were required (**9**).

```
SELECT A.ROWID A_ROWID
  FROM JOB_QUEUE A
 WHERE JOB_TYPE = :b1
   AND JOB_STATUS = :b2
 ORDER BY A.JOB_TYPE,A.JOB_STATUS,A.JOB_SEQUENCE
```

call	count	cpu	elapsed	disk	query	current	rows
Parse	1	0.00	0.00	0	0	0	0
Execute	1	0.01	0.00	0	0	0	0
Fetch	1	0.00	0.00	0	2	0	1
total	3	0.01	0.00	0	2**9**	0	1

```
Rows    Execution Plan
-------  ------------------------------------------------
      0  SELECT STATEMENT   OPTIMIZER HINT: CHOOSE
      1    INDEX (RANGE SCAN) OF 'JOB_QUEUE_1IX' (NON-UNIQUE) 8
```

FIGURE 13.10 *Tkprof* output for the first of the two queries implemented for Case Study 3.

Figure 13.11 shows *tkprof* output for the second of the two queries in the PL/
SQL function. We can see that the query was able to find the required rows using
the ROWID without recourse to an index lookup or table scan (**10**) and required
only three block reads to do so (**11**).

```
SELECT *
  FROM JOB_QUEUE
 WHERE ROWID = :b1
   AND JOB_TYPE = :b2
   AND JOB_STATUS = :b3
   FOR UPDATE
```

call	count	cpu	elapsed	disk	query	current	rows
Parse	1	0.00	0.01	0	0	0	0
Execute	1	0.01	0.01	0	3	3	0
Fetch	1	0.00	0.00	0	0	0	1
total	3	0.01	0.02	0	3	3 **11**	1

```
Rows     Execution Plan
-------  ------------------------------------------------------------
      0  SELECT STATEMENT    OPTIMIZER HINT: CHOOSE
      1    FOR UPDATE
      1      TABLE ACCESS    OPTIMIZER HINT: ANALYZED (BY ROWID) 10
                  OF 'JOB_QUEUE'
```

FIGURE 13.11   *Tkprof* output for the second of the two queries implemented for Case Study 3.

The new approach retrieves the required row with only five block reads while
the previous approach required as many as 5,053 block reads.

This example illustrates a number of the principles we've encountered in previous chapters:

❏ The FOR UPDATE clause can often defeat an attempt to minimize
response time since it requires that all eligible rows be retrieved and
locked, even if only a single row is actually fetched.

❏ PL/SQL can often provide an efficient alternative to a single SQL
statement which has excessive I/O requirements.

❏ A query can sometimes be resolved entirely by an index access with
good results.

❏ Saving the ROWID of a row for future processing can reduce I/O
requirements when a row is likely to be re-accessed in a subsequent
step.

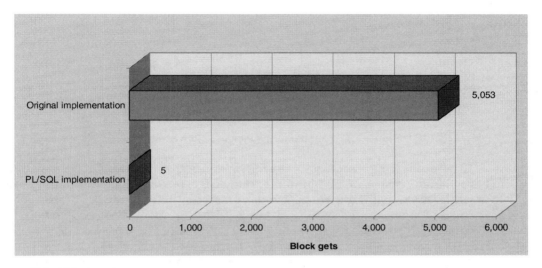

FIGURE 13.12 Improvement in I/O obtained by re-implementing the SQL query in Case Study 3 using a PL/SQL function.

CASE STUDY 4: A NUMBER RANGE LOOKUP

A high-load transaction processing system needed to convert the phone number of every order coming into the system. It did this by comparing the phone number included within the order to a phone number range table which contained about 10,000 rows. Each row contained a high and low phone number, which defined the range of numbers covered by the row. There were no overlapping numbers. Not all phone numbers needed conversion, and it was expected that a match would not be found in the conversion table in the majority of cases.

Initially, the high and low phone number were indexed and a query was issued using the BETWEEN operator. Results of this query were disappointing. *Tkprof* output in Figure 13.13 shows that 13 I/Os and over 2,000 index row accesses were required to obtain a match.

```
select conversion_code
  from number_range
 where :1 between low_number and high_number
```

call	count	cpu	elapsed	disk	query	current	rows
Parse	1	0.01	0.01	0	0	0	0
Execute	1	0.00	0.00	0	0	0	0

```
Fetch        1      0.03       0.03           0          13          0             1
-------  ------  --------  ----------  ----------  ----------  ----------    --------
total        3      0.04       0.04           0          13          0             1

Rows     Execution Plan
-------  -------------------------------------------------------
      0  SELECT STATEMENT   HINT: CHOOSE
      1   TABLE ACCESS (BY ROWID) OF 'NUMBER_RANGE'
   2087    INDEX (RANGE SCAN) OF 'NUMBER_RANGE_HILOW_IDX' (NON-UNIQUE)
```

FIGURE 13.13   Number range lookup before optimization.

The performance problem with this query occurs because Oracle does not have the advantage of our intuitive knowledge of the table distribution. We would assume that there are no overlaps between number ranges in the table. Furthermore, we would know that LOW_NUMBER is always going to be less than HIGH_NUMBER. Knowing this, we would know that once we find a single matching row, there is no need to look for further rows. Oracle cannot assume that there are no overlapping ranges and does not know that LOW_NUMBER is always less than HIGH_NUMBER. Consequently, Oracle scans every row in the index where the low number is less than the number provided to determine if the high number is greater than that number.

The first attempt to improve the performance of this statement involved adding a "Rownum=1" condition to the query in order to prevent the query from continuing to search once a match has been found. Unfortunately, the ROWNUM condition was applied after the index lookup and no performance improvement was achieved.

```
select conversion_code
  from number_range
 where :1 between low_number and high_number and rownum=1

call     count      cpu    elapsed        disk       query     current        rows
-------  ------  --------  ----------  ----------  ----------  -------    ----------
Parse        1      0.01       0.01           0           0          0             0
Execute      1      0.00       0.00           0           0          0             0
Fetch        1      0.03       0.03           0          12          0             1
-------  ------  --------  ----------  ----------  ----------  ----------    --------
total        3      0.04       0.04           0          12          0             1

Rows     Execution Plan
-------  -------------------------------------------------------
      0  SELECT STATEMENT   HINT: CHOOSE
      1   COUNT (STOPKEY)
      1    TABLE ACCESS (BY ROWID) OF 'NUMBER_RANGE'
   2086     INDEX (RANGE SCAN) OF 'NUMBER_RANGE_HILOW_IDX' (NON-UNIQUE)
```

FIGURE 13.14   First unsuccessful attempt to optimize the range query.

Since Oracle is seemingly unable to take advantage of the characteristics of the data distribution, it was decided to use PL/SQL to explicitly force an execution plan. The following pseudo-code illustrates the program logic:

```
FETCH the first row where high_number is greater than our
        phone number
IF the low_number is less than our phone number THEN
        A match has occurred
ELSE
        There is no matching row
END IF
```

Figure 13.15 shows a PL/SQL function which implements this logic.

```
CREATE function range_lookup(p_phoneno varchar2)
        return number as

  CURSOR range_csr (cp_phoneno varchar2) is
        select low_number,high_number,conversion_code
          from number_range
         where high_number >= cp_phoneno
         order by high_number;

  range_row range_csr%ROWTYPE;

BEGIN

-- FETCH the first row where high_number is greater
-- than the supplied phone number

  OPEN range_csr(p_phoneno);
  FETCH range_csr into range_row;

  IF range_row.low_number <= p_phoneno THEN
     -- A match was found
     CLOSE range_csr;
     RETURN(range_row.conversion_code);

  ELSE
     -- No match was found
     CLOSE range_csr;
     RETURN(-1);

  END IF;
END;
```

FIGURE 13.15 PL/SQL function to perform an efficient range lookup.

Implementing this logic using an index on HIGH_NUMBER resulted in the execution plan shown in Figure 13.16.

```
SELECT LOW_NUMBER,HIGH_NUMBER,CONVERSION_CODE
FROM
 NUMBER_RANGE  WHERE HIGH_NUMBER >= :b1 ORDER BY HIGH_NUMBER
```

call	count	cpu	elapsed	disk	query	current	rows
Parse	0	0.00	0.00	0	0	0	0
Execute	1	0.00	0.00	0	0	0	0
Fetch	1	0.00	0.00	1	3	0	1
total	2	0.00	0.00	1	3	0	1

```
Rows     Execution Plan
-------  ---------------------------------------------------
      0  SELECT STATEMENT   HINT: CHOOSE
      1   TABLE ACCESS (BY ROWID) OF 'NUMBER_RANGE'
      1    INDEX (RANGE SCAN) OF 'NUMBER_RANGE_HIIDX' (NON-UNIQUE)
```

FIGURE 13.16 *Tkprof* output after implementing the PL/SQL solution.

Implementing the PL/SQL solution reduced I/O requirements from 13 to 3—a good result. However, it was possible to squeeze a little more performance out of the solution by creating an index on HIGH_NUMBER, LOW_NUMBER and CONVERSION_CODE. This index allowed the table access to be avoided altogether, reducing the I/O requirements to 2.

```
SELECT LOW_NUMBER,HIGH_NUMBER,CONVERSION_CODE
FROM
 NUMBER_RANGE  WHERE HIGH_NUMBER >= :b1 ORDER BY HIGH_NUMBER
```

call	count	cpu	elapsed	disk	query	current	rows
Parse	1	0.00	0.00	0	0	0	0
Execute	1	0.00	0.00	0	0	0	0
Fetch	1	0.00	0.00	0	2	0	1
total	2	0.00	0.00	0	2	0	1

```
Rows     Execution Plan
-------  ---------------------------------------------------
      0  SELECT STATEMENT   HINT: CHOOSE
      1   INDEX (RANGE SCAN) OF 'NUMBER_RANGE_HI_LOW_SWITCH' (NON-UNIQUE)
```

FIGURE 13.17 *Tkprof* for PL/SQL number range lookup after adding LOW_NUMBER and CONVERSION_CODE to an index on HIGH_NUMBER.

This case study illustrates the following principles:

❏ The Oracle optimizer never knows as much about your data as you do. Things which seem intuitively obvious to us can be completely ignored by the optimizer.

❏ Range lookups are difficult for the optimizer to perform efficiently.

❏ As we've seen previously, a procedural approach using PL/SQL can pay off handsomely in performance terms.

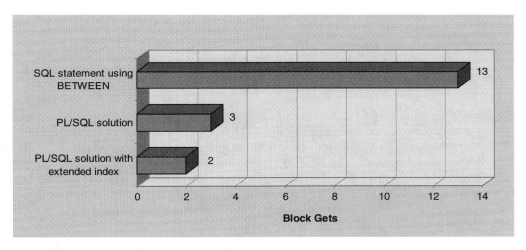

FIGURE 13.18   Performance of the PL/SQL solution to the range lookup problem in Case Study 4.

CASE STUDY 5: THE FIRST ROWS APPROACH

An interactive application for a work management system displayed a list of outstanding activities on the initial application screen. This list consisted of all work items displayed in priority and date order. The system was originally implemented using Oracle 7.1.

Performance of this screen during development was acceptable, but it degraded rapidly once the application was deployed. Suspicion focused on the query which populated the initial screen, since performance seemed to be degrading as the number of active activities increased. *Tkprof* output for the primary query is shown in Figure 13.19.

```
select   *
  from WORK_LIST
 where job_status='READY'
 order by priority, job_due_date

call      count       cpu     elapsed       disk      query    current       rows
------- ------   -------- ----------- ---------- ---------- ----------   --------
Parse         1      0.03        0.04          0          0          0          0
Execute       1      0.00        0.00          0          0          0          0
Fetch         1      3.42       14.29       1490       1489         32         15
------- ------   -------- ----------- ---------- ---------- ----------   --------
total         3      3.45       14.33       1490       1489         32         15

Rows       Execution Plan
-------   -------------------------------------------------------
      0   SELECT STATEMENT    HINT: CHOOSE
    966     SORT (ORDER BY)
  14999       TABLE ACCESS    HINT: ANALYZED (FULL) OF 'WORK_LIST'
```

FIGURE 13.19 Work management screen query before optimization.

The *tkprof* output shows that a full table scan of the 15,000 row table was performed. Rows with the appropriate STATUS_CODE were then sorted into priority and JOB_DUE_DATE order. Although only 15 rows are retrieved from the query, 15,000 rows are retrieved from the table and 966 rows are sorted. Although the screen only displays the first 15 rows of the query, the need to retrieve the rows in sorted order results in all eligible rows being fetched and sorted before the first rows can be displayed on the screen. As the number of rows held in the system increases, the response time rapidly degrades.

An index had been created on JOB_STATUS, PRIORITY and JOB_DUE_DATE. However, because JOB_STATUS contained only a few unique values, the Oracle 7.1 cost based optimizer chose not to use this index.

Since the user typically only displays the first pageful of information, it was essential that these rows be retrieved as quickly as possible. Essentially, this means that the rows must be retrieved in pre-sorted order using an index rather than by performing an explicit sort. The FIRST_ROWS hint is designed to favor such an optimization plan and it was hoped that using this hint would be sufficient to force an index-based retrieval plan.

Unfortunately, the FIRST_ROWS hint was not sufficient encouragement for Oracle 7.1 to use the desired plan and the retrieval plan was virtually unchanged (see Figure 13.20).

```
select /*+ first_rows */ *
  from WORK_LIST
 where job_status='READY'
 order by priority, job_due_date

call      count       cpu     elapsed       disk      query    current       rows
------- ------   -------- ----------- ---------- ---------- ----------   --------
Parse         1      0.02        0.02          0          0          0          0
```

```
Execute     1      0.00      0.00         0          0         0          0
Fetch       1      3.26     11.65      1490       1489        32         15
------- ------ -------- ---------- ---------- ---------- ---------- --------
total       3      3.28     11.67      1490       1489        32         15

Rows       Execution Plan
-------    ------------------------------------------------------
     0     SELECT STATEMENT   HINT: FIRST_ROWS
   966       SORT (ORDER BY)
 14999       TABLE ACCESS   HINT: ANALYZED (FULL) OF 'WORK_LIST'
```

FIGURE 13.20 Results of a failed attempt to force a better work management retrieval plan using the FIRST_ROWS hint.

Due to the failure of the FIRST_ROWS hint, it was necessary to force an index based retrieval using the INDEX hint. Figure 13.21 shows *tkprof* output of the resulting plan. I/Os required to retrieve the first 15 rows using the index have been reduced from 1521 to just 31. Furthermore, increases in the size of the WORK_LIST table will not result in increases in response time. \

```
select /*+ index(WORK_LIST,WORK_STAT_PRI_DATE_IDX) */ *
  from WORK_LIST
 where job_status='READY'
 order by priority, job_due_date

call       count       cpu    elapsed       disk      query    current       rows
------- ------ -------- ---------- ---------- ---------- ---------- --------
Parse       1      0.02      0.03          0          0          0          0
Execute     1      0.00      0.00          0          0          0          0
Fetch       1      0.03      0.21          6         31          0         15
------- ------ -------- ---------- ---------- ---------- ---------- --------
total       3      0.05      0.24          6         31          0         15

Rows       Execution Plan
-------    ------------------------------------------------------
     0     SELECT STATEMENT    HINT: CHOOSE
    15     TABLE ACCESS    HINT: ANALYZED (BY ROWID) OF 'WORK_LIST'
    15     INDEX   HINT: ANALYZED (RANGE SCAN) OF 'WORK_STAT_PRI_DATE_IDX' (NON-UNIQUE)
```

FIGURE 13.21 Optimization of the work management query using the INDEX hint.

Although the INDEX hint does the job, it's better in general to use more general hints such as FIRST_ROWS. It's easier for the SQL programmer to make a mistake in the INDEX hint and the hint will be invalidated should the name of the index change. Furthermore, the FIRST_ROWS instruction can be specified as a database configuration parameter or an ALTER SESSION command, whereas the INDEX hint must be embedded in the SQL statement concerned.

After upgrading to Oracle 7.3, the FIRST_ROWS hint worked as we would have hoped. It caused the index to be used to optimize the return of the first set of rows.

```
select /*+ first_rows */ *
  from WORK_LIST
 where job_status='READY'
 order by priority, job_due_date

call       count       cpu    elapsed        disk       query     current        rows
-------    ------   -------- ----------  ----------  ----------  ----------   ---------
Parse          1      0.02       0.02           0           0           0           0
Execute        1      0.00       0.01           0           0           0           0
Fetch          1      0.02       0.01           7          31           0          15
-------    ------   -------- ----------  ----------  ----------  ----------   ---------
total          3      0.04       0.04           7          31           0          15

Rows       Execution Plan
-------    ----------------------------------------------------------
      0    SELECT STATEMENT    GOAL: HINT: FIRST_ROWS
     15     TABLE ACCESS    GOAL: ANALYZED (BY ROWID) OF 'WORK_LIST'
     15       INDEX    GOAL: ANALYZED (RANGE SCAN) OF
                   'WORK_STAT_PRI_DATE_IDX' (NON-UNIQUE)
```

FIGURE 13.22 Optimizing the work management query using the FIRST_ROWS hint in
Oracle 7.3.

This case study illustrates some notable points:

❑ By default, the cost based optimizer optimizes for throughput. That
is, it tries to minimize the time taken to retrieve all eligible rows from
a query. However, for interactive applications, it is often the time
taken to retrieve the first row which is more significant. Using the
FIRST_ROWS hint, or setting the optimizer preference to
FIRST_ROWS using the OPTIMIZER_MODE configuration parameter or ALTER SESSION SET OPTIMIZER_GOAL command will
encourage the cost based optimizer to seek a FIRST_ROWS solution.

❑ Avoiding a SORT step in an execution plan is often the key consideration when optimizing for response time. If an ordered result set is
required, then an index should be used to retrieve the rows in the
required order.

❑ Improvements to the cost based optimizer are made in each release of
Oracle. In releases prior to 7.2, the cost based optimizer can make
questionable decisions and it may be necessary to override these with
explicit hints.

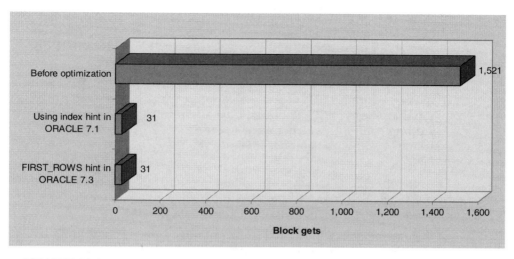

FIGURE 13.23 Improvement in retrieval of the first row obtained by using the INDEX or FIRST_ROWS hint in Case Study 5.

CHAPTER SUMMARY

In this chapter, we've examined some real life examples of SQL statement tuning. You have seen how the tools and techniques introduced in previous chapters can be used in the real world to improve the performance of SQL statements. The improvements we've seen in these examples—in terms of reductions in response time or database I/O—ranged from 80% to 99.9%. Obtaining these sorts of improvements from SQL tuning is not at all uncommon and is why SQL tuning is so effective.

The examples presented in this chapter do not incorporate all of the SQL tuning principles and techniques presented in previous chapters. They do however, illustrate the following fundamental principles:

❏ Measurement of SQL statement execution time, execution plan and resource usage is a key component of SQL tuning. The most widely available tool which can perform these measurements is the SQL_TRACE option and the *tkprof* tool.

❏ When SQL is untuned and I/O intensive, the overhead of parsing the SQL statement is relatively small. However, once the SQL is I/O efficient, the proportion of time spent parsing can be significant. Reducing parse overhead can make well-tuned SQL even faster.

❏ Effective indexing is one of the most effective ways of improving query performance. A concatenated index which contains all the columns in the WHERE clause will usually result in best performance. Adding columns (which appear in the SELECT list) to the index can result in additional gains if it allows the query to resolve without a table access.

❏ Some operations which seem to be impossible to perform efficiently in a single SQL statement may be more efficiently performed using a procedural approach—possibly using PL/SQL.

❏ SQL statements which need to be optimized for response time may benefit from a "first rows" approach using the FIRST_ROWS hint. Statements which return rows in sorted order or use the FOR UPDATE clause to lock rows may present obstacles to the "first rows" approach.

Chapter 14

DATA MODEL AND APPLICATION DESIGN

INTRODUCTION

In previous chapters, we've looked at writing SQL statements which will perform well against an established data model. Although we've felt free to create indexes when appropriate—and in a few cases, to de-normalize or replicate data—in general, we have assumed that the data model is fundamentally unchangeable. This assumption is realistic, because in real life, changing the data model of a production (or even preproduction) application is prohibitive—it requires rebuilds of affected tables and reworking of multiple program modules.

The data model can have an overwhelming impact on the performance of SQL statements. It's common at the end of a tuning exercise to conclude that an SQL statement cannot be made efficient without a change to the data model—and that such a change is impractical. It follows that the ultimate success of our SQL tuning endeavors is dependent on the quality of our data model, and that the time to tune the data model is before implementation.

In this chapter, we'll develop some basic principles for constructing a data model which can support efficient SQL and high performance applications. Data modeling itself is a large topic which could—and does—fill many books. We can't hope to comprehensively cover the topic here and will instead try to focus on the transition from a *logical model*—which models the data in a performance-and implementation-independent way—to a physical model—which describes the actual tables, indexes and other structures which will exist in the actual database.

Some of the data modeling techniques which we will consider are:

❑ Mapping entities which contain subtypes into tables.

❑ The use of "natural" and "artificial" primary keys.

❑ The effective use of Oracle datatypes.

❑ The use of NULLS.

❑ De-normalization.

The architecture of your application can also limit the ultimate performance of your SQL. Some of the application issues we'll look at are:

❑ Building tracing and profiling into your application.

❑ Using an appropriate locking strategy.

❑ Caching data to reduce database load.

❑ Division of client-server processing loads.

❑ Ensuring the application supports concurrency and parallelism.

BUILDING TUNING INTO THE DESIGN PROCESS

Guidelines such as those contained in this chapter can be very useful in avoiding common performance pitfalls in database and application design. However, given the wide variety of application architectures and performance requirements, it is not possible to provide guidelines which will suit every situation. It's therefore important to build performance tuning into the design process itself.

DEFINE YOUR PERFORMANCE REQUIREMENTS EARLY

Many applications are developed under seemingly unrealistic timeframes and it's quite common for these applications to fail to consider or define performance requirements until after the system is delivered. This approach is not suitable for a performance-critical application.

The performance requirements for an application are every bit as real and often as important as its functional requirements. The performance requirements for the system and for specific modules or transactions should be defined early in the system's development lifecycle—usually during requirements analysis.

By defining the performance requirements early, we ensure that the requirements are available to those involved in modeling, designing and constructing the system. As part of a formal systems requirement, performance becomes something which must be considered in system and acceptance testing phases.

If performance requirements are not defined early, then it's possible that no effort to provide an acceptable level of performance will be made and that the ultimate performance of the system will be disappointing.

IDENTIFY CRITICAL TRANSACTIONS

Most applications have a number of critical modules or transactions which can make or break the system. For instance, in a banking system, deposit and withdrawal transactions might comprise 99% of all transactions. Identify these critical transactions and ensure that all features of the design support their effective implementation.

MEASURE PERFORMANCE AS EARLY AS POSSIBLE

During the build phase, measure the performance of the system regularly. This might require obtaining realistic test data volumes and may not be a trivial task. However, by measuring the performance of the system at an early phase you allow performance problems to be identified and corrected as they occur. The "traditional" approach of ignoring performance until a volume or stress test is conducted right before implementation increases the risk of delivering a poorly performing system.

CONSIDER PROTOTYPING CRITICAL PORTIONS OF THE APPLICATION

If the performance requirements of your system are critical, it may be worth prototyping critical transactions before commencing a full-blown construction phase. Doing this allows you to prove that the data model and system design can deliver the required performance. If the prototype indicates that the required performance cannot be achieved, there will at least be time to modify the design before too much of the system has been constructed.

Prototyping with SQL can be quite practical, since you may only need to code a few critical pieces of SQL, rather than writing many lines of procedural code. However, you will need to assemble realistic test volumes and this may present difficulties.

Build performance tuning into your data modeling and application design process. Define performance requirements in the system requirements specification
and measure performance during the build phase, or even earlier, by using prototype transactions.

DESIGNING AN EFFICIENT PHYSICAL DATA MODEL

A well-designed data model can serve as a solid foundation for building a robust
and efficient database application. In contrast, a poorly constructed data model
can lead to persistent difficulties in meeting performance targets and can considerably shorten the life of your application.

As in most aspects of software development, the cost of correcting deficiencies in the data model multiply as the development lifecycle progresses. When the
data model exists only in a CASE repository or on paper, it may take a few minutes or hours to remodel some performance-critical aspect. When the data model
is implemented in a mission-critical production system, reworking the same
aspect may require reworking and re-testing dozens of software programs, con-
ceivably incorporating hundreds of SQL statements. The conversion from the old
to the new model in a very large database may also require significant downtime.

This is why it is important to incorporate performance requirements into the
data model as early as possible, and why the extra effort spent in tuning the data
model will be repaid many times in reduced tuning effort following system
implementation.

LOGICAL AND PHYSICAL DATA MODELING

Application data models are commonly created in two phases. The *logical data
model* results from a process of identifying the data items which must be stored
and processed by the application. For relational database implementations, this
usually involves constructing a normalized entity-relationship model although
other representations—such as an object-oriented model—are emerging. The purpose of the logical model is to ensure that the information requirements of the
proposed system are correctly defined and to serve as the basis for further design.

The logical data model is then mapped to the *physical data model*. For a relational database, the physical data model describes the tables, indexes, views, keys and other characteristics of the database. In traditional methodologies, performance requirements are ignored during the logical modeling process and are first considered during the physical modeling process.

An alternative to the "purist's" approach—in which performance requirements are ignored during logical design—might be termed the "pragmatist's" approach. The pragmatic logical data modeler will be aware of performance requirements and will attempt to produce a logical model which supports these without compromising business requirements. When the physical model is constructed, any divergence from the logical model for performance reasons will be minimized—which will improve maintainability of both models and enhance the performance of the physical system.

CONVERTING FROM A LOGICAL TO A PHYSICAL MODEL

Since most methodologies regard the physical modeling phase as the most appropriate stage for introducing performance considerations, this phase is critical to the ultimate performance of our application.

Unfortunately, the professionals who are concerned with data modeling usually specialize in logical modeling and have little expertise in SQL tuning. Conversely, those charged with developing and managing the application usually have little input into the data modeling process. The sad result is that many physical models are no more than exact replicas of the source logical model. Performing a one-to-one mapping of a logical model to a physical model is usually simple to achieve (perhaps requiring only a single click in a CASE tool). However, such a translation rarely results in a physical design which will support a high performance application. Invest time in the physical modeling process—the dividend will be a physical model which can support your performance requirements.

Don't create a physical model which is a one-to-one representation of the logical model. Take the time to build a physical model which allows your application to reach its full performance potential. Remember that time spent during physical modeling is likely to be repaid many times during production tuning.

Mapping entities to tables

An entity in a logical model often translates to a table in the physical model. This transformation is usually straightforward except when the entity contains subtypes.

Subtypes are used to categorize or partition a logical entity and help to classify the types of information which is within the entity. A subtype will usually have a set of attributes which are held in common with the parent entity (the super-type) and other attributes which are not shared with the super-type or other subtypes.

Figure 14.1 shows how a PEOPLE entity could be split into subtypes of CUSTOMER and EMPLOYEE.

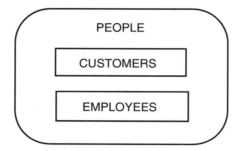

FIGURE 14.1   Representation of subtypes in an entity-relationship diagram.

When translating entity subtypes into tables, we have the following options:

1. Create a table for the super-type and for each subtype. The super-type table contains only columns which are common to both subtypes.

2. Create a table for the super-type only. Attributes from all subtypes become columns in this "super-table." Typically, columns from subtype attributes will be nullable, and a category column indicates the subtype in which a row belongs.

3. Create separate tables for each subtype without creating a table for the super-type. Attributes from the super-type are duplicated in each table.

Figure 14.2 illustrates three options for translating the entities in Figure 14.1 from a logical to physical model.

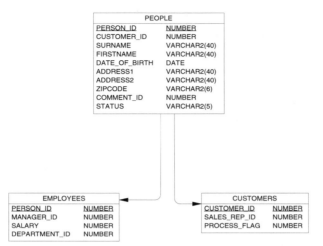

1. Implement subtypes as a master table with detail tables for each subtype

2. Implement subtypes in a single table

3. Implement as two unrelated tables

FIGURE 14.2 Options for physically modeling logical subtypes.

The three solutions will result in very different performance outcomes. In particular, creating tables for the super-type and each subtype is likely to reduce performance in most circumstances, except where only the super-type is subject to a full table scan. Table 14.1 compares the performance of each of the three solutions for common database operations.

TABLE 14.1   Performance of various subtype/super-type implementations.

Operation	Single Table	Separate subtype and super-type tables	Separate subtype tables only—no super-type table
Inserting a new row	Single insert only.	Two inserts will be required.	Single insert only.
Updating a row	Single update only.	Usually a single update. If you need to update super-type and subtype columns, then two updates will be required.	Single update only.
Fetching a single row via an index	Single table access.	If you need rows from both subtype and super-type, then a join will be required.	Single table access.
Full table scan— super-type columns only	Slowest, since row length may be increased by columns from both subtypes.	Fastest, since super-table row length will be short.	OK. Row length will be greater than for a super-type/subtype split but shorter than for the single table solution.
Full table scan— subtype and super-type columns	Good.	Poor, since a join to one or more subtype tables will be required.	Best. No joins are required and no irrelevant columns need be scanned.

When implementing tables derived from subtypes, avoid implementing both super-type and subtype tables. Instead, implement a single table for all subtypes, or multiple subtables without a super-type table.

Using artificial primary keys

A *natural key* is one constructed from unique attributes which occur normally within the entity. An *artificial key* is one which contains no meaningful column information and which exists only to uniquely identify the row. There is a continual debate within the database community regarding the merits of "artificial" primary keys versus the "natural" key.

Natural keys may consist of multiple columns and may be composed of any datatype. In contrast, artificial keys are usually sequential numbers. For instance, the natural key for a CUSTOMER table might be a combination of the "government allocated corporation number" together with department or address (if we anticipate multiple "customers" within a single large corporation). An artificial key could be comprised of a single numeric column populated by an Oracle sequence.

Without entering into the wider debate of the merits of natural keys from a data modeling and design perspective, it is worth considering the merits of artificial keys from a performance perspective. There is little doubt that artificial keys generally result in superior performance:

❑ An artificial key will usually consist of a single numeric column. If a natural key consists of non-numeric or concatenated columns, then the key length will be longer and joins and index lookups will be less efficient.

❑ Since an artificial key contains no meaningful information, it should never need to be updated. If a natural primary key is updated, then updates to any referencing foreign keys will be required—which may significantly increase I/O overhead and lock contention.

❑ Artificial keys result in smaller indexes and may result in a shallower index tree. This will help optimize index lookups.

Clearly there will often be a requirement for the "natural" key columns to exist within the table and for these columns to be accessible via an index lookup. To allow for this, you can simply create an index on these columns.

Where possible, use numeric artificial keys, populated by sequences, in preference to natural keys comprising concatenated or non-numeric columns.

Choosing between VARCHAR2 and CHAR datatypes

Oracle provides two datatypes for character columns—VARCHAR2[1] and CHAR.

The CHAR datatype stores fixed length character data. If a string value shorter than the length of the CHAR column is inserted, it is blank padded to the length of the CHAR column. For instance, if the value "Fred" is inserted into a CHAR(12) column, it will be stored as "Fred." Thus a CHAR(12) column always requires 12 bytes of storage.

As the name implies, the VARCHAR2 datatype stores variable length character strings. VARCHAR2 columns are never implicitly blank padded and require storage only for the length of the data value inserted.

VARCHAR2s and CHARs behave differently in some comparison operations and it is generally regarded as unwise to mix them arbitrarily within a data model.

Because VARCHAR2 columns tend to require less storage, rows which are comprised of VARCHAR2s tend to be shorter than rows based on CHAR columns; and hence tables which are constructed with VARCHAR2s will also be smaller. Smaller tables will be less expensive to scan, and indexes on VARCHAR2s will be smaller and somewhat more efficient.

CHAR datatypes do have at least one performance advantage over VARCHAR2s. When a CHAR column is updated so that it becomes longer, free space within the row for the update is guaranteed. On the other hand, if a VARCHAR2 column is updated, it is possible that there will not be sufficient free space to support the update. This may result in the row being *chained* to a separate block, degrading index lookups on this row.

Use VARCHAR2s in preference to CHARs in order to reduce the row length and optimize table scans unless the risk of row chaining is excessive.

Using LONG columns

The LONG datatype can be used to store large amounts of data—up to 2 gigabytes. The long datatype has a number of restrictions from a functional point of view. From a performance point of view, we should remember that LONGs

---

[1] Oracle also supports a VARCHAR datatype, which is identical in operation to the VARCHAR2. However, the ANSI standard has yet to finalize the definition of the VARCHAR datatype and hence its definition in Oracle may change in the future. Therefore, it is recommended that you use the VARCHAR2 datatype, for which upward compatibility is assured.

may not appear in the WHERE clause and cannot be indexed. If we wish to select rows based on the contents of a LONG column, we will be forced to perform a full table scan and to perform the evaluation of the LONG data within our client program. This could result in excessive I/O and network traffic.

The VARCHAR2 datatype can store up to 2,000 bytes of information—compared with the CHAR datatype, which can store only 255 bytes. In many cases, a VARCHAR2 can be used in place of a LONG column and can be indexed or used in the WHERE clause.

EMPLOYEES2	
EMPLOYEE_ID	NUMBER
SURNAME	VARCHAR2(40)
FIRSTNAME	VARCHAR2(40)
ADDRESS1	VARCHAR2(40)
ADDRESS2	VARCHAR2(40)
ZIPCODE	VARCHAR2(6)
DATE_OF_BIRTH	DATE
PHONENO	VARCHAR2(12)
MANAGER_ID	NUMBER
SALARY	NUMBER
STATUS	VARCHAR2(9)
DEPARTMENT_ID	NUMBER
COMMENTS	LONG

FIGURE 14.3   Using a LONG column to store freeform text.

If the data to be stored is greater than 2,000 characters and there is an identified need to search for information within the data, then you may wish to consider storing the data in multiple rows within a subtable. For instance, consider the need to store freeform text, such as comments, in an EMPLOYEE table. We could use a LONG column, as is shown in Figure 14.3. However, by using a LONG, we would be unable to search for particular text within a comment—something we might realistically want to do.

An alternative approach is to store the freeform text in multiple VARCHAR2 columns in a separate table. This approach is illustrated in Figure 14.4. Of course, we now need to join to the COMMENTS table in order to retrieve the comments and, in some circumstances, the use of the LONG may be justified on the basis of reducing join overhead. However, if we ever want to search on comment text, the detail table solution will probably be preferred.

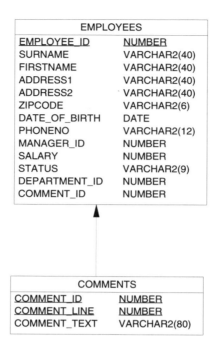

FIGURE 14.4   Storing freeform text in a detail table.

Don't use LONG columns where there may be a need to search for values within the column. Instead, use VARCHAR2 or a subtable (if the data is greater than 2,000 characters).

OPTIONAL ATTRIBUTES

Standard modeling guidelines suggest that optional attributes should become NULL columns. As we have seen in Chapter 6, NULL values can have a significant effect on performance of your SQL. The characteristics of NULL values which should be kept in mind are:

❑ NULL values cannot be indexed and it will usually require a full table scan to find NULL values with the IS NULL clause.

❑ The use of NULL values can reduce average row lengths, thus improving full table scan performance.

❑ If most column values are NULL and queries seek only values which are not NULL, then an index on the column will be compact and efficient.

Therefore, when determining the nullability of a column, consider whether it will ever be required to search for a row where the column is NULL. If the answer is "yes," then don't make the column NULL. Instead, define the column as NOT NULL and apply a default value.

Don't define a column as nullable if it is expected that queries will be constructed which will search for the NULL values. Instead, define the column as NOT NULL with a default.

In the case of character data, the default value will usually be a string such as "UNKNOWN." In the case of numeric data, it can be more difficult to determine an appropriate default value. For instance, consider a statistical database which contains the column AGE. Index based scans on age are common, as are queries to find rows where the age is unknown. If we create a default value for such a column, we will distort attempts to retrieve average, maximum or minimum ages in the database. In cases such as this, it may be necessary to use NULLs and either accept the consequent difficulty in quickly identifying unknown ages, or use de-normalization to create an indexed indicator column (AGE_KNOWN=N) which flags rows where the age is unknown.

DE-NORMALIZATION

Normalization is the process of eliminating redundancy and repeating groups from the data model and ensuring that key attributes are correctly defined. A normalized data model is the usual output from the logical modeling stage.

De-normalization is the process of reintroducing redundant, repeating or otherwise non-normalized structures into the physical model—almost always with the intention of improving performance.

Normalized data models tend to be inherently reasonably efficient and they are certainly easier to maintain. De-normalization—although sometimes desirable—entails certain risks:

❑ De-normalizing may improve the performance of certain key transactions or queries, but may inadvertently make other operations awkward, inefficient or impossible. For instance, repeating groups often seem to be a useful de-normalization because they avoid a join to a detail table. However, producing statistical information—such as averages—from repeating groups may be difficult.

❑ De-normalization will almost always lead to higher insert and update overhead.

❑ Because de-normalization introduces redundant information, it can also allow for inconsistent information. This can occur if the application code which is maintaining the de-normalized data develops software faults or if the use of an ad-hoc tool avoids the de-normalization routines. These inconsistencies may be difficult to detect and correct. The cost of the inconsistencies may be huge (for instance, if the de-normalized aggregate invoice total was inaccurate).

❑ There will be a software development and maintenance cost associated with maintaining the de-normalized data. Database triggers and snapshots reduce this cost since the code to maintain any replicated or redundant data can be stored within the database and need not be embedded in the application code. Database triggers also help to avoid inconsistencies arising if data is manipulated from outside of the application (from SQL*PLUS, for instance).

De-normalization is therefore not something that should be undertaken lightly. Make sure you have fully compared the costs and benefits of each proposed de-normalization. Ideally, test the performance gains (and costs!) of the de-normalization within your performance-tuning environment.

Replicating column values to avoid joins

One common de-normalization is the replication of a column in a related table so as to avoid a join. We saw an example of this kind of de-normalization in Chapter 10 when we replicated the DEPARTMENT_NAME column into the EMPLOYEES table. This is a very common form of de-normalization and can be very effective, since joins can multiply the cost of a query considerably.

> **Consider replicating columns to avoid excessive joins in critical queries. This can be very effective when the de-normalized data is stored on static lookup tables.**

"Roll up" aggregation

Queries which generate totals or aggregations can be very expensive and are often too resource-intensive to be run in prime time. One solution is to maintain a "totals" table which allows ready access to this information.

Such a summary table can be maintained in the following ways:

❑ If real-time summary data is required, the summary data can be updated whenever the source data is changed. For instance, a trigger could be used to update a SALES_TOTAL_BY_CUSTOMER table whenever the SALES table was changed. While this approach will allow real-time totals to be accessed without the overhead of on-line aggregation, it will have a small negative impact on sales transaction processing. There is also a danger that the heavy update activity on the summary table may lead to unacceptable lock contention.

❑ If real-time summary information is not essential, then the summary table can be populated by regularly scheduled jobs—possibly during off-peak processing periods. Oracle's snapshot mechanism provides a convenient means of implementing such an approach. The approach has the advantage of eliminating any overhead during peak transaction processing periods but does provide a less up-to-date view of the summary information.

Queries which perform aggregate operations can be very resource intensive. Consider maintaining de-normalized aggregate information, either real-time via triggers or at regular intervals using Oracle snapshots.

Indexing calculated columns or functions

Another common de-normalization technique involves replicating an amended version of a column within the source table. We used this technique in Chapter 10 to create uppercase versions of surname and given names to allow for case-insensitive indexed queries. Maintaining derived columns can allow index searches on functions to be performed and can reduce the overhead of performing complex manipulation on the source columns.

Maintain columns containing derived data if it's required to perform indexed searches on derived data to reduce the overhead of performing complex calculation during queries.

Creating artificial subtypes

We discussed in an earlier section the issues involving the translation of logical subtypes into physical tables. In general, we found that implementation of subtypes as detail tables generally diminished the performance of commonplace SQL operations.

However, if a large table is to be subjected to frequent table scans, but only a small portion of columns are usually queried, then it can be worthwhile splitting the table in two, especially if the infrequently accessed columns are very long.

We considered a good example of this technique in Chapter 6. If the EMPLOYEE table contained a LONG column with a high resolution image of each employee, then we would expect a full table scan performance to be poor. However, we wouldn't normally require that the image be accessed when performing a full table scan—it might only be accessed when accessing all details for a specific employee via an on-line query. In this case, we could improve the performance of full table scans and improve *buffer cache* efficiency by moving the LONG column to a subtable.

If a large table is expected to be subject to frequent table scans, consider moving long, infrequently accessed columns to a separate subtable to reduce row length and improve table scan performance.

Implementing de-normalization

Prior to the introduction of Oracle version 7, implementing redundant or derived columns required extensive changes to all application code to ensure that the redundant information was kept current. Even if this code was successfully implemented, there was still a danger that an update might be issued from an ad hoc tool (SQL*PLUS, for instance) and fail to update the redundant or derived columns.

Database triggers provide an easier, safer and often more efficient means of maintaining de-normalized information. A database trigger will fire regardless of the tool used to update the source data, so the risk of inconsistent data is reduced. By using triggers, application logic can be kept simpler and independent of changes to the database schema.

Use database triggers to maintain de-normalized data in preference to application code. Database triggers reduce the risk of inconsistent de-normalized data, simplify application code and will often perform more efficiently.

PARTITIONING TABLES IN LARGE APPLICATIONS

Very large tables can often present special maintenance problems. Operations requiring full table scans may become impractical and storage may degrade as rows are deleted, necessitating a table rebuild which may itself be impractical.

Partitioning these very large tables may help to avoid some of these problems. The partitioning allows rows for specific column value ranges to be stored separately and to be scanned, dropped or rebuilt independently.

Only Oracle8 supports true table partitioning. In Oracle8, tables may be composed of multiple partitions—each of which is associated with a specific range of data values. Oracle8 will automatically insert data into the correct partition and can limit table scans to appropriate partitions only. Partitions can be dropped or added as required.

Although Oracle7 does not support partition tables, Oracle version 7.3 allows you to create partitioned union views which have some of the same properties. A partition view defines a union of tables—each of which contains a constraint which limits the data in the table to a specific range of values. Oracle7 can limit a query against the view to the appropriate tables in a similar way to Oracle8's ability to limit a scan to appropriate partitions.

Unlike Oracle8 partitioned tables, Oracle7 partition views require that application code insert into the correct table. The view must be dropped and re-created if a "partition" is to be added or removed.

Consider partitioning large tables to improve parallelism, table scan performance and table maintenance. In Oracle8, use the partition option of the CREATE TABLE statement. In Oracle7, consider partition views.

APPLICATION DESIGN

Application design won't have the same direct and fundamental effect on a SQL statement's performance as the data model. However, there are some application design considerations which affect your ability to tune your SQL or to get the maximum benefit from well-tuned SQL.

SQL_TRACE

We've made extensive use of SQL_TRACE/*tkprof* trace output throughout this book. It is very convenient to be able to enable SQL_TRACE when required.

Although Oracle provides facilities for enabling SQL_TRACE for an entire database or for a specific session, it is most convenient if SQL_TRACE is enabled by the application itself. SQL_TRACE might be enabled:

❏ By a command line switch.

❏ By the presence of an environment variable.

❏ From a menu option on an interactive application.

After SQL_TRACE has been enabled, it is handy to issue a dummy SQL statement to "tag" the trace file. For instance:

```
select 'Tracing Program117' from dual;
```

The SQL statement will be written to the trace file and so traces for "Program117" will be easy to locate.

Build the ability to enable SQL_TRACE into your application. "Tag" the trace files by issuing a dummy SQL statement.

Profiling your application

Generating SQL traces will be invaluable when performance-tuning your application. However, SQL tracing only provides one part of the puzzle. To get the complete picture, your application should be able to generate performance data such as:

❏ Critical transactions per second.

❏ Elapsed time for a critical transaction.

❏ Elapsed time spent in various critical sections.

❏ Number of times key modules were visited.

This information can help you locate the "hot spots" within your application that will be most suitable for tuning. This may not always relate to SQL tuning, but will often point to the need for related measures, such as caching or array processing.

Some tools and environments allow profiling information, such as function call counts and elapsed times, to be generated automatically. In other tools, you may need to write your own code to collect this information.

> **Build into your application the ability to report on critical performance indicators. Consider the use of profiling tools to determine the time spent in various subroutines.**

LOCKING STRATEGY

Oracle locks database rows either when they are modified or when they are selected with the FOR UPDATE clause. If another session wishes to lock or update an already locked row, it will normally wait until competing locks have been released. Extended waiting for database locks can have a ruinous effect on both throughput and response time. The designers of a high performance application will adopt a locking policy which minimizes lock waits.

The pessimistic locking strategy

The pessimistic locking strategy is based on an assumption that it is possible that a row will be updated by another user between the time you fetch it and the time you update it. To avoid any contention, the pessimistic locking strategy requires that you lock the rows as they are retrieved. The application is therefore assured that no changes will be made to the row between the time the row is retrieved and the time it is updated.

The optimistic locking strategy

The optimistic locking strategy is based on the assumption that it is very unlikely that an update will be applied to a row between the time it is retrieved and the time it is modified. Based on this assumption, the optimistic locking strategy does not require that the row be locked when fetched. However, to avoid the possibility that the row *will* be updated between retrieval and modification, it will be necessary to check that the row has not been changed by another session when being modified or locked. This can be done by checking a time-stamp value, or by checking that the original selection criteria still applies. If it is detected that the row has been modified, then it will be necessary to either re-try the transaction or return an error to the user.

The optimistic and pessimistic locking strategies are diagrammed in Figure 14.5. Each strategy has its strengths and weaknesses and the choice of strategy can affect the performance of your application. Consider the following points when deciding upon an appropriate locking strategy:

❏ The optimistic locking strategy tends to hold locks for shorter periods of time, thus reducing the potential for lock contention.

❏ In an interactive application, the pessimistic locking strategy can allow locks to be held indefinitely. This is a common phenomenon in an interactive application which fetches and locks data pending and waits for the user to hit the "OK" button. It's quite possible for the row to remain locked for hours if the user "goes to lunch"—not realizing that a lock has been placed on the row displayed.

❏ If the optimism in the optimistic locking strategy is misplaced—if it is reasonably common for rows to be updated by other sessions between retrieval and update—then the optimistic locking strategy can lead to poor batch performance or user frustration as a high proportion of updates are rejected with a "try again" message.

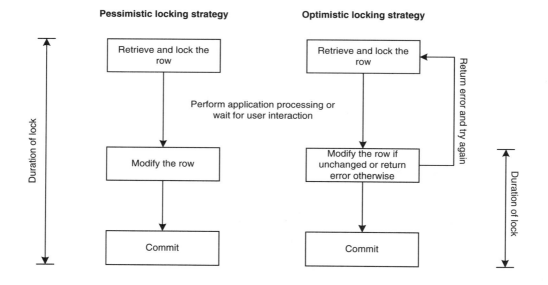

FIGURE 14.5   Optimistic and pessimistic locking strategies.

Choose a locking strategy which is right for your application. When possible, implement the optimistic locking strategy—which tends to reduce the duration of locks.

CACHING

No matter how well you tune your SQL, each SQL query will involve a substantial overhead. Control must be passed from your application to the Oracle server—often across a network—which must undertake complex processing. Any steps which reduce the number of SQL statement executions will usually be effective in improving the performance of your application.

One of the most effective ways of reducing SQL calls is to *cache* frequently accessed data within your application. This involves allocating an area of local memory—usually an array variable or PL/SQL table—and storing data items retrieved from the database in this memory. When a new data item is required, the program will first scan the cache to see if it has already been read. If found in the cache, a database access has been avoided. If not found, then the data item can be retrieved from the database and stored in the cache. We saw an example of caching in Chapter 10.

Caching particularly suits small, frequently accessed tables which contain static "lookup" values. For instance, a table of product codes, status codes, etc.

Here are some considerations to keep in mind when implementing caching:

❑ Caches consume memory on the client program. In many environments, memory is abundant and is of little consequence. However, for large tables and memory constrained environments, the implementation of a caching strategy could actually degrade performance by inducing *paging* or *swapping* (see Chapter 16 for a discussion on paging and swapping).

❑ When caches are relatively small, sequential scanning (i.e., examining each entry in the cache from the first entry to the last) will probably result in adequate performance. However, if the cache is larger, the sequential scan may start to degrade performance. To maintain good performance, it may be necessary to implement advanced search techniques such as *hashing* or *binary chop*.

❑ If the table being cached is updated during program execution, then the changes may not be reflected in your cache unless you implement some sophisticated synchronization mechanism. For this reason, local caching is best performed on static tables.

Caching frequently accessed data from small or medium-sized static tables can be very effective in improving program performance. However, beware of memory utilization and program complexity issues.

CLIENT-SERVER PARTITIONING

Oracle's ability to store and execute PL/SQL programs within the database server provides you with the capability to locate application logic either within the client environment or within the server environment. If client and server are located on computers with different processing capacities (for example, PC clients and a high-end UNIX server), client-server partitioning configurations may substantially affect performance.

Guidelines from the early days of client-server environments suggested moving as much processing logic as possible to the server, since the processing capacities of the server would typically be several times greater than the capabilities of the client platform. With the increasing processing capabilities of client machines in recent years, and the increased use of lower-end hardware as database servers, the differential is not so great and each case must now be judged on its merits.

Transactions which perform substantial database manipulation, but which have minimal input and output requirements are good candidates for server side processing, since a server side implementation will reduce network traffic.

Alternatively, operations which require user interaction, or are required to return sets of data, are difficult to implement in Oracle stored programs and may not perform efficiently. These operations may be best implemented in client code.

If the sum of processing power in the client machines outstrips the processing power available in the server—for instance, Pentium-based client workstations interacting with a Novell-based server—then implementing substantial application logic on the server may result in a server bottleneck and poor performance.

If the processing power of the server hardware is much greater than that available on the client side—for instance, a high-end UNIX SMP server and low-end 486 clients—then it may be advantageous to reduce the processing requirements of the clients by moving application logic to the server.

Carefully consider the break-up of application processing between client-based processing and server-based PL/SQL stored programs. Keep in mind the level of user interaction and database processing required by each transaction and the relative power of client and server hardware.

CONCURRENCY AND PARALLELISM

We noted in Chapter 12 that the full power of computers with multiple CPUs will often not be realized unless some degree of parallel processing can be implemented. Oracle has implemented parallel processing capabilities for a wide range of SQL statements, but it is still not possible to use Oracle's parallel capabilities in all circumstances. Even if database operations can be parallelized, this might be of no avail if all application processing occurs in serial.

When writing long-running, database-intensive programs, it is important to ensure that multiple instances of the same job can be run in parallel.

For example, consider a monthly billing program written in C, COBOL or some other procedural language. The job might run through the SALES table and generate invoices for outstanding sales. We could, of course, use the parallel query option to scan the SALES table in parallel, but because only one instance of the billing program would be running, it is unlikely that we would be able to fully exercise all of the host's CPU capacity since the billing program itself would only be able to utilize a single CPU.

The obvious solution—to run multiple billing programs concurrently—may not be as simple to implement as it might seem. If each instance of the billing program is to perform a full table scan of SALES, then an I/O bottleneck would be likely. Further, how do we prevent multiple instances of the program from issuing invoices to the same client?

One solution would be partitioning the invoices to be issued by the customer and executing background billing jobs for each customer. The master program would need to ensure that the required number of jobs were kept active concurrently. Simplified pseudo-code for the job might look like this:

```
FOR each customer
   SUBMIT billing job for customer
   INCREMENT jobs_running BY 1
   IF jobs_running = number_of_jobs_to_run THEN
        WAIT for a job to finish
        DECREMENT jobs_running BY 1
   END IF
NEXT customer
```

More complex logic may be required in many circumstances; and job schedulers available on some platforms may remove the need to explicitly control the number of jobs running.

In general, when requiring to run multiple jobs in parallel:

❑ Implement a mechanism of partitioning work to each job.

❑ Implement a means of keeping a specified number of jobs active at any given time.

❑ Eliminate any contention for resources between jobs such as database locks, output files, etc.

Ensure that long-running batch jobs can make use of available processing power by running in parallel.

CHAPTER SUMMARY

Although SQL tuning can lead to impressive improvements in application performance, the data model and the application design often provide the ultimate constraints on the performance that can be achieved. It is quite common to find that SQL performance cannot be improved without substantial and costly changes to the underlying database architecture.

In this chapter, we've developed some guidelines for developing high performance data models and application designs.

Of fundamental importance in effective high performance design is to incorporate tuning into the design process. Identify the performance requirements of the system early and build measurement and testing of these requirements into the project plan.

When developing the physical data model, keep these basic principles in mind:

- ❏ Avoid implementing separate tables for each subtype entity because of the probable join overhead.

- ❏ Make use of sequences to create "artificial" primary keys. These will often be more efficient in joins and lookups than natural keys, which might be non-numeric or concatenated.

- ❏ Use the VARCHAR2 datatype in preference to the CHAR attribute because it reduces row length and improves the efficiency of full table scans.

- ❏ Avoid LONG columns if possible—consider implementing the LONG as a VARCHAR2 or as a subtable of VARCHAR2s.

- ❏ Be careful when creating columns which can be NULL. If a query will search for these NULL values, an indexed retrieval will not be possible. Consider using NOT NULL together with the DEFAULT option.

De-normalization is the process of introducing redundant or derived information into the data model in order to improve performance. De-normalizing the data model has a number of risks on maintainability and performance grounds and should not be undertaken lightly. However, if properly implemented, de-normalization can greatly improve query performance. Some of the de-normalizations which you might wish to consider are:

- ❏ Replicating columns to avoid joins.

- ❏ Maintaining derived values to reduce aggregate operations, or to allow indexed lookup of derived values.

❑ Moving long, infrequently accessed columns to a detail table.

❑ Maintaining real-time or regularly updated summary data tables.

Where possible, implement de-normalization using Oracle triggers and snapshot technology. This reduces the risk of inconsistencies, simplifies application logic and is often the most efficient mechanism.

Partitioning large tables can improve queries which need to access only some of the tables partitions and can allow for easier table maintenance. True partition tables are only available in Oracle8, but you can achieve some of the benefits in Oracle7 by using partition views.

Effective application design will allow you to get the most out of your SQL by avoiding processing bottlenecks and building tuning facilities into the application.

❑ Ensure that your application supports some mechanism for invoking the SQL_TRACE facility and for reporting performance metrics.

❑ Adopt an appropriate locking model for your application. The optimistic locking model reduces the duration of locks and will usually provide good performance—providing that there is little contention for the same rows. If contention for rows is high, use the pessimistic model. Never allow locks to be held indefinitely at a user's discretion.

❑ Where possible, use caching in your application to reduce the number of requests made to the database. If possible (and this usually depends on the size of the tables), never ask the database for the same data twice.

❑ In a client-server environment, ensure that the split of processing between the client and the server is optimal. Using stored procedures and triggers moves much of the processing load from the client to the server and reduces parse overhead. If you have "big" servers and "little" clients, moving the processing load to the server is probably a wise move.

❑ Make sure that your application design doesn't prevent concurrent processing. For instance, exclusive locks on a file or on a single row in the database may allow only a single thread of execution to proceed concurrently. This will lead to poor performance in interactive applications and failure to leverage the power of all CPUs in a batch environments.

BUILDING A HIGH-PERFORMANCE ORACLE DATABASE SERVER

INTRODUCTION

The term *database server* can refer to an Oracle database instance or may be used to refer to both the Oracle instance and the host computer on which it resides. In this chapter, we will provide an introduction to sizing and configuring a database server which will support your application and allow your SQL to perform to its peak potential.

Although the database server can have a significant effect on the performance of SQL, you cannot usually compensate for untuned SQL by improving your database server. When SQL is untuned, its resource requirements might easily be magnified tens or hundreds of times. In this case, improving the configuration of your database server is likely to have a marginal effect at best on your SQL's performance. On the other hand, once your SQL is tuned, it's possible that the database server configuration can become the limiting factor. A well-sized and configured database server allows your SQL to reach its peak performance potential.

In this chapter, we provide a brief overview of server configuration issues. Some of the topics we'll discuss are:

❏ Establishing a realistic configuration for your computer hardware in terms of memory, disk devices, network and CPU.

❏ Using RAID devices.

❑ Designing the Oracle instance, including redo log placement and backup strategy.

❑ Creating tablespace layouts to suit your application.

❑ Configuring the Oracle shared memory area (SGA).

❑ Using optional features such as multi-threaded servers and parallel query.

❑ Advanced Oracle configuration issues.

A REVIEW OF THE ORACLE ARCHITECTURE

Before we can begin configuring our high performance server, we need to ensure that we have a firm grasp on basic Oracle database components. A detailed examination of the Oracle architecture is beyond the scope of this book—refer to Oracle documentation or other texts (see Appendix F) for more detailed coverage.

Figure 15.1 illustrates some of the basic components of an Oracle server at the memory, database and disk layers.

❑ *Database files* are files which contain the data which comprise an Oracle database.

❑ A *tablespace* is a logical structure which contains and groups the segments (mainly tables and indexes) which comprise a database. A tablespace may consist of more than one database file, but any given database file may belong to only one tablespace.

❑ Database *segments* include user objects, such as tables, indexes, *rollback segments* and *temporary segments*. A segment can belong to only one tablespace.

❑ *Rollback segments* are used to store original (or "before image") copies of database blocks which have been changed but not committed. Rollback segments contain the information which must be restored if a ROLLBACK command is issued.

❑ *Temporary segments* are used to store data needed for large sorts or for large intermediate temporary tables created during SQL statement execution.

❑ *Redo logs* contain details of transactions which may not as yet have been written to the datafiles. The primary purpose of redo logs is to allow for the recovery of the database in the event of a system or database failure.

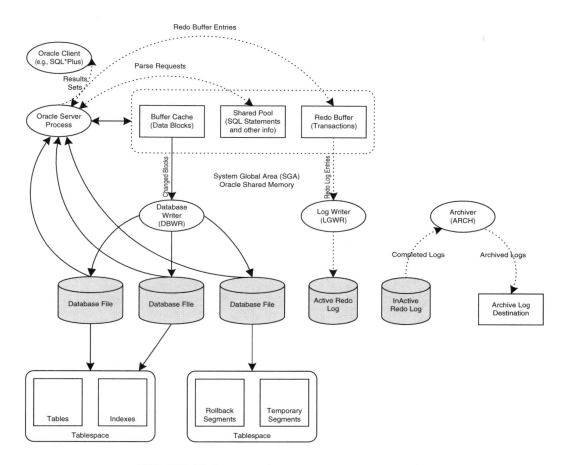

FIGURE 15.1 Basic Oracle database components.

❏ The Oracle *System Global Area* (SGA) is an area of shared memory which is used to store information which can be shared by multiple sessions.

❏ The *buffer cache* is an area in the SGA which contains copies of blocks from database files. The buffer cache exists primarily to reduce disk I/O by allowing sessions to access frequently or recently accessed data in memory.

❏ The *shared pool* contains cached SQL and PL/SQL statements, *data dictionary* information and sometimes private session information (if *multi-threaded servers* are enabled).

❑ The *redo buffer* contains redo log entries which have not yet been written to the redo logs. The redo buffer is flushed periodically and is always flushed when a COMMIT occurs.

❑ *Server processes* perform SQL processing on behalf of an Oracle session. A server process can perform processing for a single session only (a *dedicated server*) or for multiple sessions (a *multi-threaded server*). In some operating systems (VMS, for instance), the server process and the user process can be combined. In other operating systems and in client-server configurations, the user process and the server process are separate.

❑ Background processes perform specialized tasks on behalf of the all sessions. For instance, the *database writer (DBWR)* is responsible for writing changed blocks from the buffer cache to the database files. The *log writer (LGWR)* is responsible for writing blocks from the redo buffer to the redo logs. The *archiver* (ARCH) processes copies completed redo logs to backup storage. Other processes (*SMON, PMON*) perform housekeeping functions and some processes may be enabled only if certain Oracle options are enabled.

SIZING THE HOST COMPUTER

Determining the optimum hardware configuration for an application is a complex procedure which cannot always be reduced to a simple set of guidelines. The four main resources to size are:

Memory	Which is required by each database and user process and by Oracle's shared memory areas.
Disks	Which must be sufficient in size to store the data required by the database and sufficient in number to support the I/O requirements of the database.
CPU	Which must support the processing requirements of Oracle and user processes.
Network	Which must support communication between processes on multiple machines in a client-server configuration.

DETERMINING MEMORY REQUIREMENTS

Ensuring that there is sufficient free memory on your host computer is essential to maintain reasonable performance levels. In most operating systems, memory requirements can be calculated using the following formula:

$$memory = system + (\#users^*user\_overhead) + SGA + (\#servers^*server\_size)$$

The terms in the formula are:

❏ *System* is the system memory overhead. This includes memory required for the system kernel, buffers and other purposes. The value is operating system dependent. On a mid-range UNIX server, the value may be between 50-150MB.

❏ The *#users* is the number of user processes which are resident on the server. In a client-server configuration, there may be no clients on the server; whereas in a batch system, the "users" are batch programs which are resident on the server machine.

❏ *User_overhead* is the memory required by each user program. This is application specific and you would generally have to measure the memory utilization of your program using an operating system utility to determine its value.

❏ *SGA* is the size of the System Global Area. The optimal size of the SGA depends on your application and adjusting the size of the SGA is a common tuning measure. On a mid-range UNIX server, most SGAs use between 50 and 150MB of memory, although very large SGAs are often implemented. If you use multi-threaded servers, you will need to allocate additional storage for session information within the SGA.

❏ The *#servers* is the number of database server processes implemented on your system. If you implement *dedicated servers*, then the value will be equivalent to the number of users on your system plus the number of background processes. If you use *multi-threaded servers*, then the number can be much smaller—perhaps one server per 10 users—plus the number of background processes. There will be a minimum of four background processes on your system, but a more common minimum is six. Additional background processes may be created for parallel query servers, distributed database operations and for archiving of redo logs.

❏ *Server_size* is the amount of memory required for each Oracle server process. This can be dependent on the version of Oracle and the operating system, but in UNIX, the value is almost always 1.5-2MB.

To take an example, let's suppose we are sizing a UNIX database server. We know that the number of concurrent users will be about 500 and that a client-server configuration will be used. A large high-end UNIX machine is required, so let's assume that the system overhead is about 150MB. We plan to use dedicated database servers and to enable the parallel query option with a maximum of 50 query processes. We can't be totally sure what the size of the SGA will be, but it's unlikely to be more than 200MB.

From the above, we know that the number of background processes will be 6+50 (minimum + parallel query processes). The number of user server ("shadow") processes will be 500 (one per user). Assuming 1.5MB of memory per process, the total requirement for server processes is (500+6+50)*1.5MB = 834MB. Adding our system requirement and SGA requirement gives a total of 834MB+200MB+150MB=1,184 MB.

It's wise to add some additional memory to allow for errors or unanticipated load.

Some 32-bit architectures support a maximum of 2GB of memory. If your memory requirements exceed the maximum memory requirements for the hardware, you could try implementing multi-threaded servers, a *Transaction Monitoring* software or a *three-tier architecture* to reduce memory requirements.

The architecture of Oracle under Windows NT is somewhat different. Oracle background processes run as threads within the same memory space, and shadow (server) threads are limited to 256MB of memory. To support large user populations, you may need to implement *multi-threaded servers*.

ESTIMATING DISK DEVICES

A major aim of configuring an Oracle server is to ensure that disk I/O does not become a bottleneck. While there may be some differences in the performance of disk devices from various vendors—especially if the devices are in some sort of RAID configuration (discussed in detail later)—the major restraining factor on disk I/O is the number of disks acquired and the spread of I/O between these devices.

If possible, estimate the physical I/O which will be generated by your database, and use this figure to determine the number of devices which would be required to support the configuration.

How many disks are required for datafiles?

For a simplistic example, consider a transaction processing system in which 99% of the transactions were simply GET ROW, UPDATE ROW and COMMIT. The peak transaction rate has been specified at 50 transactions per second.

We know that we will be using an index lookup to retrieve the row which will require three or four index block lookups (index head block, one or two branch blocks and one leaf block) and one table block lookup. Therefore:

$$\text{I/Os required to fetch row} = 4.5$$

We will use the FOR UPDATE clause to lock the row as it is retrieved. This will require a further I/O to update the transaction list in the block itself and an I/O to update the rollback segment.

I/Os required to lock row = 2

Updating the row using the ROWID or *current of cursor* (see Chapter 10) will require an I/O to update the block and the rollback segment.

I/Os required to update the row = 2

Committing the row will involve an I/O to the redo log, but because the redo log should be on a dedicated device, we can overlook that I/O while we calculate the datafile's I/O. The total number of datafile I/Os for our transaction would appear to be about 8.5 (4.5+2+2). To be safe, let's double that estimate to account for overheads and special circumstances (data dictionary reads, chained rows, etc.) and allow 17 I/Os per transaction.

We expect Oracle's buffer cache to allow many of our I/Os to be satisfied in memory without requiring a disk I/O. Eighty percent is at the low end of hit rates in the buffer cache, so let's assume that disk I/Os will be about 20% of "logical" I/Os. Remember that our peak transaction rate is about 50/second, so we can estimate that datafile I/O will be:

Disk I/Os per second = 17 * 20% * 50 = 170

Disk capacities vary, but a disk in common usage can perform 20 random I/Os per second comfortably and as much as 50/second in bursts. Using the figure of 20 I/Os per second, we expect to require as many as 170/20=8.5 disk devices, and to spread our data evenly over these devices, in order to comfortably satisfy database file I/O.

There are a number of factors which bear on the accuracy of this estimate. For instance:

❏ We assumed a hit rate in the buffer cache of about 80%. However, hit rates of 90 to 95%—or even higher—are not uncommon, so our estimate is conservative (that is, our estimate errs on the side of caution).

❏ Disk capacities can vary, and the implementation of *disk caches, solid state disk* or RAID technology can have a big influence on the performance of your disk devices. Your disk vendor should be able to provide accurate random I/O rates.

❏ We've assumed an efficiently implemented transaction: efficient index lookup, using the ROWID to update the rows and so on. If the transaction turns out to be implemented less efficiently, then our disk requirement estimate may be inadequate.

Disks for redo devices

When the transaction is committed, the redo log entry in the redo log buffer must be written to disk. The characteristics of the redo log writes are very different from those of the data file I/O. First, they are *sequential I/Os*, which means that each access follows the previous access on the disk. The disk drive does not have to "seek" the disk block to access, and so, sequential I/Os are much faster than random I/Os. Most disk devices can perform about one hundred sequential I/Os per second. Second, the I/Os are write-only and will attempt to *write through* any disk cache. These factors combine to suggest that transaction processing will be optimized if a redo log is on a dedicated disk device. Of course, if your database is primarily read-only, then redo log I/O is unlikely to be an issue and the redo logs can be placed in virtually any convenient location.

The number of disk devices available to your database determines the maximum I/O rate which can be achieved. Try and calculate the likely I/O rates and use these rates to estimate the number of disk devices required by your application. Redo logs should be on a dedicated device if there is significant update activity.

Disk sizes

From the above discussion, it might be apparent that small capacity disk devices will result in a potentially greater I/O rate than large disk devices for a database of a known size. Unfortunately, disks are getting bigger and the best megabyte/dollar ratio is obtained with larger disks. Consequently, there is a temptation to buy bigger disks. Try and resist this temptation. Remember that in most cases, an 8GB disk is twice as slow as two 4GB disks.

RAID

RAID (Redundant Array of Inexpensive Disks) arrays are an increasingly popular way of delivering fault tolerant, high performance disk configurations. There are a number of levels of RAID and a number of factors to take into consideration when deciding upon a RAID configuration and the level of RAID to implement.

There are three levels of RAID commonly provided by storage vendors:

❏ *RAID 0* is sometimes referred to as "striping" disks. In this configuration, a logical disk is constructed from multiple physical disks. The data contained on the logical disk is spread evenly across the physical disk and hence random I/Os are also likely to be spread evenly. There is no redundancy built into this configuration, so if a disk fails, it will have to be recovered from a backup.

❏ *RAID 1* is referred to as disk "mirroring." In this configuration, a logical disk is comprised of two physical disks. In the event that one physical disk fails, processing can continue using the other physical disk. Each disk contains identical data and writes are processed in parallel, so there should be no negative effects on write performance. Two disks are available for reads, so there can be an improvement in read performance.

❏ In *RAID 5*, a logical disk is comprised of multiple physical disks. Data is arranged across the physical devices in a similar way to disk striping (RAID 0). However, a certain proportion of the data on the physical devices is *parity data*. This parity data contains enough information to derive data on other disks should a single physical device fail.

It's common to combine RAID 0 and RAID 1. Such striped and mirrored configurations offer protection against hardware failure together with spread of I/O load.

Performance implications of RAID

Both RAID 0 and RAID 5 improve the performance of concurrent random reads by spreading the load across multiple devices. However, RAID 5 tends to degrade write I/O, since both the source block and the parity block must be read and then updated.

Neither RAID 0 or RAID 5 offer any performance advantages over single disk configurations when sequential reads or writes are being undertaken.

The performance of RAID 0 + RAID 1 for database files, and RAID 1 for redo logs, is generally superior to any other configuration and offers full protection from media failure. However, RAID 5 requires less disk space than a RAID 0+1 configuration and may provide acceptable performance in many circumstances.

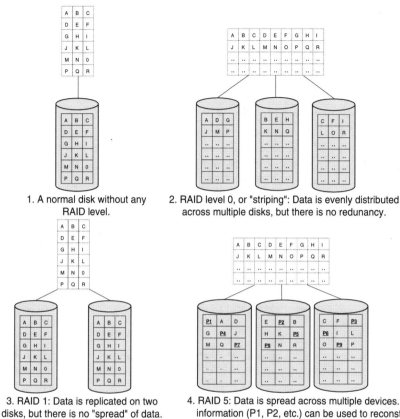

1. A normal disk without any RAID level.

2. RAID level 0, or "striping": Data is evenly distributed across multiple disks, but there is no redunancy.

3. RAID 1: Data is replicated on two disks, but there is no "spread" of data.

4. RAID 5: Data is spread across multiple devices. Parity information (P1, P2, etc.) can be used to reconstruct data if any single disk fails.

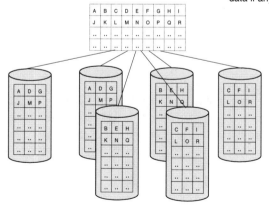

5. RAID 0 + 1 can be combined to provide both spreading of data and redundancy.

FIGURE 15.2 RAID configurations.

TABLE 15.1   Characteristics of different RAID levels.

Situation	RAID 0	RAID 0	RAID 0 + RAID 1	RAID 5
Database files are subject to high-read activity	Good performance	Unless datafiles are striped across disks using Oracle striping, disk bottlenecks may result	Good performance	Good performance
Database files are subject to high-write activity	Good performance	Unless datafiles are striped across disks using Oracle striping, disk bottlenecks may result	Good performance	Poor performance, since the parity block and the source block must both be read and updated
Redo logs	Striping is of limited benefit, since I/Os are all sequential	Good performance	Striping is of limited benefit, since I/Os are all sequential	Poor performance, since the parity block and the source block must both be read and updated
Protection from media failure	None	Yes	Yes	Yes
Disk overhead (amount of addition disk required)	None	100%	100%	Varies, depending on the number of devices in the array but usually 20-25%

> **RAID 5 results in degraded write performance and should never be used for Oracle redo logs. RAID 0+1 is the high performance/availability configuration of choice for Oracle database files, but RAID 5 can be used if the database has a high-read/low-update profile.**

Battery backed caches in RAID devices

The write penalty associated with RAID devices, and with disks in general, can be reduced by the use of a non-volatile cache. The non-volatile cache is a memory store with a battery backup, which ensures that the data in the cache is not lost in the event of a power failure. Because the data in the cache is protected against loss, it is allowable for the disk device to report that the data has been written to disk as soon as it is stored into the cache. The data can be written down to the physical disk at a later point in time.

Battery-backed caches can improve the performance of writes immensely, especially when the application requests confirmation that the data written has actually been committed to disk. Such caches are very common in RAID devices, mainly because they help to alleviate the overhead of disk writes in a RAID configuration. With a large enough cache, the RAID write overhead can be practically eliminated for some applications. However, if the cache fills with modified data, disk performance will reduce to that of the underlying disks and a substantial and sudden drop in performance may occur.

If considering a RAID 5-based solution, give preference to RAID arrays which are configured with a non-volatile cache. Such a cache can reduce the write I/O overhead associated with RAID.

CPUS

While we can estimate disk and memory requirements fairly accurately before a system is built, it is far more difficult to accurately estimate an application's CPU requirements.

The CPU requirements for an Oracle database server will be determined by:

❏ Operating system type.

❏ Hardware type.

❏ Database I/O rates.

❏ Frequency and types of transactions.

Since CPU requirements are so hard to estimate, you could use some of the following methods to arrive at a suitable CPU configuration:

❏ Consider the CPU requirements of "similar" systems. A similar system is one with a similar transaction type (e.g., OLTP or OLAP), transaction rate, network model (e.g., client-server or batch), data volumes and application characteristics.

❑ Measure the CPU requirements of your application before acquiring hardware. It may be possible to defer hardware acquisition until after volume testing. In this case, you may be able to measure the CPU requirements of the system in a test environment and extrapolate those requirements to a production configuration.

❑ Benchmark test your system on multiple hardware configurations. If your system is likely to require a substantial hardware investment, or if your organization is a significant client, vendors will often be willing to make hardware available for benchmark testing. You'll need to develop a simulation of your application and this may not be trivial. However, the vendor will often provide access to performance tuning experts and at the conclusion of the benchmark test you should have a good idea of your application's CPU requirements.

❑ Acquire a configuration with room for growth. The majority of large-scale Oracle applications are currently implemented on Symmetric Multi-Processor (SMP) UNIX minicomputers with the capacity for multiple CPUs. Windows NT-based servers are also available which allow for multiple CPUs. By acquiring a machine with the capability to add more CPU capacity, you insure against the possibility that the initial configuration may have insufficient CPU capability. You may have to buy more CPUs, but you will not have to replace the entire host computer.

Improvement gained by adding more CPUs

As more CPUs are added to an SMP machine, the overhead of coordination between the multiple CPUs increases. This means that a diminishing return is obtained as more CPUs are added. Moving from a single CPU to two CPUs may result in an almost doubling of processing capacity. However, moving from four to eight CPUs might result in only a 50% improvement (see Figure 15.3).

Because of the scalability deficiencies of multi-CPU systems, it is better to have a smaller number of more powerful CPUs than to have a large number of less powerful CPUs. Don't assume that doubling the number of CPUs will double the processing capacity.

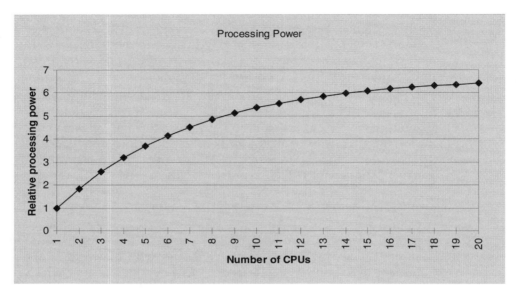

FIGURE 15.3   Processing improvements achieved by adding CPUs to an SMP computer.

NETWORKS

For many application architectures, particularly distributed database designs and client-server systems, the configuration of the network can have a major influence on overall application performance.

As with CPU requirements, it is can be difficult to calculate network requirements before a system has been built and measured. Therefore, a similar approach to CPU sizing is recommended:

❏ Determine the network requirements of your system. When client and server programs share a single host, the network component will be minimal. Client-server applications may generate a moderate network component. Distributed databases and applications which transfer large quantities of data in bulk will have a high network component.

❏ Consider the requirements of similar systems.

❏ Talk to vendors and networking experts.

❏ Benchmark test or trial your application.

❏ Configure a solution with room for growth.

When designing or selecting a network, bear the following principles in mind:

❏ For most client-server applications, Ethernet will be used to link client workstations into the wider network. For very network-intensive applications (such as multi-media applications), an ATM or other advanced networking solution may be preferable, although at much greater expense.

❏ When the Ethernet network becomes saturated, the solution is usually to split the network into a number of subnetworks. These subnetworks can then connect to a high speed "backbone."

❏ The backbone of a client-server network may be based on Ethernet, but recently is based on fiber optic solutions such as FDDI, Fiber channel and ATM.

BUILDING THE ORACLE DATABASE

Having ensured that the host computer is suitably configured to support the resource demands of your application you are now in a position to design a high performance Oracle database.

PROCESSING CHARACTERISTICS

First, ensure that you have a very clear understanding of the processing characteristics of the applications which are to run on your high performance database. For instance, is the database being used for on-line transaction processing or is the database more suited to long-running queries? Will there be overnight batch loads? How many on-line users will be required? Will there be large sorts? And so on.

Most of the recommendations in this chapter are based on the assumption that the database will be subject to long-running queries, on-line transactions and bulk loads. In other words, the recommendations are for a database which is ready for anything.

BACKUP STRATEGY

The backup mechanism selected for your database has a significant influence on its optimal configuration. Oracle allows database backups to occur when the database is on-line and allows a database to be restored to any point in time. To enable the on-line backup and point-in-time recovery, the database must be running in *archivelog* mode.

Archivelog mode requires that redo logs be copied to a separate location (the *archivelog destination*) as they are filled. This involves additional I/O on redo log devices and on the archivelog destination. If a redo log file needs to be reused before it has been archived, then the database operations will suspend until the archive completes. It's therefore essential that archive logging is optimized and that bottlenecks and processing interruptions are avoided.

Before designing the high performance database, it's wise to determine the backup requirements of the database. If in doubt, assume that archivelog mode will be enabled.

DATABASE BLOCK SIZE

The database block is the smallest unit of Oracle storage. Datafiles, buffer cache entries, tables and almost all Oracle structures are composed of database blocks. The size of the database blocks is set when the database is created and cannot be changed thereafter unless the database is recreated.

Oracle recommends that the database block size be set to a multiple of your operating system block size. However, the default value (2K on many systems) is often substantially less than the block size used by the operating system.

For a high performance database system, ensure that the database block size is at least the size of the operating system block size. Because operating system I/O on partial blocks can be very inefficient, and it might actually be slower to process a 2K block than an 8K block if the operating system block size is 8K. On many UNIX operating systems, the operating system block size is 8K. On Windows NT, the block size is 2K.

Ensure that your database block size is at least as large as your operating system block size.

Increasing the block size beyond the operating system block size will be most beneficial for applications which frequently perform full table scans, since the number of I/Os required to scan the table may be reduced. For OLTP applications, smaller block sizes (but not usually below the operating system block size) are recommended, since most table accesses will be via an index which will only be retrieving a single row.

REDO LOG CONFIGURATION

When a transaction is committed, a physical write to the redo log file must occur. The write must complete before the commit call returns control to the user; and hence, redo log writes can provide a limit to throughput of update intensive applications.

Redo log I/O will be optimized if the log is on a dedicated device and there is no contention for the device. If this is achieved, then the disk head will already be in the correct position when the commit is issued and write time will be minimized (the disk won't need to "seek").

Since the log writes are sequential and are performed by the Logwriter processes only, there is little advantage in striping. Since LGWR is write-only to these devices, the performance degradation caused by RAID 5 is likely to be most significant, even if the volume is dedicated to redo logs (because of contention with the archiver process).

In order to insure against any loss of data in the event of a media failure, it is essential that the redo logs be mirrored. Oracle provides a software mirroring capability (redo log multiplexing), although hardware mirroring (RAID 1) is probably more efficient.

To maximize transaction processing performance, locate redo logs on a fast dedicated disk device.

Because switching between redo logs results in a database *checkpoint*, and because a log cannot be reused until that checkpoint is completed, large and numerous logs can result in better throughput. By increasing the number of logs, we reduce the possibility that a log will be required for reuse before its checkpoint is complete. By increasing the size of the logs, we reduce the number of checkpoints which must occur.

The optimal size for your redo logs will depend on your transaction rate. You will want to size the logs so that log switches do not occur too rapidly. Since you will usually allocate dedicated devices for redo logs, there is likely to be substantial disk capacity available for logs. It's often easiest to overconfigure the log size and number initially. Log sizes of 64 to 256M are not uncommon. Configuring up to 10 to 20 redo logs is also not unusual.

OPTIMIZING ARCHIVING

Archived logs are copies of on-line redo logs which can be used to recover a database to point of failure or another point in time after a backup has been restored. Archive logging is also required if on-line backups are desired.

Once a redo log file is filled, and Oracle moves to the next log file, the archiver process (ARCH) copies the recently filled log to an alternate location. If the archiver reads from a log on the same physical device as the current log being written, then the sequential writes of the log writer will be disrupted. If the log writer falls sufficiently behind, then the database may stall since a log file cannot be reused until it has been archived.

It is therefore important to optimize the performance of the archiver. Contention between the archiver and the log writer can be minimized by alternating redo logs over two devices. The redo log writer can then write to one device while the archiver is reading from the other device. Since the archiver must be capable of writing at least as fast as the log writer, the archive destination should either be a dedicated device or a dedicated set of disks in a RAID 0+1 (mirrored and striped) configuration.

If running in archivelog mode and in a high-update environment, allocate an additional dedicated device (for a total of two) for the redo logs and another dedicated device (or devices) for the archive destination.

OPTIMIZING DATA FILE I/O

Oracle server processes read from database files when a requested data item cannot be found within the Oracle buffer cache. Waiting for data from disk is one of the most common reasons for delays experienced by server processes and so any reduction in these delays will help improve performance.

Writes to the database files are made on behalf of the user by one or more DBWR processes. These I/Os are random in nature. Although user processes do not wait for DBWR to complete its writes on their behalf, if DBWR falls behind sufficiently the Oracle buffer cache will fill up with "dirty" blocks and waits will occur when user processes try to introduce new blocks into the cache.

Optimizing datafile I/O can be achieved by:

❏ Getting a good hit rate in the buffer cache.

❏ Striping datafiles across a sufficient number of disks.

❏ Optimizing database writer performance.

Buffer cache hit rate

If a data block requested for read is already in the buffer cache, then a disk read will be avoided. Avoiding disk reads in this manner is one of the most significant optimizations which can be made to an Oracle database. In the next chapter, we'll see how to monitor database hit rates. If the hit rate is low, or the absolute number of disk reads too high, then increasing the size of the buffer cache can significantly improve disk performance.

We speak more on sizing the buffer cache later in this chapter and on monitoring buffer cache performance in Chapter 16.

Reduce your disk read overhead by adequately sizing your buffer cache.

Striping

We saw at the beginning of this chapter how the ultimate limit on I/O performance is dictated by the number of devices and the spread of data across these devices. You should first ensure that there are a sufficient number of disks to support your projected I/O rates. You should also ensure that data is spread as evenly as possible across these disks and that there are no disk "hot-spots."

There are three ways to spread data across devices:

❏ RAID 0 or "striping."

❏ RAID 5.

❏ Oracle striping.

We discussed RAID 5 earlier in this chapter. Remember that RAID 5 can decrease write performance unless the RAID array is associated with a battery-backed memory cache—and quite often even then.

Generally, RAID 0 is recommended on performance grounds. If RAID 0 is not available, you should manually stripe your tablespaces across multiple devices. Manual or Oracle striping is achieved by allocating many small files to each tablespace and spreading these files across multiple disks.

Because a table extent must be located within a single database file, tables consisting of a single extent will not be able to be manually striped. In this case, you will probably want to ensure that heavily utilized tables (and indexes) are composed of a large number of extents. You may wish to reduce the size of your datafiles to that of a single extent (plus a one block overhead).

> Use some form of striping for your database files, but avoid RAID 5 unless your update activity is very low or the disk array has a non-volatile cache. Oracle striping can be used if operating striping is not available.

Optimizing database writers

The database writer process (DBWR) is the only process which writes modified database blocks from the buffer cache to the database files. The database writer writes *asynchronously*. This means that a user process never needs to wait for the database writer write to complete. However, if the DBWR falls behind sufficiently, then the buffer cache will fill up with "dirty" blocks and waits will occur while user processes try to introduce new blocks into the cache.

Keeping the database writer optimized is therefore critical to maintaining database throughput. The best way to optimize database writer throughput is to spread I/O across multiple disk devices and allow the database writer to write to these disk devices in parallel.

Parallelizing database file writes can be achieved in two ways:

❑ Multiple database writers can be configured using the DB_WRITERS configuration parameter.

❑ Operating system *asynchronous I/O* or *list I/O* can be enabled. This will allow the database writer to issue write requests against multiple disk devices simultaneously.

Experience shows that the operating system asynchronous I/O performs more efficiently than multiple database writers. However, asynchronous I/O may not be available on all platforms or may require special measures. In some operating systems, asynchronous I/O may require that the database be built on *raw devices*.

If configuring multiple database writers, you may benefit from configuring as many database writers as you have physical disks.

> Optimize database writer performance by striping database files across multiple devices and enabling some form of parallel database write capability. Asynchronous or list I/O is preferred. If these facilities are not available, create multiple database writers with the *db_writer* parameter.

TABLESPACE DESIGN AND EXTENT SIZING POLICY

Tablespaces should be used to group objects with similar storage and access requirements. From a performance point of view, it is important to store objects with similar extent sizes and growth patterns together so as to avoid fragmentation, which can lead to performance degradation and database failures.

The following tablespaces should be created as standard:

❑ The SYSTEM tablespace contains objects owned by SYS (mainly data dictionary tables).

❑ The TOOLS tablespace contains objects created and used by development tools such as SQL*FORMS. In general, objects in this tablespace should be owned by SYSTEM.

❑ The ROLLBACK tablespace contains rollback segments only. Rollback segments can grow and contract, and it's important that they are located in their own tablespace so that the free space does not fragment or get used by other objects.

❑ The TEMPORARY tablespace contains temporary segments created by disk sorts and intermediate results sets.

❑ The USER tablespace contains ad hoc tables created by users. These might include temporary tables explicitly created by programs.

Once these standard tablespaces have been created, we can move on to creating tablespaces to hold application data.

There is a very strong argument for arranging objects into tablespaces based on uniform extent sizes. In this scheme, all objects in a tablespace have extents which are the same size. This requires that the tablespace be defined with the default initial extent size equal to the default next extent size and *pctincrease* set to "0." Segments (tables, indexes, etc.) never specify extent sizes in their CREATE statement, but always adopt the default storage for the tablespace.

The advantage of this uniform extent sizing policy is that it completely eliminates free space fragmentation within your database. Free space fragmentation occurs when tables with varying extent sizes are stored together. When an object is dropped (perhaps to be rebuilt), odd-sized areas of free space are created. Eventually, all the free space in the tablespace tends to consist of fragmented unevenly sized pockets of free space. When an object needs to create a new extent, it needs to scan these pockets for a suitably sized fragment. If one cannot be found, it must coalesce adjacent pockets. If a suitably sized area of free space still cannot be found, the segment will fail to extend.

If every extent in the tablespace is the same size, then the problems of free space fragmentation will never occur. Every extent in the free space will be reuseable and you will be able to drop and rebuild database objects without risking tablespace degradation. This will both improve performance when objects extend and give you more freedom to rebuild objects as a tuning measure (to create multiple free lists or eliminate chained rows, for instance).

To implement a standard extent sizing policy, you perform the following steps:

1. Determine the number of tablespaces. Usually at least six will be required (SMALL_TABLE, MEDIUM_TABLE, BIG_TABLE, SMALL_INDEX, MEDIUM_INDEX, BIG_INDEX).

2. Estimate the sizes for all your tables and indexes.

3. Assign an extent size to each tablespace. This will probably be a guess at first, but you will later refine the size.

4. Allocate tables and indexes to the appropriate tablespace. An object is in the correct tablespace if there is not too much wasted space (for instance, a 50K table in a tablespace with 50M extents) and if the table will not require too many extents.

5. Vary extent sizes and object allocations until all objects are in an appropriate tablespace.

One controversial aspect of the uniform sizing policy is that it leads to some objects having a large number of extents. In the past, Oracle recommended that objects be maintained in a single extent, if possible, to optimize scan performance. However, more recent research has shown that in the modern Oracle environments, multiple extents cause only a marginal performance degradation at worst, and may actually improve performance in some cases by spreading I/O.

> **Consider implementing a uniform extent policy for your tablespaces. This will eliminate free space fragmentation, improve performance and allow easier maintenance.**

ROLLBACK SEGMENT CONFIGURATION

The configuration of your rollback segments can have an important effect on the performance of your database—especially for transactions which modify data. Any operation which modifies data in the database must create entries in a rollback segment. Queries which read data that has been modified by uncommitted transactions will also need to access data within the rollback segments.

Poorly tuned rollback segments can have the following consequences:

❏ If there are too few rollback segments, transactions may need to wait for entries in the rollback segment.

❏ If rollback segments are too small, they may have grown dynamically during the transaction and later shrink back (if the rollback segment has an *optimal* size specified).

As well as these performance-related problems, poorly tuned rollback segments can lead to transaction failure (failure to extend a rollback segment) or query failure ("snapshot too old").

The following guidelines may serve as a starting point for rollback segment configuration for a transaction processing environment:

❏ The number of rollback segments should be at least one-quarter of the maximum number of concurrently active transactions. In batch environments, this may mean allocating a rollback segment for each concurrent job.

❏ Set OPTIMAL or MINEXTENTS so that the rollback segment has at least 10 to 20 extents. This minimizes waste and contention when a transaction tries to move into an already occupied extent.

❏ Make all extents the same size.

❏ Allow ample free space in the rollback segment tablespace for rollback segment expansion. Large, infrequent transactions can then extend a rollback segment when required. Use OPTIMAL to ensure that this space is reallocated when required.

It's very difficult to determine the optimal setting for rollback segments by theory alone. Rollback segments should be carefully monitored and storage should be adjusted as required. We discuss ways of monitoring rollback segments in Chapter 16.

TEMPORARY TABLESPACE

As discussed in Chapter 8, a sort operation which cannot be completed in memory must allocate a temporary segment. Temporary segments may also be created to hold intermediate result sets which do not fit in memory. The location of these temporary segments will be determined by the TEMPORARY tablespace clause in the CREATE or ALTER USER command. You should always allocate at least one tablespace for temporary segments.

Prior to Oracle 7.3, a temporary tablespace had the same characteristics as ordinary tablespaces, and temporary segments allocated space in much the same way as other segments, such as tables and indexes. An initial extent would first be allocated and if this was insufficient, further extents would be allocated as required. The size for these extents would be determined by the default settings for the tablespace as determined by the CREATE or ALTER tablespace commands.

Prior to Oracle 7.3, allocating additional extents for temporary segments often resulted in contention for the space transaction lock. As a result, best performance would be achieved by setting the size of extents such that temporary segments would require only one extent.

If you are using a version of Oracle prior to 7.3, use the INITIAL setting of the CREATE TABLESPACE command to ensure that most temporary segments require only one extent.

From Oracle 7.3 onwards, the TEMPORARY clause was added to the CREATE TABLESPACE command to explicitly create a tablespace for temporary operations. This tablespace will contain a single sort segment which can be used by all sessions. The segment never gets de-allocated, so the overhead and contention caused by allocating segments and extents is removed.

The extent size in the temporary tablespace should be at least the same as the memory allocation provided by the SORT_AREA_SIZE parameter (plus one block for the segment header).

If using Oracle 7.3 or later, use the TEMPORARY clause of the CREATE TABLESPACE statement to create a true temporary tablespace.

Whichever version of Oracle you are using, the temporary tablespace should be large enough to hold all concurrent temporary segments. If it is not, then errors may be returned to SQL statements which attempt to allocate additional space. It's not easy to predetermine how large disk sorts will be, so it may be necessary to refine your first estimates. You can measure the size of temporary segments using DBA_SEGMENTS (SEGMENT_TYPE="TEMPORARY") in Oracle 7.2 or earlier or V$SORT_SEGMENT in Oracle 7.3 or later.

SIZING THE SGA

The size and configuration of the SGA can have a substantial effect on the performance of your database. This is not surprising, since the SGA exists primarily to improve performance by buffering disk reads and reducing the need for SQL statement parsing.

It's difficult to determine in advance exactly how large the various components of the SGA should be. In this chapter, we'll provide an overview of the components of the SGA and some general sizing considerations. In the next chapter, we'll see how we can monitor the usage of the SGA and amend its storage to improve performance.

In general, oversizing areas of the SGA will not hurt performance, providing that the SGA can still fit in main memory. So if you have memory to spare, increasing the size of the SGA is usually not a bad thing.

Buffer cache

As we saw earlier, the buffer cache area of the SGA holds copies of data blocks in memory to reduce the need for disk I/O. The following principles are relevant to the sizing of the buffer cache:

❑ You aim to size the buffer cache so that sessions rarely need to read data blocks from disk. In general, you should attempt to get a "hit rate" of 90% or better—this means that 90% of all read requests are satisfied from the cache without requiring a disk access.

❑ In general, the higher rate of I/O activity, the greater your incentive to obtain a high hit rate. For instance, if your logical I/O rate is only 500 reads per second, then a hit rate of 90% translates into 50 reads/second—a rate which could probably be satisfied comfortably by two disk devices. However, if the logical I/O rate is 5,000 reads/second, then the physical I/O rate associated with a 90% hit rate will be 500 reads/second—which will probably overtax a disk configuration under 12 or more disks. In this case, you might need to aim for a hit rate of 95% or better.

❑ Applications which perform frequent full table scans of very large tables are unlikely to achieve a good hit rate in the buffer cache.

Adjusting the size of the buffer cache is one of the most fundamental tuning options. You need to ensure that there is enough free memory on your system to allow for an increase if required.

Buffer cache sizes vary depending on application characteristics and I/O rates. Many applications get good performance from a buffer cache as small as 10MB. High performance applications may have buffer caches of 50 to 100MB and caches of over 200MB are not rare.

Shared pool

The shared pool is another large and performance-critical area of memory held in the SGA. The major components of the shared pool are:

❑ The *library cache*, which stores parsed representations of SQL and PL/SQL blocks. The purpose of the library cache is to reduce the overhead of parsing SQL and PL/SQL by the caching and sharing of parsed SQL statements.

❑ The *dictionary cache* (sometimes called the *row cache*) caches *data dictionary* information. The data dictionary contains information about the database objects, users and other information defining the database. Because the data dictionary is referenced so frequently, it is cached separately in this special area.

❑ If using the *multi-threaded server*, then some user session information, such as cursor structures, will be stored in the shared pool. This section of the shared pool is called the *User Global Area* (UGA).

The size of the shared pool is determined by a single database configuration parameter (SHARED_POOL_SIZE) and the individual components of the shared pool cannot be separately sized. As with the buffer cache, it's not really possible to determine the exact optimal size in advance. It's necessary to monitor and adjust the shared pool until the optimal setting is found.

The following considerations are relevant when sizing the shared pool:

❑ The default value for the shared pool (3.5MB) tends to be too small for many applications.

❑ If your application makes extensive use of large PL/SQL stored packages, your shared pool requirements will be higher.

❑ If your database will use the multi-threaded server option, then your shared pool may need to be much larger. The amount of memory depends on the memory allocated for session information and on the number of concurrent cursors open by a session. The memory required usually does not exceed 200K per concurrent session unless large sort areas or hash areas are allocated.

It's not uncommon for shared pools of 50MB or higher to be allocated, although smaller allocations may also be adequate. If MTS is used, shared pools of several hundred megabytes may be required, although memory allocation for server processes will be reduced by a commensurate amount.

Redo buffer

The redo buffer contains redo entries destined for the redo log (see Figure 15.1). The redo log is flushed periodically or when a COMMIT occurs. Unlike the other areas in the shared pool, it is not wise to oversize the redo buffer. If the redo buffer is too large, the log writer process may have to work harder when a flush is required.

USING MULTI-THREADED SERVERS

Oracle's multi-threaded server (MTS) option allows multiple client programs to share Oracle server processes.

Without MTS, each Oracle session will usually acquire a dedicated server process.[1] If MTS is enabled, processes can share servers. This reduces the overall number of server processes required.

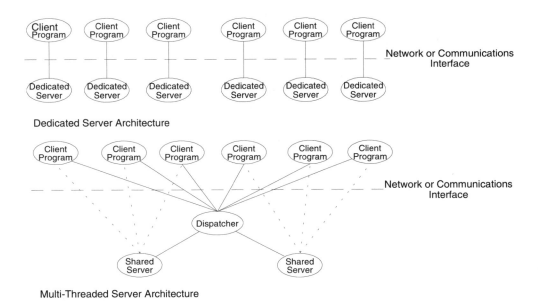

FIGURE 15.4 Comparison of the multi-threaded server and dedicated server architectures.

---

[1] Some operating systems allow user and server processing to occur in the same process if both exist on the same host—VMS is the usual example.

If implemented appropriately, MTS can reduce the overall memory requirements for an Oracle implementation. In some circumstances, implementing MTS may avoid Oracle internal bottlenecks by reducing the number of server processes competing for limited resources. However, if implemented inappropriately, MTS can have a very negative effect on performance. If user processes must wait for a server or dispatcher process to become available, then performance will degrade substantially.

Before implementing MTS, you need to make two decisions:

❑ Is MTS appropriate for your application?
❑ What is the optimal user to server process ratio?

MTS is suitable for interactive applications, since an interactive application will involve a substantial amount of "think time" while the user assimilates data, decides upon a course of action or is simply busy typing. With these applications, high user to server ratios will be possible, since server processes will usually be idle. On the other hand, applications which are continually busy, such as intensive batch processing or data loads, will tend to consume all the resources of a dedicated server and so will not benefit from shared servers.

If it's decided that MTS is appropriate, the user to server ratio will depend on the estimated proportion of time that user processes are idle, at least in terms of database activity. If you expect your processes to be idle 90% of the time, you might consider implementing one shared server per ten users. The number of dispatchers will usually be less than the number of servers—a ratio of one dispatcher per 5 to 10 servers might be appropriate.

In the next chapter, we'll see how the server processes can be monitored and these ratios adjusted. In Appendix D, configuration parameters which affect MTS are defined.

PARALLEL SERVER PROCESSES

Another important consideration is the configuration of parallel server processes to support parallel SQL. As we saw in Chapter 12, parallel SQL can contribute substantially to performance of individual queries. However, many environments are totally unsuitable for parallel query option. For instance, a transaction processing environment is unlikely to benefit from parallel query option—the transactions are unlikely to use table scans and parallelism is usually achieved by multiple sessions executing concurrently. However, parallel SQL may still be used in overnight batch processing where a few sessions must perform a great deal of processing in a short time.

Review the guidelines in Chapter 12 carefully to determine if parallel SQL is appropriate for your application. Then configure the number of parallel slaves appropriately. Guidelines for configuring the database for parallel processing are given in Appendix D.

RAW PARTITIONS

Under some operating systems (for instance, UNIX and Windows NT), Oracle database files may either be created on operating system filesystems (FAT, NTFS, UFS, JFS, etc.) or on "raw" partitions. Raw partitions allow I/O to go directly to the disk, avoiding the buffering of operating system filesystems. In UNIX, updates to datafiles on UNIX filesystems often need to update UNIX *inodes* (a sort of directory entry). Because inodes are often located in the first blocks of the filesystem, they can become a "hot spot," even when the filesystem is striped across multiple disks.

Using raw partitions entails a significant administrative overhead and complicates database backup and configuration. Some of these disadvantages are alleviated by the use of Logical Volume Management software.

The use of raw partitions is a controversial topic in the Oracle community and there is no clear consensus on the appropriate use of raw partitions. However, the following positions seem fairly well accepted:

❑ Where there is no bottleneck in the I/O subsystem, no improvement in application performance will be gained by a switch to raw devices.

❑ For very heavily loaded, I/O bound applications, some improvement in performance will be realized by the move to raw devices.

Under the UNIX or NT operating systems, consider the use of raw devices for databases with very high I/O requirements.

CHAPTER SUMMARY

In this chapter, we've briefly reviewed the principles of Oracle database design for high performance systems. These guidelines should help you construct an Oracle database which will provide a sound foundation for high-performance SQL. However, remember that database server configuration is not a replacement for tuning of SQL statements.

Ensuring that your host computer is appropriately sized is an essential prerequisite for good database and SQL performance:

❏ Memory requirements can be estimated fairly accurately from the size of your user population.

❏ The performance which can be obtained from your disk subsystem is essentially dependent on the number of disks allocated to your system and the technique used to spread datafiles across these disks. When determining disk requirements, remember that it's the number of disks—not the size of disks—which limits the I/O capacity of your system.

❏ RAID 5 arrays are an increasingly popular means of spreading disk I/O and economically providing fault tolerance, but have definite drawbacks for write-intensive Oracle databases. Redo logs should almost never be located on a RAID 5 array, and datafiles subject to high update activity should be located on RAID 5 only if the database is predominantly read-only.

❏ It is far more difficult to accurately estimate CPU and network requirements for a system. Experience, expert vendor advice and comparison with similar systems can help when formulating an initial estimate. Benchmark testing or simulations of your system can be used to obtain more accurate estimates. Ensuring that your configuration is capable of growth is usually a wise decision.

When building a high performance database, ensure that there is no inherent contention for resources and that all processing flows within the database architecture are free to proceed full speed.

❏ Understand the uses to which the database will be put. Know the transaction types, timings and backup strategy.

❏ Setting the database block size is an important decision and the block size cannot easily be changed after the database is created. Choose a block size which is at least as big as your operating system block size. Decision support databases or data warehouses may benefit from a larger block size while transaction processing databases may benefit from a smaller block size.

❏ Redo log throughput is a critical factor for databases with high update rates (for instance, bulk updates and OLTP). Redo logs should be on a fast device with low contention. Ideally, at least one disk should be allocated exclusively for redo logs. Redo logs should not be located on RAID 5 devices.

❏ If the database is in archivelog mode, then best performance will be achieved if redo logs are alternated between two dedicated devices. The archivelog destination should also be on a dedicated device.

❏ Database files should be striped across multiple disks. RAID 5 may be a barely acceptable way of doing this for read-intensive databases, although RAID 0+1 will usually give better performance. If no striping or RAID technology is available, tablespaces can be manually striped.

❏ There should be separate tablespaces for system objects, rollback segments, tables installed by tools and for temporary segments. In addition, application tables and indexes should be in separate tablespaces. One very effective way of arranging objects in multiple tablespaces is to do so in such a way that all extents in a tablespace are the same size. This eliminates free space fragmentation and improves performance and maintainability.

❏ Rollback segments should be configured so that there are sufficient rollback segments for concurrent transactions, as well as no need for rollback segment expansion in the event of normal transactions, but sufficient free space for expansion if an unusually large transaction is encountered.

❏ Create a temporary tablespace large enough to contain all concurrent temporary segments. In Oracle 7.3 and above, use the TEMPORARY keyword to optimize extent allocation and make the extent size a multiple of the SORT_AREA_SIZE+1 block. Before Oracle 7.3, make the extent size large enough so that sorts do not normally have to allocate a second extent.

❏ Implementing multi-threaded servers (MTS) can conserve operating system memory. However, if the demand for multi-threaded servers exceeds the number available, then contention for the servers will occur and performance will diminish.

❏ Ensure that database writer performance is optimal. This involves ensuring an effective spread of database files across multiple disks and allowing the database writer to perform writes to multiple disks in parallel. On some operating systems, a single database writer can write in parallel using asynchronous or list I/O. On other operating systems, it will be necessary to configure multiple database writers using the DB_WRITERS parameter.

❏ In the UNIX or NT operating system, consider the use of raw disk partitions instead of operating system filesystems for your database files and redo logs. Raw partitions are complex to administer and do not suit all applications, but applications with high I/O rates may benefit.

TUNING THE DATABASE SERVER

INTRODUCTION

Even after your SQL is perfectly tuned, you may still be disappointed with the SQL's performance. A common cause of this disappointment is a bottleneck or inefficiency in the database server. If you configured your server using the guidelines introduced in Chapter 15, you will have reduced the chances of such bottlenecks occurring. Even so, a database server may require fine-tuning to match specific application requirements. If the initial configuration of the server was not perfect, server tuning may be able to detect or compensate for deficiencies in server configuration.

This chapter will provide an overview of Oracle server performance diagnosis and treatment. Some of the topics we'll cover are:

❏ Monitoring the operating system to detect and remedy contention or resource shortages in memory, CPU or disk subsystems.

❏ An overview of Oracle processing flows architecture and the bottlenecks and inefficiencies that can develop.

❏ Methods of monitoring an Oracle server with an emphasis on the tools distributed on the CD-ROM which accompany this book.

❏ Key efficiency indicators which reveal the effectiveness of the various Oracle processes and memory stores.

❏ Using Oracle wait events to detect bottlenecks and contention for key resources.

❏ Advanced tracing options.

❏ Other common Oracle performance problems and tuning opportunities.

EVALUATING OPERATING SYSTEM PERFORMANCE

A good place to start when diagnosing a poorly performing Oracle system is at the operating system level. It is the operating system which provides key resources such as CPU, memory and disk I/O. By monitoring the operating system,we will be able to detect any shortfall in system resources (for instance, insufficient memory) or contention for resources (such as a "hot" disk).

OPTIONS FOR MONITORING THE OPERATING SYSTEM

Oracle is available on a wide range of operating systems and hardware platforms, and it's not possible to provide detailed guidance for them all. However, all modern operating systems provide some form of monitoring which can reveal the usage of computer resources. You should consult your operating system documentation for detailed descriptions of these tools.

"Standard" UNIX contains only very minimal monitoring tools. Most UNIX versions will include a version of the *sar* (System Activity Reporter) program. This program can collect system performance indicators such as CPU, memory and disk utilization. It reports only in text mode. Older BSD-based UNIX systems may not include *sar*, but will provide a program called *vmstat* which can provide similar, although less comprehensive, performance statistics.

Because *sar* and *vmstat* are difficult to use and provide no graphical display, most vendors implement alternative performance monitors. Additionally, a character-based program called *top* is available on most UNIX systems, which provides summary performance information and a "top processes" display.

Windows NT provides a graphical performance monitor appropriately named "Performance Monitor." This tool allows access to memory and CPU utilization, paging and disk activity.

VMS provides a character mode program called *monitor* from which all system resources may be monitored.

As well as the standard tools outlined above, there are third-party tuning and monitoring tools available for most of the operating systems—especially for variants of the UNIX operating system.

MEMORY BOTTLENECKS

A shortage of available memory on a host computer will usually lead to severe performance degradation.

Most host operating systems (Netware is a notable exception) support *virtual memory*, which allows the memory accessed by processes to exceed the actual memory available on the system. The memory in excess of actual memory is stored on disk. Disk accesses are several orders of magnitude slower than memory accesses, and so applications which need to access virtual memory located on disk will typically experience significant performance degradation.

When a process needs to access virtual memory which is not in physical memory, a *page fault* occurs and the data is retrieved from disk (usually from a file known as the *swapfile* or from the program's executable file) and loaded into main memory. If free physical memory becomes very short, most operating systems will look for data in main memory which has not been accessed recently. They will move it from main memory to the swapfile until sufficient free memory is available. The movement of data between the swapfile and main memory is known as *paging*.

The *scan rate* reveals the rate at which the operating system searches for memory to page out of the system. Increases in the scan rate can indicate increasing pressure on available memory.

If free physical memory becomes very short, the operating system may move an entire process out of main memory. This is known as *swapping*. Any level of swapping is usually a sign that a memory shortage has reached the crisis point.

Acceptable levels of swapping, paging and free memory vary between operating systems. However, the following principles apply to most operating systems:

❏ There should be no swapping.

❏ Paging activity should be low and regular. Sudden peaks of paging activity may indicate a shortage of memory.

❏ There should be sufficient free physical memory for all database processes and the Oracle SGA. Although virtual memory allows the computer to continue operation when all physical memory has been exhausted, the cost in performance terms is usually too high.

Options for treating memory shortages

If monitoring of the operating system leads to the conclusion that memory resources are inadequate, two options are available:

❏ Acquire additional memory.

❏ Reduce memory consumption.

If acquiring additional memory is not an option, we can attempt to reduce Oracle's memory consumption. Some of the ways this can be done are:

❑ Reduce parameters which control the size of the Oracle server processes. The two main options are SORT_AREA_SIZE and HASH_AREA_SIZE. These parameters control the amount of memory allocated for sorts and hash joins. If they are set unnecessarily high, memory may be being wasted.

❑ Reduce the size of the SGA. It's possible that the buffer cache or shared pool is oversized and also wasting memory.

❑ Reduce the number of server processes. This can be achieved by implementing shared server processes (multi-threaded servers, discussed in Chapter 15). This may be an effective way of reducing memory requirements, but may backfire if performance degrades because of contention for the shared servers.

> **If you observe a shortage of free memory, swapping or excessive paging, you probably have a memory bottleneck. Acquire more memory or take action to reduce memory requirements.**

I/O BOTTLENECKS

Disk I/O bottlenecks are also a common cause of poor database performance. Disk I/O bottlenecks occur whenever the disk subsystem cannot keep up with read or write requests. This may be recognized from a number of performance metrics:

❑ Disk %busy. If a disk is perpetually more than 50% busy, then it is likely that I/O requests to that disk are being delayed.

❑ Disk queue length. This is a measure of the number of requests queued against the disk. This should not average more than one or two. If the queue is long, but the disk is not busy, then the bottleneck may reside in the *disk controller* rather than the disk itself.

If you perceive that a particular disk is forming a bottleneck, the action depends on the types of files stored on the disk.

❑ If the disk contains Oracle database files, you should attempt to spread the files across multiple disk devices. The options for spreading I/O were discussed in Chapter 15 and include using RAID, operating system striping or Oracle striping.

❑ If the disk contains redo logs, ensure that no other active files exist on the same device. If you're in archivelog mode, alternate redo logs across multiple devices to eliminate contention with the Archiver process.

❑ If the disk contains archived redo logs, ensure that there is no process competing with the archive process for the device. It's common for this device to become very busy in bursts because when a log is archived, the archiver will copy the log to the archive destination in one operation.

Ensure that no disk devices are forming a bottleneck for your system. Spread data files across multiple devices and ensure that the redo logs are on fast dedicated devices.

CPU BOTTLENECKS

In a well-tuned Oracle database, memory and disk resources do not form a bottleneck. As load on such a database increases, the CPU becomes the critical resource and eventually no further increases in throughput are possible due to CPU limitations.

In one sense, such CPU bottlenecks are healthy, since they indicate that other subsystems are not constraining performance and that all available CPU can be used. However, excessive CPU utilization can also indicate that the application or Oracle is performing inefficiently. Possible causes of excessive CPU requirements in Oracle are:

❑ **Inefficient SQL**. SQL which has excessive I/O requirements will not only tax the I/O subsystem, but may also heavily load the CPU. This is because most of the overhead of Oracle logical I/O occurs in memory and the manipulation of Oracle shared memory is a CPU intensive operation.

❑ **Excessive sorting**. Sorts can be very CPU intensive. If your application performs very frequent in-memory sorts, then it may result in a CPU bottleneck. It may be possible to reduce this overhead by eliminating accidental sorts or using indexes to retrieve rows in the desired order. These issues are discussed in Chapter 7.

❑ **Excessive parsing**. We discussed the overheads of SQL statement parsing in Chapter 3. Applications with discard SQL cursors or which force re-parsing by using literals instead of bind variables will cause

Oracle to perform CPU intensive parse operations more frequently. Later in this chapter, we will see how to measure the degree and cost of the parse overhead. Guidelines for implementing cursor re-use and bind variables for various development tools are given in Appendix C.

If your application is CPU bound, you have the option of either increasing the amount of available CPU or reducing the demand for CPU. You may be able to add additional CPUs to your system or to upgrade your CPU to a faster model. Keep in mind that the improvement gains realized by adding CPUs diminish as more CPUs are installed. It is usually better to have faster CPUs rather than more CPUs.

To reduce the CPU requirements of your application, tune the application's SQL and minimize unnecessary re-parsing by using bind variables and performing efficient cursor management (Appendix C).

If your application is CPU bound, consider reducing CPU load by tuning SQL or eliminating unnecessary parsing. If adding CPU, remember that the benefit of additional CPUs diminishes as the number of CPUs added increases.

If your database server has multiple CPUs, it's possible that individual processes can become CPU bound even if the system as a whole is not. Since a single process can only make use of a single CPU, a single process blocked on a CPU will only consume 25% of the CPU resources of a 4-CPU machine. If you detect or suspect that a process is blocked in this manner, you could try and parallelize the operation—either by using parallel SQL (Chapter 12) or by parallelizing the application (Chapter 14).

RECOGNIZING ORACLE DATABASE BOTTLENECKS

ORACLE PROCESS FLOWS

Effective operation of the Oracle database depends on an efficient and unconstricted flow of SQL and/or data between user processes, Oracle processes, Oracle shared memory and disk structures. Figure 16.1 illustrates some of these process flows.

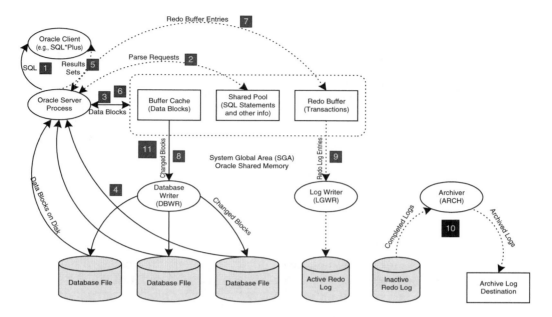

FIGURE 16.1 Process flows within an Oracle instance.

In Chapter 15, we briefly defined the components of the Oracle architecture, such as database files, redo logs and the SGA. Please refer to that chapter if you are unsure of the definition of any of those items.

In the following discussion, we will make frequent references to "latches." These are Oracle internal locks which prevent processes from concurrently updating the same area within the SGA. We will elaborate on the use of latches and latch contention later in this chapter.

To understand the process flows within an Oracle instance, consider the following short SQL transaction:

```
select * from employees
 where employee_id=:1
   for update of salary;

update employees
   set salary=:2
 where employee_id=:1;

commit;
```

The numbered labels in Figure 16.1 correspond to the following activities:

1. The client program (SQL*PLUS, Oracle power objects or some other tool) sends the SELECT statement to the server process.

2. The server process looks in the shared pool for a matching SQL statement. If none are found, the server process will parse the SQL and insert the SQL statement into the shared pool. Parsing the SQL statement requires CPU, and inserting a new statement into the shared pool requires a *latch*.

3. The server process looks in the buffer cache for the data blocks required. If found, the data block must be moved on to the most recently used end of the *Least Recently Used (LRU)* list. This, too, requires a *latch*.

4. If the block cannot be found in the buffer cache, then the server process must fetch it from the disk file. This will require a disk I/O. A latch must be acquired before the new block can be moved into the buffer cache.

5. The server process returns the rows retrieved to the client process. This may involve some network or communications delay.

6. When the client issues the UPDATE statement, the process of parsing the SQL and retrieving the rows to be updated must occur. The UPDATE statement then changes the relevant blocks in shared memory and also updates entries in the rollback segment buffers.

7. The UPDATE statement will also make an entry in the redo log buffer, which records the transaction details.

8. The database writer background process copies modified blocks from the buffer cache to the database files. The Oracle session performing the update does not have to wait for this to occur.

9. When the COMMIT statement is issued, the log writer process must copy the contents of the redo log buffer to the redo log file. The COMMIT statement will not return control to the Oracle session issuing the commit until this write has completed.

10. If running in archivelog mode, the archiver process will copy full redo logs to the archive destination. A redo log will not be eligible for re-use until it has been archived.

11. At regular intervals, or when a redo log switch occurs, Oracle performs a *checkpoint*. A checkpoint requires that all modified blocks in the buffer cache be written to disk. A redo log file cannot be re-used until the checkpoint completes.

Our aim in tuning and monitoring the Oracle instance is to ensure that data and instructions flow smoothly through and between the various processes and that we ensure that none of these flows becomes a bottleneck for the system as a whole. Monitoring scripts and tools can be used to detect any blockages or inefficiencies in each of the processing steps outlined above.

TUNING AND MONITORING TOOLS

To effectively diagnose and remedy server bottlenecks, we need tools which can help us to measure the load and efficiency of the various process flows. The available tools are:

❏ Monitoring tools which are provided with the Oracle software.

❏ Third-party tools.

❏ "Home grown" and public domain tools.

Oracle monitoring tools

The ultimate source of Oracle instance performance information is the dynamic performance table (or "V$" table). These are not "true" tables, but are instead representations of Oracle internal memory structures which can be queried using SQL. These tables contain a wealth of information from which we can derive very significant performance information. However, using the V$ views directly requires some experience.

Oracle *server manager* provides dynamic access to information in the V$ views. The display is in character mode only and provides very little in the way of interpretation.

The Oracle distribution includes a pair of SQL scripts which can be used to collect useful SQL statistics for a time interval. The script *utlbstat.sql* is run at the commencement of the period of interest and the *utlestat.sql* is run at the end of the period. The *utlestat* script produces a report on changes in the values of significant columns in the V$ tables. While this information can be highly significant, the report provides little interpretation and reports mainly raw data.

Oracle provides an optional add-on to the Oracle enterprise manager known as the *Oracle performance pack*. This product includes real-time graphical monitoring of Oracle databases together with analysis and diagnostic facilities. However, as an add-on product, the tool is not always available.

Third-party tools

A wide variety of third-party tools are available for monitoring and diagnosing Oracle performance. Some of these tools include:

❏ BMC Patrol (www.bmc.com)

❏ Menlo DBAware (www.menlosoftware.com)

❏ AdHawk

❏ Bradmark DbGeneral

All of these tools aim to monitor Oracle load, diagnose performance problems and advise on corrective action. The use of such a tool is highly recommended, since the native performance monitoring provided by Oracle leaves much to be desired.

The author's toolkit

Because the tools provided with a default Oracle instance are inadequate for detailed performance analysis, and because sophisticated third-party tool sets are often not available, many professionals develop their own tool kit for monitoring Oracle performance. The companion CD-ROM contains some utilities for performing basic monitoring of Oracle databases which have been developed by this author. Two of these tools will be used to illustrate the tuning principles outlined in this chapter:

❏ A set of SQL*PLUS tuning scripts are provided; they can report on the contents of the V$ tables either overall or for a specific period. These scripts bear some similarity to the *utlbstat* and *utlestat* scripts provided by Oracle, but also report significant performance ratios directly and attempt to flag significant or problem results. Two versions of each script are provided. Scripts ending in "stA" calculate statistics for the period since the database was last started. Scripts ending in "stS" calculate statistics for a sample time period which you define using the *samp_srt* and *samp_end* scripts.

❏ Monet is a Microsoft Windows-based tool which displays real-time graphical performance indicators for an Oracle instance. Figure 16.2 shows an example of the MONET main Monitor screen.

Appendix G includes details of the installation and use of these tools. These tools are free and are provided in the hope that they will be useful. However, they provide only a subset of features which are available in some commercial tools. Nonetheless, they are capable of detecting most of the common performance problems experienced by Oracle servers.

MONITORING LOAD

The performance of an SQL statement is often related to the overall load placed on an Oracle database. It is therefore important to have some idea of the average loads to which your Oracle instance is subjected. Some of the more frequently used measures of load are:

❏ Logical I/Os per second. This is a measure of the number of requests for Oracle data blocks made by Oracle sessions.

❑ SQL executions per second. This statistic reflects the number of SQL statements submitted to the database each second. A related measure is the number of parse requests per second, which is the number of times a session requests an SQL statement be parsed.

❑ Transactions per second. This measure indicates the number of COMMIT or ROLLBACK statements issued each second.

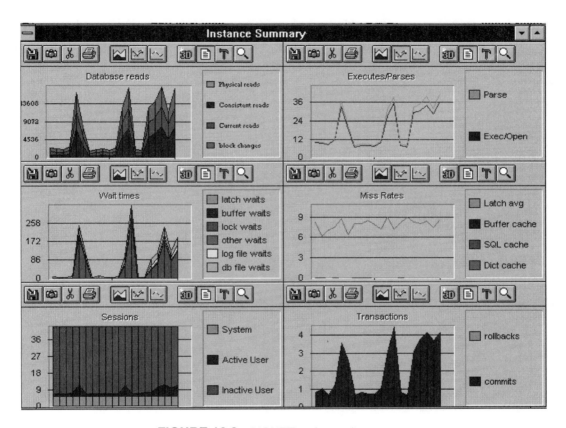

FIGURE 16.2 MONET main monitor screen.

Sudden changes in these load indicators may result if unusually resource-intensive ad hoc SQL is issued or if application usage patterns suddenly change. The Monet main screen and many of the third-party monitoring tools can display these load indicators.

KEY EFFICIENCY RATIOS

Certain key ratios can be used to determine the efficiency with which the Oracle database is being used. For instance, the buffer cache hit ratio indicates the frequency with which required blocks are not found in the buffer cache and must be fetched from disk. A low value indicates an inefficient use of the SGA and potential for performance improvements.

The *db_stA.sql* or *db_stS.sql* scripts can report on these ratios. Figure 16.3 shows sample output from this script.

```
Database efficiency indicators: MYDB  08/10/96:15:06
Sampled since database startup at 08/10/01:32:56

Ratio (mostly percentages)    Value      Comments
--------------------------    ----------  ------------------------------------
buffer cache hit ratio        84.0257    *** May need to increase db_block_buffers

dictionary cache hit rate     95.8915    *** high dictionary cache miss
library cache get hit ratio   97.9864
library cache pin hit ratio   98.6949

Immediate latch get rate      91.7468    *** Poor latch hit rate
Willing to wait latch get rate 99.0635

buffer busy wait ratio         0.2189
free buffer wait ratio         0.0014

chained fetch ratio            1.6892    *** PCTFREE too low for a table

CPU parse overhead             1.1423
cached cursor efficiency      53.4631
parse/execute                101.7552    *** high parse rate

redo space wait ratio          0.0000

disk sort ratio                1.2517

rows from idx/total rows      43.1392
short/total table scan ratio  89.9202

blk changes per transctn      11.4724
calls per transctn            15.4401
commits/(commits+rollbacks)   99.9807
rows per sort                 31.1387
```

FIGURE 16.3   Database efficiency indicators from the *db_stA* script.

Buffer cache hit ratio

This ratio describes the percentage of time a required data block was found in the buffer cache. For most applications, a value in excess of 90%—and often much higher—is desirable.

The buffer cache hit ratio is one of the most significant tuning ratios. Untuned values can lead to unnecessarily high disk I/O rates and contention for internal resources (*latches*).

To improve the buffer cache hit ratio, increase the size of the buffer cache by increasing the size of the DB_BLOCK_BUFFERS configuration parameter (see Appendix D).

Applications which perform frequent table scans of large tables may see little benefit from increasing the buffer cache. For these applications, low buffer cache hit ratios may be unavoidable.

> **To improve the buffer cache hit ratio, increase the number of buffer cache blocks with the db_block_buffers configuration parameter.**

Library cache get hit ratio

The *library cache get hit* ratio describes the frequency with which a matching SQL statement is found in the shared pool when an SQL parse request is issued by a session. If a matching SQL statement is not found in the library cache, then the SQL statement must be parsed and loaded into the library cache. Low hit rates will therefore result in high CPU consumption (from parsing) and possible contention for *library cache latches* (when the new SQL is loaded into the library cache). An acceptable rate for the library cache get hit rate is 90 to 95% or higher.

The most frequent cause of high miss rates in the library cache is the use of literals rather than *bind variables* in SQL statements. Bind variables reduce parse overhead by allowing otherwise identical SQL statements with different query parameters to be matched in the shared pool. However, bind variables preclude the use of column histograms and are not suitable in all circumstances. The trade-off between bind variables and histograms was discussed in Chapter 6.

> **To increase the get hit rate in the library cache, ensure that bind variables rather than literals are used in your SQL statements. But beware of disabling column histograms.**

Library cache pin hit ratio

A library cache pin miss occurs when a session executes an SQL statement which it has already parsed, but finds that the statement is no longer in the shared pool. This will happen if the statement has been "aged out" of the library cache to make way for new SQL statements. We expect a very high ratio for the pin hit ratio, since we would hope that once parsed, an SQL statement stays in the shared pool if we continue to execute it.

Low values (below 99%) for the library cache pin hit ratio usually imply that the shared pool is too small and that SQL statements are being "aged out" of the library cache prematurely.

Dictionary cache hit rate

The dictionary cache contains information about the structure of objects within the database. This information is frequently accessed during SQL statement parsing and during storage allocation.

The dictionary cache is stored in the shared pool and low hit rates (below 95%) probably indicate that the shared pool is too small.

> **Low hit rates for the library cache pin hit ratio (<99%) or for the dictionary cache hit ratio (<95%) probably indicate that the shared pool is too small. Increase the size of the shared pool with the SHARED_POOL configuration parameter.**

Latch get rates

Latches are Oracle internal locks which protect memory structures in the SGA. The latch get rate reflects the proportion of times that requests for latches are satisfied without waiting. Latch hit rates should be high—usually over 99%.

For a more detailed discussion, see the section on latches which appears later in this chapter .

Chained fetch ratio

This ratio represents the number of times sessions attempting to read a row had to perform an additional read because the row had been chained to another block. This will occur when an update to a row causes the row length to increase, but there is insufficient free space in the block for the expanded row.

The typical cause of chained rows is an inadequate value for PCTFREE— which is the amount of space within a block reserved for updates. PCTFREE is discussed in detail in Chapter 6. You can find tables which contain chained rows with the ANALYZE TABLE command, which will store a count of the chained rows in the USER_TABLES view. Tables with chained rows may need to be rebuilt using a higher value for PCTFREE.

> **A high value for the chained fetch ratio (>.1%) suggests a need to rebuild tables with a higher value for PCTFREE.**

Parse ratios

The parse/execute ratio reflects the ratio of parse calls to execute calls. Because parsing is an expensive operation, we hope that statements will be parsed once and then executed many times. High parse ratios (>20%) may result from the following circumstances:

❑ If literals rather than bind variables are used as query parameters, then the SQL will need to be re-parsed on every execution. You should use bind variables whenever possible, unless there is a pressing reason for using column histograms (see Chapter 6).

❑ Some development tools or techniques result in SQL cursors being discarded after execution. If a cursor is discarded, then the parse will be required before the statement can be re-executed.

If an application is discarding cursors, it may be possible to relieve some of the parse overhead by creating a *session cursor cache*. This can be done by using the SESSION_CACHED_CURSORS configuration parameter. This setting allows Oracle to maintain a "cache" of SQL statements in the session memory. If a session requests a parse of a statement which it has already parsed previously, then it might be found in the cache and re-parsing avoided.

The cached cursor efficiency ratio shows the efficiency of the session cursor cache. It reflects the proportion of times that a parse request was satisfied from an SQL statement in the session cursor cache. If the parse ratio is high, but the cached cursor efficiency is low, then it is likely that the high parse rate is caused by a failure to use bind variables.

CPU parse overhead

The CPU parse overhead describes the proportion of CPU time consumed by server processes due to the parsing of SQL statements. If this ratio is low, then reducing the parse ratio will probably not result in a significant performance boost. The higher the ratio, the more incentive you have to reduce parsing. The CPU parse overhead can be low even if the parse ratio is high—if the SQL being generated is very I/O intensive. In these circumstances, it may not matter that the statement is parsed every time.

If both the parse/execute ratio and the CPU parse overhead are high, then you have a strong incentive to reduce the parse overhead of your application. Use bind variables, re-use SQL cursors or try enabling a session cursor cache.

Redo space wait ratio

When a change is made to an Oracle data block, an entry must be made to the *redo log buffer*. If there is insufficient space for the redo log entry, then a redo space wait will occur. The redo space wait records the proportion of time a redo buffer had to wait because of insufficient space. If this ratio is high—certainly if higher than 1%—the LOG_BUFFER parameter should be increased.

Increase the LOG_BUFFER configuration parameter if redo space waits exceed one percent.

Disk sort ratio

This ratio records the proportion of Oracle sorts which were too large to be completed in memory and which consequently involved sorting using a temporary segment. Disk sorts are probably unavoidable if your application performs sort merge joins, aggregation or ordering of large tables.

However, if your application performs only small sort operations, you can attempt to reduce the disk sort ratio by increasing SORT_AREA_SIZE. But only do this if you have spare memory capacity on your server computer.

Consider increasing the value of SORT_AREA_SIZE if you have a high disk sort ratio.

Index fetch ratio

This ratio describes the proportion of rows which were obtained via a ROWID lookup (almost always from an index scan) versus those retrieved from a full table scan.

The appropriate value for this statistic depends on your application. You should bear in mind that a single large scan can retrieve a very large number of rows and hence disturb this ratio.

However, in transaction processing environments, you will probably want the index fetch ratio to be high.

UNDERSTANDING ORACLE WAIT EVENTS

In a perfect Oracle implementation, the Oracle server process would be able to perform its tasks using its own resources without experiencing any delays. However, in reality, Oracle sessions often wait on system or database requests or for resources to become available.

Using our earlier example—where a session selected a row, updated it and then committed—and using Figure 16.4, let's see where the server process might have to wait:

1. While the application is idle, the server process will be waiting for a message from the client.

2. When the server process parses a new SQL statement and the statement has not previously been executed, it will have to acquire a latch to add the new statement to the library cache. If the latch required is held by another session, then the server process may have to wait for the latch to become available.

3. The server process also has to acquire a latch when executing an SQL statement held in the shared pool and may have to wait on the latch if it is currently held by a different session.

4. When accessing a data block in the buffer cache, the server process will have to change the location of the block on the *Least Recently Used (LRU)* list. This will require obtaining, and possibly waiting, for the appropriate latch.

5. If the block is not in the buffer cache, the session will have to issue and wait for an I/O request to obtain the block. Moving a new block into the buffer cache also requires a latch which might also be unavailable and cause a wait.

6. Changing the data block requires obtaining latches both to change the block itself and to make an entry in the redo log buffer. Additionally, if there is insufficient free space in the redo log buffer, the session will need to wait for the log writer process to make space available.

7. When a COMMIT is issued, the session will need to wait for the log writer process to write the blocks in question to the redo log file.

8. The log writer session itself may need to wait if the redo log is full and the next redo log has an outstanding checkpoint or archive operation.

We can see that there are many reasons why an Oracle session may need to wait. Some of these waits—such as waiting for I/O operations—are inevitable, although we can reduce them in many cases by tuning I/O, the buffer cache or the SQL involved. Other operations—such as waiting for latches—can indicate inefficiencies in your configuration and opportunities for further tuning.

```
                 Top Oracle Wait events: MYDB 08/10/96:15:07
                Sampled since database startup at 08/10:01:32:56

                        No of      Pct of    Time      Pct of   Avg
Event name              waits      Waits     Waited    Time     Wait
--------------------    --------   -------   ---------  -------  -------
db file sequential read 20127526    96.83    1688243    66.46     .08
db file parallel write     53266      .26     322213    12.68    6.05
latch free                111956      .54     207144     8.15    1.85  *
free buffer waits           1767      .01      77792     3.06   44.02  *
log file sync              35746      .17      75615     2.98    2.12
log file parallel write    39347      .19      69333     2.73    1.76
db file scattered read    124715      .60      52930     2.08     .42
buffer busy waits         287488     1.38      26590     1.05     .09  *
write complete waits         362      .00        284      .37   23.65
rdbms ipc reply             2253      .01       8685      .34    3.85
```

FIGURE 16.4   Wait events report from *wait_stS* or *wait_stA* scripts.

The *wait_stA.sql* and *wait_stS.sql* scripts report on the occurrences and duration of the various wait categories either for a sample period or since the database was last started. Figure 16.4 shows some sample output from this report. Waits which indicate idle sessions or no activity are excluded from the report. For the remaining waits, the report shows the number and duration (in 1/100ths of a second) for the waits both as an absolute value and as a percentage of total waits.

Db file waits

Wait conditions starting with the phrase "db file" (*db file parallel write, db file scattered read, db file sequential read* or *db file single write*) all occur when an Oracle session issues an I/O request against an Oracle datafile. The session will use the operating system's read system call and wait while the I/O subsystem performs the I/O.

As noted earlier, database file writes are performed only by the database writer, and so *db file* write waits are never experienced by user sessions. User sessions do, however, read data from database files directly and will almost always experience *db file* read waits.

Unless your entire database is cached in memory, waiting for *db file* I/O is inevitable and the presence of *db file* waits does not indicate that anything is amiss within the database. In most healthy databases, *db file* waits account for about 80 to 90% of all non-idle wait times.

Db file waits can be reduced by:

❏ Optimizing disk I/O and striping datafiles.

❏ Reducing I/O requirements by increasing the size of the buffer cache.

❏ Reducing the I/O requirements of SQL statements through SQL tuning.

Log file sync/write waits

Just as Oracle sessions must inevitably wait for *db file* I/O, they must also wait for log file I/O. These waits occur when a COMMIT is issued. As revealed earlier, a COMMIT will cause the redo log writer session to flush the contents of the redo log to the redo file. The user session must wait for this write operation to complete before the COMMIT statement will return control.

The session issuing the COMMIT will wait on the *log file sync* event. When the log writer process issues the I/O request, it will wait on the *log file parallel write* event.

Both these wait events are inevitable and usually account for 10 to 20% of total non-idle wait times in a healthy database.

The average wait time for a log file parallel write is an important measure. It indicates how quickly the log writer process can flush the redo buffer and is a good indicator of the efficiency of the redo log device. Values of 0.2 (hundredths of a second) are good, and values of up to 5 (hundredths of a second) are not unusual. Values above this range may indicate contention for the redo log device.

Log file space/switch

This event occurs when you cannot make a redo log entry because there is no free space in the redo log buffer, or when you cannot write to a redo log because it is in the process of being switched. The incidence of this event should be negligible in a well-tuned database.

If waits of this category are occurring, check the redo space wait ratio from the *db_stA.sql* or *db_stS.sql* scripts. If this ratio is not close to zero, try increasing the size of the redo log buffer (with the LOG_BUFFER configuration parameter).

Also look at the *alert log* for the database instance. If you see instances of the message "cannot allocate new log.... checkpoint not complete" or "cannot allocate new log.... All on-line logs need archiving," then the log writer is stalling because a redo log has not been checkpointed or archived since it was last used. The usual remedy is to increase the size or number of on-line logs and make sure that there is no contention for the archive destination device.

> **Any significant waits for "log file space/switch" indicates that either the redo log buffer is too small, there are insufficient redo logs or the archiver process needs tuning.**

Buffer busy waits

This event occurs when a session cannot access a needed block because it is in use by another session. The two most common causes are insufficient *free lists* for a table or too few rollback segments.

If buffer busy waits are significant, run the *busy_stA* or *busy_stS* scripts. These scripts will report on the category of buffers being waited for. Figure 16.5 shows some sample output from these scripts.

```
                  Buffer busy statistics: MYDB 08/10/96:15:07
               Sampled since database startup at 08/10:01:32:56

                                             Time
                         Waits      Pct of   waited       Pct of
     Class               (/1000)    waits    (s)          Time
     ------------------   --------   -------  ----------   -------
     data block          287        99.97    271          97.24
     undo header         0          0.02     6            2.28
     undo block          0          0.01     1            0.47
     segment header      0          0.00     0            0.01
     sort block          0          0.00     0            0.00
     free list           0          0.00     0            0.00
     system undo block   0          0.00     0            0.00
     system undo header  0          0.00     0            0.00
     save undo header    0          0.00     0            0.00
     save undo block     0          0.00     0            0.00
```

FIGURE 16.5   Buffer busy statistics generated by the *busy_stS* or *busy_stA* script.

If the predominant buffer waits are for data blocks, then it is likely that you need to create multiple FREELISTS (using the FREELIST clause of the CREATE TABLE statement) for tables which are subject to very heavy concurrent inserts. If the leading category is for either "undo header" or "undo block," then you may need to create additional rollback segments.

> **"Buffer busy" waits usually indicate that heavily inserted tables should be re-created with multiple free lists or that there are insufficient rollback segments.**

Free buffer waits

Free buffer waits occur when a session wishes to read a data block from a database file on disk into the buffer cache. If there are no unmodified ("clean") blocks in the buffer cache, then the session will have to wait for the database writer process to write modified ("dirty") blocks to disk in order for free buffers to be made available.

Normally, the database writer is constantly writing dirty buffers to disk, so this event should rarely occur. When it does occur, it is usually due to one of the following reasons:

❏ Untuned disk layout. If datafiles are not spread evenly across disk devices, then a single disk may form a bottleneck to both read and write performance. In this circumstance, the database writer may not be able to clear dirty blocks from this device as rapidly as they are created.

❏ Untuned database writers. To efficiently write to multiple disk devices, it is essential that you either configure multiple database writers or implement *asynchronous* or *list I/O*—as discussed in Chapter 15. This will help the database writer keep up with changes to the buffer cache.

❏ Untuned sorts. Prior to Oracle 7.2, large sorts which required a temporary segment would write the sort blocks to the buffer cache and rely on the database writer to move them into the temporary segment. This would often "flood" the buffer cache and cause other sessions to encounter free buffer waits. In Oracle 7.2, this can be avoided by setting the configuration parameter SORT_DIRECT_WRITE to "true," which allows sorts to avoid the buffer cache completely. In Oracle 7.3 and above, the sort direct writes are enabled by default in most circumstances.

Write complete waits

This wait occurs when a session tries to modify a block which is currently being written to disk by the database writer process. This will, of course, happen occasionally; but if it is contributing significantly to overall waits, then it may indicate inefficiencies in the database writer. The treatment may involve optimizing datafile I/O and database writer configuration by spreading datafiles across multiple disks, using multiple database writers or employing asynchronous or list I/O.

> **"Free buffer"** and **"write complete"** waits often indicate inefficiencies in the database writer process or untuned disk I/O. Prior to Oracle 7.3, free buffer waits would often occur due to excessive or untuned disk sorts.

Enqueue waits

Enqueue waits occur when a session waits to obtain a lock. In most cases, this will occur because of a lock on a table or row which the waiting session wishes to lock or modify. In some circumstances, the lock involved may be an Oracle internal lock. If the database is well tuned and the application design is sound, then enqueue waits should be negligible. Common causes of excessive enqueue waits are:

❑ Contention for a specific row in the database. The application design may require that many processes update or lock the same row in the database. Once common example of this phenomenon is when primary keys are generated using a *sequence table* (see Chapter 11).

❑ Table locks caused by unindexed foreign keys. If an unindexed foreign key is updated, then the parent table will be subjected to a table lock until the transaction is complete. This was discussed in Chapter 9.

❑ "Old-style" temporary tablespaces. If the tablespace nominated as the temporary tablespace has not been identified with the TEMPORARY clause (introduced in Oracle 7.3), then sessions may contend for a "space transaction" lock.

❑ The space reserved for transactions within a data block is too small. By default, only one *transaction slot* for tables or two for indexes is allocated when the table or index is created. If additional transaction slots are required, they are created providing there is free space in the block. However, if all transaction slots are in use and there is no free space in the block, then a session wishing to lock a row in the block will encounter an enqueue wait, even if the row in question is not actually updated or locked. This phenomenon can occur if both PCT-FREE and INITRANS were set too low.

> **"Enqueue"** waits occur when a process is waiting to obtain a lock. This may mean contention for specific rows in the database, table locks resulting from unindexed foreign keys or contention for Oracle internal locks.

Row cache lock

This wait event occurs when a session needs to update information in the *data dictionary*. The data dictionary contains information about the structure of the database, including tables, indexes, users and storage allocation.

Row cache lock events should be negligible. They have been observed when sequences are created with the ORDER clause or NOCACHE clause. This causes each sequence access to write to the data dictionary and results in heavy loading on the row cache lock.

Latch free waits

Latches are Oracle internal locking mechanisms which prevent multiple sessions from simultaneously updating the same item within Oracle shared memory (SGA). If a session needs to acquire a latch which is held by another session, then a *latch free wait* may occur.

The presence of latch free waits of any significant magnitude may indicate a bottleneck within the SGA. The specific action depends on the latch and is discussed in the upcoming section on latches.

Events which are safe to ignore

There are some events which occur when a session is idle or waiting for instructions and which are not significant from a performance point of view. Some of these events are:

- ❏ NULL event
- ❏ SQL*NET message from client
- ❏ SQL*NET more data from client
- ❏ parallel query dequeue wait
- ❏ client message
- ❏ *smon* timer
- ❏ *rdbms ipc* message
- ❏ *pmon* timer
- ❏ WMON goes to sleep
- ❏ virtual circuit status
- ❏ dispatcher timer
- ❏ pipe get

Recording wait events to the trace file

There is an undocumented mechanism for recording wait information in the Oracle trace file. By using this mechanism, you cannot only record the waits experienced for a specific session, but you can also determine the exact "location" of a wait. For instance, for a *db file* sequential read wait, you could identify the table being accessed. For an enqueue wait, you could identify the type of lock for which you are waiting.

To add wait information to the trace file, you can use the ALTER SESSION SET EVENT command. Be aware that the functionality provided by events was primarily intended for Oracle support personnel and that you use these events at your own risk. However, this particular trace event is considered safe to use.

To set the trace event, you can use the following syntax:

```
alter session set events '10046 trace name context forever, level n';
```

where *n* is a number from 0 to 12 which can take the following values:

0	Turn tracing off
1	Basic tracing (equivalent to "alter session set sql_trace true")
4	Include bind information in the trace
8	Include event wait statistics in the trace
12	Include both event and bind statistics in the trace

Although the event causes wait information to appear in the raw trace file, the information is hard to interpret and *tkprof* does not format the information. The PRO*C *tk_waits* program contained on the companion CD-ROM can summarize and interpret these waits. It can also display the detailed wait information (for instance, name of object, latch or lock for which you are waiting). Figure 16.6 shows some sample output from this program.

```
Analysis of wait events in trace file ora_18686.trc

                      Summary of waits by category
                      ----------------------------

Event                            No of    Pct of    Time     Pct of
Name                             Waits    Total     Waited   Total
----------------------------     ------   -------   ------   -------
db file sequential read            658    18.42     19.48    42.30
latch free                        2311    64.70     17.18    37.31
log file sync                      514    14.39      6.46    14.03
log file space/switch                4     0.11      1.39     3.02
buffer busy waits                   82     2.30      1.08     2.35
write complete waits                 1     0.03      0.37     0.80
enqueue                              2     0.06      0.09     0.20
```

```
                        Breakdown of waits by resource
                        ------------------------------

Event or resource                       No of     Pct of    Time     Pct of
Name                                    Waits     Total     Waited   Total
--------------------------------------- -------- -------- -------- --------
                                        ** db file sequential read
SQLTUNE.CUSTOMERS                           157    23.86     6.51    33.42
SQLTUNE.CUSTOMERS_CONS_UNIQUE_2             200    30.40     6.48    33.26
SQLTUNE.CUSTOMERS_CONS_UNIQUE_1             156    23.71     5.19    26.64
SQLTUNE.SALES                                75    11.40     0.54     2.77
..................
** Sub Total **                             658              19.48

                                        ** latch free
enqueues                                    659    28.52     5.71    33.24
cache buffers lru chain                     318    13.76     3.16    18.39
session idle bit                            314    13.59     2.47    14.38
.............
                                        ** buffer busy waits
SQLTUNE.SALES                                25    30.49     0.46    42.59
RS13                                          6     7.32     0.12    11.11
SQLTUNE.PROGRAMS                              1     1.22     0.06     5.56
```

FIGURE 16.6   Partial output from the *tk_waits* PRO*C program.

LATCH WAITS

We saw in our example scenario that most operations which affect the contents of the SGA require that the process acquire a latch. A latch is similar to a lock, but instead of preventing two sessions from concurrently changing the same row, a latch prevents two sessions from altering the same area in shared memory at once.

Latches are usually held for a very brief interval and in a healthy database, there should be little or no contention for latches. Unfortunately, very busy databases often suffer considerably from latch contention.

If a process requires a latch and cannot obtain it on the first attempt, a *latch miss* will result. The session will repeatedly attempt to obtain the latch up to the value of the configuration parameter *spin_count*. This technique is known as acquiring a *spin lock*. If the session still cannot obtain the latch, then the session will relinquish the CPU and a *latch sleep* will result. A latch sleep will be recorded as a *latch free* wait. When the session "wakes up," it will repeat the attempt to obtain the latch.

Problems obtaining latches will have already been revealed in the "latch get rate" section of the *db_stA* or *db_stS* report. This ratio records what proportion of latch requests could be satisfied on the very first attempt.

Contention for latches is revealed by low overall latch get rates and by significant "latch free" waits. Both ratios should normally be less than 1%.

Latch problems will also be revealed by the *wait_stA* or *wait_stS* report. If latch free waits are significant—say more than 1% of total waits—then there may be a latch contention problem.

If you observe indications of latch contention, run the *latch_stA* or the *latch_stS* report. This report will show the relative frequency of gets, misses and sleeps for the various latches. Figure 16.7 shows some sample output from this report.

```
              Oracle latch statistics:MYDB 08/10/96:15:08
          Sampled since database startup at 08/10:01:32:56

                                                        spin    Waits
Latch                   % of  % of   Sleep   % of   Miss  success holding
Name                    gets  Sleeps rate %  Misses rate %   %       %
-------------------------------------------------------------------------
cache buffers lru chain  7.4   84.6   0.44    75.6   9.60*  95.7    99.0
cache buffers chains    88.7   14.4   0.01    23.6   0.25   98.3     .0
library cache             .6     .6   0.04      .2   0.23   85.8     .0
library cache pin        1.0     .2   0.01      .3   0.28   97.8     .2
messages                  .3     .1   0.01      .1   0.20   94.1     .0
shared pool               .1     .1   0.02      .0   0.07   71.3    39.1
row cache objects         .7     .1   0.00      .1   0.11   97.1     .0
redo allocation           .2     .0   0.01      .1   0.58   99.0     .0
system commit number      .2     .0   0.00      .0   0.02   97.8    11.1
multiblock read objects   .1     .0   0.00      .0   0.00   87.5    31.3
session idle bit          .3     .0   0.00      .0   0.02   99.4     .0
```

FIGURE 16.7   Latch statistics as shown by the *latch_stA* or *latch_stS* report.

The latches which contribute to a high proportion of misses or sleeps deserve attention. Not surprisingly, the latches which are used most heavily and which therefore typically suffer the most contention are the latches associated with the three major areas of the SGA: the *buffer cache latches*, the *library cache latches* and the *redo buffer latches*.

Buffer cache latches

Two main latches protect data blocks in the buffer cache. The *cache buffer lru chain* latch must be obtained in order to introduce a new block into the buffer cache and when writing a buffer back to disk.

A *cache buffer chains* latch is acquired whenever a block in the buffer cache is accessed (*pinned*).

Contention for these latches usually typifies a database which has very high I/O rates. It may be possible to reduce contention for the *cache buffer lru chain* latch by increasing the size of the buffer cache and thereby reducing the rate at which new blocks are introduced into the buffer cache.

Reducing contention for the cache buffer chains latch will usually require reducing logical I/O rates by tuning and minimizing the I/O requirements of application SQL.

You can create additional *cache buffer lru chain* latches by adjusting the configuration parameter DB_BLOCK_LRU_LATCHES. You may be able to reduce load on the *cache buffer chain* latches by increasing the configuration parameter _DB_BLOCK_HASH_BUCKETS.

Contention for the cache buffer lru chain and cache buffer chain latches can occur if a database sustains very high physical or logical I/O rates. Reduce I/O rates by tuning SQL or increasing the size of the buffer cache. Increasing the values of DB_BLOCK_LRU_LATCHES or _DB_BLOCK_HASH_BUCKETS may help.

Library cache latches

The library cache latches protect the cached SQL statements and objects definitions held in the library cache within the shared pool.

The *library cache* latch must be obtained in order to add a new statement to the library cache. During a parse request, Oracle searches the library cache for a matching statement. If one is not found, then Oracle will parse the SQL statement, acquire the library cache latch and insert the new SQL. Contention for the library cache latch can occur when an application generates very high quantities of unique, unsharable SQL—usually because literals have been used instead of bind variables. If the library cache latch is a bottleneck, try to improve the use of bind variables within your application. Misses on this latch may also be a sign that your application is parsing SQL at a high rate and may be suffering from excessive parse CPU overhead as well.

The *library cache pin* latch must be obtained when a statement in the library cache is re-executed. Misses on this latch occur when there are very high rates of SQL execution. There is little you can do to reduce the load on this latch, although using private rather than public synonyms (or even direct object references such as OWNER.TABLE) may help.

The _KGL_LATCH_COUNT parameter controls the number of library cache latches. The default value should be adequate, but you may wish to increase it if contention for the library cache latch cannot be resolved.

Contention for library cache and library cache pin latches can occur when there is heavy parsing or SQL execution rates. Misses on the library cache latch is usually a sign of excessive re-parsing of non-sharable SQL.

Redo buffer latches

Two latches control access to the redo buffer. The *redo allocation* latch must be acquired in order to allocate space within the buffer. If the redo log entry to be made is greater than the configuration parameter LOG_ENTRY_MAX_SIZE, the session which acquires the redo allocation latch may copy the entry into the redo buffer immediately while holding the allocation latch.

If the log entry is greater than LOG_ENTRY_MAX_SIZE, then the session will release the redo allocation latch and will acquire the *redo copy latch* in order to copy the entry.

There is only one redo allocation latch, but there may be up to LOG_SIMULTANEOUS_COPIES allocation latches.

If you see contention for the redo allocation latch, reduce the number of redo buffer copies which occur on this latch by decreasing LOG_ENTRY_MAX_SIZE. If you see contention for the redo copy latch, increase the number of copy latches by increasing the value of LOG_SIMULTANEOUS_COPIES.

Contention for the redo allocation latch can be reduced by lowering LOG_ENTRY_MAX_SIZE. Contention for the redo copy latch can be treated by increasing LOG_SIMULTANEOUS_COPIEs.

Spin count and latch sleeps

If a session "sleeps" because it cannot obtain a latch response, time will be significantly degraded. You can decrease the probability of the session sleeping by increasing the value of the configuration parameters _LATCH_SPIN_COUNT or SPIN_COUNT. This parameter controls the number of attempts the session will make to obtain the latch before sleeping. "Spinning" on the latch consumes CPU, so if you increase this parameter, you may see an increase in your system's overall CPU utilization. If your computer is near 100% CPU utilization and your application is throughput rather than response time driven, you could consider decreasing SPIN_COUNT in order to conserve CPU.

Adjusting SPIN_COUNT is a trial and error process. In general, only increase SPIN_COUNT if there are enough free CPU resources available on your system; and decrease it only if there is no spare CPU capacity.

'If you encounter latch contention and have spare CPU capacity, consider increasing the value of SPIN_COUNT. If CPU resources are at full capacity, consider decreasing the value of SPIN_COUNT.

MULTI-THREADED SERVER AND PARALLEL QUERY BOTTLE-NECKS

When you configure the Oracle multi-threaded server or parallel query option, additional background processes are created. The processes created are:

❑ Dispatchers, which receive SQL requests from client processes and pass these requests to shared servers.

❑ Shared server processes, which perform SQL operations on behalf of client processes.

❑ Parallel slave processes, which are used for the parallel execution of SQL statements.

The number of these processes will vary within high and low values determined by Oracle configuration parameters. These parameters are detailed in Appendix D.

```
                Shared and Parallel server statistics: MYDB 08/10/96:15:08
Sampled since database startup at 08/10:01:32:56

Statistic                                         Value
--------------------------------------------    -----------
COMMON queue avg wait %                            0.000
DISPATCHER queue avg wait %                        0.000
OUTBOUND queue avg wait %                          0.000
ipc dispatcher busy%                               0.000
tcp dispatcher busy%                               0.000
Parallel Query Servers Highwater                   0.000
mts_servers                                       25.000
mts_max_servers                                  200.000
mts_max_dispatchers                              100.000
parallel_min_servers                               0.000
parallel_max_servers                               5.000
```

FIGURE 16.8 Parallel query and multi-threaded server statistics reported by *serv_stA* or *serv_stS* scripts.

The *serv_stA.sql* script or *serv_stS* scripts display statistics for multi-threaded and parallel servers. Example output is shown in Figure 16.8.

Contention for shared servers or parallel slaves may be occurring sporadically or for short intervals and, for this reason, may not be showing up in the *serv_st* reports. The server monitor screen on the Monet tool allows you to monitor the state of these servers in real-time and detect bottlenecks which are of short duration.

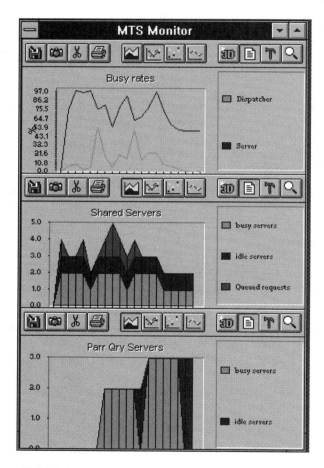

FIGURE 16.9   Server monitor from the Monet tool.

If MTS dispatchers or servers show high busy rates, or if you observe high wait rates in the common or dispatch queues, there may be a bottleneck in your MTS configuration. In this case, consider adding more dispatchers or shared servers.

If all parallel servers are busy, statements requesting parallel execution may run serially or at a reduced level of parallelism. You should ensure there is an appropriate number of parallel servers to service the parallel processing demand.

> **Ensure that the number of dispatchers, parallel servers and shared servers is properly configured. Too few servers can degrade the performance of sessions connecting via MTS or parallel servers. Too many servers may overload CPU, disk or memory resources.**

ROLLBACK SEGMENTS

Any session which modifies a row must make an entry in a rollback segment. If there are too few or too small rollback segments, then delays may occur as sessions wait for a free extent within a rollback segment or entry in the rollback segment's *transaction table*. You may have seen evidence of these delays as buffer busy waits when using the *wait_stS* or *busy_stS* scripts.

The scripts *rbs_stS* or *rbs_stA* can display detailed statistics for all rollback segments. Example output is provided in Figure 16.10.

```
              Rollback segment statistics: MYDB          18/10/96:07:22
                     Sampled since database startup

                 Current            High
   Rollback         Size  Optimal  Water  No. of Avg Shrink
   Segment          (KB)    (KB)    (KB) Shrinks      (KB) Extents
   ------------  -------- -------- -------- ------- ---------- -------
   SYSTEM             552             552        0          0       7
   RS01             52912    5120   69432       40       3535     189
   RS02              9232    5120    9792        5       1120      33
   RS03             43952    5120   43952        0          0     157
   RS04              5312    5120   18472        3       5040      19
   RS05              5312    5120    8112        4       1330      19
   RS06              5312    5120   23512        5       4760      19
   RS07              5312    5120   88752        5      17416      19
   RS08              5312    5120   11192        3       2240      19
   RS09              5312    5120   88192        3      27720      19
   RS10              5312    5120   82872        3      26320      19
   RS11              5312    5120   89592       18      10624      19
   RS12              5312    5120   14272        3       3640      19

   Rollback
   Segment            Gets        Writes waits/writes % waits/gets %
   ------------  ----------- ------------- -------------- ------------
   SYSTEM               454          6393         .0000        .0000
   RS01            3361391     458440991         .0032        .4365
```

RS02	157243	50727517	.0003	.0808
RS03	50264	24475613	.0001	.0318
RS04	454204	71203482	.0003	.0493
RS05	102979	43441644	.0001	.0418
RS06	253273	116848368	.0000	.0197
RS07	1160275	134877511	.0001	.0114
RS08	452659	70006858	.0004	.0566
RS09	1134542	131937362	.0014	.1666
RS10	782929	99279203	.0001	.0068
RS11	6550807	602308131	.0053	.4893
RS12	162088	52741664	.0001	.0339

FIGURE 16.10 Output from the *rbs_stA* script.

Ideally, Oracle sessions will not need to wait for rollback segments and rollback segments will extend or contract only occasionally.

The "waits/writes" and "waits/gets" columns in the *rbs_st* scripts indicate the proportion of read and write requests made to a rollback segment which needed to wait. If waits are significant (perhaps greater than 0.5%), then you may need to add more rollback segments. Also remember that it helps to have many extents in a rollback segment—at least 10 are recommended, but not usually more than 20.

The values for *optimal*, *high water mark* and *shrinks* can be used to determine if our rollback segments are appropriately sized:

❑ If the average size of the rollback segment is less than the optimal setting, then OPTIMAL is probably too high.

❑ If there are large numbers of shrinks, but the average size shrunk is small, the rollback segment is probably shrinking too often. Try increasing the value of OPTIMAL.

❑ If there are only a few shrinks, but the average size of the shrinks is high, then the rollback segment is probably well-configured and only expanding occasionally for very large transactions.

If sessions are waiting to make entries in the rollback segments, increase the number or size of rollback segments. Set the OPTIMAL size of the rollback segment so that dynamic extention and contraction occurs only rarely.

RESOURCE-INTENSIVE SQL

It's not uncommon for an otherwise well-tuned application or database server to experience performance degradation caused by a single untuned SQL statement. Two tools on the companion CD-ROM can help you to detect such "problem" SQL.

The *shared_s* program scans the shared pool and extracts and explains SQL with the highest resource requirements. You can filter SQL statements by number of executions, user who first parsed the SQL or text within the SQL statement. The SQL statements can be ordered by overall I/O requirements, I/O requirements per execution or by the number of executions. Figure 16.11 shows sample output from this program.

```
                 Analysis of SQL in Oracle Shared Pool
                 -------------------------------------
Sorted by buffer_gets desc
Maximum of 10 statements analyzed
Where executions > 0


-----------------------------------------------------------
Address        : 455F7DF0 Hash value:     400152181
First loaded   : 09/08:15:22
Parsing user   : SYS

 select "A".rowid, 'SALES', 'CUST_FK'
   from "SALES" "A" , CUSTOMERS" "B"
  where( "A"."CUSTOMER_ID" is not null)
    and( "B"."CUSTOMER_ID" (+)= "A"."CUSTOMER_ID") and( "B"."CUSTOMER_ID" is null)


Execution statistics
--------------------
                 Total   Executions    Per Exec    Per Row     %Total
Buffer gets      5823398          9      647044  5823398.00      21.94
Rows                   1          9           0
buffers/rows     5823398
Disk reads          9143          9        1015     9143.00
Parse Calls            9          9        100%
Sorts                  0          9           0          0
Hit Rate              99

Explain Plan
------------
Optimizer: CHOOSE  Cost=26

  SELECT STATEMENT
    FILTER
      NESTED LOOPS OUTER
        INDEX RANGE SCAN SALES_CUSTOMER
        INDEX UNIQUE SCAN PK_CUSTOMERS
```

FIGURE 16.11 Partial output from the *shared_s* program.

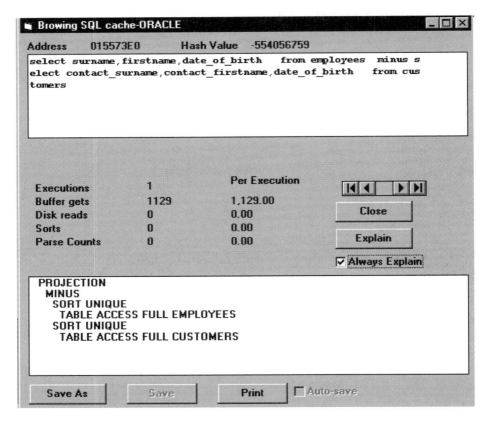

FIGURE 16.12   SQL cache browser in the Monet tool.

The Monet program also contains a shared pool browser which allows you to scroll through the statements in the shared pool.

CHAPTER SUMMARY

In this chapter, we've explored methods of monitoring an Oracle database server and detecting bottlenecks and inefficiencies in Oracle process flows.

A good place to start in the diagnosis of Oracle server performance problems is with an examination of operating system performance indicators. The various operating systems differ in the details of performance tuning and in the performance monitoring tools available, but share some fundamental principles:

❏ Shortages in available physical memory will almost always lead to dramatic performance degradation. You should ensure that there is adequate physical memory available at all times. Shortages in memory often show up as high rates of *paging* and *swapping*. The most effective remedy for memory shortages is to add additional memory to the configuration, although Oracle's memory requirements can be reduced by downsizing the SGA or implementing multi-threaded servers.

❏ I/O bottlenecks may occur if a particular disk or disks is continually busy. You can eliminate I/O bottlenecks by distributing database files evenly across physical devices or reducing I/O requirements by increasing the size of the buffer cache or tuning SQL.

❏ Oracle is designed so that the CPU will provide the ultimate limitation on performance. If CPU utilization is continually high, it may indicate a need to upgrade the server hardware. Reducing CPU requirements in Oracle may be possible by tuning SQL and reducing parsing.

The Oracle architecture implements a complex interaction between user and database processes, shared memory and datafiles. If a bottleneck prevents an efficient flow of processing through this architecture, then your SQL may be unable to perform to its potential.

The default monitoring tools provided by Oracle are not very powerful, but there are many third-party tools which can assist in monitoring and there are free tools on this book's companion CD-ROM.

There are a number of critical efficiency indicators which can help you determine if Oracle is operating efficiently. Some of the main indicators are:

❏ The buffer cache hit ratio, which reflects the proportion of database I/Os which were satisfied by data blocks held in the buffer cache. For transaction processing systems, high ratios are recommended—greater than 90 to 95%. For applications which perform frequent scans of large tables, it may not be possible to achieve such a high hit rate.

❏ The library cache hit ratio reflects the number of parse requests which found a matching SQL statement in the library cache. Low ratios can occur when literals are used in place of bind variables and can result in excessive CPU overhead and *latch contention*.

❏ The library cache pin hit ratio and the dictionary cache hit ratio reflect the efficiency of the Oracle shared pool. Low hit ratios usually mean that the shared pool should be increased in size.

❏ The parse ratio represents the proportion of calls to the database which were requests to parse new SQL statements. High ratios may indicate poor SQL statement handling in the application and may result in excessive CPU consumption.

❏ The redo space ratio reflects the proportion of redo log entries which had to wait for free space in the redo log buffer. High values may indicate the redo log buffer should be increased in size.

❏ The disk sort ratio reports the percentage of sorts which could not be satisfied in memory and therefore had to allocate or use a temporary segment. Disk sorts may be unavoidable, but if your disk sort ratio is very high, you might consider allocating more memory to sorts via the configuration parameter SORT_AREA_SIZE.

❏ The index fetch ratio shows you the proportion of rows which were obtained via an index or ROWID lookup. In a transaction processing environment, low values may indicate excessive full table scans.

Oracle sessions often have to cease SQL processing in order to wait for a resource to become available. Analyzing waits and eliminating unnecessary waits is an important step in curing server bottlenecks.

❏ Waits for database file reads are inevitable and usually account for the vast majority (80 to 90%) of waits in a well-tuned system.

❏ Waits for redo log writes are also inevitable and may account for 10 to 20% of waits.

❏ The presence of buffer busy waits can be an indication of free list or rollback segment contention.

❏ Free buffer waits and write complete waits may indicate database writer inefficiencies or, in earlier versions of Oracle, heavy disk sort activity.

❏ Enqueue waits indicate contention for database locks.

❏ Latch waits indicate contention for structures within the SGA. Cache buffer latches indicate heavy activity in the buffer cache and may indicate excessive I/O rates. Library cache latches indicate contention for the SQL cache in the shared pool and possibly excessive unsharable SQL. Redo allocation and redo copy latches indicate contention for the log buffer.

Other areas of contention which might be experienced are:

❏ If you are using multi-threaded servers, sessions may be waiting for a server or dispatcher to become available. If you observe this, you should increase the number of available servers or dispatchers.

❏ Parallelized SQL statements may encounter dramatic reductions in performance if there are not sufficient parallel slave processes to allow execution to proceed in parallel.

❏ Sessions may wait for rollback segments if there are too few rollback segments or if the number of extents or size of segments is too small. Excessive dynamic extension and contraction of rollback segments can also lead to performance problems.

❏ A few resource-intensive SQL statements can degrade the performance of the entire system. Use shared pool browsers to identify these SQL statements.

REFERENCE

In this section, we summarize commands and options which you may need on a day-to-day basis when writing and tuning high-performance SQL. The concepts and facilities referred to here are covered in greater depth in the main sections of this book.

HINTS

Hints are used to influence the decisions made by the Oracle query optimizers. Note that all hints except for RULE implicitly invoke the Cost Based Optimizer, irrespective of optmizer mode or the presence or absence of statistics.

HINTS must be enclosed in a comment block immediately following the first keyword in an SQL statement or in a subquery and are preceded by the plus sign "+". Remember that if a table alias is specified in the SQL then it must be used in the hint. For instance:

```
SELECT /*+PARALLEL(N,8) */  name FROM names N;
```

Hint	Usage
ALL_ROWS	Use the cost based optimizer and optimize for the retrieval of all rows.
AND_EQUAL(*table_name index_name index_name ....*)	Retrieve rows from the specified table using each of the specified indexes and merge the results.
BITMAP(*table_name index_name*)	Retrieve rows from the specified table using the specified bitmap index.

Hint	Usage
CACHE	Encourages rows retrieved by a full table scan to remain in the buffer cache of the SGA.
CHOOSE	If statistics have been collected for any table involved in the SQL statement, use cost-based/all-rows optimization, otherwise use rule based optimization.
CLUSTER(*table_name*)	Use a cluster scan to retrieve table rows.
DRIVING_SITE(*table_name*)	For a distributed SQL statement, causes the site at which the specified table resides to be the driving site.
FIRST_ROWS	Specifies that the cost based optimizer should optimize the statement to reduce the cost of retrieving the first row only.
FULL(*table_name*)	Use a full table scan to retrieve rows from the specified table.
HASH(*table_name*)	Use a hash scan to retrieve rows from the specified table. The table must be stored in a hash cluster.
HASH_AJ	Perform a anti-join using hash join methodology. This hint must appear after the SELECT statement of a NOT IN subquery.
INDEX(*table_name [index_name]*)	Use the specified index to retrieve rows from the table or, if no index specified, use any index.
INDEX_DESC(*table_name [index_name]*)	Scan the specified index in descending order.
MERGE_AJ	Perform a anti-join using sort-merge join method. This hint must appear after the SELECT statement of a NOT IN subquery
NOCACHE(*table_name*)	Discourages Oracle from keeping rows retrieved by a full table scan in the buffer cache of the SGA. Overrides the CACHE setting on the CREATE or ALTER TABLE statement.
NOPARALLEL(*table_name*)	Don't use parallel processing for the SQL statement. Overrides the PARALLEL setting on the CREATE or ALTER TABLE statement

Hint	Usage
NO_EXPAND(*table_name*)	Oracle will sometimes expand statements with OR conditions into multiple SQL statements combined by a union operation. This hint instructs the optimizer not to do this, even if it calculates that such a transformation would be beneficial.
NO_MERGE(*table_name*)	Instructs the optimizer not to consider a sort merge join for the table in question.
ORDERED	Instructs the optimizer to join the tables in exactly the left to right order specified in the FROM clause.
PARALLEL(*table_name*, *degree_of_parallelism*)	Instructs the optimizer to perform parallel scans on the nominated table. If no degree of parallelism is specified, the default will be used.
PUSH_SUBQ	This hint causes sub-queries to be processed earlier in the execution plan. Normally subqueries are processed last unless the SQL statement is transformed into join.
RULE	Use rule based optimization.
STAR	Consider the STAR join methedology in preference to other methods.
USE_CONCAT	Oracle will sometimes expand statements with OR conditions into multiple SQL statements combined by union all. This hint instructs the optimizer to do this, even if it calculates that such a transformation would not be beneficial.
USE_HASH(*table_name*)	When joining to this table, use the hash join method.
USE_MERGE(*table_name*)	When joining to this table, use the sort-merge join method.
USE_NL(*table_name*)	When joining to this table, use the nested-loops join method.

FIGURE A.1 Optimizer Hints.

EXPLAIN PLAN AND SQL TRACE

CREATING THE PLAN TABLE

To create the plan table, run the script utlxplan.sql from SQL*PLUS. The script can usually be found in the rdbms/admin subdirectory of the Oracle distribution.

RUNNING EXPLAIN PLAN

The syntax of the explain plan statement is:

```
EXPLAIN PLAN [SET STATEMENT_ID='text']
             [INTO table_name]
         FOR sql_statement
```

- ❏ If "INTO table_name" is not specified then a plan table named PLAN_TABLE will be used.
- ❏ The "SET STATEMENT_ID" option allows multiple plans to be stored in a single table.

FORMATTING EXPLAIN PLAN OUTPUT

The following query generates formatted output from the plan table:

```
SELECT LPAD(' ',2*(LEVEL-1))||operation||' '||options
              ||' '||object_name
              ||' '||DECODE(id, 0, 'Cost = '||position) "Query Plan"
  FROM plan_table
 START WITH id = 0 AND statement_id = 'statement_id'
CONNECT BY PRIOR id = parent_id AND statement_id ='statement_id'
```

ENABLING SQL_TRACE

SQL trace can be initiated from within a session by the command:

```
ALTER SESSION SET SQL_TRACE TRUE;
```

"Advanced" tracing—which includes details of resource waits—can be enabled with the command:

```
ALTER SESSION SET EVENTS '10046 TRACE NAME CONTEXT FOREVER, LEVEL 8';
```

FINDING THE TRACE FILE

Trace files generated by the SQL trace facility are written to the directory specified by USER_DUMP_DEST. You can determine the location of this directory with the following query:

```
select value
   from v$parameter
 where name='user_dump_dest'
```

RUNNING TKPROF

Basic usage for tkprof:

```
tkprof trace_file_name output_file_name
       table=name_of_alternate_plan_table.
       explain=username_and_password_to_use_with_explain
       sort=sort_options
```

Commonly used sort options are:

```
(prsela,exeela,fchela)sort statements by elapsed time
(prscpu,execpu,fchcpu)sort statements by CPU time
(exeqry,execu,fchqry,fchcu)sort statements by logical I/O
(exedsk,fchdsk)sort statements by physical I/O
```

A more complete list of options is included in Chapter 5.

SQL*PLUS AUTOTRACE OPTION

The autotrace option can be used in SQL*PLUS 3.3 and above to display execution plans and statistics. The AUTOTRACE command has the following usage:

```
SET AUTOTRACE OFF;ON[EXPLAIN|STATISTICS]|TRACEONLY
```

OFF	Normal behavior, generate no trace output.
ON EXPLAIN	Following each SQL statement execution, display the execution plan in the normal "nested" format.
ON STATISTICS	Following each SQL statement execution, print a report detailing I/O, CPI and other resource utilization.
ON	After SQL statement execution, display both the execution plan and the execution statistics.
TRACEONLY	Same as the "ON" setting, but suppresses the display of data from an SQL statement so that only the execution plan and statistics are shown.

ALTERING SESSION SETTINGS

You can alter the configuration of your session with the ALTER SESSION command. The general form of the alter session command is:

```
alter session set option = value
```

The following performance-related options can be set with alter session:

Option	Effect
SQL_TRACE	TRUE causes SQL trace information to be written to the trace file. FALSE stops tracing.
OPTIMIZER_GOAL	Sets the optimization strategy for the session. Valid values are: RULE CHOOSE FIRST_ROWS ALL_ROWS
SESSION_CACHED_CURSORS	Defines the number of cursors to be cached locally. High values improve the performance for programs which discard cursors for SQL statements which are eventually re-executed.

Option	Effect
CLOSE_OPEN_CACHED_CURSORS	If TRUE, cached cursors are closed when a COMMIT is executed. A value of TRUE saves memory, but FALSE can reduce parse overhead.
HASH_JOIN_ENABLED	If TRUE, hash joins will be performed if the optimizer determines that they are beneficial. A value of FALSE prevents hash joins in any circumstances.
HASH_AREA_SIZE	Amount of memory available for hash join operations. Larger values can improve performance of hash joins.
PARTITIONED_VIEW_ENABLED	If TRUE, Oracle will perform partition view optimizations as described in Chapter 11.

FIGURE A.2   Some of the options of the ALTER SESSION statement.

SQL COMMANDS

This section documents some SQL commands and options which may be useful when tuning SQL. It is not intended that this section substitute for the SQL reference manual and neither all SQL statements, nor all options of selected SQL are included. Rather, the section concentrates on options and statements which are significant to SQL tuning.

ANALYZING TABLES

The analyze command collects and stores table and index statistics which are essential for the efficient operation of the cost-based optimizer.

The simple form of the analyze command is:

```
ANALYZE INDEX|TABLE|CLUSTER object_name
                COMPUTE STATISTICS |
   ESTIMATE STATISTICS SAMPLE number ROWS|PERCENT
```

To create histograms on selected columns:

```
ANALYZE TABLE table_name
   COMPUTE STATISTICS
FOR COLUMNS column_names SIZE number_of_bands;
```

To drop statistics:

```
ANALYZE TABLE table_name
    DROP STATISTICS;
```

To list the chained rows in a table:

```
ANALYZE TABLE table_name
    LIST CHAINED ROWS INTO chained_row_table;
```

You should first create a "chained rows" table using the script utlchain.sql found in the rdbms/admin subdirectory of the Oracle distribution.

For more information on the ANALYZE command see Chapter 3 and the *Oracle server SQL language reference*.

CREATING INDEXES

The general form of the create index command is:

```
create [unique] [bitmap] index index_name on table_name
(column_list)
    [initrans no_of_transaction_entries]
    [storage and tablespace clauses]
    [pctfree pctfree]
    [recoverable|unrecoverable]
    [nosort]
    [parallel(degree parallel_degree)]
```

Some of these options can reduce the time required to build the index:

❏ The UNRECOVERABLE option avoids generation of redo log information and can dramatically reduce creation time. However, the index created in this way cannot be recovered from redo log information until the next tablespace backup occurs.

❏ The NOSORT option indicates to Oracle that the table rows are in sorted order and reduces the sort overhead of the index create.

❏ The parallel clause allows multiple processes to be allocated to the index create.

The size of the index can be reduced slightly by reducing the PCTFREE setting if the index keys are rarely updated. INITRANS should be set to the expected number of concurrent transactions—especially if PCTFREE is very low.

Rebuilding an index

An index can be rebuild in place—using the existing index as the data source for the new index—using the rebuild option of the ALTER INDEX command. This will be substantially faster than dropping and recreating the index. Parallel and unrecoverable options can further reduce index rebuild time.

```
alter index index_name rebuild [parallel (degree
parallel_degree)]
   [unrecoverable|recoverable]
```

CLUSTERS

The general form of the create cluster command is:

```
create cluster cluster_name
(
   cluster key
)
size average_entry_size
index|hashkeys no_of_hashkeys
parallel(degree parallel_degree)
other_storage_clauses;
```

If the HASHKEYS clause is specified then a hash cluster will be created with the specified number of hash key entries. If the INDEX keyword is specified then an index cluster will be created.

The SIZE clause specifies the amount of space to reserve for all rows which share the same cluster or hash key. If this value is too high then space will be wasted and scan performance will be degraded. If the value is too low then overflow blocks will need to be allocated to store additional rows and lookup performance will be degraded.

Once a cluster has been created, the CLUSTER clause of the CREATE TABLE statement can be used to add a table to the cluster (see below).

OPTIONS OF THE CREATE TABLE STATEMENT

A simplified form of the CREATE TABLE statement is:

```
create table table_name
(column_specifications)
table_options
AS subquery
```

Some of the options which have performance implications are listed below. Some of these options can also be specified in the ALTER TABLE statement.

Option	Effect
PCTFREE n	When the percentage of free space in this block reaches this point no new rows will be inserted. If rows are rarely updated then this value can be reduced resulting in a higher number of rows per block and improved table scan performance. However, if set too low, UPDATE statements which increase the row length may cause the row to *chain*, reducing lookup efficiency.
PCTUSED n	When DELETES reduce the percentage of space used within a block to this point INSERTS will again be allowed into the block. Increasing this value can improve scan performance by reducing the number of blocks which make up the table but may reduce insert performance.
INITRANS n	Specifies the number of transaction slots within each block. This should be set to the estimated maximum number of concurrent transactions in each block. It is particularly important to increase INITRANS if PCTFREE is reduced.
UNRECOVERABLE	If the create table statement is based on a subquery, this clause specifies that redo log information not be generated. This option, together with PARALLEL, radically reduces the time required to perform a table rebuild or temporary table creation. However tables created with this option cannot be recovered from log information until a backup of the relevant tablespace is undertaken.
CLUSTER cluster_name (columns)	Add the table to the specified cluster.
PARALLEL (DEGREE n)	Specifies the default degree of parallelism for queries which access the table. Where the table is based on a subquery, this setting also determines the number of parallel processes used to create the table.
CACHE	Specifies that table blocks read into the *buffer cache* as a result of a full table scan will be kept at the most recently used end of the *LRU list*. This increases the probability that these blocks will still be in memory when a subsequent full table scan is performed but may result in blocks read in from index accesses being pushed out of the buffer cache.

FIGURE A.3   Options of the CREATE TABLE statement.

GLOSSARY

Aggregate operations	Aggregate operations are those which group related rows and return a single row for each group. For example, returning the total number of employees in each department. Aggregate operations are invoked with the GROUP BY operator.
Array processing	Array processing allows a single SQL call to process multiple rows. For instance, a single execution of an INSERT statement could add multiple rows, or a single fetch from a SELECT statement could return multiple rows.
	In programming environments, array variables are used to hold the rows fetched or inserted. In many development and enquiry tools, array processing is enabled transparently and automatically.
Artificial key	An artificial key is a unique key which is contains no real-world information. Artificial keys are usually generated using Oracle *sequences*. Compare with *natural key*.
B*-Tree index	An index structure which takes the form of an hierarchy or inverted "tree." This is the default format for Oracle indexes.
Binary chop	A procedure for searching a sorted list of items. The list is successively divided into two sections and the section which must contain the desired item further sub-divided. Eventually the remaining portion is sufficiently small to

enable a sequential scan. This technique is useful in programs which cache table data to avoid excessive database access.

Bind variables

Bind variables allow the variable portions of an SQL statement, such as data values to be inserted or a search key, to be defined as "parameters" to the SQL statement..

The use of bind variables allows SQL statements to be re-executed without re-parsing the SQL statement. The alternative approach, where substitution variables are embedded as literals within the SQL statement requires that the SQL statement be re-parsed when re-executed.

Block

The basic unit of storage in an Oracle instance. Block sizes most commonly range between 2 and 8 KB.

Branch blocks

The middle level of blocks in a B*-tree index. Each branch block contains a range of index key values and pointers to the appropriate leaf blocks.

Cardinality

A measure of the number of unique values within a column or an index. The higher the cardinality of the index, the fewer the number of rows which will be returned by an exact lookup of a key value and hence the more useful the index will be.

Concatenated index

An index which is comprised from more than one column.

Consistent Read

Oracle queries return rows which are consistent with the time at which the query commenced. This consistent read may require access to rows which have changed since the query commenced—these rows are accessed from rollback segments.

Cursor

A memory structure which contains an SQL statement or PL/SQL block. Otherwise referred to as a *context area*.

Denormalization

The process of re-introducing redundant or derived information into a data model with an aim to improving performance.

Driving table

The driving table is the table which is accessed first in a table join. Choosing the best driving table is a key decision when optimizing join order.

Extent

Segments are composed of a number of distinct storage allocations known as extents. As a segment grows it will allocate extents as required, up to the limit of available space and the value of MAXEXTENTS.

Foreign key	A column or columns within one table which relate to the primary key of a "master" or "parent" table. These matching foreign and primary key columns can be used to join the two tables.
Hashing	In general, hashing refers to the technique of mathematically transforming a key value into a relative address which can be used to rapidly locate record. Oracle uses hashing as a table access method (hash clusters) and to optimize certain join operations (hash join). Hashing is also used extensively within internal SGA operations.
Hierarchical queries	Hierarchical queries are a special case of a self-join in which each row accessed child rows in a hierarchy of parent-child relationships. This is sometimes referred to as "explosion-of-parts."
High water mark	The high water mark indicates the highest block in a segment which has ever contained data. The high water mark increases as rows are inserted into the segment. However, deleting rows will not reduce the high water mark. Full table scans access all rows in the segment up to the high water mark.
Leaf blocks	The lowest level of blocks in a B*-tree index. Each leaf block contains a range of index key values and pointers (ROW-IDs) to appropriate blocks.
Natural key	A unique identifier for a table which is composed of naturally occurring columns in the table. Compare with *artificial key*.
Nested loops join	A join method in which each row of the outer table is read. For each row, a lookup of the inner table is undertaken. This best suits joins where the inner table is accessed via an index lookup.
NULL values	NULL values indicate that a value is missing, unknown or inapplicable. The use of NULL values extends the normal two valued logic to a three-valued logic. NULL values are important in SQL tuning because they are not generally stored in indexes and therefore present unique tuning problems.
OLAP	On-Line Analytical Processing. On-line analytical processing involves the real-time manipulation of large quantities of data generally for the purpose of facilitating business

decisions. OLAP databases are typified by large data volumes and infrequent, long running queries.

OLTP

On-Line Transaction Processing. OLTP databases typically have a very high rate of update and query activity. OLTP is typified by high rates of index lookups, single-row modifications and frequent commits.

Optimistic locking strategy

A locking strategy based on the assumption that a row is unlikely to be changed by another session between the time the row is queried and the time it is modified. Optimistic locking minimizes the lock duration but requires that the transaction be aborted if the row is changed by another session.

Outer table

The outer table is the first table processed in a join of two tables.

Parallel execution

The execution of an SQL operation using multiple processes or threads. This allows some of the stages of execution to be executed simultaneously and large tables to be scanned by multiple processes.

Parsing

The process of preparing a SQL statement for execution. This involves checking the statement for syntax errors, checking for a matching statement in the *shared pool* and determining the optimal execution plan. Parsing can contribute significantly the processing overhead, especially in OLTP like environments.

Pessimistic locking strategy

A locking strategy based on the assumption that a row might be changed between the time it is fetched and the time it is updated. Pessimistic locking involves locking the row when it is selected to prevent any concurrent updates.

Primary key

A column or columns which uniquely identify a row in a table.

Process

A unit of execution in a multi-processing environment. A process will typically execute a specific program and will have a unique and private allocation of memory. The operating system will determine the process's access to resources such as CPU, physical memory and disk.

RAID

Redundant Array of Inexpensive Disks. RAID is nowdays used to describe configuration of multiple physicals disks into one or more logical disks. RAID 0 is commonly referred to a "striping" and RAID 1 and "mirroring". The other popular RAID configuration, RAID 5, stripes data across multi-

	ple drives while storing sufficient parity information on all drives to allow data to be recovered should any single drive fail.
Random I/O	I/O in which a specific disk block are directly accessed. This is typical of the I/O which results from indexed lookups.
Redo logs	Oracle files which are used to record all changes made to objects with a database. When a COMMIT is issued, the changes made within the transaction are recorded in the redo log. The redo log can be used to restore the transaction in the event of a system failure.
Referential integrity	Referential integrity ensures that foreign keys correctly map to primary keys. A referential constraint will prevent the insert or update of foreign keys for which there are no matching primary keys and will either prevent the deletion of primary keys if foreign keys exist or delete these foreign key rows (delete cascade).
	Referential integrity can result in table-level locking if there are no indexes on the foreign keys.
Result sets	The output from a SQL query is a result set. Results sets have the same tabular construction as tables. Results sets are also created during intermediate SQL operations. For instance in a multi-table join, each successive join create a result set. The final result set is the output of the query.
Rollback segments	Rollback segments store the contents of a row before it is modified by a DML (UPDATE, INSERT DELETE) statement. This information is used in the event of a ROLLBACK, to provide a consistent view of the table for queries which commenced before the transaction was committed and to record the eventual success of a transaction.
Row level locking	In general, Oracle only locks a row which is modified by a DML statement. Page, block or table locks are not normally applied and read locks are never applied.
ROWID	The ROWID uniquely identifies a row by it's physical location. The ROWID of a row—if known—is the fastest way to access a row. An index will contain the ROWIDs for rows matching specific key values thus providing quick access to these rows.
Selectivity	A measure of the number of table entries for each index key. The less rows in the table which match specific index keys, the more selective is the index.

Segment   A segment is an object within an Oracle database which
                            consumes storage. Examples are tables, indexes, rollback
                            segments, temporary segments and clustsers.

Sequential I/O   I/O in which disk blocks are read in sequence. This is typi-
                            cal of the I/O which results from full table scans.

Serial execution   The execution of an SQL statement using a single process or
                            thread. This requires that each stage of the SQL operation be
                            processed one after the other. Compare with parallel.

Server process   See shadow process.

Shadow process   In many environments, the Oracle program runs in a sepa-
                            rate process from the client program (for instance,
                            SQL*PLUS). This "server" process is referred to as the
                            shadow process.

Shared pool   An area of the SGA which stores parsed SQL statements,
                            data distionary information and some session information.
                            The shared pool reduces parse overhead by caching fre-
                            quently executed SQL statements.

SMP   Symmetric Multi-processing. An SMP machine contains
                            multiple, equivalent CPUs. The SMP architecture domi-
                            nates mid-range UNIX computers and is increasingly popu-
                            lar on Microsoft NT systems.

Striping   A familiar term for RAID 0. Striping involves spreading
                            data evenly across a number of disks, thus allowing higher
                            data transfer rates than would otherwise be possible.

Thread   A thread is a unit of execution which shares it's memory
                            space with other threads. Threads can be implemented
                            within processes on some systems or may be used in place
                            of processes in others (for instance, in Windows NT).

Transaction   A transaction is a set of DML (update, delete or insert) oper-
                            ations which succeed or fail as a unit. A transaction is suc-
                            cessfully terminated by the COMMIT statement or aborted
                            with the ROLLBACK statement.

CONFIGURING DEVELOPMENT TOOLS

This appendix provides a concise overview of some of the configuration considerations affecting SQL performance in some popular development tools.

The most significant performance improvements for SQL embedded in these development environments will be realized by following the guidelines contained in the main sections of this book. However, when the SQL is tuned, overheads resulting from untuned client tools can prevent the SQL from reaching its full potential.

The development tools we'll be considering are:

❑ Powerbuilder

❑ SQL*Windows

❑ Oracle Power objects

❑ Oracle Precompilers

❑ Oracle Forms

❑ Oracle Objects for OLE

❑ ODBC

❑ Oracle Call Interface (OCI)

The configuration issues we'll consider are:

❑ Enabling array fetch to improve query performance. Using the array fetch facility reduces the number of calls to Oracle and network traffic—especially in the client server environment. The use of the array fetch was discussed in Chapter 6.

❑ Ensuring that SQL statement, or *cursors,* are re-used within the application. This reduces the number of parse calls to Oracle and thus reduces CPU overhead and database contention. SQL statement parsing was discussed in Chapter 3.

❑ Using bind variables to ensure that SQL is sharable across sessions. This reduces parse overhead by increasing the chance that if a matching SQL statement will be found in the *shared pool.* SQL statement parsing was discussed in Chapter 3.

POWERBUILDER

Powerbuilder is a popular client-server development tool which runs on multiple platforms—but most typically Microsoft Windows. It support numerous back-end databases through proprietary database interfaces or through *ODBC.*

Powerbuilder configuration parameters are specified in the *DBParm* property of the Transaction object or database connection.

ARRAY FETCH IN POWERBUILDER

Array fetches for PowerBuilder data-windows is controlled by the BLOCK setting within the *DbParm.* The default array size of 100 should be adequate for most situations.

USING BIND VARIABLES IN POWERBUILDER

Any powerbuilder variable may be used as a bind variable within an SQL statement. Within an SQL statement, the bind variable is preceded by a colon (":").

If the *DisableBind DbParm* parameter is set to 1 then bind variables will not be used and literal values will be substituted into the SQL which Powerbuilder sends to Oracle. In earlier releases of PowerBuilder, the DisableBind option was often set to avoid problems executing certain types of SQL. However, you should ensure that DisableBind is not set unless absolutely necessary.

CURSOR REUSE IN POWERBUILDER

Powerbuilder will not reuse cursors unless the SQLCache *DBParm* is set to a non-zero value. The value of the parameter tells powerbuilder how many cursor definitions to save. If the number of cursors opened exceeds SQLCache then least recently used cursors will be discarded to make room for new cursors.

The default value of SQLCache is 0—which means that no cursors will be cached and cursors will be discarded. You should generally set SQLCache to a higher value—20 to 30 is a reasonable setting.

SQL*WINDOWS

SQL*Windows is a popular client-server development environment for the Microsoft Windows environment. It supports multiple back-end server databases—including Oracle—through proprietary database interfaces known as SQL/Routers.

ARRAY HANDLING IN SQL*WINDOWS

SQL*Windows transparently implements array fetch on your behalf. The size of the array is primarily determined by the value of the *fetchrow* keyword in your sql.ini file.

BIND VARIABLES IN SQL*WINDOWS

Bind variables are fully implemented in the SQL*Windows environment. As in other environments, bind variables in SQL*Windows are prefixed with a colon. For instance:

```
bOk=SqlPrepare(hSql2,"select * from customers
                where customer_id=:dfCustomerId")
```

CURSOR RE-USE IN SQL*WINDOWS

SQL*Windows makes it rather difficult for the programmer to preserve and reuse cursors. A cursor in SQL*Windows is implemented as a SQL handle which is also usually used to define the database connection. In most SQL*Windows implementations, a single SQL handle is used for all the SQL statements in the application. Each time a new statement is executed (usually using the SQLPrepareAndExecute call), the SQL handle associated with the previous statement is effectively destroyed. As a result, most SQL*Windows applications have a very high parse to execute ratio (see Chapter 16) since an SQL statement must be re-parsed before each execution.

It is possible—with some effort—to preserve SQL*Windows cursors. This technique requires the following :

❏ The DBP_PRESERVE parameter is set to prevent SQL handle information being destroyed on commit or rollback.

❏ A SQL statement handle is allocated for each frequently executed SQL statement using the SqlConnect statement. This does not result in additional Oracle sessions being established (this only happens when the SqlConnectTransaction function is used).

❏ A SQLPrepare statement is issued for each frequently executed statement using the SQL statement handle created for that purpose. This step (and the allocation of the handle) can be performed in an global initialization function or whenever the statement is first required. The SQLPrepare call is issued once only for each SQL statement.

❏ A SQLExecute call is made when the SQL is first executed or the result set refreshed.

❏ For SQL which is executed infrequently or once only the SQLPrepare-AndExecute approach would still be used.

SQL*Windows Example

In some initialization function (or in an static initialization area of individual sub-routines), SQL handles for frequently executed SQL are declared and the SQL statements prepared:

```
!
! Implement cursor context preservation (don't destroy context
areas
! after a commit).
!
bOK=SqlSetParameter(DBP_PRESERVE,TRUE)


!
! Declare handles for the statements we execute more than once
!
!
bOK=SqlConnect(hSql1)
bOk=SqlPrepare(hSql1,"select some_columns from some_table
                    where some_column=:some_bind_variable")

bOK=SqlConnect(hSql2)
bOk=SqlPrepare(hSql2,"select some_columns from some_table2
```

```
                              where some_column=:some_bind_variable")
bOK=SqlConnect(hSql3)
bOk=SqlPrepare(hSql3,"update some_table set
some_column=:some_bind_variable
                        where some_column=:some_other_bind_var")

!
! This is a general purpose handle for statements which are in-
frequently executed
!
bOk=SqlConnect(hSql)
```

Once the SQL handles are created and the SQL prepared, the SQL can be executed at any time by issuing a SQLExecute against the appropriate SQL statement handle:

```
!
! Execute the SQL statement
!
call sqlExecute(hSql1)
while nRetVal != FETCH_EOF
    Call SqlFetchNext(hSql1,nRetVal)
```

As you can see, it requires some coding to implement SQL*Windows reuse. However, in a high-performance application the overhead of continually reparsing SQL statements may be unacceptable and it could be worth implementing this technique for commonly executed SQL statements.

If you can't implement cursor re-use in your SQL*Windows application, ensure that your database has the SESSION_CACHED_CURSORS parameter set—this will substantially reduce the parse overhead.

ORACLE POWER OBJECTS

ARRAY HANDLING IN ORACLE POWER OBJECTS

Oracle power objects implements array processing transparently and automatically for the *recordsets* which underlie Oracle Power Object controls. You can manipulate the degree of array processing by adjusting the RowFetchMode property for a form. If RowFetchMode is set to 1 (Fetch as needed), then rows will be fetched in arrays of at least 20 items when required. If RowFetchMode is set to 3 (fetch all immediately) then all rows will be fetched when the recordset is first accessed. When RowFetchMode is set to 2 (Fetch Count First) then a count of all rows will be undertaken after which rows will be fetched as needed.

RowFetchModes of 2 and 3 both require that Oracle retrieve all rows from the associated query before the first row can be processed. This may lead to dramatic degradation of response time for large tables and it is recommended that Row-FetchMode generally be set to 1.

The RecSrcMaxMem property defines the amount of memory available to store record set data. The default is 4K. Increase this value if your control displays a large number of rows or has a long row length and free memory is abundant on the computer running your application.

BIND VARIABLES IN ORACLE POWER OBJECTS

Bind variables are implemented in the normal way within Power Objects. Any Oracle basic variable can serve as a bind variable and is referred to in the standard way with a leading colon (":").

CURSOR RE-USE

Oracle Power Objects does not use explicit cursors. A recordset is analogous to a cursor and is kept open as required. Cursor re-use in Oracle Power Object applications is therefore usually good.

ORACLE PRECOMPILERS

The Oracle precompilers are a set of pre-processors which allow SQL statements to be embedded in high level languages such as C, COBOL, FORTRAN, Pascal, Ada and PL/1.

ARRAY PROCESSING IN THE PRECOMPILERS

All of the Oracle precompilers fully support array processing. However, array processing must be explicitly specified within the program code: it is never transparently implemented.

When using array processing, bind variables are defined in the host language as single dimensional arrays. These arrays can be FETCHed into, used in the values clause of an INSERT statement or in a WHERE clause. The FOR clause of the EXEC SQL statement can be used to limit the number of elements processed. If the FOR clause is not specified, the entire array is used.

BIND VARIABLES IN THE PRECOMPILERS

The pre-compilers fully support bind variables. In versions 1.x of the precompilers bind variables should be declared within EXEC SQL BEGIN DECLARE SECTION and EXEC SQL END DECLARE SECTION statements. In version 2.x of the precompilers any variable may be used as a bind variable.

CURSOR RE-USE IN THE PRECOMPILERS

The Oracle pre-compilers implement a cursor cache to enable frequently executed cursors to be re-executed without re-parsing. This cursor cache is automatic and requires no special action to implement, but can be tuned using compile time options. These options are:

MAXOPENCURSORS	To specify the minimum size of the cursor cache.
HOLD_CURSOR	To specify that subsequent cursors should not be aged out of the cursor cache.
RELEASE_CURSOR	To specify that subsequent cursors should not be stored in the cursor cache.

During a pre-compiler session, Oracle will keep open as many cursors as necessary, even if this exceeds MAXOPENCURSORS. However, if a cursor is closed and then reopened, the precompiler program can avoid a re-parse if it finds the statement in the cursor cache. Therefore, it is usually worth increasing MAXOPENCURSORS from it's default of 10. The optimum value is the number of re-executable SQL statements in the program.

However, each cursor takes memory and in some circumstances you may need to set MAXOPENCURSORS lower than optimal. If this happens, you can determine which SQL statements get cached by using the HOLD_CURSOR and RELEASE_CURSOR options.

If RELEASE_CURSOR=YES is in effect, subsequent SQL statements will not be placed in a local cursor cache. This is useful for SQL statements which are not likely to be re-executed.

If HOLD_CURSOR=YES is in effect, subsequent SQL statements be added to the SQL cache permanently and will not be "aged out". This is useful for SQL statements which will be re-used frequently when MAXOPENCURSORS has a low value.

If neither RELEASE_CURSOR or HOLD_CURSOR is in effect then SQL statements will be placed in the cursor cache but may be "aged out" of the cache if a new SQL statement requires an entry in the cache.

RELEASE_CURSOR and HOLD_CURSOR options take effect at compile time, not at run time. This means that they effect all subsequent statements in the program file, regardless of module structure or run-time flow of execution. The usual way to control these options is to surround an SQL statement. For instance, in the following example, the fetch from dual is not added to the cursor cache:

```
EXEC Oracle OPTION(RELEASE_CURSOR=YES);

EXEC SQL SELECT USER
              INTO :USER
              FROM DUAL;

EXEC Oracle OPTION(RELEASE_CURSOR=NO);
```

ORACLE FORMS

Oracle Forms is the forms generation tool included in Oracle's Developer/2000 product.

ARRAY PROCESSING IN ORACLE FORMS

Oracle Forms transparently implements array processing for Form blocks. The size of the array is set to the number of rows displayed plus 3 additional rows, but can be adjusted using the "Records Buffered" property for the block.

You can disable array processing altogether by specifying array=NO on the command line. Doing this is not recommended.

BIND VARIABLES IN ORACLE FORMS

Bind variables are automatically and transparently implemented for SQL generated from Oracle Forms blocks. In procedure and trigger code, PL/SQL variables are translated by PL/SQL into bind variables.

CURSOR RE-USE

Oracle Forms assigns and re-uses individual cursors for each SQL statement contained in the form unless you specify the OptimizeTP=NO option on the command line, in which case only SELECT statements are allocated separate cursors. Setting OptimizeTP=NO may save memory, but is likely to increase parse overhead.

ORACLE OBJECTS FOR OLE

Oracle objects for *OLE* is an Oracle product which allows application environments which support OLE automation to access an Oracle database. It is most commonly used with Microsoft Visual Basic.

ARRAY PROCESSING WITH ORACLE OBJECTS FOR OLE

Array processing is implemented transparently in Oracle Objects for OLE. The size of the array is defined by the FetchLimit setting of the "[Fetch Parameters]" section of the ORAOLE.INI file. The default value is 20.

BIND VARIABLES IN ORACLE OBJECTS FOR OLE

Oracle Objects for OLE supports bind variables. They are represented by the Ora-Parameter object and the OraParamaters collection of an OraDatabase object. Within an SQL statement the parameters are referenced using the usual leading-colon convention.

To create a bind variable, you must use the Parameter.Add method of the database object. For example, the following code fragment creates an "employee_id" bind variable.

```
OraDatabase.Parameters.Add "employee_id", 0, 1

sql_text = "select * from employees where
employee_id=:employee_id"
Set EmployeeDyn = OraDatabase.DbCreateDynaset(sql_text, &H0&)
```

CURSOR RE-USE IN ORACLE OBJECTS FOR OLE

Cursors are represented as dynasets in Oracle objects for OLE. Providing that your dynasets are not de-allocated, your cursors will be re-usable.

ORACLE CALL INTERFACE (OCI)

The Oracle Call Interface (OCI) is the fundamental programming interface to Oracle. All the Oracle development tools discussed in this appendix are constructed directly or indirectly on OCI. As the lowest level interface to Oracle, OCI includes all of the performance facilities present in higher-level environments. However, more work is often required to implement these features.

ARRAY PROCESSING IN OCI

OCI fully supports array processing. To use array processing, you must use the appropriate OCI calls. To issue array DML, you must use the OEXN call instead of the OXEC call. To fetch an array of data you should use OFEN in place of OFETCH. You declare the input or output arrays using the standard techniques for your programming language.

BIND VARIABLES IN OCI

Any host variable can become a bind variable in OCI. Bind variables are prefixed by colons in the SQL statement in the normal manner. If using the largely obsolete OBNDRN call to bind your variables then the bind variables are denoted by numbers (e.g., ":1",":2") in the SQL statement, otherwise the bind variables are defined as colon-prefixed names (e.g., ":SURNAME").

You bind each variable to the SQL statement with a separate call to the bind function. Three bind functions exist in OCI (OBNDRN, OBNDRV and OBNDRA). The OBNDRA call provides the most functionality and should be used in new applications.

CURSOR RE-USE IN OCI

Cursor re-use is completely under the control of the programmer in OCI.

In OCI, a cursor memory area is created with the OOPEN call and associated with an SQL statement (e.g., parsed) with the OPARSE call. Once the cursor is created, it can be bound to host variables (OBNDRA), executed (OEXN or OXEC), fetched from (OFEN) or closed (OCLOSE).

For SQL statements which are to be re-executed, allocate a distinct and dedicated cursor. Do not close the cursor (OCLOSE) after statement execution—this completely de-allocates the memory and the SQL statement. You can re-use the cursor simply by re-binding and re-executing the cursor. If a query cursor has not yet retrieved all rows, you can cancel the query using OCAN without destroying the cursor area.

For statements which are not re-used you can either destroy the cursor (OCLOSE) or parse a new statement into the existing memory area using OPARSE.

ODBC

ODBC (Open Database Connectivity) is a server independent API which allows client programs to issue SQL against virtually any back-end database. ODBC drivers are available for a very wide variety of back-end database servers, including Oracle. Client programs issue generic SQL requests which the ODBC driver translates into server-specific SQL.

The ODBC API fully supports bind variables, array processing and cursor re-use. However, the ODBC API is a very low-level implementation and is commonly accessed using middleware layers which allow a more high-level and productive programming environment.

The vendors who develop ODBC based middleware products must often compromise performance for portability. For instance, not all server databases support bind variables and as a result many ODBC products do not implement a bind variable capability. Array fetch and cursor re-use are more frequently, but not universally, implemented.

If contemplating and ODBC interface to an Oracle database evaluate ODBC middleware carefully and ensure that it implements bind variables, array processing and cursor re-use. In Visual Basic, you may wish to consider Oracle Objects for OLE as a high-performance alternative to ODBC.

ORACLE SERVER CONFIGURATION

In this appendix we look at Oracle server configuration parameters which may affect the performance of your SQL. These parameters are contained in a configuration file, typically referred to as the *init.ora* file, although the actual name will usually include the Oracle instance identifier (*Oracle_SID*). DBA authority is required to alter these parameters.

You can determine the current values for these parameters with the following query (see your DBA if you don't have access to the V$PARAMETER view):

```
select name,value,description from v$parameter;
```

You will need to omit the "description" column if your version of Oracle is earlier than Oracle 7.3.

Configuration parameters which commence with an underscore ("_") are undocumented parameters. These are not included in Oracle documentation and are not included in the v$parameter view. You can list the names and values of these parameters with the following query (which must be run while connected as SYS or INTERNAL):

```
select ksppinm name ,
         ksppstvl, ksppdesc
   from x$ksppi x, x$ksppcv y
  where x.indx = y.indx
    and  translate(ksppinm,'_','#') like '#%'
```

If your version of Oracle is prior to 7.3, you will need to use the following query:

```
select ksppinm name, ksppivl value
  from x$ksppi
 where substr(ksppinm,1,1)='_'
  order by ksppinm
```

You should change Oracle server parameters—especially undocumented parameters—with care. Always keep a backup copy of the init.ora file, preferably via version control software, so that you can revert to previous settings if you experience any problems.

Oracle server configuration parameters change from release to release and some parameters are operating system specific. This appendix details only parameters which are performance related and specifically related to SQL statement performance. You should refer to Oracle documentation—specifically the *Oracle server Reference Manual*—for detailed documentation of all parameters.

PARAMETERS AFFECTING SQL TRACING

Adjusting these parameters are useful when using the SQL trace facility (discussed in some detail in Chapter 5).

_TRACE_FILES_PUBLIC	This undocumented parameter causes Oracle to generate trace files which can be read by any user. If this parameter is not set, Oracle may generate trace files which are readable only to DBA accounts. Set this parameter to true if you want users to be able to analyze their own trace files and you are satisfied that no sensitive information is hard-coded into SQL statements
MAX_DUMP_FILE_SIZE	The maximum size of a trace file in Oracle blocks. Setting this parameter to a low value can conserve disk space but you may lose valuable information in the trace file.
SQL_TRACE	If set to TRUE, all Oracle sessions with generate SQL trace files. You should normally have this parameter set to FALSE, since a significant disk space and performance overhead will result if all sessions are being

	traced. However, there may be circumstances in which setting this parameter temporarily is the only way to obtain required trace output.
TIMED_STATISTICS	If this parameter is set to TRUE, then Oracle sessions will maintain elapsed and cpu timings for internal operations. This will allow tkprof to report cpu and elapsed times for SQL statement execution and will allow a number of server performance metrics to be accessed (for instance the TIME_WAITED column in V$SYSTEM_EVENT which records the time spent waiting for various system resources).
	Because the overhead of setting TIMED_STATISTICS to TRUE is fairly low, and the information is provides is so useful, many DBAs leave TIMED_STATSITICS=TRUE always.
USER_DUMP_DEST	This parameter specifies the directory to which user trace files initiated by the SQL trace facility will be written.

PARAMETERS AFFECTING SQL PROCESSING

These parameters affect the way in which Oracle processes your SQL and the resources available for certain SQL operations.

ALWAYS_ANTI_JOIN	If set to TRUE, Oracle will use the anti-join optimizations automatically. If set to FALSE, Oracle will only perform an anti-join if the HASH_AJ or MERGE_AJ hints are used. See Chapter 7 for more information on anti-joins.
	Since Oracle's anti-join methods usually improve performance, it is recommended that this parameter be set to TRUE.

CLOSE_CACHED_OPEN_CURSORS

If set to TRUE, cursor definitions are discarded in PL/SQL when a COMMIT is issued. This frees memory but increases the parse overhead, since SQL statements must be re-parsed in each transaction.

The default value of FALSE allows cursor definitions to be retained across COMMITS and is recommended unless memory is very scarce.

CURSOR_SPACE_FOR_TIME

Setting this parameter to true ensures that SQL statements are never aged out of the shared pool providing that there is at least one open cursor referencing the statement. A value of TRUE also causes cursor information which is not shared to be retained between executions.

The default value of FALSE allows SQL statements to age out of the shared pool even if a cursor is open on the statement. However, this should rarely occur.

Set this value to TRUE if you are sure that your shared pool is large enough to hold all concurrently opened SQL statements (you should probably increase it anyway if it is not) and there is ample free memory available for client processes.

DISCRETE_TRANSACTIONS_ENABLED

If set to TRUE, discrete transactions (see Chapter 9) are permitted.

HASH_AREA_SIZE

This parameter controls the amount of memory available (in bytes) to a session performing a hash join. Increasing this parameter will improve hash join performance up to the point at which the entire hash table fits in memory. After this point, increasing hash_area_size will have no effect.

HASH_JOIN_ENABLED

If set to FALSE, hash joins are not permitted. Since hash joins are very efficient there is usually no reason to change the default value of TRUE.

OPTIMIZER_MODE

Sets the default optimization mode for the instance. Valid values are CHOOSE (the default), RULE, FIRST_ROWS, and LAST_ROWS. Chapter 3 discusses the optimizer_mode setting in some detail.

PARTITION_VIEW_ENABLED

If FALSE, partition view processing is disabled. Partition view processing allows Oracle to skip unneeded tables in a view which contains multiple UNIONed tables.

Set to TRUE if you wish to take advantage of partition views as described in Chapter 11.

SESSION_CACHED_CURSORS

This parameter controls the number of cursors cached in a session-specific cache. If the client program is re-using cursors efficiently, this cache will have little effect. However, if a program is discarding cursors which are later re-executed, increasing this parameter can have a significant effect on parse overhead.

PARAMETERS AFFECTING SORTING

SORT_AREA_SIZE

The amount of memory available to an Oracle session for sorting. Increasing this value reduces the possibility that a large sort will have to write to temporary segments and will improve the performance of sorts.

Setting an appropriate value of SORT_AREA_SIZE is the most significant server-side optimization for sorting.

Since each session will allocate it's own SORT_AREA_SIZE and because this memory is never released back to the operating system, you should ensure that SORT_AREA_SIZE is increased only to the degree necessary to reduce disk sorts.

See Chapter 16 for information on monitoring sort activity.

SORT_AREA_RETAINED_SIZE

SORT_AREA_SIZE sets the maximum amount of session memory available for all concurrent sort while SORT_AREA_RETAINED_SIZE specifies the maximum amount of session memory available for any individual sort. A single query may need to perform more than one sort (a good example is a sort merge from a non-indexed join), although it's unusual for more than two to be required concurrently. If each sort can fit into a SORT_AREA_RETAINED_SIZE and all sorts can fit into SORT_AREA_SIZE, then the sort can be performed in memory.

SORT_AREA_RETAINED_SIZE defaults to SORT_AREA_SIZE and there is usually little incentive to change this default.

SORT_DIRECT_WRITES

If set to TRUE or AUTO, the sorts which exceed SORT_AREA_SIZE will write directly to disk bypassing the buffer cache. This improves performance for the session performing the sort and also avoids filling the buffer cache with sort blocks.

Prior to Oracle 7.3 this feature was not enabled by default and should be set to TRUE. On version 7.3 and above, the default value of AUTO is preferred.

SETTINGS AFFECTING PARALLEL PROCESSING

OPTIMIZER_PERCENT_PARALLEL

This parameter determines the amount of weight the optimizer gives to parallel processing in determining the optimal execution plan.

A value of 0 will cause the optimizer to ignore parallel processing when determining an execution plan, while a setting of 100 will cause the optimizer to fully "discount" the estimated cost of a parallel query based on the degree of parallelism selected. Intermediate settings result in a proportional reduction in parallel query costs.

High values should only be used if your system and application are well suited to parallel query. Low values will encourage the use of indexes and other access methods which prevent parallelism.

PARALLEL_MAX_SERVERS

The maximum number of parallel servers which can run concurrently.

If this value is set too low, SQL which would otherwise be executed in parallel will either be executed serially or will return an error (depending on the value of PARALLEL_MIN_PCT). If set too high, your server may be overloaded by parallel processes.

PARALLEL_MIN_PERCENT

This parameter defines the minimum acceptable percentage of parallel slaves which must be available for the SQL to run. If less than the PARALLEL_MIN_PCT% slaves are available an error is returned.

For instance, if your query required 8 and only 5 were available (5/8=62%) then your query would execute in parallel if PARALLEL_MIN_PERCENT were below 62. If PARALLEL_MIN_PERCENT were above 62 your statement would terminate with an error.

PARALLEL_MIN_SERVERS

This setting determines the minimum number of parallel servers allocated to your instance. These servers will be allocated when the instance is started and will never be removed.

Idle servers can take up system memory whereas creating new server processes takes time. If you have sufficient memory, set this parameter to the value of PARALLEL_MAX_SERVERS to avoid any delay while starting servers.

PARALLEL_SERVER_IDLE_TIME   This parameter defines the number of minutes that a server can be idle before being deactivated. Servers will never be deactivated unless the total number exceeds PARALLEL_MIN_SERVERS.

Avoid setting this parameter too low, since constant activation and deactivation of parallel processes will waste system resources.

PARAMETERS AFFECTING THE SGA

These parameters affect the size and composition of the *System Global Area* or SGA. This is an area of shared memory which exists primarily to improve performance and enable communication between Oracle sessions.

DB_BLOCK_BUFFERS   The size of the buffer cache in database blocks. The buffer cache maintains database blocks in memory using a *Least Recently Used* (LRU) algorithm. If a required block can be found in the buffer cache then a disk read will be avoided and performance will be improved. This is possibly the most significant performance-related parameter.

You can increase the size of the buffer cache if you have sufficient free memory and you determine that the "hit rate" is too low. See Chapter 16 for details on monitoring the buffer cache hit rate.

DB_BLOCK_SIZE   The database block size in bytes. This cannot be changed once the database has been created. It should be at least as high as the operating system block size.

See Chapter 15 for more information on setting this parameter.

LOG_BUFFER   Size of the redo log buffer in bytes. When processes change a data block, they create an entry in this buffer. When a COMMIT occurs, or when the reaches a certain threshold, the buffer is flushed to disk. You should normally increase the size of the redo log buffer if you observe *log space waits* (see Chapter 16).

SHARED_POOL_RESERVED_MIN_ALLOC The shared pool may be partitioned into two partitions based on the size of the objects stored. This parameter defines the minimum size for objects to be stored in the "reserved" area of the shared pool.

The purpose of the reserved area is to provide an area of memory unaffected by the fragmentation caused when small objects are moved in and out of the shared pool.

SHARED_POOL_RESERVED_SIZE Size in bytes of the reserved area of shared pool. Objects—typically PL/SQL objects—which are larger than SHARED_POOL_ RESERVED_MIN_ALLOC will be stored in this area of the shared pool.

SHARED_POOL_SIZE The size in bytes of the shared pool. The shared pool is a part of the SGA which stored data dictionary information, cached SQL statements and object definitions and some session information.

There are a number of metrics which can indicate if your shared pool is too small. See Chapter 16 for more details.

SERVER TUNING PARAMETERS

These parameters affect the overall performance of the Oracle server. Many of these parameters are described in Chapter 16.

DB_BLOCK_LRU_LATCHES Number of *LRU* latches. A session must acquire an LRU chain latch whenever a block is read in from disk. You may need to increase this value if you encounter contention for the *cache buffer lru chain* latch.

SPIN_COUNT Number of times to spin on a latch miss. Increasing the value of this parameter increases the probability that a latch can be obtained without a latch sleep, but will increase CPU utilization. Increase this parameter only if there is free CPU on the database server.

CHECKPOINT_PROCESS — Create a dedicated process to perform updates of file headers during *checkpoints*. Enabling this process increases process overhead (by one process) but reduces the overhead of checkpoints on the *logwriter*, especially for database with a large number of data files.

COMPATIBLE — This parameter enables features of Oracle which are specific to particular releases of Oracle. Setting this value to the current version of Oracle will usually result in increased performance by enabling new features but may impede any attempt to downgrade the version of Oracle.

LOG_SIMULTANEOUS_COPIES — The number of redo buffer copy latches. Increase this value if you observe contention for *the redo copy latch*.

LOG_SMALL_ENTRY_MAX_SIZE — redo entries smaller than this value will make redo log entries while holding the *redo allocation latch*. Redo entries larger than this will use *the redo copy latch*. Since there are multiple copy latches but only one allocation latch, contention is reduces when the copy latch is used.

Reduce this value (but keep it greater than 0) if you observe contention for the *redo allocation latch*.

SEQUENCE_CACHE_ENTRIES — The number of sequences which can be cached in memory. If this value is not as large as the number of sequences concurrently in use then processes which require a new sequence number may incur a disk I/O and degraded performance.

DB_FILE_MULTIBLOCK_READ_COUNT — Maximum number of blocks read in a single I/O during a sequential read. Higher values can significantly improve the performance of table scans. The amount read cannot exceed 64K on many platforms. On at least some versions of UNIX, setting USE_READV to true can allow larger values.

DB_WRITERS

Number of database writer processes. If *asynchronous* or *list I/O* is available, then such I/O should normally be used in preference to multiple database writers. However, when asynchronous or list I/O is not available and datafiles are located on multiple disks, setting db_writers to the number of disk can result in a very significant performance improvement.

USE_ASYNC_IO

On some operating systems, this parameter must be set to TRUE if asynchronous I/O is to be used. On other platforms it is sufficient to use raw devices and set db_writers=1.

DIFFERENCES BETWEEN ORACLE VERSIONS

Each version of Oracle introduces substantial new functionality. This appendix summarizes features which are not common to all versions. Not all differences between versions are listed here—only those that are relevant to SQL tuning. You should refer to the *Oracle server migration guide* for more detailed information about facilities available in each new release.

Activating SQL_TRACE for a remote session	The dbms_system.set_sql_trace_in_session package, which allows SQL trace to be activated from a remote session, was introduced in Oracle 7.2.
Anti join	The anti-join mechanism, which allows fast execution of NOT IN subqueries was introduced in Oracle 7.3.
CACHE clause	The CACHE clause of the CREATE or ALTER TABLE statement was introduced in Oracle 7.1. This option encourages rows retrieved by a full table scan to remain in the buffer cache of the SGA.

Cost based optimization	Cost based optimization is common to all versions of Oracle from version 7.0 onwards. However, the capabilities of the optimizer have been improved with each release. It is commonly accepted that cost based optimization should not normally be used with Oracle version 7.0 and possibly not in Oracle 7.1.
	The cost based optimizer appeared to reach usable maturity in Oracle version 7.2 and later.
Fast index rebuild	The rebuild option of the alter index command can be used to recreate an index based on the existing index. This functionality was introduced in version 7.3.
Hash joins	The hash join method was introduced in Oracle 7.3.
Histograms	Historgrams were introduced in Oracle version 7.3. Histograms improve the performance of the cost based optimizer by storing information about the distribution of data within a column.
In line PL/SQL functions	The ability to reference PL/SQL functions from within SQL statements was introduced in Oracle 7.1.
Index only tables	Index only tables were introduced in Oracle 8.0. An index only table allows table rows to be stored in a B*-tree index structure.
In-line views	The in-line view facility allows SQL statements to be embedded in the FROM clause of a SELECT statement. This facility was officially introduced in Oracle 7.2, but was available (undocmented and unsupported) in Oracle 7.1.
Parallel CREATE TABLE AS SELECT	The parallel option of the CREATE TABLE statement (when used in conjunction with a query) was introduced in Oracle 7.2.
Parallel DML	Parallel DML allows Data Manipulation statements (insert, update and delete) to be processed in parallel. This facility was introduced in Oracle 8.0 and can only be used with partitioned tables.
Parallel index build	First available in Oracle 7.1.

Parallel query	Parallel query first became available in Oracle 7.1.
Partition tables	Partition tables allow a logical table to be divided into partitions, each of which contain only a specified range of values. This facility first became available in Oracle8.
Partition views	Partition view processing allows Oracle to avoid scanning all tables within a constrain partitioned UNION ALL view.
	This facility was introduced in Oracle 7.3
SESSION_CACHED_CURSORS	This initialization parameter, which creates a local cache for session cursors, cannot be set in versions earlier than Oracle 7.1.
Sort direct writes	The SORT_DIRECT_WRITES parameter, which allows disk sorts to avoid writing through the Oracle *buffer cache*, was introduced in Oracle 7.2.
Temporary tablespaces	Prior to Oracle 7.3, temporary tablespaces had the same characteristics as other tablespaces. Oracle 7.3 introduced true "temporary" tablespaces which store temporary segments only. This is enabled by the temporary clause of the CREATE or ALTER TABLESPACE command.
Unrecoverable table and index creation.	The UNRECOVERABLE option of the CREATE TABLE and CREATE INDEX statements was introduced in Oracle 7.2. This option improves create table and create index by avoiding the necessity for Oracle to generate redo log information.
User defined hash function for hash clusters.	The ability to specify your own hash function in hash clusters was introduced in Oracle 7.2.

BIBLIOGRAPHY AND RESOURCES

In this section, you will find pointers to resources which can provide Oracle information to enhance topics included in this book or to explore topics beyond the scope of this book.

INTERNET SITES

By far the newest and most exciting sources of Oracle information can be found on the internet. Here are some of the other useful resources:

NEWSGROUPS AND MAILING LISTS

Even before the advent of the World Wide Web, the internet was alive with Oracle-related news groups and mailing lists. These newsgroups are still one of the best ways to exchange Oracle information and keep abreast of new developments. Some of the groups you may wish to join are:

comp.databases.oracle.misc	Oracle related topics
comp.databases.oracle.marketplace	Oracle-related jobs, etc
comp.databases.oracle.server	Oracle database administration/server topics

comp.databases.oracle.tools   Oracle software tools/applications

Oracle-L mailing list.   General mailing list for Oracle-related
                                          information. To join, send email to LIST-
                                          SERV@KBS.NET with "SUBSCRIBE ORA-
                                          CLE-L your_real_name" in the message
                                          body

WEB SITES

Attempting to create a definitive list of web sites is a futile task. However, here are just a few of the sites which offer useful information:

DBMS Magazine   http://www.dbmsmag.com

Oracle informant Magazine   http://www.informant.com/oracle/
                                          oi_index.htm

Oracle magazine interactive   http://www.oramag.com/

Oracle Performance Tuning   http://www.mindspring.com/~hayden/

Oracle Underground   http://www.onwe.co.za/frank/faq.htm
Frequently asked questions

Oracle User forum and fan club   http://www.orafans.com/

OraPub of Earth—white papers   http://www.europa.com/~orapub/

Oracle White papers   http://tiburon.us.oracle.com/odp/
                                          public/library/cr/data.html

OReview: Magazine   http://www.oreview.com/
(formally Oracle Technical Journal)

Oracle Frequently asked questions   http://www.bf.rmit.edu.au/OracleFAQ

International Oracle users group   http://www.ioug.org

Oracle Corporation   http://www.oracle.com/

ORACLE TECHNICAL DOCUMENTATION

The Oracle documentation set is comprehensive, well-organized and accurate. All too often it seems that users of the Oracle system reach for the manuals only as a last resort. Always have a current set of Oracle documentation available and use them as a primary resource. Oracle now makes all documentation available on a single CD-ROM.

The following Oracle documents particularly useful when tuning SQL:

Oracle Server SQL language reference	This manual completely documents Oracle SQL including all options and facilities discussed in this book.
Oracle Server Tuning guide	This manual contains valuable guidance on the optimization of the Oracle server. Although the guidelines for tuning SQL are not extensive, good documentation of hints, explain plans and *tkprof* are included.
Oracle Server Concepts manual	Explains the architecture and operation of the Oracle server, including details of query optimization and SQL statement processing.
Oracle Server reference	Documents the Oracle data dictionary, including *dynamic performance views* and documents server initialization parameters.

ORACLE BULLETINS

In addition to the standard Oracle documentation set, Oracle staff produce a number of interesting and useful whitepapers and bulletins. Some of these are available on the *Oracle Support Notes* CD-ROM, which you can obtain from your local Oracle worldwide support contacts. Other documents may be available from the internet sites listed above.

Some of the more useful papers available are:

Configuring Oracle Server for VLDB.	Cary V Millsap. Oracle System Performance Group Technical Paper, 1996.
Tuning the Oracle Server—Identifying Internal Contention.	Virag Saksena. Oracle System Performance Group Technical Paper, 1996.
Identifying Resource Intensive SQL in a production environment.	Virag Saksena. Oracle System Performance Group Technical Paper, 1996.
How to Control the Cost Based Optimizer in Oracle7.	Deepak Gupta. Oracle internal publication.
Optimizing Oracle 7.3 Database Performance.	Deepak Gupta. Oracle internal publication.
Tuning the Performance of the Oracle7 Parallel Query Option	Gary Hallmark. Oracle internal publication.

Avoiding a Database Reorganization.   Craig Shallahamer. Oracle internal Publication.

Archiver Best Practices.   ORACLE bulletin 10477121.6.

Oracle for UNIX Performance Tuning Tips.   ORACLE Part A22535.

BOOKS

A number of books are available which cover Oracle server tuning and concepts. Here are the author's favorites:

Understanding the Oracle Server   Marina Krakovsky, 0-13-190265-2, Prentice Hall PTR, 1996.

ORACLE Performance Tuning and Optimization   Edward Whalen, 0-672-30886-X, SAMS Publishing, 1996.

ORACLE Backup & Recovery Handbook   Rama Velpuri, 0-07-882106-1, Osborne McGraw-Hill, 1995.

Oracle Performance Tuning, Second Edition   Mark Gurry and Peter Corrigan, 1-56592-237-9, O'Reilly & Associates, 1996.

INTERNATIONAL ORACLE USERS GROUP

The International Oracle Users Group (IOUG) is an independent, nonprofit organization which exists to encourage and facilitate the use of Oracle software. Local chapters of the IOUG exist in most countries and municipalities.

By joining an Oracle user group, you get access to other users of Oracle software. Local user groups may hold special presentations or issue local newsletters. In addition to these local benefits, IOUG issues an international magazine "SELECT" and participates heavily in the various annual regional conferences.

Visit the IOUG web site at www.ioug.com for more information.

MAGAZINES AND PERIODICALS

There are a number of excellent periodicals focusing on Oracle software. None of these magazines concentrate exclusively on SQL tuning, but all have an interest in Oracle server and application performance.

OReview Magazine (formally Oracle Technical Journal)	www.oreview.com	An independent magazine focusing on Oracle technology, management and strategic issues.
Oracle Informant Magazine	www.informant.com/ oracle/oi_index.htm	An independent magazine focusing primarily on Oracle development issues.
Oracle Magazine	www.oramag.com	Oracle Corporation's magazine for Oracle users. Available on-line.
SELECT Magazine	www.ioug.com	The magazine of the International Oracle Users Group

CONTENTS OF THE CD-ROM

This appendix outlines the contents of the companion CD-ROM.

The companion CD-ROM contains tools which can assist in writing and tuning high-performance SQL. Some of these tools—such as the author's toolkit—are free software, while others are demonstration or limited trial editions of the products.

THE AUTHOR'S TUNING TOOLKIT

The TUNEKIT directory contains tools developed by the author for Oracle SQL and server tuning. Many of these tools have been used to illustrate tuning principles throughout the book.

These tools are free software and provided in the hope that they will be useful. However, they come with no warrantee. Requests for assistance with these tools should be directed to the author at gharriso@werple.net.au.

WINDOWS TOOLS

The windows directory includes two Microsoft Windows-based tools for SQL and Oracle tuning. To install the tools, run the SETUP.EXE file found in the directory. The programs will be installed together with readme and help files outlining their use. The programs require either a local Oracle database (e.g., Personal Oracle for Windows) or Oracle SQL*NET for Windows.

Xplain

Xplain is a Microsoft Windows program which allows execution plans for SQL statements to be generated from within a windows environment. Some of the features of the Xplain tool are:

❏ Change SQL statements and immediately see the changed execution plan.
❏ Display SQL sent to remote nodes for distributed statements.
❏ Display parallelised steps of Parallel SQL.
❏ Record execution statistics such as block gets, CPU times, elapsed times and resource waits.
❏ Produce a tree-structured drawing of the SQL's execution plan.

Monet

Monet is a Microsoft Windows-based program which monitors Oracle server and displays load and efficiency information in graphical format.
Some of MONET's features are:

❏ Graphical displays of I/O rates, hit rates for latches, buffer cache and library cache, transaction rate, event waits and call rates.
❏ SQL cache browser which displays the text, execution counts, I/O rates and execution plans for SQL statements in the shared pool.
❏ Checks critical efficiency measures and reports anomalies.
❏ Writes statistics to CSV files for import into spreadsheet programs for further analysis.

ShrPool

ShrPool is an Oracle Shared Pool browser which displays SQL statements in the shared pool. It generates execution plans and displays execution statistics. It is similar to the shared sPRO*C program, also included on the CD-ROM, but runs in the Microsoft Windows environment.

The program was written by Elio Bonazzi. The version included on the CD-ROM is an early version; updates can be obtained from Elio's Web site:
http: yallara.cs.mit.edu.au.~bonazzi.

SQL*PLUS SCRIPTS

This directory contains SQL*PLUS scripts for displaying useful performance metrics, for generating explain plan output and for reporting table definitions.

Server monitoring scripts

These scripts collect Oracle server performance statistics. Sample output and guidelines for interpreting the reports are provided in Chapter 16.

The scripts are:

samp_srt.sql	Start a sampling period
samp_end.sql	End a sampling period
stat_ctl.sql	Configuration script
db_stA.sql	Display some key performance ratios since instance startup
db_stS.sql	Display some key performance ratios for a sample time period
wait_stA.sql	Display event wait statistics since instance startup
wait_stS.sql	Display event wait statistics for a sample time period
ltch_stA.sql	Display latch statistics since instance startup
latch_stS.sql	Display latch statistics for a sample time period
busy_stA.sql	Display buffer busy statistics since instance startup
busy_stS.sql	Display buffer busy statistics for a sample time period
rbs_stA.sql	Display rollback segment statistics since instance startup
rbs_stS.sql	Display rollback segment statistics for a sample time period
file_stA.sql	Display table/file IO statistics since instance startup
file_stS.sql	Display table/file IO statistics for a sample time period
serv_stA.sql	Display MTS or parallel server statistics since instance startup
serv_stS.sql	Display MTS or parallel server statistics for a sample time period

Some of the scripts can use data collected for a specific time period, while others use statistics since the last database startup. To commence a sample, run samp_srt.sql. To end a sampling period (or to create a new sample since the end of a previous sample) run samp_end.sql.

Output from the scripts is written to a set of files in the format $ORACLE_SID.st?—where ? is a number 0-9. These files are written to the directory specified by the spool_dir variable in stat_ctl.sql.

You need to have read access to all dynamic performance ("v$") tables and create table privilege for the temporary tables.

Explain plan scripts

Two scripts to assist in generating execution plans are provided:

eplan.sql   Generates an explain plan for a SQL statement stored in a separate file. The file may not contain anything other than the SQL statement. Eplan handles the create of the plan table and displays parallel and distributed query details

xtree.sql   Draws a "picture" of an explain plan using ASCII characters. Requires that the SQL be stored in a file which contains only the SQL statement to be drawn.

Schema report

The dbschema.sql report displays definitions of tables indexes and views in a users account. You are prompted for the account name and a table mask.

PRO*C PROGRAMS

This directory contains a couple of PRO*C programs to aid in tuning Oracle databases and applications.

To compile these programs under UNIX, try:

> make -f $ORACLE_HOME/proc/lib/proc.mk shared_s
> make -f $ORACLE_HOME/proc/lib/proc.mk tk_waits

shared_s   This program interrogates the dynamic tables containing cached SQL details and formats output in a *"tkprof*-like" style. This can be useful to find the most expensive SQL in an application system.

tk_waits   This program extracts and reports on event wait statistics from trace files which have been generated using event 10046 level 4 or 8. Versions of *tkprof* prior to 7.1 used to report on wait events, but Oracle, in their wisdom, removed the ability.

THIRD-PARTY SQL TUNING TOOLS

Included on the CD-ROM are demonstration versions of commercial software which can assist in SQL tuning. These software products vary in their approach to SQL tuning, but all are capable of generating execution plans in the windows environment.

SQLAB

SQLab is a SQL tuning environment for Oracle. SQLab identifies and tunes offensive SQL statement generated by any Oracle application. SQLab provides the following functionality:

❏ Graphical Explain plan.
❏ Extract SQL statements from the SQL cache in the *shared pool* based on I/O characteristics or by tables accessed.
❏ SQL statement editor.
❏ Display of table, index and other object definitions.

License and Registration

SQLab requires a license number to be able to connect to a database instance. You can obtain a free temporary license number by calling in the US (800)306.9329 or outside the US (714)720.1434. You can also obtain a temporary license number by e-mailing your request to *info@quests.com*. For more information you can point your browser to *http://www.quests.com*.

The installation process will ask for the license number. It is recommended that you have the number at that time. The installation will succeed without the license number but the SQLab will NOT be able to connect to the Oracle instance. If you run the installation without the temporary license number you will have to modify the sqlab.ini file using a text editor such as Notepad. You can find the file within the SQLab directory created during the installation. The first section of the .ini file should look like this:

```
[License]
        Number=Enter the number here
```

After typing the license number, save the file and try to connect again. Please read the read.me file for further setup instructions and the getting.doc for additional product information.

❏ SQLab is a Windows-based application tuning tool for Oracle. SQLab identifies and tunes offensive SQL statement generated by Oracle Applications, SAP, PeopleSoft and home-grown applications.

Quest Software,
610 Newport Center Drive Suite 1400
Newport Beach, CA 92660
Electronic mail: *info@quests.com*
Web: *www.quests.com*
Telephone: (714)720-1434, East Coast: (609)279-0709
Fax: (714)720-0426

SQL NAVIGATOR

SQL Navigator is a complete SQL programming environment from Technosolutions. Although SQL Navigator is not a dedicated tuning tool, it does have an integrated Execution plan generator.

SQL Navigator includes the following features:

❏ SQL and PL/SQL editor.

❏ Graphical Explain plan facility.

❏ Visual database object browser and data browser.

❏ Graphical object creation and maintenance.

TechnoSolutions Corp.
8101 NE Parkway Drive
E-2, Suite 501
Vancouver, WA 98662
USA
Email:*info@TechnoSolutions.com*
Voice:(360)-260-0710
Fax:(360)-260-0717

ORACLE TRIAL SOFTWARE

Included on the CD-ROM are full function 90-day trial versions of Personal Oracle for Windows 3.1 and Personal Oracle for Windows 95. Personal Oracle for Windows is a complete implementation of Oracle for the Windows operating system. Demonstration and utility software on the CD-ROM should run fine under Personal Oracle.

Oracle Corporation
500 Oracle Parkway
Redwood City, CA 94065
Internet: *www.oracle.com*

INDEX

LICENSE AGREEMENT AND LIMITED WARRANTY

READ THE FOLLOWING TERMS AND CONDITIONS CAREFULLY BEFORE OPEN-
ING THIS CD PACKAGE. THIS LEGAL DOCUMENT IS AN AGREEMENT BETWEEN YOU AND
PRENTICE-HALL, INC. (THE "COMPANY"). BY OPENING THIS SEALED CD PACKAGE, YOU
ARE AGREEING TO BE BOUND BY THESE TERMS AND CONDITIONS. IF YOU DO NOT
AGREE WITH THESE TERMS AND CONDITIONS, DO NOT OPEN THE CD PACKAGE.
PROMPTLY RETURN THE UNOPENED CD PACKAGE AND ALL ACCOMPANYING ITEMS TO
THE PLACE YOU OBTAINED THEM FOR A FULL REFUND OF ANY SUMS YOU HAVE PAID.

1.   **GRANT OF LICENSE:** In consideration of your purchase of this book, and your agreement to abide by the terms and conditions of this Agreement, the Company grants to you a nonexclusive
right to use and display the copy of the enclosed software program (hereinafter the "SOFTWARE") on a
single computer (i.e., with a single CPU) at a single location so long as you comply with the terms of this
Agreement. The Company reserves all rights not expressly granted to you under this Agreement.

2.   **OWNERSHIP OF SOFTWARE:** You own only the magnetic or physical media (the
enclosed CD) on which the SOFTWARE is recorded or fixed, but the Company and the software developers retain all the rights, title, and ownership to the SOFTWARE recorded on the original CD copy(ies)
and all subsequent copies of the SOFTWARE, regardless of the form or media on which the original or
other copies may exist. This license is not a sale of the original SOFTWARE or any copy to you.

3.   **COPY RESTRICTIONS:** This SOFTWARE and the accompanying printed materials and
user manual (the "Documentation") are the subject of copyright. The individual programs on the CD are
copyrighted by the authors of each program. Some of the programs on the CD include separate licensing
agreements. If you intend to use one of these programs, you must read and follow its accompanying
license agreement. If you intend to use the trial version of Internet Chameleon, you must read and agree
to the terms of the notice regarding fees on the back cover of this book. You may not copy the Documentation or the SOFTWARE, except that you may make a single copy of the SOFTWARE for backup or
archival purposes only. You may be held legally responsible for any copying or copyright infringement
which is caused or encouraged by your failure to abide by the terms of this restriction.

4.   **USE RESTRICTIONS:** You may not network the SOFTWARE or otherwise use it on
more than one computer or computer terminal at the same time. You may physically transfer the SOFT-
WARE from one computer to another provided that the SOFTWARE is used on only one computer at a
time. You may not distribute copies of the SOFTWARE or Documentation to others. You may not
reverse engineer, disassemble, decompile, modify, adapt, translate, or create derivative works based on
the SOFTWARE or the Documentation without the prior written consent of the Company.

5.   **TRANSFER RESTRICTIONS:** The enclosed SOFTWARE is licensed only to you and
may not be transferred to any one else without the prior written consent of the Company. Any unautho-
rized transfer of the SOFTWARE shall result in the immediate termination of this Agreement.

6.   **TERMINATION:** This license is effective until terminated. This license will terminate
automatically without notice from the Company and become null and void if you fail to comply with any
provisions or limitations of this license. Upon termination, you shall destroy the Documentation and all
copies of the SOFTWARE. All provisions of this Agreement as to warranties, limitation of liability, rem-
edies or damages, and our ownership rights shall survive termination.

7.   **MISCELLANEOUS:** This Agreement shall be construed in accordance with the laws of
the United States of America and the State of New York and shall benefit the Company, its affiliates, and
assignees.

8.   **LIMITED WARRANTY AND DISCLAIMER OF WARRANTY:** The Company war-
rants that the SOFTWARE, when properly used in accordance with the Documentation, will operate in
substantial conformity with the description of the SOFTWARE set forth in the Documentation. The
Company does not warrant that the SOFTWARE will meet your requirements or that the operation of the

SOFTWARE will be uninterrupted or error-free. The Company warrants that the media on which the SOFTWARE is delivered shall be free from defects in materials and workmanship under normal use for a period of thirty (30) days from the date of your purchase. Your only remedy and the Company's only obligation under these limited warranties is, at the Company's option, return of the warranted item for a refund of any amounts paid by you or replacement of the item. Any replacement of SOFTWARE or media under the warranties shall not extend the original warranty period. The limited warranty set forth above shall not apply to any SOFTWARE which the Company determines in good faith has been subject to misuse, neglect, improper installation, repair, alteration, or damage by you. EXCEPT FOR THE EXPRESSED WARRANTIES SET FORTH ABOVE, THE COMPANY DISCLAIMS ALL WARRANTIES, EXPRESS OR IMPLIED, INCLUDING WITHOUT LIMITATION, THE IMPLIED WARRANTIES OF MERCHANTABILITY AND FITNESS FOR A PARTICULAR PURPOSE. EXCEPT FOR THE EXPRESS WARRANTY SET FORTH ABOVE, THE COMPANY DOES NOT WARRANT, GUARANTEE, OR MAKE ANY REPRESENTATION REGARDING THE USE OR THE RESULTS OF THE USE OF THE SOFTWARE IN TERMS OF ITS CORRECTNESS, ACCURACY, RELIABILITY, CURRENTNESS, OR OTHERWISE.

IN NO EVENT, SHALL THE COMPANY OR ITS EMPLOYEES, AGENTS, SUPPLIERS, OR CONTRACTORS BE LIABLE FOR ANY INCIDENTAL, INDIRECT, SPECIAL, OR CONSEQUENTIAL DAMAGES ARISING OUT OF OR IN CONNECTION WITH THE LICENSE GRANTED UNDER THIS AGREEMENT, OR FOR LOSS OF USE, LOSS OF DATA, LOSS OF INCOME OR PROFIT, OR OTHER LOSSES, SUSTAINED AS A RESULT OF INJURY TO ANY PERSON, OR LOSS OF OR DAMAGE TO PROPERTY, OR CLAIMS OF THIRD PARTIES, EVEN IF THE COMPANY OR AN AUTHORIZED REPRESENTATIVE OF THE COMPANY HAS BEEN ADVISED OF THE POSSIBILITY OF SUCH DAMAGES. IN NO EVENT SHALL LIABILITY OF THE COMPANY FOR DAMAGES WITH RESPECT TO THE SOFTWARE EXCEED THE AMOUNTS ACTUALLY PAID BY YOU, IF ANY, FOR THE SOFTWARE.

SOME JURISDICTIONS DO NOT ALLOW THE LIMITATION OF IMPLIED WARRANTIES OR LIABILITY FOR INCIDENTAL, INDIRECT, SPECIAL, OR CONSEQUENTIAL DAMAGES, SO THE ABOVE LIMITATIONS MAY NOT ALWAYS APPLY. THE WARRANTIES IN THIS AGREEMENT GIVE YOU SPECIFIC LEGAL RIGHTS AND YOU MAY ALSO HAVE OTHER RIGHTS WHICH VARY IN ACCORDANCE WITH LOCAL LAW.

ACKNOWLEDGMENT

YOU ACKNOWLEDGE THAT YOU HAVE READ THIS AGREEMENT, UNDERSTAND IT, AND AGREE TO BE BOUND BY ITS TERMS AND CONDITIONS. YOU ALSO AGREE THAT THIS AGREEMENT IS THE COMPLETE AND EXCLUSIVE STATEMENT OF THE AGREEMENT BETWEEN YOU AND THE COMPANY AND SUPERSEDES ALL PROPOSALS OR PRIOR AGREEMENTS, ORAL, OR WRITTEN, AND ANY OTHER COMMUNICATIONS BETWEEN YOU AND THE COMPANY OR ANY REPRESENTATIVE OF THE COMPANY RELATING TO THE SUBJECT MATTER OF THIS AGREEMENT.

Should you have any questions concerning this Agreement or if you wish to contact the Company for any reason, please contact in writing at the address below.

Robin Short
Prentice Hall PTR
One Lake Street
Upper Saddle River, New Jersey 07458